Renaissance Thinkers

James McConica is a Fellow of All Souls College, Oxford. His previous books include *English Humanists and Reformation Politics* and *The Collegiate University*, volume 3 of the History of the University of Oxford.

Anthony Quinton was President of Trinity College, Oxford from 1978 to 1987. His books include *The Nature of Things* (1973), *Utilitarian Ethics* (1973), *The Politics of Imperfection* (1978) and *Thoughts and Thinkers* (1982). He was created a life peer in 1982, and was chairman of the British Library Board from 1985 to 1990.

Sir Anthony Kenny is President of the British Academy and Warden of Rhodes House, Oxford.

Peter Burke is reader in Cultural History at the University of Cambridge and Fellow of Emmanuel College. His books include *The Italian Renaissance* (3rd edn., 1987); *Popular Culture in Early Modern Europe* (4th edn., 1988); and *The Fabrication of Louis XIV* (1992).

Renaissance Thinkers

Erasmus
James McConica

Bacon
Anthony Quinton

More
Anthony Kenny

Montaigne
Peter Burke

Oxford   New York

OXFORD UNIVERSITY PRESS

Oxford University Press, Walton Street, Oxford OX2 6DP

Oxford New York Toronto
Delhi Bombay Calcutta Madras Karachi
Kuala Lumpur Singapore Hong Kong Tokyo
Nairobi Dar es Salaam Cape Town
Melbourne Auckland Madrid

and associated companies in
Berlin Ibadan

Oxford is a trade mark of Oxford University Press

Erasmus © James McConica 1991
Bacon © Anthony Quinton 1980
More © Anthony Kenny 1983
Montaigne © Peter Burke 1981
This composite volume © Oxford University Press 1993
Foreword © Sir Keith Thomas 1993
Each section was first published
separately in the Past Masters '
series as an Oxford University Press
paperback

This edition first published 1993

British Library Cataloguing in Publication Data
Data available

Library of Congress Cataloging in Publication Data
Renaissance thinkers. p. cm.
"Each section was first published separately in the Past masters
series as an Oxford University Press paperback"—P.
Includes bibliographical references and index.
Contents: Erasmus / James McConica—Bacon / Anthony Quinton—
More / Anthony Kenny—Montaigne / Peter Burke.
1. Philosophy, Renaissance. 2. Classical education—History—16th
century. 3. Humanism. I. Past masters.
190'.9'031—dc20 B775.R46 1993 92-34276

ISBN 0-19-283106-2

3 5 7 9 10 8 6 4

Printed in Great Britain
Biddles Ltd.
Guildford and
Kings Lynn

Foreword

The four thinkers discussed in this book were all products of the European Renaissance. That is to say they were all learned in the literary classics of ancient Greece and Rome and they all assumed that the insights of pagan antiquity retained their validity in the Christian era. Moreover, their writings displayed those powers of literary eloquence which classical humanism had made central to education. But whereas Erasmus and More believed that the highest human good lay in a union of classical wisdom and Christian teaching, Montaigne displayed a more sceptical temper, while Bacon sketched out a scientific programme which was intended to supersede the authority of classical antiquity and literary humanism altogether.

In Erasmus the humanist ideal of Christian erudition reached its peak. He believed in an education which, by shaping morals as well as intellect, would incline the virtuous man to a life of public service. The prodigious literary output of this cosmopolitan figure included educational treatises, works of piety and apologetic, proverbs, satires and letters. But his most important achievement was the first printed Greek text of the New Testament, designed to buttress a new Latin translation with substantial annotations. Erasmus stressed the interior disposition of the soul rather than theological dogma; and he brought a gentle satirical wit to bear upon the follies of his time. The contending parties of the Reformation era largely ignored his eirenic position, but his educational programme determined the shape of liberal education for the next four hundred years.

Thomas More attracts our attention as much for the quality of his life and personality as for the interest of his thought. For Dr Johnson he was 'the person of greatest virtue these islands ever produced'. An accomplished classical scholar and friend of Erasmus, he exemplified the humanist doctrine that learning should be used for public service. He rose to the office of

Lord Chancellor, only to surrender both the office and his life through his unwillingness to compromise his belief in the spiritual authority of the international Catholic Church. What distinguishes him from so many of the other martyrs of that bloody century was the wit and self-deprecating modesty with which he comported himself in the face of adversity. In his controversial writings on religion, however, More used his rhetorical skills to compose diatribe and invective against the Lutherans. As Sir Anthony Kenny shrewdly remarks, it was partly the pugnacious conventions of humanist debate which made the Reformation so divisive. More's greatest achievement, however, was *Utopia*, a work which imitates Plato in depicting an imaginary society in order to criticise existing institutions and attitudes, but whose true meaning continues to fascinate and divide its innumerable commentators.

Unlike most learned humanists, Michel de Montaigne forsook public involvement as far as possible, choosing to spend much of his life in his library in a round tower in Gascony. The *Essais* which he wrote and revised over several decades were a set of reflections on the human mind and they originated a new literary genre for which there was no classical precedent. Although Montaigne's favourite authors were all ancients, there is something deceptively 'modern' about his cast of mind. His scepticism, his irony, his informality and his cultural relativism make him an author who appeals readily to the twentieth-century reader. Yet his exploration of the human self and his sense of the diversity of human customs and opinions owe much to classical influences. For him, as for earlier humanists, the greatest age was the age of Greece and Rome.

Only with Francis Bacon does the emphasis shift firmly from the past to the future. Bacon shared with Erasmus a distaste for the medieval scholastic philosophy which had been founded on the logic of Aristotle; and he was indebted to Montaigne for the idea of presenting his hard-headed reflections on worldly prudence in an aphoristic series of *Essays*. Like More, he was a man of affairs who held the office of Lord Chancellor. But he was wholly unlike the other three in being a large-scale systematic thinker. His 'Great Instauration' was a philosophical programme designed to restore to man the dominion over nature which he had supposedly lost at the Fall. He sought to replace the 'contentious' learning of scholasticism, the 'delicate' learning of literary humanism and the 'fantastic' learning of magic and astrology by a new science of nature, independent of religion, founded on inductive logic and carried out co-operatively for the material benefit of mankind. Following More, he depicted in his *New Atlantis* a utopian island containing in 'Salomon's House' a model establishment devoted to scientific research. Bacon was a deeply influential prophet of modern science, though, ironically for so creative a writer, the scientific method he propounded greatly underrated the part played by creativity and imagination in scientific research.

Three of these four thinkers normally wrote in Latin, in the sixteenth century the accepted language of international communication. All of them were deeply imbued in the culture of the classical world. Today, when Greek and Latin play little part in most people's education, it is important to recall the extent to which European intellectual life once rested upon the classical inheritance. It is also useful to be reminded that these four thinkers – a Dutchman, a Frenchman and two Englishmen – were in no sense limited by national horizons, but wrote and argued as members of a common European culture.

KEITH THOMAS
General Editor
Past Masters

Contents

Erasmus

James McConica

Contents

Note on abbreviations

The following abbreviations are used in references given in the text:

A	*Antibarbari, Collected Works of Erasmus* (CWE), vol. 23
Ad	*Adagia*, CWE, vol. 31
Ax	*Axiomata*, in *Christian Humanism*, ed. Olin
Bo	Boyle, *Erasmus on Language and Method in Theology*
C	*Colloquies*, ed. Thompson
E	*Enchiridion*, CWE, vol. 66
I	*Institutio principis Christiani*, CWE, vol. 27
M	*Praise of Folly*, CWE, vol. 27
Mc	McConica, 'Erasmus and the Grammar of Consent', in *Scrinium Erasmianum*, ed. Coppens
P	*Paraclesis*, in *Christian Humanism*, ed. Olin
Ph	Phillips, *The 'Adages' of Erasmus*
Q	*Querela pacis*, CWE, vol. 27
R	Rummel, *Erasmus' Annotations*
Ru	Rupp, *The Righteousness of God*
S	*De ratione studii*, CWE, vol. 24
V	Letter to Volz, CWE, vol. 66
W1, W2, W3, etc	Volumes of the correspondence series within the *Collected Works of Erasmus*.

Full bibliographical details of these and other works are given in the suggestions for further reading at the end of the book.

Introduction

Erasmus is the Reformation's orphan. Illegitimate at birth and deprived of his parents as a boy, his origins seem in retrospect oddly prophetic of his role in history. He was passionately concerned to promote the faith and enlightenment of Christendom, but quite unable to give unqualified assent to any of the rival orthodoxies which the civil war among Christians had spawned. Before the time of Luther, he was the most widely read and persuasive critic of the Church which he wanted—like Luther—to reform, but Luther found him equivocal and faint-hearted. To the end of his life he was as stubbornly loyal to Catholic unity as he was independent of conventional ecclesiastical authority, yet he suffered the posthumous excommunication of having all of his works placed on the Index of prohibited books. He lived away from his native Holland and found his most lasting domicile with the Froben press in Basle, but his true homeland was the one he constructed with his pen, through his vast correspondence, his tireless publication—works of devotion, the sources of Christian faith, educational texts and treatises, coruscating satire and social commentary—and withal, through the alluring warmth of his intimate, lucid, and insinuating style. In the centuries that followed, it is not surprising that the defenders of confessional religion have been slow to claim him as their own, nor that his general reputation has been that of the dauntingly witty, erudite, and corrosive critic of official belief and popular devotion. For his irenic and rational faith, however, he has received the unwavering esteem of such as Lucius Cary, Viscount Falkland, who regarded him as one 'who thought himself no Martyr, yet one who may passe for a Confessor, having suffered, and long, by the Bigotts of both Parties'.

In our sceptical and self-consciously tolerant age, Erasmus seems at times to be coming into his own. Until quite recently, the modern revival of Erasmus and his legacy has rested chiefly on the great critical edition of his correspondence by Percy Stafford Allen, who from 1924 to 1933 was President, appropriately enough, of the outstanding Erasmian foundation at Oxford, Corpus Christi College. The appearance of a comprehensive edition of Erasmus' letters naturally drew the interest of historians to this new window on the Reformation, to concentrate their attention, not so much on Erasmus' vast legacy of scholarship preserved in the Leiden folios of 1703–6 as on this more accessible material, the most important single archive for the intellectual history of the time. But the letters, which were often written or revised expressly for publication, inevitably throw into relief the Erasmus of the public forum, responding to criticism, moving to the attack, adapting to change, pursuing patrons, and justifying his work. Seen through the eyes of the first scholars to exploit Allen's researches in detail, what emerged was the face of the cultivated religious *politique*, the founder of the 'third Church' of Augustin Renaudet, a prophet of the Enlightenment who led his followers 'au doute discret, à une sorte de scepticisme de bonne compagnie, et qui se trahit par le sourire ou par les silences respectueux'. The cloistered smile, the discreet silence, the artful ambiguity, the irreverent wit—these traits still dominate the received view of Erasmus in most classrooms and lecture halls, so that, even among the scholars of today, echoes of the old hostilities can be heard from those who feel that the history of the Reformation really belongs to the confident dogmatists, and that Erasmus, for all of his erudition (or even because of it?) was not, somehow, really serious about religion.

In recent years, however, this appreciation has begun to develop a new dimension. The reasons for this are many, but all derive from a growing interest in the things about which Erasmus was expert—the sources of the Christian faith, the theory and practice of education, the uses of language, the arts of persuasion and satire, the need for social harmony, and concern with the official ideals of our society contrasted against the behaviour not only of those in power, but of the populace who support them.

Within the Christian faith itself, the ecumenical urge to draw together in the face of a diffident world has worked finally to the advantage of the one commanding moderate of the Reformation who refused to fall silent, or to surrender his convictions in the face of warring orthodoxies. The reform programme which he saw founder in his own day has won new attention from those who would like to reappraise the causes of that signal catastrophe in the history of western Christendom. To others, Christian or not, Erasmus' cosmopolitanism and irenicism, his hatred of war and violence, and his championing of international order recommend him equally as a figure for our time. And for those responsible for education in school or university, who lament the loss of a humanism effective in disposing the young to moral and intellectual discipline in the service of the common good, he remains a figure as challenging as he is remote.

The history of Erasmus' reputation should not deceive us into thinking that his influence lay dormant until the Second Vatican Council. In the realm of biblical scholarship, in the theory and practice of education, the articles of devotion, the sharpening of critical attitudes, the propagation of moral wisdom—in all of these spheres his largely unacknowledged presence has been so pervasive that even a century after his death, it became impossible to record.

In this book I have tried to present in brief compass the leading ideas and concerns that explain the importance of Erasmus for our moral and intellectual culture. I have begun with an account of his own formation, which explains not only why his approach to the crucial issues of his day was so unlike that of many of his contemporaries, but also so radically unlike anything to be found in our time. Paradoxically, it also explains why his influence has persisted, flowing quietly around the confessional fortresses to nourish the broad streams that bore the European mind and spirit into the age we call modern. I have dealt with his personal history only in passing, since it was his pen that made him important, and I have concentrated on a few texts, readily available, in which an epitome of his enterprise can be discovered.

1 The making of the grammarian

Erasmus was born in Rotterdam during the night of 27/28 October, some time in the latter years of the decade 1460–70. Our uncertainty over the exact year (1467 is now rather favoured) deserves to be reported, since it indicates at the very outset how little precise information survives about his origins. That this is so is chiefly his own doing. He was regularly inconsistent in reporting his age, and the fullest account we have of his early life, the *Compendium vitae*, is of disputed authorship and certainly tendentious. Tendentious too are the shorter versions he wrote to the authorities, Julius II and Leo X, in order to gain the dispensations he needed to earn his own living while still in religious vows.

His father's family seems to have originated near Gouda, and there is enough casual evidence in the correspondence to support the indications in the *Compendium vitae*, that both his parents' families were reasonably substantial, if not precisely wealthy, people. His parents were unmarried, a circumstance that left him with a relatively routine canonical impediment to ordination to the priesthood. It had also, and for the same reason, to be mentioned by him whenever he sought a dispensation for exemption from any of the obligations of his religious vows, leaving some modern historians with the groundless impression that Erasmus was haunted by his illegitimacy. He had a brother, Pieter, three years his elder; his mother was a widow, and his father at some stage became a priest. The father was himself an educated man who earned his living as a scribe, lettered in humanistic Latin and Greek. Erasmus owned books from his library, and Greek manuscripts copied by him in Italy. Just why the parents did not marry is not clear. The most reliable information is contained in the Brief of Leo X, dated 26 January 1517, which was a private document meant to be kept secret and confidential, and to be used by Erasmus only if the propriety of his clerical status was questioned. It is clear from this, not that his father was a priest at the time of Erasmus' birth, but that there was a canonical impediment to the marriage of his parents, owing perhaps to consanguinity or affinity in a collateral line. If so, it would have required the consent and co-operation of both families to obtain the needed dispensation. The argument of the *Compendium vitae*, that the father's numerous brothers were determined that the youngest of them enter the priesthood, suggests at least one reason why such co-operation was perhaps not forthcoming. At any rate, it is difficult to believe that in this secret document, the Brief of Leo X, intended to serve Erasmus as a last line of defence if his clerical credentials were challenged, we have anything other than an exact remedy for the awkward difficulties surrounding his birth. Otherwise, we must suppose that in a matter of the most vital importance to his personal welfare, he deliberately deceived the highest authority in the Church in order to obtain a document which, used as intended, would have been worthless and even damaging if the account of his birth that it contained were contrary to common knowledge. We know, moreover, that contact between Erasmus and his relatives continued through his later life. The *Compendium vitae*, at least, mentions his having seen two of his mother's brothers at Dordrecht when they were nearly ninety; on another occasion, an unidentified kinsman visited Johann Froben at Basle in 1515 while Erasmus was absent, prompting Beatus Rhenanus to remark to him in a letter, 'the resemblance in feature at once proclaims him a relative of yours'. There is a reference to a paternal uncle Theobald in a letter from Brussels in 1498, and Erasmus was clearly in touch with his brother Pieter until the latter's death in 1527. Such people would have known the truth about the father.

With the death of their parents about 1484, the two boys were placed under the protection of three guardians, one of whom was Pieter Winckel, who had also been Erasmus' first teacher. He taught in the school attached to the church of St John at Gouda. Although Winckel's competence both as a guardian of their inheritance and as a teacher is questioned in Erasmus' various recollections, he is known to have transcribed a manuscript of Juvenal at Louvain, and may be credited reasonably with having helped to lay the foundation for what was to become one of the most prodigious scholarly accomplishments in the history of learning. The two brothers were then sent (about 1478) for further schooling at the famous school of the chapter at St Lebuin in Deventer. The school was not run by the Brethren of the Common Life, as is often asserted, nor was the running of schools the work of the Brethren. Typically, they ran hostels for boarders and poor pupils, and such was the case at Deventer. One of their number, a Jan Synthen, did teach in the school and taught Erasmus, possibly along with the better-known Alexander Hegius. Hegius was a friend of the famous humanist Rudolph Agricola, and by 1483 he had become headmaster of St Lebuin's school. If Hegius did not arrive at Deventer until then, he could not have taught Erasmus for more than a year, since Erasmus appears to have left the school and Deventer when the plague struck in 1484. Later, in his *Spongia*, he remarked that he owed little to Hegius, but he spoke of him always with praise. Certainly under the influence of Hegius the Deventer school rose to prominence as a centre of humanistic education, and it seems likely that the school was already well along the road to distinction before Hegius's arrival. At the time of his death in 1498, the school was attended by more than two thousand pupils, and had become a nursery for a generation of Dutch humanists.

About the humanists and their interests a preliminary word must be said. Their bent was opposed to that of the established intellectual culture of the medieval university—of the 'Schools'. In particular they rejected any emphasis upon logic and speculative sciences like metaphysics, in favour of the practical arts of life in society—of persuasion (rhetoric), and its ancillary disciplines like politics, history, and poetry— although they shared an interest in dialectic, the art of argument. More broadly, it may be said that the humanists were absorbed with the place and potentialities of the human individual in this world, without excluding the perspective of an eternal destiny. These preoccupations reflected the needs of an increasingly urban and literate, lay society first in Italy, then in northern Europe. In classical antiquity they felt they found a distant but seemingly recognizable culture contrasting with that prevailing about them, and having a particular authority for solution of the questions they faced. It became urgent therefore to study the texts bequeathed by that culture, to master the languages which would give immediate access to them, to adopt the stylistic training and standards which produced them, and to take from them the lessons of man's humanity, *humanitas*. This concept implied relation to the community, the exercise of effective freedom of the will, and the obligation as a citizen of a particular town or state, there to serve the common good. The texts of the *litterae humaniores*, of humane letters, of *bonae litterae*—these provided a schooling, therefore, in civic virtue. It must be stressed in our time that this 'humanism' did not imply hostility to or rejection of traditional religion; indeed, it could and did at times form a powerful synthesis with it. In the developing philosophy of Erasmus we shall see all of this demonstrated in magisterial form.

With his mother a victim of the plague in 1483, and his father's death shortly thereafter, Erasmus was sent with his brother to the school at Bois-le-Duc or 's-Hertogenbosch, where once again they stayed in a hostel run by the Brethren. This was a crucial period for the young men, since (in Erasmus' admittedly highly coloured account) Winckel and the guardians pressed them to enter religious life as a solution to their orphaned poverty, while Erasmus at least was keen to go to university. His later account is bitter indeed. Of the Brethren: 'Their chief purpose, if they see a boy whose intelligence is better bred and more active than ordinary, as able and gifted boys often are, is to break their spirit and depress them with corporal punishments, threats, and recriminations, and various other devices—taming him, they call it—until they make him fit for the monastic life. On this ground they are pretty popular with the Dominicans and Franciscans, who say their Orders would soon come to an end if it was not for the young entry bred up by the Brothers, for it is out of their yards that they pick their recruits.' Then, addressing the substance of their teaching, he continues: 'Personally, I believe that even among them there are some quite worthy people, but suffering as they do from a lack of the best authors, and living by customs and rites of their own in a darkness of their own making ... I do not see how they can give the young a liberal education. Experience shows, at any rate, that no places produce young men more coarsely educated or more depraved in character.'

These quotations are taken from a disguised biographical account written in 1516, and known as the 'Letter to Grunnius' (W 4.11). It was published in the *Opus epistolarum* in 1529, and was composed to support his appeal for a further dispensation from his monastic commitments (the first having been granted by Julius II in 1506). It was part of a campaign agreed upon in London with Andrea Ammonio, the sub-collector of papal taxes, who was one of Erasmus' closest friends. The campaign was successful, and brought as its trophy the dispensation of 1517 from Leo X. It is important to understand that essential to the canonical case Erasmus wished to make was the contention that he had not entered monastic life with mature judgement and of his own free will, but under age, and only in response to the relentless pressure of his guardians, intensified by his wish to escape from an intolerable situation, including the way of life of the Brethren at 's-Hertogenbosch.

Whatever the exact truth of the matter, after two more years at 's-Hertogenbosch Erasmus' older brother Pieter entered the house of the Augustinian canons at Sion, near Delft, and, a little later, Erasmus joined the same order at Steyn, a few miles away. This was in 1487, seemingly, and Erasmus was about twenty years old (not sixteen, as he would later claim). His only extant letter to his brother is from this time. It is affectionate and cordial, and speaks warmly of a friend in the monastery, Servatius, with whom Erasmus formed a close attachment. To a casual reader the most striking thing about this letter and others of the period is the evidence of familiarity with the style and conventions of classical rhetoric, and of pleasure in the exercise of the epistolary arts. Moreover, Erasmus asks his brother to lend Servatius his small copy of Juvenal's satires, one suggestion among many that the Augustinian cloisters were not entirely inhospitable to humanistic learning. Erasmus' exchanges with Servatius Roger and other of his early correspondents from this time— Franciscus Theodoricus, Cornelis Gerard, and Willem Hermans in particular—all show that the same enthusiasms for the study of good letters were widely shared, while it is also clear that Erasmus was the dominant member of this growing literary sodality. It was the first of many occasions in which he would become the focus and inspiration of a whole literary circle.

Beyond this broad framework of events and our general knowledge of the religious milieu in which he now lived, we have little detailed or clearly unprejudiced information about the early formation of Erasmus, either in the monastery or earlier in his schooling. To say that this formation was humanistic is so general as to be misleading. The details we need we find instead in his own treatises on education, and in his first important work, the *Antibarbari*—'Against the Barbarians'.

The *Antibarbari* is effectively the manifesto of the young Erasmus. It is also an impassioned defence of the study of the classics, and so provides an ideal access to his preoccupations and personal culture. It was begun, as he tells us, before he was twenty, which is to say at about the time he entered the monastery. It had a remarkable history, and like many of his major works, was revised and developed over some years. It was originally conceived in four books, of which only the first survives. This was recovered by Erasmus while he was in Louvain after the entire manuscript disappeared from the custody of friends in Italy, then revised once more and published by Froben in 1520. Erasmus explained that he had found the manuscript circulating unofficially (as was to happen sometimes also to his letters), and to protect his reputation from the juvenile mistakes these versions contained, he produced an official edition. Margaret Mann Phillips, in her English version, has pointed out that in 1520, the *Antibarbari* also contained unmistakable allusions to some of his detractors in Louvain.

The work was originally conceived as a rhetorical speech in defence of the classics, and it retains essentially that form, although the first recasting imposed on it some of the form of a dialogue. The principal speaker is Jacob Batt of Bergen op Zoom, a faithful friend whom Erasmus met shortly after ordination to the priesthood on 25 April 1492, while he was in the service of Hendrick van Bergen, bishop of Cambrai. It was in the bishop's country house at Halsteren, near Bergen, that Erasmus revised the *Antibarbari*, and in the bishop's gardens he created the neoclassical setting for the meeting of friends which opens the piece.

Batt, a graduate of the University of Paris, had been back about two years, having been appointed rector of the municipal school. He then became town secretary, not long before the dialogue begins, which permits a fairly precise dating for Erasmus' reworking of the original speech, between the spring and autumn of 1495. Further additions, including the allusions to theologians and religious orders at Louvain, were added in 1520.

In the *Antibarbari* we seem to have a résumé of Erasmus' personal philosophy, based on the experiences of his youth and early manhood. By the time it was sent to Froben for printing he was in his early fifties, and he had suddenly become at once famous and notorious with the appearance between 1515 and 1517 of two new editions of the *Adagia*, and, above all, the publication of the Greek New Testament, the *Novum Instrumentum*, in February 1516. While its principal theme is a defence of classical learning against the attacks of Christian fundamentalists, the *Antibarbari* moves toward an understanding of the Christian mission which informs all of Erasmus' writing. We are also able to identify the masters from whom Erasmus derived his own inspiration, and to locate him precisely in the history of Christian thought.

In the dialogue, Erasmus plays the part simply of host and

(as events prove) recorder of discussion. Batt, cast in the role of the defender of pagan learning, begins with an impassioned account of the difficulties he had encountered as a schoolmaster in trying to improve the curriculum of his school. He is soon given a serious challenge by the burgomaster, in the role of the devil's advocate: Batt's programme implies ('let us be frank') the introduction of heathen authors who are not only difficult to get to know, but who write licentious, even obscene works. 'Now admit the facts: you are rejecting Christian writers and bringing in heathen ones . . . you are forbidding the young to read chaste authors and offering them lascivious ones.' (A 38)

Batt's first line of defence is to plead for genuine knowledge of the pagan authors before judgements are made, since, after all, the entire legacy of our learning comes from those sources. 'If we are to be forbidden to use the inventions of the pagan world, what shall we have left I ask you, in the fields, in the towns, in churches and houses and workshops, at home, at war, in private and in public? To such an extent is it true that we Christians have nothing we have not inherited from the pagans. The fact that we write in Latin, speak it in one way or another, comes to us from the pagans; they discovered writing, they invented the use of speech.' (A 57) He insists on the excellence and virtue of many pagan authors, as he does on the frailty and error of many Christians. 'The books of Origen, censured as heretical in many passages, are read by the Christian church with profit to scholarship; and yet we shun the divine writings of men on whose moral character we cannot pass judgement without the greatest impertinence.' (A 58) It is true that some of the inventions of the pagans are doubtful and unwholesome, but others are useful, health-giving, and even necessary. Why should we not take over the good for ourselves?

From this Batt moves to a more profound reflection: the achievements of the pagans were a part of the divine plan. 'When I look a little more closely at the wonderful arrangement, the harmony as they call it, of things, it always seems to me that it was not without divine guidance that the business of discovering systems of knowledge was given to the pagans.' God, after all, is Wisdom itself, 'establishes all things with consummate skill, differentiates them with beautiful play of interchange, and orders them with perfect rightness'. It was he who willed that the Son, the incarnate Word, should be born in an age which was sovereign over all epochs before or after, and it pleased him that whatever existed in nature should be put to use for increasing the happiness and glory of that time. It was his own promise: 'I, if I be lifted up from the earth, will draw all unto me.' Why did all this happen, if not to ensure that the best religion should be adorned and supported by the finest studies? (A 59)

At this point we find stated the central theme of the book, and indeed the ground of the whole of Erasmus' enterprise: 'Everything in the pagan world that was valiantly done, brilliantly said, ingeniously thought, diligently transmitted, had been prepared by Christ for his society.' (A 60) Later on he adds, 'None of the liberal disciplines is Christian, because they neither treat of Christ nor were invented by Christians; but they all concern Christ.' (A 90) While Christ revealed in his own time the highest good, 'he gave the centuries immediately preceding a privilege of their own: they were to reach the thing nearest to the highest good, that is, the summit of learning'. On this point, God also considered the predicament of the Christians, 'who were likely to have much to do elsewhere' (A 61). Batt goes further: Christians have added nothing to the pagan legacy of learning; more typically, they have brought damage and confusion to the legacy. Batt is not speaking of the mysteries of religion, but of systems of learning. He is adamant: 'In my opinion there is no erudition in existence except what is secular (this is their name for the learning of the ancients) or at least founded on and informed by secular literature.' (A 62)

We are here on the familiar territory of an ancient debate, as Erasmus was well aware. Of particular importance is his invocation of the *preparatio evangelica*—the evangelical preparation of the ancient world to be the cultural cradle of the Christian mystery. In this view, there is less of a gap than one might think between the state of humanity before and after Christ. Man's aptitude for virtue and wholeness existed in part before, not only in pious Israelites, but also in the pagan sages. Their excellence was possible because the grace which abounds since Christ was not lacking before, and the Fall damaged but did not altogether destroy human nature. The acquisition of the finest pagan learning by the Christian will add enormously to his usefulness; 'how much the power of his virtue will be increased, more brilliantly and more widely known as if a torch had been set before it'. But moral worth without learning 'will die with its possessor, unless it be commended to posterity in written works'. He is even prepared to compare the usefulness of martyrs and scholars: 'The martyrs died, and so diminished the number of Christians; the scholars persuaded others and so increased it. In short, the martyrs would have shed their blood in vain for the teaching of Christ unless the others had defended it against the heretics by their writings.' (A 83)

In defence of his views, Batt invokes the famous testimony of Jerome and Augustine, although these were perhaps less favourable to his cause than one might believe from reading Erasmus. He invokes Jerome's analogy of the captive slave woman cleansed and turned into a daughter of Israel, to insist that 'we should not run away from any heathen literature, but should hand it over, cleansed, to Christian learning' (A 92–3). From Augustine he cites the classic metaphor of the Hebrews taking spoils from the Egyptians for their own use. Implied in this is the rejection of what is evil and superstitious. 'But if there is among them any gold of wisdom, any silver of speech, any furniture of good learning, we should pack up all that baggage and turn it to our own use, never fearing to be accused of thieving, but rather venturing to hope for reward and praise for the finest of deeds.' (A 97)

The last serious challenge to Batt's argument is the stark truth that, as the founders of the Christian religion, God chose unlettered apostles whom, surely, we should wish to emulate? Batt replies that while it is most desirable to imitate the apostles in faith, we should also imitate in learning the finest of the doctors of the Church, among whom Jerome is pre-eminent. What is more, Peter, with greater authority, consented to be instructed by Paul, the most highly educated among the apostles. Paul, alone possessing liberal learning, stands out among the other apostles as fitted to bear arms against the schools of Athens, 'and to range Roman eloquence under the sway of Christ'. Significantly, Batt cannot resist pointing out further that the supposedly rustic John was capable of 'that sublime utterance, "In the beginning was the Word, and the Word was with God, and the Word was God."' (A 103) Of this we shall have more to say. Batt also admits, more soberly, that 'it was not for nothing that it was arranged for the Christian religion to take its beginnings from untutored founders. That indeed was right, and its purpose was that the glory of such an event should not appertain to human effort but be attributed entirely to divine power.' (A 113) That was appropriate to those times, but what of the present? The apostles surely never reproved secular learning, and today, it is desperately important to meet the needs of Christendom.

The stylistic authority of this work (as of other among his early letters and writings), its classical citations and allusions, its vivacity and ease, betray not only unusual gifts but, already, a remarkable erudition. This would become increasingly apparent as time passed and Erasmus took responsibility for his own instruction in putting together the *Adagia*, not to mention the editions of Jerome and the New Testament. It is also clear that he was possessed of a prodigious memory. There is charming allusion to this evidently notorious gift in the opening pages of the *Antibarbari* when the fictional Batt, persuaded to give voice to his concerns, agrees to do so only if his remarks are kept in confidence by his friends, and also, 'if only Erasmus can be got to give his pen a rest. Whatever he even dreams at night he blackens his paper with in the daytime.' Erasmus points out that he has with him neither pen nor paper. 'Quite so,' replies Batt, 'but I know what a memory you have—it is as good as a notebook to you.' (A 40–1)

There is nothing mysterious about his educational masters:

they are those of antiquity, Quintilian and Cicero among the foremost. Following thereon, inevitably, is the *De doctrina christiana* of Augustine. All are cited in the *Antibarbari* and frequently in his educational writings. Of course this is only the nucleus, since he seems to have come as near as anyone in his day might have done to fulfilling the mandate of the grammarian—the mastery of all known literature, in order properly to understand the use of speech. We recall the doctrine of a forgotten world, a rhetorical ideal of education, inherited by the Romans from the Greeks, and passed on into Christian antiquity chiefly by the Stoic writers. It conceived of education as directed to the formation of the whole individual, in intellect, and in morals. Its end was the virtuous man, fully informed about the experience of the past, nourished by knowledge of history's great achievements and tragedies, of the legacy of philosophy and literature, and devoted to the use of his talents for the good of the whole community. It is the ideal of the *doctus orator*, the learned orator, where *doctus* implies moral integrity as well as 'book learning'. It was Augustine's contribution in the *De doctrina* to build a bridge between this Ciceronian ideal and Christianity, to domesticate the life of the informed and virtuous pagan in the new religious world. His treatise was the vade-mecum for all of the Christian humanists.

For them, of course, the formative texts of the faith were added to the learning of antiquity. Scripture came first, but this was followed by the chief exponents among the Fathers of the Church, where Jerome and Augustine were foremost in learning and authority. Toward the conclusion of the *Antibarbari* there is a list of Christian writers who meet with approval: Augustine, Jerome, Lactantius Firmianus, Ambrose, Bernard of Clairvaux, Hilary of Poitiers, Bede ('even-toned and dull, but learned, considering his century'), and Gregory the Great. (A 105) The subject of the discussion is 'church writers and their eloquence', but the list reveals more; it reveals an entire tradition of theology, a tradition in which Erasmus most unmistakably stands as a late if eminent figure.

At the heart of that tradition was an ancient conception

of wisdom, invoked by Erasmus at a critical point in the *Antibarbari*, where Batt is distinguishing genuine theologians from those who 'grow old over a stack of jumbled anthologies and digests, thinking nothing learned unless it is barbarous'. By contrast he recommends 'the wise Ecclesiasticus: "the wise man will seek out the wisdom of all the ancients, and will be occupied with the prophets. He will keep the discourse of men of renown, and will enter in among the subtleties of parables. He will seek out the hidden meaning of proverbs, and be conversant in the dark sayings of parables. He will serve among great men, and appear before him that ruleth. He will travel through the land of strange nations; he will try good and evil in all things."' It is in the nature of such wisdom to join together the knowledge of things human and divine as did the wisdom of Solomon, who is also invoked with the approbation of Jerome: 'In the introduction to the Book of Proverbs he admonishes us to understand words of prudence, subtleties of language, parables and dark speeches, sayings of the sages, and riddles, which properly belong to the dialecticians and philosophers.' (A 92)

Here we have the foundation of what Batt praises as 'no confused or barren erudition, but one which is polished and rich, and founded in high antiquity' and we must recall that for Erasmus and his friends, the true theology was the 'old theology'. The wisdom on which it is founded is older than time itself, a direct gift of God, as was that of Solomon. The text of Genesis in the second chapter provides a clue: 'Out of the ground the lord God formed every beast of the field and every bird of the air, and brought them to the man to see what he would call them; and whatever the man called every living creature, that was its name.' So the naming of creatures was a divine power bestowed on Adam, a mark of his primordial understanding of the true nature of things and, individually, of their true *natures* which, of course, their names expressed. We find the same conception put by Plato: 'For the gods must clearly be supposed to call things by their right and natural names.'

The naming of creatures by the representative of the human

family was therefore a sign in ancient tradition of man's mastery over all of creation to which he alone, among God's creatures, had the key: this was divine power. If God alone could utter the creative Word, which had the power to bring into being what it expressed, only his human creature, made in his image, had in turn the power of apprehension, signified by this ability to name. This power rested upon the response of man's created intellect to that to which it was akin, the mind of God, reflected also in all creation. And the greatest deprivation of that primordial cataclysm which we know as the Fall was the darkening of the human intellect, now alienated from its creator, so that it was no longer able to penetrate the inwardness of God's creation, which in turn was reduced to disorder by that same cataclysm.

As we have seen, however, that disorder was not complete. The ineffable God could still be discerned, if only dimly, through the darkened mirror of his creation, so that the wisdom of the ancients, and the tested experience of the race (to be discovered in parables and proverbs) were part of an authentic legacy. Moreover, if the glass had been darkened by the Fall, Christ, the new Adam, had done much to remedy the situation. Was he not the incarnate Word, one with the creative Word from before the beginning of time, identified with the Wisdom which had instructed Solomon and the prophets? Through grace and the power of rebirth in Christ, a better vision could be obtained, especially for those practised in holiness. On the level of morals and practical judgement, proverbial wisdom was a lifeline to supplement the teaching of revelation. The opening of the Book of Proverbs, referred to a moment ago, tells us that these proverbs were collected, 'that men may know wisdom and instruction, understand words of insight, receive instruction in wise dealing, righteousness, justice and equity, that prudence may be given to the simple, knowledge and discretion to the youth. . . . The fear of the Lord is the beginning of knowledge; fools despise wisdom and understanding.'

In these beliefs we have the essential key to an understanding of Erasmus' enterprise in all of its aspects. They explain

21

the singular emphasis on the Word and on words, on speech and eloquence. Education in 'genuine letters'—*bonae litterae*—derives its regenerative power finally from the Word, to the degree that it is vested in traditions stemming from authentic wisdom. It must also now be grounded upon the Word incarnate revealed in the sacred page—in scripture—as well as the rhetorical word of ancient civil society. It must be directed by teachers of high moral character, themselves the product of such training, and for those who wished to apply themselves to the divine mysteries, the original languages were essential, since they alone could open the unpolluted springs of the primordial wisdom and experience of the race.

At the very conclusion of the *Antibarbari*, Batt leaves one question unanswered: 'It remains for us to refute those who say that it is not for a Christian to pay attention to eloquence.' Having to his own satisfaction made the case for the legitimacy of appropriating the wisdom of the past for Christian use, he admits, 'Those who condemn the study of eloquence are many in number, and they have perhaps something to say, if not true at least plausible.' (A 121) It is into this issue that we shall now follow Erasmus in his own voice, to learn why the mastery of eloquence by those capable of it was indeed indispensable to the Christian life.

2 The educational mission

Antibarbari is our most important source, at least for Erasmus' personal development, about the years spent in the monastery in Steyn. The surviving letters from that time are highly conventional exercises in epistolary style, and none at all survive from the last two or three years. We see only an Erasmus avid for literary studies and resentful of the 'barbarism' which is attacked in the *Antibarbari*, whose tones and attitudes are entirely supported by these few letters. In one, he lists his 'authorities in poetry'—Virgil, Horace, Ovid, Juvenal, Statius, Martial, Claudian, Persius, Lucan, Tibullus, and Propertius; in prose, Cicero, Quintilian, Sallust, and Terence. For style, he turns to Lorenzo Valla and to Rudolph Agricola, who was clearly his early inspiration among the northern humanists. After his ordination to the priesthood by the Bishop of Utrecht in 1492, he was permitted to take the post of Latin secretary to Hendrick van Bergen, bishop of Cambrai, who in the next year was named Chancellor of the Order of the Golden Fleece. Both bishops were well-educated, well-connected men of noble family, and Erasmus admired the pastoral and personal qualities of David of Burgundy, his ordaining bishop. From Hendrick van Bergen he presumably looked for further opportunity to study, especially since the bishop was hoping for a red hat, which posed the prospect of a visit to Italy. His hopes however were dashed, and, with them, Erasmus' expectations. Erasmus' letters become gloomy and fretful, and he speaks of 'endless distractions' which keep him from letter-writing and his studies. It is clear that with the assistance of Jacob Batt, who was influential with the bishop's family, he was allowed to go at last to university, to Paris, with the expressed intention of securing a doctor's degree in theology. The year was 1495. Except for occasional visits home, the next four years were spent in Paris, only the first of them at the Collège de Montaigu, where he found the life intolerable. By 1497 he was compelled to take pupils to support his studies. His educational programme germinated in this atmosphere, while he was giving lessons to young men who seem to have been foreigners in Paris, like himself. We have letters from Erasmus to Christian and Henrich Northoff, sons of a merchant from Lübeck, and to two young Englishmen of good family, Thomas Grey and Robert Fisher. Fisher was a kinsman of the future bishop, John Fisher, who was then chaplain and confessor to the Lady Margaret Beaufort and Master of Michaelhouse, Cambridge, and who was later to play an important part in Erasmus' career. The idea of providing teaching materials and helps to study for schoolboys in their assault on the Latin language would have come to Erasmus naturally enough, and in his letters to his pupils in Paris we find authors and precepts recommended also in his treatise on 'The Method of Study'— the *De ratione studii*, published by Erasmus in 1512. His epitome of Lorenzo Valla's *Elegantiae linguae latinae*, first composed for a schoolmaster while Erasmus was still at Steyn, was revised and expanded at this time, and he continued to lend the text to his friends. Valla's work was a landmark in humanist philology, first appearing in the 1440s and widely circulated thereafter. Erasmus finally brought out his paraphrase after his earlier version was published in 1529, without his knowledge, in Cologne and Paris. His revised and authorized version was published in Freiburg in 1531; nevertheless like many of his later publications it began at Steyn and in Paris.

Another of his principal works, on the acquisition of a rich rhetorical style, was in existence at least by 1499 as a manuscript entitled 'A brief instruction on abundance of style'— *Brevis de copia praeceptio*. This was in effect the first draft of what came to be the *De copia verborum ac rerum*— 'Foundations of the Abundant Style', finally published in Paris in 1512. Other of his educational aids began to take shape. For the Northoffs he composed a small handbook of useful and polite conversation (there were many examples by others), 'Rules for familiar conversation', which grew eventually into one of his best-known and best-loved works, the *Colloquia*, or 'Colloquies'. For Robert Fisher he wrote the first version of his extensive treatise on the composition of Latin Letters, *De conscribendis epistolis*. All of these works, like those written shortly after specifically for St Paul's school in London, and like his later translation of the first two books of Theodore of Gaza's important Greek grammar, were intended in the first place to supply the want of sound instruction in the foundations of fine and fluent Latin and Greek. While of itself such an aim has a limited appeal, we must remember that eloquence was perhaps the foremost objective of the educational philosophy espoused by Erasmus and his colleagues. Without it, the informed and moral person could not be an effective, persuasive presence in Christian society.

Of all the works conceived and initiated during the Paris years, the one most informative for us is the *De ratione studii*. It is heavily indebted to Quintilian's *Institutio oratoria*, and also to Lorenzo Valla. It provides not only an account of how to organize study, and how to ensure a mastery of the authors deemed essential to the equipment of the effective citizen, but also how to keep such learning at hand. All authors are to be annotated, and the pupil is to collect notebooks of aphorisms and proverbs he finds striking and useful while reading his authors.

Since a true foundation must be laid, Erasmus wrote, 'Grammar claims primacy of place and at the outset boys must be instructed in two—Greek, of course, and Latin. This is not only because almost everything worth learning is set forth in these two languages, but in addition because each is so cognate to the other that both can be more quickly assimilated when they are taken in conjunction...' (S 667). The voice of the schoolmaster is sure and direct. The authors studied should be very limited in number 'but carefully chosen': Theodore of Gaza, followed (in second place) by Constantine Lascaris. The fourth-century grammarian Diomedes is recommended 'among ancient Latinists', but Erasmus finds little to choose among the more recent, excepting only Niccolo Perotti, secretary to Cardinal Bessarion and a member of the distinguished literary circle which included Theodore of Gaza and Lascaris. His *Rudimenta grammatices*, printed in Rome in 1473, was the first modern Latin grammar. In any case, Erasmus is reluctant to multiply the names of printed grammars, and it seems certain that he would rely principally on the teacher. He disagrees 'with the common run of teachers who, in inculcating these authors, hold boys back for several years'. No doubt his own experience was in his mind, but we must remember also that he is concerned above all that the young pupil should be taught to speak correctly, a skill 'best fostered both by conversing and consorting with those who speak correctly and by the habitual reading of the best stylists'. For the beginner he recommends Lucian, then Demosthenes, and thirdly, Herodotus. Among the poets, Aristophanes first, Homer second, and Euripides. Among Latin writers, Terence is first and foremost; 'he is pure, concise, and closest to everyday speech'. His subject-matter is also congenial to the young. He would add a few, well-selected comedies of Plautus, 'free from impropriety'. Virgil occupies the second place, then in order, Horace, Cicero, and finally Caesar. He would not object to the addition of Sallust. 'These, then, I believe to be sufficient for a knowledge of each language.' (S 669)

Once a pure linguistic foundation is laid, the youthful mind must be directed toward 'an understanding of things' as well as of words. Some of this will be absorbed in the course of reading the authors already listed, and almost all is to be sought in the Greek authors.

Further study with such masters as Lorenzo Valla will instruct the student in elegant style; he must also memorize the rules of poetry, and the chief points of rhetoric. Whenever reading, passages are to be marked at any striking word or expression, brilliance of argument or style, any adage, historical parallel, or maxim worth committing to memory. At the same time, 'the best master of style is the pen and you must therefore give it plenty of practice in poetry, prose and every sort of literary material' (S 671). The memory must also be cultivated, and while Erasmus does not disapprove of memory systems, he asserts, 'nevertheless, the best memory is based on three things above all: understanding, system and

care. For memory largely consists in having thoroughly understood something.' Things which are necessary but difficult
to remember may be written 'as briefly and attractively as
possible on charts and hung up on the walls of a room where
they are generally conspicuous'. The beginnings and ends of
books will be likewise adorned with 'brief but pithy sayings',
while other such will be inscribed on rings or drinking cups,
painted on doors and walls or even in the glass of a window
so that what may aid learning is constantly before the eye.
Finally, the greatest instruction of all comes from teaching
others. 'For there is no better means of grasping what you
understand and what you do not. Sometimes new ideas occur
to one in preparing a lesson, and everything is more firmly
fixed in the mind when teaching.' (S 672)

Accordingly, Erasmus concludes his treatise by considering
the method of teaching pupils. Quintilian is again acknowledged as the master, 'so that it would seem the height of
impertinence to write about a subject he has already dealt
with' (S 672). Preparation of the teacher is first: he must have
a firm grasp of the fundamentals of each discipline. Erasmus
is in accord with the principles of the ancient grammarians,
who insisted that a complete knowledge of all literature was
needed if the understanding of any given word in its place was
to be complete. He insists that the teacher must have much
more than the usual 'select list' of authors at his command.
'He must range through the entire spectrum of writers so that
he reads, in particular, all the best, but does not fail to sample
any author, no matter how pedestrian.' Accordingly, he should
have at hand his commonplace books where he notes 'systems
and topics, so that wherever something noteworthy occurs
he may write it down in the appropriate column' (S 672).
An account of the commonplace book, which became one of
the great conventions of learning in the two centuries that
followed, is set forth at more length in the *De copia*, which
was published together with the *De ratione studii*. Above all,
Erasmus insists, 'recourse must be had to the sources themselves, that is, to the Greeks and the ancients. Plato, Aristotle,
and his pupil Theophrastus will serve as the best teachers of

27

philosophy, and then there is Plotinus who combines both
these schools. Among theological writers, after the Scriptures,
no one writes better than Origen, no one more subtly or
attractively than Chrysostom, no one more devoutly than
Basil. Among the Latin Fathers, two at least are outstanding in
this field: Ambrose who is wonderfully rich in metaphors, and
Jerome who is immensely learned in the sacred Scriptures.'
In studying the poets it will also be necessary to command
a good supply of mythological lore, 'and from whom is it
better to seek this than Homer, the father of all myth?' The
Metamorphoses and *Fasti* of Ovid are recommended, 'although
written in Latin', as of no small importance. Geography,
needed for history and poetry both, can be learned from
Pomponius Mela, Ptolemy ('most eruditely'), and Pliny ('most
comprehensively'). (S 673)

In this passage we find crystallized Erasmus's view of education as a grammarian: the totality of all good learning includes
not only the ancient pagan masters, but scripture and the
doctors of the Church. This is a single fabric, woven in many
hues and from more than one fibre, but it is the fabric of
Christian culture, from which the adornment of men and
nations must, he holds, be fashioned. In his final sentence, he
addresses the French friend to whom the work was dedicated
as follows: 'Forge ahead as you have begun; apply yourself
zealously to the cause of learning, and adorn your native
France, so illustrious in other spheres, with ennobling studies
as well.' (S 691) It is too easy to read such words as mere
convention and dismiss them, but the intent was serious and,
in the author's mind, the cause the most urgent and fundamental of any facing the nations of Europe. For reasons indicated in the previous chapter, education in the works of
worthy authors, both sacred and profane, was an immersion in
the mystery of the Word, an ascesis that cleansed the soul and
turned the nature of the learner to good and holy ends.

We left Erasmus with his pupils in Paris, among them two
Englishmen, Thomas Grey and Robert Fisher. By November
1498, he was also acting as tutor to William Blount, fourth
Baron Mountjoy, whose grandfather had been ennobled by

Henry VI for loyal service during the Wars of the Roses. Mountjoy became a patron and firm friend, and the next year he invited Erasmus to accompany him when he returned to England. This first stay was brief, but it may have been during that visit, in conversation with Mountjoy, that Erasmus conceived of another work which was, in time, to become a cornerstone of the revived classical culture of Europe, the *Adagia*. Once again, Paris and the circle of pupils there provided the place and occasion; the first version was published there in 1500 with a prefatory letter dedicating the work to Lord Mountjoy. It was called the *Adagiorum collectanea*, and it contained 818 adages, Greek and Latin. Like the *De copia*, it emerged directly from Erasmus practising what he preached, and from edition to edition it grew abundantly with the passage of time. It is the centrepiece of Erasmus' secular learning, and occupied the same position in that sphere of knowledge and understanding as did the edition of the New Testament in sacred learning. Some explanation of it is therefore essential in this place.

In his dedicatory letter to Mountjoy, Erasmus explains, with pleasing fiction, that the work came about when he set aside more serious studies owing to a fever, 'and strolled through divers gardens of the classics, occupied in this lighter kind of study, and so plucked, and as it were arranged in garlands, like flowerets of every hue, all the most ancient and famous of the adages'. And he hopes as well that the collection will be of use to others, 'those, I mean, who dislike the current jargon and are searching for greater elegance and a more refined style' (W 1.257).

The printer of this modest book of 152 pages was a German named Master Johann Philipp, who had set up his presses on the south bank of the Seine, near the Collège de Montaigu and the Abbey of Sainte-Geneviève, in a district well known to Erasmus. The printer's blurb described it as 'A collection of *paroemiae* or adages, old and most celebrated, made by Desyderius Herasmus Roterdamus: a work both new and wonderfully useful for conferring beauty and distinction on all kinds of speech and writing'. The book was printed in Roman

29

type, to identify its kinship with Italian humanism. It was a book of Latin scholarship—Erasmus was still struggling to master Greek—but it provided Greek versions for 154 of the proverbs it contained and 143 more were added in the second edition. It was thus one of the first books issued from the Paris presses to print some words in Greek, which in itself gave it great cachet. The *Collectanea* would be of small intrinsic importance if it had not been the seed from which a massive achievement would grow, yet to the literary circles in Paris and England it was a landmark. In 1508 it re-emerged in wholly new form as from a chrysalis, as the *Adagiorum Chiliades* ('ordered in thousands'), a book beautifully printed by Aldus in Venice, in which the number of adages had risen to 3,260. This version reflected Erasmus' reading of the Greek authors since 1500, containing a large proportion of Greek passages, and its aim was not simply to explain the proverb, but to give its whole pedigree, as the saying moved from author to author, from poetry to prose. The proverb was also a convenient peg, quite often, on which to hang picturesque information about the ancient world, or telling commentary about the issues of the day. It was this possibility which led to some of the adages taking on an independent literary existence of their own. The Froben edition of 1515 envisaged a yet wider public, added new adages and long commentaries, and Latin translations of all the Greek. The process of enrichment continued in the edition of 1517/18 and in each of the six editions up to that of 1536. At Erasmus' death in that year, the number of adages was 4,151.

In his introduction to the *Adagia* Erasmus opens with the topic 'What a proverb is'. He first cites the Latin grammarian, Donatus, as follows: 'A proverb is "a saying which is fitted to things and times". Diomedes however defines it as follows: "A proverb is the taking over of a popular saying, fitted to things and times, when the words say one thing and mean another."' Then, noting that many definitions exist among the Latin and Greek writers, Erasmus sums up the leading elements on which there is agreement: a proverb has in it something of the allegory, and it contains something gnomic or didactic, which is helpful in the conduct of life. Despite the great variety, he continues, 'I would not deny that the majority of adages have some kind of metaphorical disguise. I think the best of them are those which equally give pleasure by their figurative colouring and profit by the value of their ideas.' He proposes then a complete definition of his own: 'A proverb is a saying in popular use, remarkable for some shrewd and novel turn.' (Ad 4)

In this passage, 'proverb' represents the Greek *paroemia*, which we read also in the printer's blurb advertising the *Collectanea*. The term could mean a byword, but it could also carry the sense of an enigma or parable. When the disciples of Jesus say that their master is now speaking plainly and not in any figure (John 16: 29), the Greek word is *paroemia*. There may be something numinous, therefore, about an adage, which, like an analogy, alludes to more than it signifies directly. Erasmus emphasizes the antiquity of proverbs, and how they were respected by the greatest among the ancients, from Aristotle and Plato through Plutarch and the poets, even to their use by Christ himself: 'by their fruits shall ye know them', 'they strain at a gnat and swallow a camel'. They encapsulate ancient wisdom and the experience of the race, and 'there appears to be no form of teaching which is older than the proverb. In these symbols, as it were, almost all the philosophy of the Ancients was contained. What were the oracles of those wise old Sages but proverbs? They were so deeply respected in old time that they seemed to have fallen from heaven rather than to have come from men. "And *Know thyself* descended from the sky", says Juvenal.' (Ad 13)

This primordial quality is of course of the greatest interest to Erasmus. He is prepared to hint that proverbs derive from that time of ancient harmony and understanding before the cataclysm of our first parents. In explaining why he has said that they belong to the science of philosophy, he states that 'Aristotle, according to Synesius, thinks that proverbs were simply the vestiges of that earliest philosophy which was destroyed by the calamities of human history'. For that reason they are to be looked into, 'closely and deeply: for underlying them there are what one might call sparks of that ancient philosophy, which was much more clear-sighted in its investigation of truth than were the philosophers who came after. Plutarch too . . . thinks the adages of the Ancients very similar to the rites of religion, in which things which are most important and even divine are often expressed in ceremonies of a trivial and seemingly almost ridiculous nature.' (Ad 14) He suggests that these sayings, brief as they are, give a hint in their concealed way of those very things which were propounded in so many volumes by the princes of philosophy. For instance, that proverb in Hesiod, 'The half is more than the whole', is exactly what Plato in the *Gorgias* and in his books on the State tries to expound by so many arguments: it is preferable to receive an injury than to inflict one. What doctrine was ever produced by the philosophers more salutary as a principle of life or closer to the Christian religion?

This is a chord struck again and again throughout the entirety of the *Adagia*: the explicit desire to show the harmony between classical wisdom and Christian teaching. In the passage immediately following that above, Erasmus cites Pythagoras, 'Between friends all is common'. This is the first of the entire collection, and Erasmus hails this as enclosing in a brief saying the whole of human happiness. 'What other purpose has Plato in so many volumes except to urge a community of living and the factor which creates it, namely friendship? If only he could persuade mortals of these things, war, envy and fraud would at once vanish from our midst; in short a whole regiment of woes would depart from life once and for all. What other purpose had Christ, the prince of our religion? One precept and one alone He gave to the world, and that was love; on that alone, He taught, hang all the law and the prophets. Or what else does love teach us, except that all things should be common to all? In fact that united in friendship with Christ, glued to Him by the same binding force that holds Him fast to the Father, imitating so far as we may that complete communion by which He and the Father are one, we should also be one with Him, and as Paul says, should become one spirit and one flesh with God, so that by the laws of friendship all that is His is shared with us and all that is ours is shared with Him; and then that, linked one to another in the same bonds of friendship, as members of one Head and like one and the same body we may be filled with the same spirit, and weep and rejoice at the same things together. This is signified to us by the mystic bread, brought together out of many grains into one flour, and the draught of wine fused into one liquid from many clusters of grapes. Finally, love teaches how, as the sum of all created things is in God and God is in all things, the universal all is in fact one. You see that an ocean of philosophy, or rather of theology, is opened up to us by this tiny proverb.' (Ad 15)

This abrupt flight into the most serious issues of the Christian faith is utterly characteristic of Erasmus, and it occurs equally in another, more controversial work which appeared not long after the publication of the *Chiliades*, the *Praise of Folly* (1511). Nothing gives more vivid witness to his personal vision of the unity of human understanding and experience.

The *Adagia* then found followers for many reasons. It was a treasury of stylistic adornments; it was, equally, a handbook of erudition in which the user, learned or not, could claim an acquaintance with the classical heritage to astonish and delight his readers. As a vade-mecum of ancient culture, it also provided a historical perspective on the past which distinguishes it from its medieval antecedents, the encyclopaedias and compendia of knowledge. Not that the *Adagia* professes to teach history. Its information about the past is fragmentary, although animated by Erasmus' critical sense and commentaries on his sources. At the same time it is unsystematic and disorganized, and filled with gossip, which gives its contents the savour of actuality. An example at random might be the adage *Frons occipitio prior*, 'Forehead before occiput'—the occiput being the back part of the head. Erasmus delights in the riddling quality of this ancient saw, finds it in Cato *On Agriculture*, chapter 4, in Pliny, and in Aristotle's *Economica*, Book 1, where it is used to mean that the presence of the master was the most important thing in the successful conduct of affairs. Erasmus is then reminded of a passage in Columella, of a story in Aulus Gellius, of a passage in Plutarch's essay 'On the Education of Children', and of the same simile used by Aeschylus in the *Persians*. He then proceeds through Livy and Terence to conclude as follows:

'The person who should most take note of this is the prince, if he really has the mind of a prince and not of a pirate, that is if he has the public good at heart. But in these days bishops and kings do everything through other people's hands, ears and eyes, and think the common good is what concerns them least, kept busy as they are with their own private possessions or entirely bent on pleasure.' (Ad 165)

There was probably no other work from Erasmus' hand which had a greater direct impact on European culture than this, nor one more difficult to trace. A glance through an index of the *Adagia* will reveal phrases that are still on our lips, which many would probably attribute, vaguely, to the Bible, and which almost none would know had once been put abroad in Erasmus' great compilation: A necessary evil; There's many a slip 'twixt cup and lip; To squeeze water out of a stone; To leave no stone unturned; Let the cobbler stick to his last; God helps those who help themselves; The grass is greener over the fence; The cart before the horse; Dog in the manger; One swallow doesn't make a summer; His heart was in his boots; A rare bird; To have one foot in the grave; To be in the same boat; To sleep on it; To call a spade a spade; Up to the ears; To break the ice; Ship-shape; To die of laughing; To have an iron in the fire; To look a gift horse in the mouth; Neither fish nor flesh; Like father, like son; Not worth a snap of the fingers; He blows his own trumpet; To show one's heels. (Ph 7)

From time to time Erasmus ordered his writings into categories, with the thought in mind that one day they would be published as a whole, as indeed they were immediately on his death. The categories include educational works, *moralia* (including *Praise of Folly*), works of piety, and the many *apologiae* which he wrote to respond to his critics. Two large items in his legacy fit into none of these classes, and he listed them separately between the educational and the moral writings. One of these is the body of his letters: the second, the *Adagia*. The *Adagia* were indeed a hybrid, partly a work of literary instruction, partly the work of a moralist, partly touching on religion and piety. He explained to Colet that they came about as a by-product of his studies in Greek literature, preparatory to his study of the New Testament. There is no reason to doubt this, and it was utterly characteristic that, with his restless intellect and pen, he saw the opportunity to create a remarkable new work that would remain, not quite incidentally, a valuable commonplace book for his own use. Although he intended in principle to exclude from it proverbs in scripture, he could not resist the inclusion of some, as we have seen. We have drawn attention to his conviction that there was a genuine link between the culture represented by the classics and that revealed by God in Christ. As a grammarian, he knew that it would not be possible to understand the one without a complete grasp of the other. It is time, then, to turn to the enterprise for which the *Adagia* and many of the related educational works were really in part a propaedeutic, and that is the study of the Fathers and the New Testament.

3 Adorning the temple of the Lord

Erasmus' edition of the New Testament, which made the Greek text available in print for the first time, is remembered as his most important achievement. This is partly because his profound influence in other spheres, especially in education and Christian piety, became virtually invisible by its general absorption into the mainstream of European thought: the presence of his *Adages* throughout the works of Shakespeare is an illustrative example. Nevertheless the symbolic importance of the *Novum instrumentum* (as he called it initially) in defining the impact of Christian humanism on the intellectual culture of the day is matched by that of no other single work, including his own *Praise of Folly*. The fact that the *editio princeps* of 1516 became (rightly or wrongly) notorious for its errors, that its very status as an edition was unclear even to his contemporaries, and that its absorption into the *textus receptus* of biblical scholarship contributed to a legacy of critical problems that were not unravelled until the advent of 'higher criticism' in the nineteenth century—all of these serious qualifications notwithstanding, where the name of Erasmus is remembered, it is remembered first for the printing of the New Testament in Greek.

A new generation of scholars has given us for the first time a proper understanding of the curious inception of this famous work, and of its true nature. It is now clear that the printing of the Greek text was, in the strict sense, the last thing that mattered. Moreover, attention to it as an *editio princeps* has diverted attention away from the other two components making up the *Novum instrumentum*, a new Latin version of the text revising the Vulgate, and an assembly of copious notes known as the *Annotations*. These were not footnotes, but rather an independent work which is actually an extended commentary, not on the Greek, but on the Vulgate *textus receptus* of the day. Of the three elements contained in the *Novum instrumentum*—the Greek text, the Latin translation, and the *Annotations*—only the last was a part of his original project. In order to understand how all of this came about, and to make a proper assessment of the importance of his New Testament scholarship in the wider enterprise of the Dutch humanist, we must return to that critical period at the end of Erasmus' stay in the University of Paris.

In 1499, we recall, Erasmus accompanied Lord Mountjoy to England, at a time when he was occupied with the incipient *Adages* and the *Antibarbari*. He spent the best part of a year there, from the spring of 1499 until January 1500. The visit provided him with many valuable introductions, not least to Thomas More and, through him, to the youthful Prince Henry, who was to become Henry VIII. Most important of all was his stay in Oxford at the house of studies of his religious order, the Augustinian canons. This was St Mary's College, not far from the Oxford Castle in what is now New Inn Hall Street. He seems to have spent the Michaelmas term there. The prior of St Mary's, Richard Charnock, was a sympathetic colleague who joined with Mountjoy in urging Erasmus to persevere with what was to be the *Collectanea*, the first version of the *Adages*. John Colet had been lecturing in the university for some time on the Epistles of St Paul, bringing to them his considerable knowledge of Florentine Neoplatonism and, presumably, other resources from an earlier education of which we know but little. His lectures, although from the traditional Vulgate text, apparently inspired Erasmus as they inspired other of his hearers, by deriving theological reflection directly from scripture and the Fathers, rather than from scholastic reasoning. The method was not new; it was that of the 'old theology' practised by the authorities whom Erasmus cited in the *Antibarbari*, and which continued after the birth of scholasticism like an underground stream among the Victorines and in monastic schools. Nevertheless, to the members of Colet's university audience at Oxford in the last years of the fifteenth century, his approach came as a revelation of new possibilities, especially in combination with the newly fashionable Neoplatonism from Florence.

Colet's impact on Erasmus must be inferred from a half-dozen surviving letters. Initially, Erasmus presented himself modestly to Colet as one who 'enjoys but little experience of letters, but admits to a consuming passion for them', and who finds England most agreeable in that it is 'well supplied with that without which life itself is disagreeable to me; I mean men who are well versed in good literature' (W 1.201). However, what Colet and Erasmus discuss, and with much seriousness, is theology, and in particular, the central issue of Jesus' awareness of his own humanity, and its implications for his suffering. It is most likely that Erasmus was caught up suddenly with a frustration which had pursued him through the monastery and the schools in Paris—the sterility (in his view) of the 'modern class of theologians, who spend their lives in sheer hair-splitting and sophistical quibbling'. If he had been indifferent to theology, a devotee of pagan learning and letters and nothing more, he would have been less indignant. His response to Colet's concerns is deeply serious, since (as he wrote) he regarded theology as, indeed, 'that great queen of all sciences, enriched and adorned as she had been by the eloquence of antiquity'. In his view, the adoption of Aristotelian logic as the necessary framework for theological sciences by the university masters had imposed on the religious wisdom of the past an alien, arcane, and speculative discipline which made it inaccessible to any but the specialists, and displaced the primary authority of the text of scripture with a pagan artifice. The 'modern' theologians therefore—the Scotists and Occamists—were seen by him 'to choke up, as it were with brambles, the way of a science that early thinkers had cleared and, attempting to settle all questions, so they claim, merely envelop all in darkness' (W 1.203).

It is not necessary then to suppose that up to this time Erasmus had been simply (in the words of one scholar) 'a divided personality, the unwilling monk obliged to pursue the study of scholastic theology, and the ardent wooer of the classical Muse'. He was too well acquainted with antiquity—that antiquity which included the first four centuries of Christian history—to think that there was no alternative to the scholasticism which he found so tedious and repugnant in the schools of Paris. As one brought up in the spiritual culture of the Netherlands, in contact with the 'modern devotion' through his schooling and his religious community, as an early student of Jerome and a lover of the 'Christian Virgil', Baptista Mantuanus, he was already persuaded of the rhetorical and devotional nature of theology, supported by the tradition of the Church. It is entirely possible—indeed, likely—that not until his arrival in Oxford had he heard a theologian lecture in the manner of the 'old theology' who was also familiar with the latest enthusiasms of the classical revival, and who was therefore able to bring to life those deep affinities between classical antiquity and the Christian revelation of which Erasmus was already convinced.

This is important because of a persistent tradition that the conversion of Erasmus from poetry and elegant *belles-lettres* occurred only after his time at Paris, when he came to know the English humanists and, in particular, John Colet. We might recall an earlier correspondence with a fellow-Augustinian, Cornelis Gerard, an older man and a member of a house near Leiden. Like Erasmus he was a native of Gouda, and it is likely that their acquaintance was an early one. He was a man of letters who was crowned poet laureate by the Emperor Maximilian in 1508, and he is probably among those who gave Erasmus help and encouragement in his early studies. In the summer of 1489, writing to Gerard with his familiar complaints about those who condemn poetry as immoral ('... shall we have to censure for indecency everything that is wittily expressed or poetic?'), Erasmus invokes the authority of St Jerome: 'those worthies are only drawing a cloak over their own lack of culture, with the result that they seem to despise what they despair of achieving. If they looked carefully at Jerome's letters, they would see at least that lack of culture is not holiness, nor cleverness impiety.' (W 1.35) He also informed Gerard that he had not only read the letters of Jerome 'long ago', but copied out all of them with his own hands. It is evident that in the very years when Erasmus was discovering the Valla of the *Elegantiae* and the canon of authors in ancient Greece and Rome, he was also finding a model of Christian learning in that first master of the text of scripture, St Jerome.

As a result of their colloquies, Colet reproached Erasmus for having devoted his life entirely to secular literature. Erasmus was now in his early thirties. There was doubtless an element of self-justification in his reply. He insisted that those studies were an apprenticeship only. On the other hand, he was not yet ready to join Colet in the proper theological exposition of the Bible, and insisted that that task still lay ahead for him. He needed better preparation. In particular, he needed a mastery of Greek—a requirement which was not, it seems, so apparent to Colet. Erasmus returned to Paris to repair that want at all costs, and the first evidence of his enterprise, which was clearly already in hand before he went to England, was the Greek contained in the *Collectanea*, which appeared in the following July.

His apprenticeship was a long one, and it led through the legacy of his master, Jerome. Soon after his return to the Continent, Erasmus set out to restore and edit the letters of Jerome and to write a commentary on them. It was a great commitment, and one which combined his love of antiquity with his religion. To Jacob Batt, who was seeking financial support for Erasmus' project, he wrote that he hoped 'to restore the entire text of Jerome, which has been spoiled and garbled and confused by the ignorance of divines, for I have found many passages in his writings that are corrupt or spurious, and to restore the Greek. By so doing I shall cast light on the ancient world and illuminate his literary achievement, which I venture to say nobody hitherto has appreciated. . . . There will be no need for you to tell lies in this connexion, dear Batt, for I really am working at this.' (W 1.305)

Writing to another friend at the same time, he denounces the neglect of Jerome. 'Great Heavens: Scotus and Albertus Magnus and still more unscholarly writers than these are noisily preached in every school, while Jerome, the supreme champion and expositor and ornament of our faith . . . is the only one among all the Fathers of whom no mention is made.' And why? 'That very excellence of style, which benefitted our faith, has done harm to its creator. Many are put off by the profound learning which ought to have been the especial source of his fame; so there are few to admire an author who is comprehended by few indeed.' (W 1.141) Enlarging upon his plans, he discloses an editorial procedure which was wholly indebted to the classical grammarians, and in future to be used in his ambitious programme for the restoration of the sources of Christianity including the New Testament itself. First, he will purge Jerome's text of the errors accumulated over the centuries. Secondly, he will examine the evidence for Jerome's own learning—his classical sources, his Greek scholarship, his knowledge of ancient history—as well as 'all those stylistic and rhetorical accomplishments in which he not only far outstrips all Christian writers, but even seems to rival Cicero himself'. In a word, he would treat Jerome as a historical figure, writing in a specific time and culture, who would express himself accordingly, and who could be understood properly only with a knowledge of that time and culture. This was what the humanist approach implied, important enough in studying ancient literature, but potentially very disturbing when applied to the great religious texts whose eternal verities had been abstracted by the philosophers from the concrete realities of the world in which they were conceived and set down.

Was this decision to edit the works of Jerome an evasion of his promise to devote the rest of his life to the study of scripture? Not in the least, although it is tempting to see in his affinity with Jerome something more than a shared concern to establish the text of scripture. Jerome's vivid letters, his ardent, passionate nature, his powerful affections and hostilities, his dislike of hypocrites, his self-condemnations, his combativeness—all of these call to mind the temperament of his great humanist admirer. Jerome too was in love, famously, with the pagan classics, and was torn by guilt over this addiction in the face of his equally powerful ascetic vocation; in this he felt more unease than did Erasmus. Erasmus had, however, one problem lacking to Jerome; he had to work in relation to an acknowledged, 'received' Latin text of the

New Testament, where Jerome's task had been precisely to establish such a text. Everything points to the fact that it was this received Latin text—the Vulgate—which was the final object of Erasmus' concern. The road to it led, therefore, through Jerome. In Jerome's day there were several Latin versions in common use, some of which preserved important readings from Greek texts already lost. Jerome's new translation was made from the Greek, but incorporated important critical information retained in these 'Old Latin' versions, as they have come to be known. Jerome's text, which was accompanied by volumes of commentaries, came to be known as the 'Vulgate', or common text of Latin Christendom. Its Old Testament Jerome translated directly from the Hebrew, in place of the Greek 'Septuagint' version of the Hebrew Scriptures which was authoritative in his day. By Erasmus' time the Vulgate text had endured so many vagaries in its journey through the centuries that Erasmus declared it no longer represented Jerome's original version. His own efforts could therefore be seen in part as an extension of his editorial labours over Jerome himself.

If Erasmus were to achieve his aim of re-establishing Jerome's Latin translation of the New Testament, he had clearly to become familiar with the Greek versions which underlay it. By the same token, he had to attain the familiarity with Greek letters which would allow him to read the Greek New Testament with something of the authority that Jerome's understanding brought to it. These then are the continuing preoccupations of the years that follow his departure from Oxford.

When he returned to the Continent in 1500 he began to search for Greek texts of the Gospels and Psalms. He was also searching for a haven in which to continue his studies, since the plague at Paris and Orléans had driven him from both cities back to his native Holland, where in due course he settled at the castle of Tournehem with his friend Jacob Batt, now tutor to the young Adolph of Burgundy. Here he came into contact with an ecclesiastic whose influence on him was at least as powerful as that of John Colet—Jean Vitrier. Vitrier was an Observant Franciscan, a graduate of Louvain, and now Warden of the Franciscan convent at nearby Saint-Omer, where Vitrier had been born. He was heir to the Franciscan spiritualism of the previous century which had been touched by the apocalyptic doctrines of Joachim of Fiore. He was an intransigent reformer, a mystic influenced by Origen, and an opponent of the scholastic method. After a perhaps predictably difficult beginning, the relationship between the two men deepened with their discovery of common concerns, and in particular, Vitrier encouraged Erasmus' study of St Paul, and his appreciation of Origen. During a retreat at Courtebourne Erasmus read Origen's homilies and his commentary on the Epistle to the Romans. One immediate result was the composition of the *Enchiridion*, Erasmus' first great essay in devotional literature, which was infused with citations from Origen.

By this time, Erasmus had already decided to write his own commentary on the Epistle to the Romans, a classic undertaking for a devotee of the 'old theology'. He sought from the library at the abbey of St Bertin in nearby Saint-Omer the commentaries of Augustine, Ambrose, and Nicholas of Lyra, as well as Origen 'or anyone else who has written a commentary on Paul'. In his dedicatory preface to the *Enchiridion*, written in the autumn of 1501, he referred to his project in terms now familiar to us, as something 'to cause certain malicious critics, who think it the height of piety to be ignorant of sound learning, to realize that, when in my youth I embraced the finer literature of the ancients and acquired, not without much midnight labour, a reasonable knowledge of the Greek as well as the Latin language, I did not aim at vain glory or childish self-gratification, but had long ago determined to adorn the Lord's temple, badly desecrated as it has been by the ignorance and barbarism of some, with treasures from other realms' (W 2.53). Three years later he informed Colet that he had finished four volumes of this work 'at one rush, as it were', but interrupted himself because he needed Greek 'at every point'. He also took up the study of Hebrew, 'but stopped because I was put off by the strangeness of the language, and at the same time the shortness of life'. As for Origen, he informed Colet that 'he reveals some of the well-springs, as it were, and demonstrates some of the basic principles, of the science of theology' (W 2.87). It would be interesting to know what Colet made of all this. He certainly did not agree with Erasmus' insistence on the value of knowing the masters of pagan literature for scriptural study, as Erika Rummel has said. In his lectures on Corinthians he repudiated this view directly, asking whether such reliance 'does not make them a chief obstacle to such understanding', since in reading the pagan authors for assistance, 'you distrust your power of understanding the Scriptures by grace alone, and prayer, and by the help of Christ, and of faith' (R 12).

In 1504, in the abbey of Parc just outside Louvain, Erasmus discovered a manuscript of Valla's notes on the text of the Vulgate, his *Collatio novi testamenti*. He published it the following year as *Adnotationes in novum testamentum*. His discovery of these notes would certainly have confirmed his philological interests, although Erasmus had already begun his task. Valla's was strictly a grammarian's appraisal, comparing a number of manuscripts, including the Greek, and preferring the earlier as more authoritative. He examined the grammatical and rhetorical elements in the formation of the Vulgate text, and criticized some obscurities of meaning. It was not the work of an exegete or a theologian, and Erasmus commented later that Valla's study was 'most praiseworthy' for his energy and method, and that he was 'a man more concerned with literature than with theology... although in some things I differ from him, especially in those that relate to theological science' (W 3.137). This letter, written in 1515, confirms the impression that Erasmus conceived of his responsibility as, finally, a theological one. In restoring the text of scripture, he would also initiate a renewal of Christian theology. His models in this mission were Jerome, Augustine, and Origen, all of whom he mentions repeatedly, but, above all, his model was Jerome.

It was long believed that his discovery of Valla's annotations on the New Testament was the immediate inspiration for his own Latin version, and that his work on this began in 1505–6. This belief rested on the existence of manuscript copies intended for Colet and for Henry VIII, and bearing dates of October 1506 and September 1509. These manuscripts contain the texts both of the Vulgate and of Erasmus' version. Thanks to the scholarship of Andrew Brown, it is now known that the colophon dates in these manuscripts, which were prepared by Pieter Meghen, a copyist much favoured in the English humanist circle, applied only to the Vulgate text contained in them, and that Erasmus' translation (in an Oxford manuscript, interlinear, in the others in a wide margin) was added in the 1520s. This discovery verifies Erasmus' own statements to the effect that he had no intention of preparing an entire reworking of the Vulgate text, and that the decision to add one was made at the last minute, after the work was already ready for Froben's press.

How, then, did Erasmus proceed? We left him with his work on Jerome, his writing of the *Enchiridion*, his editing of Valla's annotations on the New Testament, and his undertaking of a commentary on the Epistles of St Paul, arrested by his deficiencies in Greek. In 1505 he made a second trip to England. Translations from the Greek are the keynote: from Lucian, with Thomas More, from Euripides, now added to his earlier translations from the writings of the rhetorician Libanius, who numbered among his pupils St John Chrysostom, whom Erasmus greatly admired. These were practice pieces, and we must assume that, if his earlier explanations to Colet have something of a self-justifying air, these exercises fit precisely into his programme for self-education in Greek. In the spring of 1506 Erasmus left England for Italy, accompanying the sons of a Genoese physician who had settled in England, professedly 'mainly in order to learn Greek'. He was to spend the next three years in Italy, where he took, perfunctorily, a doctorate in theology from the University at Turin, and stayed with Aldus in Venice to complete a much augmented edition of the *Adagia* and to work on editions of Plautus, Terence, and Seneca's tragedies. His travels took him to Padua, Siena, and Rome, and then as far as Naples, whence he visited the cave of

the Sibyl at Cumae. These years, and those that followed until
the spring of 1511, are most obscure since no letter from his
pen survives between December 1508 (to Aldo Manuzio in
Venice) and April 1511 (to Andrea Ammonio, from Dover). He
returned to England in 1509 on the accession of Henry VIII to
the throne, and it is to this period that we owe the *Praise of
Folly*. He is presumed to have lived in London during an
extended period of which, again, we know nothing. The letter
to Ammonio was written while Erasmus was on his way to
Paris, to supervise the printing of the *Praise of Folly*. He
returned to London by mid-June, and fell ill with the sweating
sickness, from which he was still feeling the effects when he
had to go to Cambridge to take up a position created for him
by John Fisher, to lecture in Greek. He translated the Mass of
St John Chrysostom from the Greek, and presented to Fisher a
translation of St Basil's commentary on Isaiah. He lectured
on the grammar of Manuel Chrysoloras and, for more senior
listeners, on that of Theodore Gaza. He completed the *De
copia*, written originally before he left for Italy, and amplified
his treatise on letter-writing, the *De conscribendis epistolis*.
His letters began to be sprinkled liberally with Greek phrases.
In 1512, he dedicated to Archbishop Warham, who had presented him with the living of Aldington in Kent, a group of
translations from Lucian. In all of this, no reference survives
to his projected work on the Epistles of St Paul. From his later
remarks we gather that he was seeking out Greek and Latin
manuscripts to compare with the Vulgate, and in the autumn
of 1512 he remarks, 'I intend to finish the revision of the New
Testament and the letters of St Jerome; if I have time, I
will also emend the text of Seneca.' The following July he
informed Colet in a postcript that 'I have finished the collation of the New Testament and am now starting on St Jerome'
(W 2.249).

In the scattered information contained in the few letters
that survive up to the time Erasmus left England for Basle, in
July 1514, we can see that his interest in Greek continued, and
that he taught himself the language by his own methods—the
study of a wide range of the best authors, the discipline of

translation, and by editing texts. It is dangerous to argue from silence, so the fact that he says practically nothing about his work on the Vulgate itself need mean nothing more than that this was all one enterprise, and that the work on the Greek New Testament was part and parcel of his work on a revision of the Vulgate. By 1514 he had completed his 'collation'. When he approached the Froben press, what exactly did he have in hand?

The most recent scholarship suggests that Erasmus intended at that point to publish the Vulgate text of the New Testament with an extended commentary—the *Annotations*. Beatus Rhenanus, fully familiar with the world of printers in Basle and destined to become a close friend of Erasmus, wrote that Erasmus had arrived in Basle, 'weighed down with good books', including his revision of Jerome, the works of Seneca, also revised, a number of translations from Plutarch, a book of *Parallels* (the *Parabolae*), the *Adages*, and 'copious notes on the New Testament' (R 23). These were unprecedented in their scope and in their extensive, consistent references to Greek texts. To follow the conjecture of Erika Rummel, it was no doubt this that suggested a much larger enterprise to Froben, one that would bring particular fame to his press and demonstrate its capacity to set up in type an extended text in Greek: the Greek text of the New Testament should be supplied also, along with Erasmus' annotations. This conjecture is supported by later statements of Erasmus himself, and by the contemporary remarks of Beatus Rhenanus. In August 1515 Erasmus informed Reuchlin personally that, 'I have written annotations on the entire New Testament, and so have now in mind to print the New Testament in Greek with my comments added.' At some point it was decided further not to print the Vulgate, but in its place a new Latin version by Erasmus, written in Basle (as he always maintained) under considerable pressure of time. His annotations however preserved his first intention, since they were cued not to Erasmus' new Latin text, but to the Vulgate which was not printed. In the first edition of 1516 the annotations were also printed quite apart from the Greek text and its parallel Latin translation. Of these three elements then—the Greek text, the Latin translation, and the *Annotations*—only the last was the product of a long and painstaking scholarly enterprise. At the same time, Erasmus' dedication to that task provided the firm foundation for his critical revision of the Vulgate, and explains why he was able to produce the text so swiftly. His personal conception of what had been done is discovered most succinctly in the long title with which the work is introduced, which, as has been observed, makes no mention of the fact that the Greek text had actually been printed for the first time. It describes: the *Novum instrumentum* revised and emended by Erasmus of Rotterdam, against the Greek original as well as many ancient manuscripts in both Latin and Greek, and against the evidences (quotations, emendations, and interpretations) to be found in the 'most approved' authors, especially Origen, Chrysostom, Cyril, Theophylact, Jerome, Cyprian, Ambrose, Hilary, and Augustine, together with Annotations which tell the reader 'what has been changed and why'. The whole is recommended to lovers of true theology, who are asked not to be offended by any changes they discover, but rather to think whether or not the text has been changed for the better.

If we ask what sources Erasmus used for his revision, it will be clear by now that we must distinguish between those consulted over many years in the preparation of his annotations and those actually used in printing the Greek text in Basle. For this latter purpose, Erasmus made use of manuscripts in Basle which had been left to the Dominicans there by Cardinal Ivan Stojkovic of Ragusa, a delegate to the Council of Basle who had died in Lausanne in 1443. Erasmus presented Froben with a manuscript—not a transcription—supplied by the Dominicans, a twelfth-century text of the Gospels which survives today, containing Erasmus' emendations between the lines and in the margins, and the printer's red chalk marks corresponding to the pages of the 1516 edition. This was a manuscript of the widely used Byzantine version, familiar in the Greek Churches since the fourth century. Another text supplied by the Dominicans had the Byzantine text with a commentary by Theophylact to which Erasmus attached much importance. Reuchlin supplied another containing the whole of the New Testament except for the Apocalypse, and this too was from the twelfth century. As a more elegant, more easily read copy, it was used by Erasmus' assistants, Oecolampadius and Nikolaus Gerbel of Pfortzheim, in correcting the text during printing, but Erasmus considered it less trustworthy than the codex with Theophylact's commentary. For the Acts and Epistles he used yet another codex of the twelfth century which belonged to Johann Amerbach. Since none of these contained the Apocalypse he borrowed a further manuscript from Reuchlin that contained the Book of Revelation. This too was of the twelfth century, but the text was so closely interlined with the commentary that Erasmus had a clean copy made, and returned the original. In the course of making the copy, a number of errors were introduced which made their way into print. Moreover, the manuscript lacked the final leaf containing the last six verses of the text (22: 16–21). To supply the defect, Erasmus translated the missing verses from the Vulgate into Greek. Perhaps this is the best indication of the real importance Erasmus attached to the printing of the Greek New Testament. It was never meant to be a 'critical' text. The burden of his scholarship, and of what he wished to achieve, lay in the *Annotations*. Current scholarly opinion is summarized by M. A. Screech: 'Inside the volume the Greek original plays much the same role as the Annotations alone were originally intended to do: to justify the improvements and emendations to the Latin Vulgate.'

As for the Annotations, the 1516 edition incorporated the material collated during his stay in England, including some from early Latin manuscripts, two of them supplied by Colet. It may well have incorporated a residue from his abortive work on the Epistles of St Paul. His search for further manuscript authority was continued for the rest of his life, by visits to libraries, borrowing, and by consultation of the Aldine and Complutensian texts when these became available. Most of this new information went into successive editions of the *Annotations*, while the Greek text remained more or less unaltered after the first general revision of 1519. Moreover, it was less the Greek text that created a furore than the *Annotations*, where the Vulgate text is regularly challenged along with many of the scholastic authorities familiar to his readers. For the present, however, Erasmus sought the approval of Leo X to whom the *Novum instrumentum* was dedicated, and who obligingly wrote in 1518, to commend the forthcoming second edition (1519), 'go forward then in this same spirit: work for the public good, and do all you can to bring so religious an undertaking into the light of day, for you will receive from God himself a worthy reward for all your labours, from us the commendation you deserve, and from all Christ's faithful people lasting renown' (W 6.108).

If the *Novum instrumentum* is regarded as an attempt to produce a critical edition of the Greek New Testament, it will certainly add little to Erasmus' reputation as a textual scholar, especially when it is measured against the critical standards of a later age. But such an assessment fails to take into account Erasmus' real purpose, which was to introduce the literate community to a substantial revision of the Vulgate, supported by extensive annotations which were his main concern, and to show the same public the standard Greek text of the day for the enlightenment of the comparatively few who could read it. A recent scholar has commented that 'the Erasmus text is a typical Byzantine text and is the only sort of text conceivable two centuries before John Fell and John Mill'. In that respect at least the more carefully edited Complutensian Polyglot New Testament from Alcala was little different. That text had been printed already in 1514, and it is often surmised that Erasmus' Greek text was rushed into print in order to anticipate its publication. The Bible from Alcala was not published however until the entire work, including the Old Testament, had been printed and papal authorization obtained. It was finally released in 1522 in only 600 sets. For all of its peculiarities, seen through modern eyes, Froben's New Testament with Erasmus' name on its title page sold some 3,000 copies in its first two editions.

There is little reason to doubt that it was the appeal of

Erasmus' fresh and more elegant Latin version which guaranteed the work its popularity, along with the controversial and critical interest of the *Annotations*. Erasmus' Latin text of 1519 appears in the windows of King's College, Cambridge, an early and striking testimony to its instant popularity, and also to the influence of Richard Foxe, bishop of Winchester, who supervised the work on the windows. The text of 1519 was the basis of Luther's German translation, and through the third edition of Robert Estienne's Greek Testament (Paris, 1550), it heavily influenced the Greek Testament of Theodore Beza. It was Beza's text that underlay the King James version and the Elzevir Greek Testament in 1633, which proclaimed it the 'received text'. In this way was created the familiar *Textus receptus* for the New Testament, the foundation of biblical scholarship for three hundred years, until the era of 'higher criticism' began in the nineteenth century.

For Erasmus, however, the *Novum instrumentum* formed only a part, if a crucial one, in a continuing effort to revitalize the Christian life and understanding of Europe, and it is to that evangelism that we should now turn.

4 The philosophy of Christ

Erasmus' New Testament appeared with a remarkable, passionate prefatory piece. He called it *Paraclesis*—a Greek word meaning a summons or exhortation. It was that, and it was also a manifesto, the second of his life, matching the *Antibarbari*. In that first manifesto Erasmus had spelled out the reason for his devotion to the wisdom of pagan antiquity, as being a part of the divine plan, an instrument of God's self-revelation in his creation. The *Paraclesis* is an exhortation precisely to the universal mastery of that revelation as it was completed in Christ, the Word of God incarnate, the fullness of wisdom, discovered in scripture and appropriated as the rule of life. If the *Adagia* was the scholarly vindication and monument of that first manifesto, so the *Novum instrumentum* justified the second.

The *Paraclesis* used a term which was to become famous for its particular association with Erasmus, 'the philosophy of Christ'. It is easily misunderstood, and can be taken to indicate a rather rationalistic, moralizing attitude to Christianity, seeking to extract from it some general principles of conduct and, perhaps, the intimations of what might be called 'higher thought'. That was not what he intended. The term *philosophia Christi* is actually of patristic origin and its critical root is *sophia*—wisdom which is loved, and is of Christ. In that love there is the transforming power which Erasmus wishes to see affect the lives of men and women of all conditions, everywhere. They cannot love what they do not know, and what they seek (whether they know it or not) they will find in scripture. Why is it, he asks, that when men devote themselves so ardently to their studies, this study—the philosophy of Christ—is so neglected and derided, even by Christians? Since the enthusiasts of the many philosophical schools—Platonists, Pythagoreans, Stoics, and so forth—fight so fiercely for their convictions, 'why do we not evince far greater spirit for Christ, our Author and Prince?' (P. 99). When we are initiated in his name by baptism, drawn to him by so many sacraments, why do we not think it shameful to know nothing of his doctrines, which alone offer certain happiness? Moreover, mastery of this teaching is as nothing compared to the intricacies of such as Aristotle. 'The journey is simple, and it is ready for anyone. Only bring a pious and open mind, possessed above all with a pure and simple faith.' (P. 100) The philosophy of Christ accommodates itself to the sophisticated as to the simple; 'not only does it serve the lowliest, but it is also an object of wonder to those at the top.... It is a small affair to the little ones and more than the highest affair to the great.... The sun itself is not as common and accessible to all as is Christ's teaching. It keeps no one at a distance, unless a person, begrudging himself, keeps himself away.' (P. 101)

Erasmus further proclaims his conviction that scripture should even be made available in the common language of the people. 'Indeed, I disagree very much with those who are unwilling that Holy Scripture, translated into the vulgar tongue, be read by the uneducated, as if Christ taught such intricate doctrines that they could scarcely be understood by very few theologians, or as if the strength of the Christian religion consisted in men's ignorance of it.... I would that even the lowliest women read the Gospels and the Pauline Epistles. And I would that they were translated into all languages...'. Certainly, some will misunderstand, but some may be captivated. 'Would that, as a result, the farmer sing some portion of them at the plow, the weaver hum some parts of them to the movement of his shuttle, the traveler lighten the weariness of the journey with stories of this kind!' (P. 101) This is the privilege, and the calling, of all. Since baptism is common in an equal degree to all Christians, and since the sacraments like the final reward of heaven are intended equally for all throughout their lives, why should the teachings of Christ be restricted to those who are called theologians and monks?

It is really sufficient to read the *Paraclesis* to grasp the heart of Erasmus' personal faith and concerns. All of the great issues are there: the universality of the Christian vocation, the enduring value of the great pagans, the dangers of formalism and mere ceremonialism, the damage done by the weakness and failures of the so-called professionals, the monks and theologians, the perverting of theology by those same professionals, who 'discuss earthly matters, not divine'—that is, who confuse and distort the Gospel of Christ by intricate syllogisms. The true theologian teaches 'by a disposition of mind, by his very expression and his eyes, by his very life'. And this vocation is open, not merely to the educated, but to the common labourer and the weaver. 'Another, perhaps even a non-Christian, may discuss more subtly how the angels understand'—an ironic thrust, surely—'but to persuade us here to lead an angelic life, free from every stain, this indeed is the duty of the Christian theologian' (P. 102).

His concern was of course a familiar one—the interiorizing of conviction, 'meaning it'. What is needed for all the world is the peace and harmony that would spring up if we could see a generation of genuine Christians everywhere emerge, to 'restore the philosophy of Christ not in ceremonies alone and in syllogistic propositions but in the heart itself and in the whole life' (P. 103). This is how Christendom's enemies should be conquered—by the allure of truth, manifested in the lives of those who profess to follow Christ. How, then, can anything be more important to us than 'the literature of Christ'? It is there that the philosophy of Christ is learned, located more truly in the disposition of the mind than in syllogisms, teaching that life means more than debate, inspiration is preferable to erudition, personal transformation to intellectual understanding. 'Only a very few can be learned, but all can be Christian, all can be devout, and—I shall boldly add—all can be theologians.' (P. 104)

As if to anticipate an outcry at such a proclamation of lay authority, he insists that the philosophy of Christ has a special connaturality with human nature, so that it may easily penetrate into the minds of everyone. He picks up the thread of earlier argument by pointing to the analogy of pagan wisdom and virtue. 'What else is the philosophy of Christ, which he himself calls a rebirth, than the restoration of human nature originally well formed?' (P. 104) Thus we find in the books of the pagans much that agrees with Christ's teaching: the Stoics, the Platonic Socrates, Aristotle in his *Politics*, and even Epicurus, are all called to witness to such parallels. Yet all of this wisdom is most fully realized in the teaching of Christ, who should come first among all teachers of the past. Yet knowledge of his doctrine is not enough; it is essential also to carry it into effect. Here is the thrust of his objection to the 'modern' theologians. 'Not that I condemn the industry of those who not without merit employ their native intellectual powers in such subtle discourse, for I do not wish anyone to be offended, but that I think . . . that the pure and genuine philosophy of Christ is not to be drawn from any source more abundantly than from the evangelical books and from the apostolic letters, about which, if anyone should devoutly philosophize, praying more than arguing and seeking to be transformed rather than armed for battle, he would without a doubt find that there is nothing pertaining to the happiness of man and the living of his life which is not taught, examined, and unraveled in these works.' In truth, in the pages of scripture we meet the living, breathing Christ himself, 'I should say almost more effectively than when He dwelt among men. The Jews saw and heard less than you see and hear in the books of the Gospels . . .' (P. 105).

Erasmus then points with dismay to the fact that while both Jews and Muslims study and venerate their scriptures from childhood on, Christians will study, seemingly, almost any other author first: authors of religious rules (he does not exempt the Augustinians), authors of the theological canon— Albertus Magnus, Aquinas, Giles of Viterbo, Richard of St Victor, William of Occam—while they neglect the writings which alone are attested by God himself. While acknowledging the merits and efforts of such writers, Erasmus is ever conscious of the wrangles and disputes which divide the various schools of theology and their adherents. In a final and moving plea for Christian nurture in the teachings of scripture he urges, 'let earliest childhood be formed by the Gospels of him whom I would wish particularly presented in such a way that children also might love him' (P. 107). He should in time form every child to full maturity; he should be the consolation of all at the end of life. How much more deserving of our devotion even than the relics of sanctity are the pages of scripture where we find the 'living and breathing likeness'. 'We embellish a wooden or stone statue with gems and gold for the love of Christ. Why not, rather, mark with gold and gems and with ornaments of greater value than these, if such there be, these writings which bring Christ to us so much more effectively than any paltry image? The latter represents only the form of the body—if indeed it represents anything of him—but these writings bring you the living image of his holy mind and the speaking, healing, dying, rising Christ himself, and thus they render him so fully present that you would see less if you gazed upon him with your very eyes.' (P. 108)

The *Paraclesis* appeared in 1516 with the first version of Erasmus' New Testament. Two and a half years later, in August 1518, there appeared another preface which confirmed his view that Christian understanding must find its fruit in a life of personal piety, and that this is the first and essential task before every Christian. This was the letter to Paul Volz, a Benedictine abbot, introducing a new edition of the *Enchiridion militis Christiani*. The *Enchiridion*, or *Handbook of the Christian Soldier*, was written, as we noted, at the time Erasmus became acquainted with Jean Vitrier and, through him, acquainted also with the works of Origen. It was first printed in Antwerp in 1503, coincidentally the very year that Volz had first taken on the life of a monk. Erasmus had come to know Volz as a member of the literary circle in Schlettstadt (Sélestat), and Volz's interest in reforming his monastic community at Hugshofen may have reminded Erasmus of Vitrier. At any rate, while the first edition of the *Enchiridion* had attracted little attention, the new edition by Froben ushered in an era when it became one of the most widely read and often translated spiritual writings of the age. Vernacular translations, almost invariably including the prefatory letter to Volz, appeared in print in Czech (1519), German (1520), Dutch (1523), Spanish (1525), French (1529), Italian (1531), English

(1533), Polish (1558), Swedish (1592), Hungarian (1627), and Russian (1783). It remained Erasmus' most influential single statement about the life of piety, and by implication, about the nature of theology and even of the Christian Church.

Despite the evidence for the remarkable impact of the *Enchiridion* on the public of Christendom—Marcel Bataillon for example revealed its popularity in Spain, where the translation was reprinted twelve times before 1556—a modern reader may find it difficult to recognize in it a work of almost revolutionary import. In order to grasp its significance we must know something of the background. A brief digression here will lead us to a better understanding of Erasmus' personal mission.

The background is the immense, sophisticated, and magisterial enterprise of scholastic theology—the theology of the 'Schools'. In the twelfth and thirteenth centuries, with the reception of Aristotle in the West and the growth of university teaching, theology began to take on the nature of a professional discipline. In place of the long-established method of a reflective reading of scripture and the Fathers following the manner of the ancient rhetorical disciplines, and structured by the liturgical cycle of the Church, there emerged the ideal of a coherent, rational system, formed by the categories of Aristotelian logic. By the middle of the thirteenth century Aristotelian rationalism had conquered the Faculty of Arts at Paris completely, and it posed an immense challenge to the traditional intellectual habits of Christendom.

In the vast synthesis of Aquinas, theology, while primarily speculative, also dealt importantly with the practical, moral life. The largest section of the *Summa theologiae*—the *Secunda pars*—was entirely concerned with this. Erasmus knew it and, seemingly, had little quarrel with its teaching. Its sheer bulk and technical organization, however, made it the preserve of the initiates, the academic theologians. Later developments of the fourteenth century led further in the direction of speculative theology and away from the Bible and the Fathers, so that the earlier view of Christian life in the Spirit as an integral whole receded. Although the earlier methods of studying the sacred page continued in the monasteries and within certain other centres, the 'new theology' associated with the names of Scotus and Occam carried the day: it was academic, rationalistic, and speculative. Those looking to theology for spiritual sustenance and practical guidance were left hungry; some, like Jean Gerson, began to develop a 'mystical theology' over against the theology of the Schools, increasingly dominated by endless disputes and subtle argumentation. These debates were to provide a wealth of illustration for Erasmus' satirical attacks. One consequence of these developments was the civil warfare among the learned which Erasmus decried as futile in principle, and, what was worse, perilous to Christian unity. A second consequence was the practical divorce of preaching and devotion among the ordinary clergy and laity from the sophisticated distractions of the academic theologians.

In their work as such it is fair to say that Erasmus took little interest. For this he paid a price, as he found in his controversy with Luther (among others). His constant preoccupation was with the calling of all the baptized to the fullness of a life lived wholly in the love of Christ. In that life of piety—*pietas*—the speculations of the intellect had, to be sure, a legitimate place, as he would occasionally admit. So did concern with right doctrine, good morals, contemplative prayer, the service of others, and, in all things, the effective preaching of the Good News by a life well-lived. This was a seamless fabric, where different gifts called forth different missions from the baptized. But no undertaking, however worthy in itself, might be allowed to obscure the message of Christ. Erasmus thus admits to Volz that his little book says nothing about Scotistic problems. 'Penetration I can do without, provided there is piety. It need not equip men for the wrestling-schools of the Sorbonne if it equips them for the tranquillity proper to a Christian. It need not contribute to theological discussion provided it contributes to the life that befits a theologian.' (V 8)

The *Enchiridion* then was meant to supply an epitome of doctrine and exhortation combined, to instruct and inspire its reader in the life of true piety. 'Who can carry the *Secunda secundae* of Aquinas round with him? And yet the good life is everybody's business, and Christ wished the way to it to be accessible to all men, not beset with impenetrable labyrinths of argument, but open to sincere faith, to love unfeigned, and to their companion, the hope that is not put to shame.' By all means let eminent professionals pore over the great tomes of theological science. None the less, 'we must take thought all the time for the unlettered multitude for whom Christ died' (V 9).

It follows also that the *Enchiridion* was not meant to be a handbook of meditation like the *Imitation of Christ* to which it is sometimes compared, unfavourably. Erasmus' aim was educational, as always. It was most simply stated in the first sentence of his original dedication: to set down 'a kind of summary guide to living, so that, equipped with it, you might attain to a state of mind worthy of Christ' (E 24). As a work both of instruction and exhortation, acquainting its reader with the essentials of the Christian faith secured by 'the sheet-anchor of Gospel teaching' and inciting as well to a love of him who is the source of that teaching, it was an effective summary of the *philosophia Christi*.

The work was dedicated to a worldly layman, possibly a successful gunsmith of Mechelen named Poppenruyter, whose family was known to Erasmus. The metaphor of the Christian soldier had an ironic relevance, therefore, but it was taken of course from St Paul, whose imagery pervades the work and whose epistles provide most of the scriptural citations. Life is a warfare waged, on the one hand, against the forces of vice without and, within, against the 'old, earthly Adam'. It is our habit to ignore our true predicament and, 'as if our life were not warfare, but a Greek symposium, we roll around in our beds ... We are garlanded with roses and the delights of Adonis rather than girded in harsh armour.' (E 25) At baptism, however, all were enrolled in the army of Christ, our general, to whom we owe our lives. We have pledged our loyalty to him. The prize of loyal service under Christ's banner is blessed immortality. We must seek it, since the worst the enemy can do is to destroy our earthly bodies, which we shall one day lose to death anyway. The supreme disaster is the death of the soul.

The Christian should prepare for service, then, by putting on the armour of the Christian militia. Two weapons in particular are important: prayer and knowledge. Prayer binds us to the goal of heaven, and knowledge fortifies the intellect with salutary opinions; each complements and guides the other. A fervent study of the scriptures is essential both to prayer and the acquisition of essential knowledge. Moreover, Erasmus does not hesitate to recommend 'a kind of preliminary training' in the pagan poets and philosophers, provided such studies are pursued with moderation and at the right stage. Basil, Augustine, Jerome, and Cyprian are all invoked in support of this opinion. While he would not want the Christian soldier to imbibe pagan morals, the pagans can instruct us well in many things which are conducive to a holy life. 'These writings shape and invigorate the child's mind and provide an admirable preparation for the understanding of the divine Scriptures, for it is almost an act of sacrilege to rush into these studies without due preparation.' Erasmus' rooted conviction about the interrelatedness of pagan and Christian wisdom is thus proclaimed at the very outset of the *Enchiridion*. He recommends in particular the poetry of Homer and Virgil, provided the reader remembers that their poetry is entirely allegorical ('no one who has had even the slightest acquaintance with ancient learning will deny this'), a rule to bear in mind in reading scripture as well. The 'obscene poets' are to be avoided. Of the philosophers, he recommends the Platonists 'because in much of their thinking as well as in their mode of expression they are the closest to the spirit of the prophets and of the gospel'. There would be profit, indeed, in a taste of all pagan literature, if it is taken at the appropriate time and with moderation, caution, and discrimination, 'more in the manner of a foreign visitor than a resident, and lastly and most important, if it all be related to Christ' (E 33).

At its best, however, the learning of the great pagans will be 'unleavened bread', temporary nourishment which will not do for the long journey. For that the Christian soldier will need the manna of heavenly wisdom, found only in the sacred scriptures. These must be approached only with great purity of mind. Regard them as nothing less than oracles. 'You will feel that you are inspired, moved, swept away, transfigured in an ineffable manner by the divine power if you approach them with respect, veneration, and humility.' (E 34) The best interpreters of scripture are those who depart as much as possible from the literal sense. Paul is first, then Origen, Ambrose, Jerome, and Augustine. 'I notice', he remarks, 'that modern theologians are too willing to stick to the letter and give their attention to sophistic subtleties rather than to the elucidation of the mysteries, as if Paul were not right in saying that our law is spiritual.' And he goes on, 'If you prefer to be strong spiritually rather than clever in debate, if you seek sustenance for the soul rather than mere titillation of the intellect, read and reread the ancient commentators in preference to all others, since their piety is more proven, their learning more profuse and more experienced, their style neither jejune nor impoverished, and their interpretation more fitted to the sacred mysteries. I do not say this because I look down upon the moderns, but because I prefer writings that are more useful and more conducive to your purpose.' (E 35)

Erasmus' concern to avoid the letter for the spirit reflects his constant preoccupation with the interior, spiritual reality. In this instance he urges the reader to care and patience in approaching scripture, where knowledgeable meditation on a single verse can provide more spiritual nourishment than 'the whole Psalter chanted monotonously with regard only for the letter'. He witnesses to this from his own experience as a failing both of the common people and of the religious professionals. 'I think the principal reason why we see that monastic piety is everywhere so cold, languid, and almost extinct is that they are growing old in the letter and never take pains to learn the spiritual sense of the scriptures. They do not hear Christ crying out in the gospel: "The flesh is of no profit; it is the spirit that gives life".' (E 35)

The object of all this endeavour is the true wisdom which

teaches us how to live. That true wisdom is found only in Christ its author, who is, indeed, wisdom itself. He is the light that banishes darkness, reflection of the glory of the Father who, 'as he became redemption and justification to us who were reborn in him according to the testimony of Paul, so he also became wisdom'. This wisdom has nothing to do with the self-styled wisdom of this world, whose end is perdition, 'because pernicious arrogance always follows after it as its attendant, arrogance is then followed by blindness of spirit, blindness by the tyranny of the emotions, and this by a whole harvest of vices and the freedom to commit every manner of sin' (E 40).

How then, do we attain to the wisdom of Christ? The beginning is to achieve self-knowledge, says Erasmus, citing one of the first of his Adages. All antiquity believed that this saying came down from heaven, but it would have little authority with us if it did not also accord with scripture. Such knowledge is not easy. Even the great Paul, who was raised to see the mysteries of the third heaven, did not presume to judge himself since he knew himself insufficiently. What self-assurance then, can ordinary creatures have? In order to assist, Erasmus now presents his reader with a likeness of human nature, 'as in a painting, so that you may have a clear knowledge of what you are on the inside and what you are skin-deep' (E 41).

There follows an anthropology which underlies all of Erasmus' thought on religion and moral duty. It is based on St Paul seen especially through the eyes of Origen, and reflects strongly the generalized influence of Plato. We have noticed already Erasmus' respect for the philosophy of Plato as being particularly congenial to the Christian outlook, but he was much less syncretic than were many of the Neoplatonic disciples of the Renaissance. Where Ficino and others drew enthusiastically and eclectically on the theories of pagan Neoplatonists such as Plotinus, Erasmus' sensitivity to the early centuries of Christianity, and to the nuances of the Christological controversies, prevented his wandering too far into the world of Philo of Alexandria or the Pseudo-Dionysius. His discrimination was probably reinforced by firm disposition towards the practical, and his dislike of any hint of teaching reserved for the initiates—hermeticism and the Cabbala were never to his taste. His Platonism came directly from Plato himself, and, indirectly, from the influence of such Fathers as those he recommends in the *Enchiridion*.

This influence is clear at the next stage of his *Handbook*, where Erasmus describes the respective claims of the inner and the outer man. Self-knowledge, it seems, is chiefly awareness of the conflict between the inward and outer natures. Erasmus' platonizing tendencies lead him consistently to imply that the body as such restrains the aspirations of man's higher nature. There is here a genuine confusion, at times, between St Paul's 'flesh' and the Platonic body, which is gross in nature and an obstacle intrinsically to the destiny of the soul. However, the Pauline 'flesh' denoted not the physical body but the entirety of the unredeemed nature, and it is sufficiently clear that no notion of the body as intrinsically evil or sinful could be reconciled with the central Christian doctrine of the incarnation. Such confusion none the less occurred among many Christian writers through the ages, as it does also in Erasmus.

Erasmus' view of the intrinsic antipathy of body and soul is apparent from the outset, when he states that man is composed of 'a soul which is like a divinity and a body which is like a brute beast'. Our bodies indeed are inferior to those of the beasts, while our souls have such a capacity for divinity 'that we can soar past the minds of the angels and become one with God'. At one time united in harmony by their Creator, these two natures have remained in unhappy discord since the Fall, so that each with regard to the other 'holds the wolf by the ears' (E 41). The mortal body pursues temporal things and sinks downward; the soul, 'remembering its heavenly origin', pursues the spiritual and imperishable, and struggles upwards against the weight of its earthly burden. Before sin broke the primal harmony of all creation, our reason commanded the body without difficulty; now, the passions strive to take reason captive. In a vaguely Platonic analogy between human nature and a turbulent republic, Erasmus likens the reason to the supreme ruler, certain worthy emotions (filial respect, love of family and friends, desire for good reputation) to the nobles, and the base passions (lust, envy, debauchery) to the 'lowest dregs of the masses' (E 42). Plato's understanding of this state of affairs Erasmus attributes to divine inspiration, since 'the authority of the philosophers would be of little effect if all those same teachings were not contained in the sacred scriptures, even if not in the same words' (E 47). What the philosophers call reason, Erasmus states, Paul calls either spirit or the inner man or the law of the mind; what they call passions he calls the flesh, the body, the outer man, or the law. While these explanations may leave one uneasy, Erasmus does not forget to acknowledge some role for divine grace, although not by that name. He states that in mastering the base passions we cannot rely upon our own strength, 'but if you have recourse to God as your helper, nothing is easier' (E 46). St Paul instructs us: when troubled by vice we must implore divine assistance immediately by repeated prayers.

To amplify these lessons and drive them home, Erasmus turns explicitly to Origen concerning St Paul's tripartite division of human nature: spirit, soul, and flesh. The body (the flesh) is the lowest part, carrier of the sin of our first parents, through which we are incited to evil; the spirit is that in which we resemble the divine author of our being, where 'the supreme maker has engraved with his finger, that is his Spirit, the eternal law of goodness, drawn from the archetype of his own mind' (E 51), and through this we are joined to God; finally, the 'middle soul' is capable of sensations and natural movements. The soul is buffeted, free to incline to one side or the other. Thus the spirit makes us gods, the flesh brute animals, and the presence of the soul constitutes us as human beings. 'Natural' virtues are the realm of the soul: love of parents and children, loyalty to friends—the pagans do as much. But if these dispositions come into conflict with a higher law, requiring us to neglect our duties to a parent, to override affection for our children or a friend, our soul is at a crossroads, solicited by the flesh on the one side, by the spirit on the other. 'The spirit says, "God is to be preferred to one's parent. To the latter you owe merely your body, to God you owe everything." The flesh suggests: "If you do not obey, your father will disinherit you, and people will say that you have no respect for your father. Be practical, think of your reputation."' (E 52)

Erasmus urges the Christian soldier to accustom himself to this mode of 'shrewd self-examination'. It is easy to think that a natural instinct is perfect piety, and Erasmus points out that personalities differ widely in their natural tastes and endowments. Some are little tempted by the pleasures of the flesh; they should beware of attributing to virtue something in itself indifferent. Others find pleasure in fasting, or in church attendance. In each case we must ask where their inclinations lie, and what they seek by what they do. If it is public reputation, then these actions smack not of the spirit, but of the flesh. 'A brother has need of your help, but you mumble your miserable little prayers to God while ignoring the need of your brother. God will not be favourable to your prayers. How will God hear your prayers when you do not hear your fellow man?' (E 53) A second example touches on marriage. A man may love his wife simply because she is his wife; the pagans do as much. Or love her because she gives him pleasure; then the love is carnal. 'But', continues Erasmus, 'if you love her above all because you perceive in her the image of Christ, for example, piety, modesty, sobriety, and chastity, and you no longer love her in herself but in Christ, or rather Christ in her, then your love is spiritual.' (E 53–4)

With this as a framework for self-examination, Erasmus turns now to some practical rules to be used 'as if they were wrestling holds' in coping with the errors of the world and attaining the pure light of the spiritual life. They will be effective especially against three evils which are vestiges of original sin, for 'even if baptism has removed the stain, nevertheless a residue of the old malady remains in us both as a safeguard of humility and as a raw material and a fertile terrain for virtue' (E 54). These three evils are blindness, the flesh, and weakness. Blindness impairs judgement, the flesh corrupts the will, and weakness destroys constancy. To avoid these evils, we must know how to distinguish between things to be avoided and those to be sought; we must hate evil once it is recognized and love good; finally, we must persevere in our undertakings for good and virtuous causes.

The twenty-one 'rules of combat' which follow vary widely in length of treatment. The Christian soldier is urged to inform himself thoroughly about the Christ whom he follows from scripture, and to believe what he learns there with his whole heart. He must be resolute in his purpose, aware that he cannot serve two masters. He must keep in view the nature of his reward, against the illusory rewards of this world. Christ should be kept before him at all times as his only goal, and all neutral goods and undertakings should be weighed solely for their use in acquiring virtue. There is an interesting personal illustration in the fourth rule drawn from the love of letters, a neutral thing in itself. It is worthy if letters are pursued for the sake of Christ, not if the possession of knowledge alone gives pleasure. 'If you have confidence in yourself and hope for an immense reward in Christ, continue on your way like a bold merchant, ranging afar in the realms of pagan letters, and convert the riches of Egypt into the adornment of the Lord's temple. But if you fear a greater loss than gain, return to the first rule, know yourself, and measure yourself by your own standard. It is better to know less and love more than to know more and not love.' (E 62)

The fifth and sixth rules deal with piety as a passage from visible to invisible goods, and with Christ as the sole archetype of the Christian. Together, they allow Erasmus to range through a variety of topics and rehearse many of his favourite themes, and, in the same way, they anticipate many passages in the *Praise of Folly*. The reader is urged under rule five to learn the value of allegory in pagan wisdom as in scripture, as a clue to the inner meaning of life. One such teaches the importance of following our natural inclinations provided they are morally acceptable; thus, 'do not entangle yourself in marriage if celibacy is more suitable to your character, and conversely, do not vow yourself to celibacy if you seem more adapted to the married state, for whatever you attempt against your natural inclination usually turns out to be unsuccessful' (E 68).

In remembering the importance of the mystery underlying the form, Erasmus gives the example of the daily celebration of mass. If this is done while living for oneself and heedless of the fortunes of one's neighbours, then the celebrant is still in the 'flesh' of the sacrament. 'But if in offering sacrifice you are conscious of the meaning of that partaking, namely, that you are one spirit with the spirit of Christ, one body with the body of Christ, a living member of the church, if you love nothing but in Christ, if you consider all your goods to be the common property of all men, if you are afflicted by the misfortunes of others as if they were your own, then you celebrate mass with great profit, since you do so spiritually.' (E 71)

The practical import of Erasmus' 'rules' is shown in the illustrations, and they are aimed clearly at those in ordinary circumstances of life, lay or clerical. We are to live only for God as members of one body, to aim at the best and, at the very least, refrain from base conduct; we cannot allow ourselves to be discouraged by temptations or failures; we must be vigilant at all times, most of all when we feel that we are succeeding. We should arm ourselves with passages of scripture against temptation, and beware of spiritual pride. In repudiating sin, we must press beyond the victory to an extra assertion of penance or further virtue. View each battle as the last, but remain alert to the danger of false, *self*-confidence. No vice is negligible; be complacent about none. When we are daunted by the task of resisting sin, we should remember the painful burden that surrender will impose.

These and like counsels are intended not to inspire immediately, but to show the aspirant how to discipline his imagination by the acquisition of knowledge and effective habits; when viewed in this light, it is less surprising that the *Enchiridion* has been seen as the basis for many of the spiritual manuals and methods (like the Ignatian *Exercises*) that followed in the next generation. Erasmus concludes with an Epilogue of remedies (E 117) against certain of the more common sins: lust, avarice, ambition ('the only honour to be sought after by a Christian is to be praised not by men, but by God'), haughtiness and arrogance of mind, anger and the desire for revenge. In these 'epilogues' there is much down-to-earth, pastoral advice to drive home the more wide-ranging precepts before. Erasmus takes his leave by pointing out what a 'vast sea of vices' still remains to be discussed, and gives these over to the resourcefulness of his reader following the method and rule already supplied. Against all vices the mind must be fortified well in advance of their attack, 'by prayer, the sayings of wise men, the doctrines of scripture, the example of pious men and especially of Christ'. Finally, the reader is exhorted to associate with those only in whom he has seen Christ's true image, and to make Paul his special friend—to be kept in his pocket and committed to memory.

What we find in the *Enchiridion* is authentically a fresh vision of the Christian life for contemporary Europeans. It was not an adapted form of monastic spirituality, like the English devotion or the *Devotio moderna* of the previous century, which had recruited followers into separate communities and something like a regular life. However important those movements proved to be, they can be seen as attempts to refurbish accepted ideals, to reassert old standards, or to broaden the base of established forms by adapting them to a laity eager for a richer spiritual life than the conventions of common worship made available.

The vision of the *Enchiridion* is of a Christian society in which the mode of life adopted is entirely secondary to the personal commitment of each of the baptized to perfection in Christ. No special prestige is attached to the clerical state, or to vows of consecrated life—these are worthy provided they are appropriate to the individuals concerned and are lived with complete integrity. Equally valid, by implication, is the vocation of those married and living 'in the world', and their charter of citizenship within the Christian polity, so to speak, is placed in the foreground with the warm reception of pagan literature both as an introduction to scripture and as a valid source of practical, ethical wisdom. Particularly evident is the lack of deference to clerical direction: each follower of this handbook is meant to be equipped as his own spiritual director, under Christ. This was a radical departure indeed— more radical, perhaps, than its author intended.

Something of Erasmus' general vision can be gathered from the most remarkable passage in the letter to Volz with which this discussion opened. This is a portrait of the Church which is original with him, and which appeared also in his important treatise on theological method, the *Ratio verae theologiae* in the same year, 1518. Here the Christian community is pictured as ranged in three concentric circles, focusing like the rings of a target on the person of Christ. (E 14) In the innermost circle, nearest to Christ, are the priests, bishops, cardinals, and popes, and 'all whose duty is to follow the Lamb wherever he shall go'. These must embrace the intense purity of the centre and pass on as much as they can to those next to them. Their neighbours in the second circle are the secular princes, whose arms and laws must be devoted to Christ's service in just war, defence of public peace, or in restraint of evil-doers through lawful punishment. Their contribution to the true ends of a Christian society then is essentially restorative: the danger is that they may turn their power to their private advantage instead of the public good. It is a prime responsibility of the members of the priestly order to call them to their duties.

In the third circle are the common people, the 'most earthy portion of this world, but not so earthy that they are not members of Christ's body just the same' (E 15). They must be nourished and encouraged, since each according to the measure that is given him must strive upwards towards Christ. Erasmus then adds as an afterthought, 'If now someone thinks that this circle is more suitable for princes, there will be no serious difference of opinion between us. For if we observe their characters, we shall hardly find Christians more rudimentary than they.' (E 16)

Outside this third circle is everything abominable: ambition, love of money, lechery, anger, revenge, and the like. These are dangerous when they disguise themselves under the mask of religion and duty, as when tyrannical power is used under a pretext of justice and right. What must be impressed upon all is that the one goal of life is Christ and his teaching in all its purity. Since the perfection of Christ is in the interior dispositions, not in the external mode of life, Erasmus makes it clear that the places people occupy in the various circles as they appear to one another do not necessarily reflect the true, invisible relationship of the members with respect to Christ.

Even on the face of it, this is a remarkable image indeed. Erasmus sees the Christian commonwealth as a polity of the baptized without elaborate institutional structure. It centres on Christ, and worldly rank within it is justified only by responsibility—the special duties of the clergy, the corresponding duties of the princes. There is also an invisible ranking, known only to God, defined by the holiness of the members. In this spiritual commonwealth, some of those in the inner circle are at the furthest remove from the centre, while some of those who are most humble in worldly terms are most exalted in their true nearness to Christ. Much could be said and more conjectured about the nuances and implications of this image. For the political and social radicalism latent within it, to comment no further, we are bound to recall Erasmus' situation when the *Enchiridion* was first written, and the radical Franciscan spiritualism to which his then host, Jean Vitrier, was heir. We must recall as well that a large part of his time and energy in the years especially after 1515 was spent in unsparing criticism of the religion, politics, and morals of his day, and in running combat with controversialists who rose on every side. It was an ironic fate for one whose professed ideals were irenicism and concord.

5 The problem of Luther

Without question, Erasmus could be infuriating. His high ideals for the reformation and renewal of Christendom—not simply, 'the Church'—could be advanced with moving sincerity and evident conviction. Almost as frequently, however, they were proposed in a way calculated to arouse the mirth of many, the ire of some, and the enmity of not a few. He invited this response in part by the use of one of his most formidable literary weapons, the coruscating satire of which he was the greatest exponent since his own master, Lucian, the first-century rhetorician of Samosata. The frustration and suspicion of his critics was provoked also by their lack of familiarity and sympathy with his humanist intellectual culture, so alien to their own. This was true not only of contemporary defenders of tradition but also of the followers of the prophetic figure who emerged as Erasmus' rival and nemesis, Martin Luther.

Erasmus' use of satire, congenial as it was to his nature, had a deeply serious intent. He beguiled his readers into examination of their accepted notions, not by challenging them directly, but by exposing contradictions and absurdities, and by the subtle flattery of presuming the harmony of their superior judgement with his own. Vulgar pieties, prelatic pride, kingly vanity, and common greed, indolence, imposture, credulity, and deceit, all were haled into the light of Lucianic wit and reason. Behind the play of irony and wit the claims of the philosophy of Christ were advanced relentlessly against the entire apparatus of religious conventions which, in his judgement, too often distracted the well-intentioned faithful from the one thing necessary—the personal claim upon their lives of 'the speaking, healing, dying, rising Christ himself' (P 108).

In order to provoke his readers to think about their religion anew he risked misunderstanding and scandal. Wittingly or not, he became a master of disenchantment, and the gibes in his *Colloquies* and elsewhere in his voluminous works could be judged with reason to have prepared the way, for many, for that great recasting of belief which became Protestant Christianity. An early convert in England, an Austin Friar who was tried by Tunstall in 1528, traced the beginnings of his apostasy from the Catholic faith to the influence of Erasmus. 'All Christian men beware of consenting to Erasmus' Fables,' he testified, 'for by consenting to them they have caused me to shrink in my faith, that I promised to God at my christening by my witnesses.' He cited the influence of the 'Colloquium' in particular, and concluded sadly, 'Thus I mused of these opinions so greatly, that my mind was almost withdrawn from devotion to saints. Notwithstanding, I consented that the divine service of them was very good and is, though I have not had such sweetness in it as I should have had because of such fables.'

Since it is perfectly clear that Erasmus approved of traditional devotions properly understood and said so repeatedly, and equally evident that his whole purpose was to increase true devotion rather than to diminish it, we are drawn to conclude that here, as with his New Testament, he failed to appreciate the potential impact of notions familiar to his learned intimates once they were disseminated in print and by translations.

Among his learned contemporaries outside the humanist community, there was little understanding of the intellectual basis of his views or of his criticisms. An important and exemplary episode concerns his rendering of the famous opening of the Gospel of St John, 'In the beginning was the Word', by translating 'Word' with the Latin *sermo* in place of the Vulgate's *verbum*. The change was made in the second edition of his New Testament (1519), and the decision was rooted in convictions about the creative power of the Word which we have discussed already. His new Latin rendering of the Greek *logos* might be translated (if imprecisely): 'In the beginning there was Speech; that Speech was in the beginning with God, and everything God made, he made by speaking' (cf. Bo 3). It altered the conception of Word from a static entity to an active presence, and it reveals a fundamental principle of Erasmus' outlook, that the divine *logos*, incarnate in Christ, continues through all of time to instruct God's people and to sustain and inform all of creation. In this conception, Christ as *sermo* incarnate was nothing less than the very eloquence of God, more vivid, more vital and present than any concept, any mere *verbum* or 'word'. In the *Ecclesiastes*, his great treatise on preaching, Erasmus refers to Christ as *sermo Dei*—the 'discourse of God'—and goes on thus: 'Through this (*sermo Dei*) the Father established the universe, through this he governs everything he established, through this he restored the fallen human family, through this he binds the Church to himself.' (Mc 84)

There was a storm of controversy. It was led by an English friar, Henry Standish, an Oxford graduate and popular preacher at court, who was provincial of the English Franciscans until 1518, when he had been appointed bishop of St Asaph's. Standish was a well-regarded professional in theology. He saw in the change not merely a philological decision but a theological meaning. In fact it was a philological decision, but it had implications of the second kind. Ill equipped as a philologist, Standish fell back upon the argument that this term violated the sacred text and was unprecedented. He was horribly wrong. Erasmus argued easily that *sermo* and *verbum* were used interchangeably in the Bible as well as patristic writing to denote the Son of God. Thomas More came to his defence both at the English court and in print, pointing to the precedents in tradition, especially in patristic commentators, noting that Gregory of Nazianzus said the Son of God was called *logos*, 'not only because he is Speech and the Word but also because he is Reason and Wisdom', and adding that, in his own view, the word might well be kept in its original form, like 'Alleluia', 'Kyrie eleison', 'Amen', and 'Osanna'.

Here was an exemplary instance of the kind of disagreement that could arise from divergence between humanistic and traditional, scholastic culture. It would be gratifying to report that Erasmus, the devoted teacher, used the opportunity to convert Standish to his own way of thinking. Nothing could be further from the truth. Much as he taught the importance of persuasion, Erasmus almost never applied his own principles in exchanges with his critics—quite the contrary. He bristled with indignation and flew to the attack. He had had Standish in his sights for some time as a suspected critic of his edition of Jerome, and named him in 1517 among theologians who rule the roost under 'some black theological planet'. He now accused Standish and his allies of ignorance, malice, and ingratitude; they were 'unfair', 'shameless', 'brainless', 'sycophants'. They were added to the growing number chiefly in the religious orders whom Erasmus saw as something close to an organized conspiracy to defame the cause of good letters in general, and Erasmus in particular. Since it was a time when public vituperation perhaps reached its apogee, it is difficult to make a final judgement, but it is clear enough that Erasmus' conduct of controversy did nothing to diminish the number of his detractors, nor to add to those converted to his way of thinking.

The Standish affair serves to illustrate a myriad of controversies which absorbed an increasing portion of Erasmus' time and energy after 1515. Inevitably the more he wrote, the more he invited criticism and attack, until polemics came to dominate his literary output. In the catalogue of works he drew up in 1523 for Johann von Botzheim he wrote, 'The eighth volume will contain the apologies. And—how sad for me!—they will make up a complete volume.' (W 9.355) None of those controversies could approach in historic importance the one which was now awaiting him, the debate with Martin Luther.

There was a generation between them; Luther could almost have been Erasmus' son. Born in November 1483, he was a young Augustinian professor at Wittenberg in the very years when Erasmus was emerging as the foremost humanist in northern Europe, as a pioneering editor of the Fathers and of the New Testament, as a master of the literary tradition and a brilliant critic of contemporary society. Like so many, Luther was Erasmus' pupil, in part. He turned to his writings for an understanding of the New Testament, for the edition of

Jerome, for the *Adages, Praise of Folly*, and works of devotion. In many ways they shared concerns about the Church, though not about the place of antiquity in education. Both rejected the supremacy of Aristotle and the system of the Schoolmen, both proclaimed the central place of the Bible in Christian life, emphasized the perils of religious formalism, denounced the abuse of indulgences, and urged the princes to take the reform of the Church in hand. The religion of the *Enchiridion* and the *Paraclesis* was common to them both. However beneath such surface agreement, which was shared after all with many others, there lay widely differing temperaments and priorities.

As early as 1516 Luther remarked, 'In the exposition of the Scripture I put Jerome as far behind Augustine as Erasmus puts Augustine behind Jerome.' A letter of the next year reveals that Luther's preoccupations were beginning to detach him from Erasmus: 'I am at present reading our Erasmus, but my mind is moving more and more away from him...I fear he does not spread Christ and God's grace sufficiently abroad...the human is of more importance to him than the divine.' (Ru 264)

For his part, Erasmus showed an immediate sympathy with the aims of the young Luther when he first encountered them. Luther had learned from friends that Erasmus admired his theses on indulgences and had seen his sympathy confirmed in the letter to Paul Volz which prefaced the 1518 edition of the *Enchiridion*. Encouraged, he evidently overcame his misgivings and reached out to the older man, acknowledging in a letter of March 1519 'that wonderful spirit of yours which has so much enriched me and all of us'. 'Though you know it not,' Luther continued, 'I possess your spirit and all that you do for us in your books, without exchange of letters or converse with you in person.... And so, dear Erasmus, kindest of men, if you see no objection, accept this younger brother of yours in Christ, who is at least much devoted to you and full of affection...' (W 6.282).

Erasmus' reply from Louvain (May 1519) is a study in rhetorical skill, since he managed almost in the same breath to extend his friendship and distance himself from Luther.

Greeting Luther as 'dearest brother in Christ' and thanking him for his letter, Erasmus at once remarked on the storm raised by his books. 'Even now it is impossible to root out from men's minds the most groundless suspicion that your work is written with assistance from me and that I am, as they call it, a standard-bearer of this new movement.' Erasmus feared with reason that their alleged association would give the enemies of humane letters a new reason to oppose them, 'as likely to stand in the way of her majesty, queen Theology, whom they value much more than they do Christ....In the whole business their weapons are clamour, audacity, subterfuge, misinterpretation, innuendo; if I had not seen it with my own eyes—felt it, rather—I would never have believed theologians could be such maniacs! One would think it was some disastrous infection...' (W 6.391). By this stage in the letter Erasmus had become wholly preoccupied with his personal situation in the university, but the main points of his public defence of Luther were clearly stated: Luther's opponents should do him the courtesy of reading what he has written; and it would behove them to discuss his views carefully and in print, or privately among specialists before attacking him in public, especially since everyone speaks highly of Luther's personal life (the deeper importance of this judgement will emerge in due course). There is a comic side to Erasmus' struggle with his own nature. Fuming with apprehension, he wrote: 'Theologians in this part of the world are unpopular at court, and this too they think is my fault.... These men have no confidence in the printed word; their hope of victory lies entirely in malicious gossip. This I despise, for my conscience is clear. Their attitude to you has softened somewhat. They are afraid of my pen, knowing their own record; and, my word, I would paint them in their true colours as they deserve, did not Christ's teaching and Christ's example point in quite another direction.' (W 6.392)

Finally, Erasmus wrote more soberly, 'Everywhere we must take pains to do and say nothing out of arrogance or faction, for I think the spirit of Christ would have it so. Meanwhile we must keep our minds above the corruption of anger or hatred, or of ambition; for it is this that lies in wait for us when our religious zeal is in full course.' (W 6.393)

Certain of Erasmus' remarks here have lasting importance: the need for a careful evaluation of Luther's views by a private discussion among the learned; the importance for his critics of Luther's reputation for an upright life; the warning to Luther to avoid discord and faction. While counsels of this sort may seem almost commonplace, they have a deeper significance, as we shall hope to demonstrate. In the meantime we shall attempt briefly to take the two men from this early community of concern to their final debate about free will which captured the attention of all of Christian Europe.

Erasmus used his influence to try to ensure a fair hearing for Luther. In October 1519 he wrote from Louvain to Albert, the cardinal archbishop and margrave of Brandenburg in whose territories Luther was living. He insisted on Luther's right to be heard. 'It is, I imagine, my Christian duty to support Luther to this extent: if he is innocent, I should be sorry to see him overwhelmed by some villainous faction; if he is wrong, I would rather he were set right than destroyed; for this agrees better with the example Christ has given us, who according to the prophet quenched not the smoking flax and did not break the bruised reed.' (W 7.111)

The fracas around Luther seemed to him a sad distraction from the true task, which was to convert to Christ those who were far from him and to raise the standard of morality among all professing themselves Christian. The source of the evil was the general state of Christian society. 'The world is burdened with ordinances made by man. It is burdened with the opinions and the dogmas of the Schools. It is burdened with the tyranny of the mendicant friars who, though they are servants of the Roman See, have risen to such influence and such numbers that the pope himself—yes, even kings themselves—find them formidable. . . . I do not condemn them all, but there are very many of this description who, for gain and for despotic power, deliberately ensnare the consciences of men. With growing effrontery they now began to leave Christ out of it and preach nothing but their own new and increasingly impudent dogmas. Of indulgences they were speaking in such terms that even the unlettered could not stomach it. This and much like it little by little was sapping the vigour of the gospel teaching; and the result would have been, with things slipping always from bad to worse, that the spark of Christian piety, from which alone the spent fire of charity could be rekindled, finally would be put out.' (W 7.112)

On 15 June 1520 Pope Leo X, pontifical patron of Erasmus' New Testament, composed the Bull *Exsurge Domine* giving Luther sixty days in which to make his submission. Erasmus was dismayed at this further rupture and joined Luther in questioning its authenticity. He tried to prevent the burning of Luther's books, and at the same time urged Froben not to print them. His whole purpose was to extinguish the fires of controversy and work for a more tranquil atmosphere. At this critical moment he did Luther a greater service than Luther ever realized. The youthful emperor Charles V was under considerable pressure to accept the condemnation of Luther without further consultation of the Imperial Diet. After his coronation at Aachen in November of 1520, the emperor passed through Cologne with his suite, and as an imperial councillor Erasmus was present as was Frederick the Wise, Luther's prince. Frederick sought counsel from Erasmus, who drew up a memorandum, the *Axiomata*, on how to deal with the affair. These 'axioms' followed the general tenor of Erasmus' views to date, but one in particular should be noted: 'It seems to the advantage of the pope that this affair be settled by the mature deliberation of serious and impartial men; in this way regard will be shown best for the dignity of the pope.' (Ax 143) In collaboration with a friar of whom he approved, a Dominican theologian of Augsburg, named Johann Faber, he devised a proposal for arbitration under the august auspices of the emperor with the kings of England and Hungary. Frederick secured from the emperor the promise that Luther would not be condemned unheard. Erasmus returned to the Netherlands.

In the months that followed, Luther's intransigence and refusal to restrain himself in the interests of concord began to take their toll, along with the growing pressure on Erasmus even from sympathetic friends clearly to dissociate himself from Luther. Luther's revolutionary tracts of 1520 had in effect made mediation impossible. Erasmus remained convinced that the real attack was directed against humane letters, and feared for that cause, so precious to his own programme for reform. In February 1521 he wrote from Louvain to Nicolas Bérault, a member of the French humanist circle, 'Luther is piling on both liberal studies and myself a massive load of unpopularity. Everyone knew that the church was burdened with tyranny and ceremonies and laws invented by men for their own profit. Many were already hoping for some remedy and even planning something. . . . Oh, if that man had either left things alone, or made his attempt more cautiously and in moderation! Luther means nothing to me; it is Christ's glory that I have at heart; for I see some people girding themselves for the fray to such a tune that, if they win, there will be nothing left but to write the obituary of gospel teaching.' (W 8.155)

The following May, Erasmus wrote a letter of great importance to Justus Jonas, a humanist graduate of Wittenberg and professor at Erfurt, who had first met him in 1519 as the bearer of Luther's first letter to Erasmus. Erasmus had learned that Jonas was siding with Luther, and his letter was meant not simply for him alone but for a whole circle of German humanists, among them Melanchthon, ready to commit themselves to Luther's cause. Erasmus pleaded that the philosophy of Christ not be sacrificed to national pride and opposition to Rome, however just the provocation. The difference in his outlook from that of Luther is nowhere better illustrated than here.

With full sympathy for the concerns that were tormenting Jonas and his friends, Erasmus recalled his own early hopes of Luther, 'except that at the very first taste of the pamphlets which had begun to appear under Luther's name, I was full of fear that the thing might end in uproar and split the world openly in two. And so I sent warning letters both to Luther himself and to friends of his who might, I thought, carry some weight with him; what advice they gave him I do not know, but at any rate the affair was handled in such a way that there is some danger of remedies wrongly applied making our trouble twice as great.' (W 8.202)

There is further evidence to show Erasmus' unwillingness to see matters of great delicacy and theological weight escape the circle of the initiated, a view at odds with those expressed only five years earlier in the *Paraclesis*. 'When a prudent steward will husband the truth ... Luther in this torrent of pamphlets has poured it all out at once, making everything public and giving even cobblers a share in what is normally handled by scholars as mysteries reserved for the initiated; and often a sort of immoderate energy has carried him, in my opinion at least, beyond the bounds of justice.' (W 8.203) With a seeming blindness to his own vulnerability to this charge, he went on, 'To give an example, when it would have sufficed to point out to the theologians that they mix in too much Peripatetic, or rather, sophistic philosophy, he calls the whole Aristotelian system the death of the soul.' Confronted by the spectacle of impending schism within his own school of reform, Erasmus now pressed the need for unity and prudence. He was not reluctant to seek scriptural support. 'That spirit of Christ in the Gospels has a wisdom of its own, and its own courtesy and meekness. That is how Christ attuned himself to the feelings of the Jews. He says one thing to the multitudes, who are somewhat thick-witted, and another to his disciples, and even so he has to bear with them for a long time while he gradually brings them to understand the celestial philosophy.' (W 8.203) He appealed to the examples of Peter and Paul, in their slow unfolding of the deeper and more difficult tenets of the Christian mystery, and also to Augustine: 'When he refutes the crazy Donatists, and the Manichaeans who are worse than madmen, his indignation stops short of what the facts deserve, and everywhere there is an endearing admixture of charity as though he thirsted for their salvation, and not their destruction. It was this gentleness in teaching, this prudence in husbanding the word of God that conquered the world and made it pass under the yoke of Christ as no military force, no subtle philosophy, no eloquent rhetoric, no human violence or cunning could ever have done.' (W 8.204)

If Erasmus had not always practised what he was now preaching, he was even-handed in asking Luther and his followers to exercise the same kind of restraint and respect for their opponents as he asked Luther's critics to show towards him. 'And I wonder very much, dear Jonas, what god has stirred up Luther's heart to make him write with such freedom of invective against the Roman pontiff, against all the universities, against philosophy, and against the mendicant orders. Had all he says been true—and those who examine what he has written declare that the case is quite otherwise—once he had challenged so many people, what other outcome was to be expected than what we see now?' (W 8.203) Speaking of his own inadequate acquaintance with Luther's works, and of his 'meagre attainments' to pronounce on such issues, he declared that he could never approve at least Luther's 'method and the way he sets to work. . . . For seeing that truth of itself has a bitter taste for most people, and that it is of itself a subversive thing to uproot what has long been commonly accepted, it would have been wiser to soften a naturally painful subject by the courtesy of one's handling than to pile one cause of hatred on another.' (W 8.203)

In January 1522 a new pope was elected, the same Adrian of Utrecht who, a seeming friend of Erasmus and of his enterprise, had told the University of Louvain to burn Luther's books and force his recantation. He twice invited Erasmus to take up residence in Rome—a compliment of ambiguous allure. The theologians of Louvain began assembling passages in Erasmus' writings which they claimed cast doubt on scriptural authority for religious vows, indulgences, confession, and fasting. Spanish critics of his New Testament living in Rome added their attacks to those of Louvain. In December 1522 Adrian wrote to Erasmus to acknowledge the dedication of his edition of Arnobius the Younger's commentary on the Psalms, and reassured Erasmus as to his confidence in his integrity and scholarship, remarking that the more excellent the learning of scholars, 'the more exposed they must be to the tooth of envy' (W 9.205). Having given this reassurance, however, the pope then asked Erasmus directly to put his learning to the service of the Church in the most pressing issue of the day. 'The affection which we feel for you and the concern we have for your reputation and true glory prompt us to urge you to employ in an attack on these new heresies the literary skill with which a generous providence has endowed you so effectually, for there are many reasons why you ought properly to believe that the task has been reserved by God especially for you.' Erasmus' great intellectual powers, his learning, his readiness in writing 'such as in living memory has fallen to the lot of few or none', his influence and popularity precisely among the Germans where the evil took its rise, such gifts should be used for Christ, who endowed Erasmus with them, for the defence of Holy Church and of the faith. (W 9.205) What is more, this will be the best way to silence those who try to fasten suspicion on him of sharing in Luther's business.

It would have been most difficult for Erasmus to deny Adrian's claims on his talents, and he did not; he temporized and still had not agreed when Adrian died in September 1523. In the meantime Erasmus had been mulling over a work which would not have been a direct challenge to Luther but something much nearer to his method and abilities, a book on peace in the form of a colloquy in three parts between a Lutheran, an opponent, and an arbitrator. The first colloquy would address the question of whether the issues of reform should be tackled in Luther's way; the second discuss his doctrines; and the third would show how the discord could be quieted in such a way that it would not easily start up again. In other words, Erasmus would have given literary reality to an event which had become impossible, a calm, even-handed discussion of the problem of Luther with a prescription for its solution.

The work was never finished, and whatever was written did not survive. Not even his friends encouraged him; he learned that his announcement alone had disappointed and angered all sides, and that by this time no country in Europe was ready for an Erasmian solution. The powerful faculty of theology at

Paris was now adding its voice to the attacks of Louvain and the Spanish theologians. A letter, now lost, came from his friend Thomas More in England. What counsel or event persuaded him to change his mind? We do not know, but he began now to sketch out his *Discourse on Free Will*.

The subject was one suggested by Henry VIII, and it had the merit of addressing an issue of deep importance for Erasmus' personal approach to reform. It was also an ancient problem for Christian theology as both Erasmus and Luther knew. In his reply *On the Enslaved Will* Luther thanked Erasmus for going to the heart of their differences instead of debating such comparatively minor issues as purgatory, indulgences, or the nature of papal authority. Erasmus sent an advance copy of his completed text to Henry VIII in March 1524, and it appeared in print in September. It pleased his patrons, but not the theologians. Luther's reply did not appear until December 1525, written with passion and in haste. It proved that Erasmus had chosen his ground well as a rhetorician, since Luther was compelled to defend a view which to the lay reader was by no means appealing. In the words of the distinguished Protestant historian, Gordon Rupp, 'Most of what Luther says and much of the way he says it must set the modern Protestant mind on edge.' (Ru 270–1) Erasmus, on the other hand, defended an attractive position with his familiar grace, courtesy, and clarity. He was the more skilful debater; Luther, the more practised theologian.

The particular issues between then cannot occupy us here, but the debate provides an important opportunity to look more deeply into Erasmus' approach to theological method and to the very nature of the Christian Church itself. Luther was not the only one who was shocked by his seeming indifference to some of the dogmatic issues of Christian tradition, and he was particularly scandalized to find that Erasmus was prepared to declare himself a sceptic in such matters. How could such an attitude be reconciled with any recognizable commitment to the gospel of Christ?

In the course of Erasmus' responses to Luther we have seen his early sympathy and growing concern with Luther's intransigence; we did not find much comment upon Luther's doctrine as such, except that it should be examined carefully by the wise and learned. What Erasmus objected to in Luther with unmistakable clarity from the beginning was his penchant for creating dissension. In his first letter to Luther of May 1519 he warned him against acting in a party spirit, as never pleasing to the spirit of Christ. Shortly after, he told Albert of Brandenburg that he had tried to prevent the publication of Luther's books because he feared the disturbance they would cause. He further stated that he would endure anything personally rather than provoke dissension.

The theme is always prominent, the more so as his fears of Luther grow. 'Tumult', 'sedition'—these are the enemies; at all costs men must strive to preserve peace and concord. By 1526, when Erasmus was ready to break off entirely from any further discussion with Luther, his final bitter accusations are not against his teaching as such, but against his 'arrogant, impudent, seditious temperament' which had brought the whole world into 'ruinous discord'. In fact the willingness of Luther and his followers to disrupt the peace of Christendom means that they are no true reformers.

These objections had been heard from Erasmus before. The charge of creating discord was a significant part of his objection to the scholastics. Their method and immersion in dialectic had brought sectarian division long before Luther appeared on the scene. Writing to Martin Dorp in May 1515, he declared that the prevailing addiction to disputations was deadening and destructive from the very fact that it produced contention and disagreement.

It is clear from this and the general tenor of his writings that concord among Christians was a matter of the utmost gravity to him; in the *Paraclesis* he even suggested that the health of the whole social body depends on it. When this view is compared with the zeal of others, both Catholic and Protestant, for dogmatic truth upon which salvation itself depends, it is easy to see how Erasmus could be dismissed as pusillanimous. Yet he paid dearly for his moderation under furious attack from both sides. There was a deeper issue at stake.

It is discovered in a concept which is almost as recurrent in the thought of Erasmus as *concordia*, and which is closely linked with it—the notion of *consensus fidelium*, the concord or agreement of the faithful. Well before the appearance of Luther, Erasmus had invoked this idea as a reforming principle in relation to the overly complex theology of the day. In his gloss on Matthew 11: 28–30 he observed that when Christendom returned at last to the concerns of true piety, theologians and preachers would leave their contentions for their true responsibility of teaching those things which are worthy of Christ, *according to a broad consensus*. With the advent of Luther, divergence from the consensus becomes the ground of Erasmus' objection to his assertions, when he is forced to confront them as such. At the heart of his argument in the *Discourse on Free Will* is Erasmus' declaration that the Holy Spirit would not overlook error in his Church for 1,300 years on a matter which is said by Luther himself to touch the very essence of evangelical teaching.

Immediately after publishing his treatise on the freedom of the will, Erasmus was caught up in a debate in Basle about the nature of the Eucharist. Erasmus insisted that he could not be persuaded by any authority to depart from the 'harmonious agreement of the Christian world'. Two years later, writing on the same matter and refusing once again to dissent from the authority of the Church, he added, 'I call "Church" the consensus of the whole Christian people.' In a subsequent letter to the same recipient, he added to this phrase, 'through the entire circle of the world' (Mc 82).

If we recall his earlier portrait of the Church in the letter to Paul Volz (repeated in the *Ratio verae theologiae* of 1518) we remember his picture of the Christian community as three concentric circles, centred like the rings of a target on the person of Christ. It was clear there that he saw the Church as a community in which there is an internal, spiritual order; nothing was said of institutional structure. That community originates in baptism, which incorporates individuals into the body of Christ. This is the work of Christ himself through the influence of the Holy Spirit, and the unity of this spiritual body is fundamental to its nature, unity in the work of the Spirit, unity in a common destiny with God.

Since concord is a distinguishing trait of the community duly formed by the action of Christ through the Spirit, the Church as such implies unanimity. In an oft-quoted preface to his 1523 edition of Hilary, Erasmus wrote, 'The essence of our religion is peace and unanimity'—*Summa nostrae religionis pax est et unanimitas*. Consider his paraphrase of John 14: 27 ('Peace I give to you, my peace I leave with you'): 'My peace, which I give to you, reconciles you to God. . . . The peace which I leave with you, binding one to another in mutual concord, renders your fellowship invincible in the face of all adversity.' In another place he wrote, 'The Church is the Christian people, cemented together by the spirit of Christ.' (Mc 84–5)

Unlike Luther, then, Erasmus insisted that Christians do not share in the headship of Christ as individuals; rather, as sharers at the same table, they are made by the Holy Spirit one among themselves. Despite his great belief in lay vocation, he opposed the radical individualism of others in proclaiming the priesthood of all believers. The thought of Erasmus always stressed the corporate identity and responsibility of the community of the Church. God's secret plan for salvation is found only in the solid consensus of the holy Fathers; teaching authority is associated with the ordained hierarchy, which must also however be well-informed about the mind of the faithful. In the *Discourse on Free Will* he reminded Luther that, other things being equal, we can presume that God will more probably communicate his Spirit to those who have been ordained, as one considers it more probable that grace will flow to the baptized rather than the non-baptized. But he saw no guarantee in any institutional form—papal, conciliar, episcopal, or congregational—of absolute authority about the teaching of Christ.

What was the meaning of his insistence on the common mind of Christendom? He held that there could be no dogmatic certainty, including that about justification, without concord. The reason is to be found in his humanistic methodology. In brief, without consensus and concord, its social concomitant, the *logos* could not speak through the Spirit to the community of the baptized. In this ancient, 'true' theology, before the advent of dialectical system, there was no rational organizing principle. The only organizing 'principle' was the text itself. The function of theology was not to produce logical system or formulations to satisfy rational curiosity; it was to penetrate mystery through theological allegory, and to proclaim the mystery in a way that will move God's people to change their lives and the world about them. Thus in Erasmus' method, grammar established the text of revelation where doctrine is discovered, and a grammatical method—that of allegory—also resolves difficulties. Wisdom and understanding accumulate in successive generations through the reflection of the devout and learned. Since the text is the immediate source of divine truth, a learned understanding of biblical languages and texts is fundamental. Necessary too, in the tradition of the classical grammarians, is knowledge of the whole cultural environment of the author, since the grammarian was expected to give general instruction in all of the arts, certainly concerning everything mentioned in the text. And he must know the traditional interpretation held by those closest in time to the moment when the text appeared. At this point Erasmus would invoke the rule in doubtful cases learned from the Fathers themselves: the frail judgement of the individual is supported by the activity of the Holy Spirit working also in the judgement of others, through the *consensus omnium*, the agreement of all.

To Erasmus this ancient method indicated a continuing dialogue of Christ with his flock throughout the ages. Compare Luther's view that 'through the Holy Spirit or the particular gift of God, each man is enlightened so that he can judge in complete certainty in what concerns himself and his own personal salvation, and decide between the doctrines and opinions of all men'. This had been his experience. His personal revelation came in his understanding of Romans 1: 17. In later recollection, Luther described this insight and its bearing on scripture as follows: 'Day and night I tried to

meditate upon the significance of these words: "The righteousness of God is revealed in it, as it is written: the righteous
shall live by faith". Then finally God had mercy on me, and I
began to understand that the righteousness of God is that gift
of God by which a righteous man lives, namely, faith, and that
this sentence—the righteousness of God is revealed in the
Gospel—is passive, indicating that the merciful God justifies
us by faith, as it is written: "The righteous shall live by faith".
Now I felt as though I had been reborn altogether and had
entered Paradise. In the same moment the face of the whole of
Scripture became apparent to me. My mind ran through the
Scriptures, as far as I was able to recollect them, seeking
analogies in other phrases, such as the work of God ... the
wisdom of God ... the strength of God, the salvation of God,
the glory of God.' (Mc 94–5) Luther had an organizing principle
of his own, a central point from which a totally non-scholastic
but nevertheless systematic theology developed. Erasmus, as
we have seen, knew no such central point. To him, scripture
was an elaborate and mysterious mosaic which, when it was
examined with purity of spirit in the light of common understanding and washed clean with the solvents of erudition,
revealed to the inward eye of the believer the very face of
Christ. If Luther's presuppositions came from his conversion
experience, those of Erasmus came from the sapiential traditions of the Patristic exegetes, strongly influenced by a Platonic
vision of the intelligible harmony of all creation. For him,
belief was always anchored in tradition, but this was not a
static order. It developed through time, with the Holy Spirit
continually at work fashioning the Church as a community
of belief. Through the common agreement of men at once
learned and pure of life (hence the importance he attached to
Luther's good reputation) we have the only assurance we can
have that we are reading correctly the luminous text of the
Holy Spirit at work among men, which is the mind of the
Church.

In this view of the essentially social character of the activity
of the Holy Spirit, Erasmus' difference with Luther is most
clear. It is clear also why peace was so important to him. It

was essential to preserve the community of discourse by which the Holy Spirit teaches, and was the very sign of truth, deriving from the creative harmony of that society which is the Holy Trinity. Interior peace was advanced as a criterion of spiritual health, and a pre-condition of receptivity to the work of the Spirit.

It is not surprising that Erasmus did not move with Luther. Despite the overlapping of many of their sympathies, Erasmus' whole outlook presupposed a tenacious adherence to the tradition and unity of the community of faith, an adherence which may be labelled 'conservative'. It is a special kind of conservatism, however, since its deepest principle made it impossible for Erasmus simply to judge Luther's doctrines right or wrong. It seems likely indeed, that Erasmus would have looked on Luther's views as he would have looked upon a striking manuscript variant: interesting and possibly significant, but needing the critical reflection of the devout, informed, and learned consensus before its true merit could be appraised.

6 In praise of Folly

In 1521 Erasmus left Louvain for the last time to settle—to the degree that he ever did or could—in Basle, driven from the one place by a rising tide of criticism, drawn to the other by the schedule of publication accumulating at the Froben press. In time, a burgeoning radicalism within the reforming party at Basle would drive him yet again from the haven of the Froben circle, and in 1529 he travelled to Freiburg with his possessions and his faithful housekeeper, Margarete Busslin, to whose patience, common sense, and sturdy independence he undoubtedly owed an unpayable debt. By 1534 a more irenic religious climate prevailed in Basle and the city council adopted a new confession acceptable to Bonifacius Amerbach, Erasmus' younger associate in letters and faithful friend. Amerbach was made rector of the University at Basle in the following May, and he travelled at once to Freiburg to bring back the great man. If a part of his purpose was to secure the prestige of Erasmus for a revival of the university it was all but too late. Erasmus died in July 1536 after a protracted illness. In February he had made Amerbach his heir and the administrator of his estate. This was a sum of five thousand florins invested with the duke of Wurttemburg and the city of Geneva at an interest rate of 5 per cent. This 'foundation', to give it a modern title, became known as the 'Legatum Erasmianum'. The beneficiaries of its earnings were to be the poor, the disabled, the aged, girls in need of dowries, and impecunious students.

Without wishing to make too much of it, this designation of the ordinary people who might be thought of as his personal legatees reminds us forcibly of a side of Erasmus' nature which remains to be dealt with in this brief survey of his vast and varied enterprise, and that is his restless preoccupation with the welfare of the society of his time, especially as that was measured against the professed ideals of those responsible for it. Here he found full scope for satire in his classical idiom, although he was unmistakably indebted to the same degree to the vivid, robust, and brawling imagery of his medieval predecessors. He was an inveterate moralist, commenting at every turn on the scene about him, excoriating injustice, delighting in absurdity, exhorting, extolling, cajoling, teasing, castigating, lamenting, reviling, and this in his letters, in his annotations, in almost everything that he wrote, but especially in certain works that fall under the general heading of *moralia*, his moral writings, which include his great satires.

Among them one important grouping might be termed 'Princes and Peace'. This would include an early rhetorical address, the *Panegyricus*, written to celebrate the return of Philip of Burgundy from Spain and printed in 1504. It would include his chief essay on the duties of the Christian prince, the *Institutio principis Christiani*, first published by Froben in 1516, and the *Querela pacis*, the 'Complaint of Peace', published in December of the same year. It would include also certain of the adages from the edition of 1515, an edition that included all of his most important essays against war: *Scarabeus aquilam quaerit*, *Aut regem aut fatuum nasci oportet*, *Spartam nactus es, hanc orna*, *Tributum a mortuo exigere*, and *Dulce bellum inexpertis*—'War is sweet to those who know nothing of it'. This last would come to rank as the most famous essay in the *Adages*. It was printed separately by Froben in 1517, and was widely reprinted and translated thereafter, surviving into the present century as a pacifist classic. Among all the duties before the Christian prince, that of preserving peace and avoiding war is the one foremost in Erasmus' mind. It appeared in the *Panegyric* of 1504, and it closed the *Institutio*, whose last few chapters have been translated separately as another peace classic. The *Institutio* was in a tradition familiar in the Middle Ages, that of the 'Mirror of Princes', designed in this case to instruct the sixteen-year-old Prince Charles, the future Charles V. It might well be included therefore among Erasmus' educational treatises and it stands in sharp contrast to the other contemporary manuals of statecraft, descriptive and analytic in their approach: Machiavelli's *Prince*, More's *Utopia*, and

Seyssel's *Grant Monarchie de France*. In his programme to form the perfect, ethical individual for this high office Erasmus drew most heavily on Plato and Aristotle, stressing in a way characteristic of the humanist outlook the need to direct action toward the 'common good'. In almost no way is it original, therefore, nor did it intend to be, since Erasmus' purpose was, as usual, to pass along the tested moral experience of the past. In one respect, however, it departed from conventional opinion, in denying the theory of the 'just war'. This view, taken over from classical times by Christian authorities like Augustine, rested on an analogy between the administration of justice in the civil state and the rectification of grievances about territorial sovereignty. Erasmus pointed out, however, that there is no such parallel, since it is precisely the lack of an impartial, judicial body to adjudicate differences that brings princes into conflict. The only way to settle such disputes peaceably, therefore, is by arbitration. This idea too, was an ancient one, but it was reinforced by Erasmus with impassioned appeals to all and sundry to apply themselves to the issue of peace among Christians, the necessary condition of all he valued and worked to achieve. The ringing climax of the Complaint of Peace, often quoted, will convey something of his passion:

'I call on you, princes, on whose assent especially the affairs of the world depend, who bear amongst men the image of Christ the Prince: heed the voice of your King, who summons you to peace. . . . I call on you, priests, dedicated to God, to express in all your endeavours what you know is most pleasing to God, and to cut out what is most hateful to him. I call on you, theologians, to preach the gospel of peace and to make your message ring unceasingly in the ears of the people. I call on you, bishops, and you others who are high in the offices of the Church, to see that your authority prevails and peace is held firm in bonds which will last for all time. I call on you, nobles and magistrates, to ensure that your will supports the wisdom of kings and the piety of pontiffs. I call on you all alike who are counted Christians to work together with united hearts. Here you must show how the combined will of the people can prevail against the tyranny of the powerful; here must be the focal point of all endeavour. Eternal concord should unite those whom nature has made one in many things and whom Christ has unified in more, and all should join in a united effort to bring about what concerns the happiness of one and all.' (Q 320–1)

If Erasmus' political writing cannot rank as a work of theoretical originality, its moralistic purpose was precisely the feature that ensured its influence. Among the German principalities, the humanistic concern that secular authority be used to bring about religious reform was particularly well received. It accorded with the established control of local princes over their local Churches. Erasmus' treatise on the *Education of a Christian Prince* bore the authority of his name and propagated an ideal of the Christian magistrate which allowed the next generation of Lutheran reformers to elaborate a doctrine of the State Church.

At the same time it should be noted that Erasmus' ideals, like those of Thomas More, were wholly at odds with the aristocratic traditions of government common to England, France, and most of the German states. This was evident from the very opening lines of the treatise, concerning the birth and upbringing of a Christian prince. 'On board ship we do not give the helm to the one who has the noblest ancestry of the company, the greatest wealth, or the best looks, but to him who is most skilled in steering, most alert, and most reliable. Similarly, a kingdom is best entrusted to someone who is better endowed than the rest with the qualities of a king: namely wisdom, a sense of justice, personal restraint, foresight, and concern for the public well-being.' (I 206) Elsewhere he wrote, 'government depends to a large extent on the consent of the people'. For Erasmus, as we might expect, there was no analogue in kingship to divine sovereignty. For him, as always, the Christian life for prince or peasant was a call to making Christ's example visible and persuasive in the life of the believer. The king who claimed a godlike majesty was imitating a pagan, not the Christian god. That the example of Christ's humility and self-sacrifice was not a plausible ideal for the rulers of his day was a point that came home to him as the years passed, and he would later acknowledge the need for coercive power as the threat of popular violence was borne in upon him. Nevertheless, the earlier, purer ideal was a genuine part of his general doctrine, and if it posed a kind of paradox, he would have much to say about that as well. In this kind of thought, which we have noted before, there is the germ of a profound social and political radicalism, and it was not by chance that Erasmus was taken to heart as a mentor of the radical reformation.

His radicalism in the widest sense is nowhere more evident than in the *Colloquies*, which took their definitive form during the years in Basle. We have alluded to these earlier among his educational works, for that is where they began. In 1518 Froben published a brief collection of conversational exchanges in Latin over Erasmus' name, probably from exercises dictated by him in Paris. Erasmus had not been informed and he was not best pleased; the work was full of faults—but it sold well. He prepared a revised edition which was even more popular. In new editions of 1522 and 1523 the potential offered by these lively introductions to conversational Latin seems to have dawned on Erasmus for the first time, in more developed plots and a broadening horizon of subject-matter. Edition followed edition, each with new dialogues added: ten in 1523, ten more in two editions of 1524, five more in 1526, two in 1527. This went on until nearly the end of his life, the last four editions appearing while he lived in Freiburg. These ebullient, irreverent, dramatic, and rollicking vignettes of common life made their way irresistibly into the schoolrooms of Europe and the imagination of Europeans despite the shock and disapproval of many who saw that, whatever their merits, they were also profoundly subversive. This was not the opinion of conservative theologians alone. Many sympathetic to Erasmus worried about their effect especially on the young; Luther said, on his death-bed, that he would forbid his children to read them.

If we wish to measure the complexity of our subject, consider the context of Erasmus' other activity during these Basle years: editions of the Fathers and of classical authors, new editions of the New Testament, of the *Adagia*, and of his letters; *Paraphrases* on the New Testament, expositions of the Psalms, and new treatises on confession, prayer, the correct pronunciation of Greek, on the Eucharist, on abstinence from meat, on Christian marriage. Above all, there was a ceaseless endeavour to reply to his critics, both Catholic and Lutheran, and, not least, the debate with Luther himself. Amidst such efforts to align himself with those defending the tradition, he continued through the *Colloquies* to present quite another, unmistakably iconoclastic face to his reading public.

Three colloquies appearing first in 1526 may be cited in illustration. 'The Pilgrimage' is one of his most famous essays, recounting his own visits to the shrine of Our Lady at Walsingham, and, in the company of John Colet, to that of St Thomas of Canterbury. At the outset it contains a letter supposedly from the Virgin Mary to Ulrich Zwingli, thanking the reformer for his attack upon her cult which has relieved her from a burden of petitions for quite unsuitable inter-cessions; 'And sometimes they ask of a Virgin what a modest youth would hardly dare ask of a bawd—things I'm ashamed to put into words.' (C 290) A merchant wishes his kept mistress's chastity protected during his absence, a hired mercenary asks for rich plunder, a gambler offers her a share of his winnings. 'A Fish Diet', an exchange between a fishmonger and a butcher, ranges over a vast canvas but serves to demon-strate the general tendency to turn some disciplinary rules into superstitious beliefs: a nun allows herself to be raped rather than break the rule of silence. 'The Funeral' contrasts the death of two men. The first, a wealthy war-profiteer, is tormented at his death-bed by the greed of his doctors, his parish priest, and a group of friars (all four of the medieval orders being represented) vying to share in his wealth to the complete detriment of his widow and children. The second, a godly man of simple life, dies in tranquillity, having four days earlier attended mass, made a confession, and received the Eucharist. He leaves all he can spare from the necessary provision for his family to the needy, and spends his final hours reading from the scriptures and comforting his family and friends. He receives extreme unction and communion from the parish priest without repeating his confession, dismissing suggestions of a ceremonial funeral and the saying of anniversary masses for the repose of his soul, for 'there is sufficient abundance of merits in Christ, and I have faith that the merits and prayers of the whole Church will benefit me if only I am a true member of it'. This final utterance of the dying man, while as much within the bounds of Catholic orthodoxy as the foregoing, was easily taken for a 'Lutheran' view in the heated atmosphere of the time:

'In two "briefs" rests my entire hope. One is the fact that the Lord Jesus, the chief shepherd, took away my sins, nailing them to the Cross. The other, that which he signed and sealed with his own sacred blood, by which he assured us of eternal salvation if we place our whole trust in him. Far be it from me that, equipped with merits and briefs, I should summon my Lord to enter into judgement with his servant, certain as I am that in his sight shall no man living be justified. For my part, I appeal from his justice to his mercy, since it is boundless and inexpressible.' (C 371) If the hand was the hand of Esau, the voice was the voice of Jacob. Or, so many thought.

The *Colloquies* in any case could not be seen alone; they would have recalled forcibly to most of their readers Erasmus' most famous and controversial work, the *Praise of Folly*. The association would be enough to set the teeth of the orthodox reader on edge. The *Folly* appeared first in 1511 in Paris, and in the next year in its authorized edition by Josse Bade. By the time of Erasmus' death there were thirty-six Latin editions, and it had been translated into Czech, French, and German. An Italian version appeared in 1539 and the English translation by Thomas Challoner ten years later. It was received with delight by his immediate circle of friends, including Thomas More and Pope Leo X, but serious criticism also appeared, like that in 1515 from the Louvain theologian, Martin Dorp. Both Erasmus and More replied to Dorp, and from 1515 most editions were accompanied by a commentary by Gerardus Listrius, a learned physician who was rector of a school at

Zwolle. Most of his information came from Erasmus. In 1527 the work was condemned by the theologians of Paris and again in 1533. The Sorbonne placed it on a list of condemned books in 1542 and 1543, a list which was the basis for the Index published at Trent in 1564. It was similarly condemned in Milan and Venice, Spain and Portugal, and was included in the works of Erasmus condemned by popes Paul IV, Sixtus V, and Clement VIII. For its life in print it depended upon the presses of England, Switzerland, and the Netherlands.

It began casually enough on a journey to England in the summer of 1509. Erasmus had been tempted to return to England by the death of Henry VII and the prospect of fresh patronage in a place where he had already made friends, people like More and Colet, William Mountjoy, and the archbishop of Canterbury, William Warham. The new king, Henry VIII, was a pupil of Mountjoy, and Erasmus would have recalled that at an earlier time he had been introduced to the youthful Prince Henry at Eltham by Thomas More. The prospect was enough to persuade him to leave the libraries and cultivated literary associates in the Rome of Leo X, where he may have been offered also a post in the Roman Curia, the gateway to further promotion. In the course of his journey he fell to musing upon a new conceit, a mock encomium in the classical manner in praise of folly—an *encomium Moriae*. It was the very thing to tickle the humanist fancy; the allusion to the name of his English friend and forthcoming host would delight More and all their friends. Paradoxical, ironic, and bantering, with Folly personified as the speaker, it would be a praise of folly by Folly (the genitive being both objective and subjective), and a praise of More, by More under the figure of a licensed fool.

This idea was written down in More's house, by his own account during an illness of a week or so. There is no reason to reject this as a literary device only, if we think of the early pages, where the playful tone is even and consistent. Later it was much rewritten and augmented, like the *Adagia* and the *Colloquies*. It contains in its final versions passages quite inconsistent with the banter of the early section, and the whole is suffused with ambiguity and paradox. From any point

97

of view it was a virtuoso exercise in literary art, by no means perfect, with stretches that invite the reader into a kind of intellectual vertigo.

By Erasmus' own insistence, the work is to be judged as a piece of his evangelical humanism, consistent with the purpose of the *Enchiridion*. This was his contention in his reply to Dorp. 'In the *Enchiridion* I laid down quite simply the pattern of a Christian life. In my book on the education of a prince I openly expound the subjects in which a prince should be brought up. In my *Panegyricus*, though under cover of praising a prince, I pursue indirectly the same subject that I pursued openly in the earlier work. And the *Folly* is concerned in a playful spirit with the same subject as the *Enchiridion*. My purpose was guidance and not satire; to help, not to hurt, to show men how to become better and not to stand in their way.' (W 3.114–15) He invokes the authority of Horace: 'To tell truth with a smile, does aught forbid?' What, then, of the unmistakably critical passages? 'I saw how the common throng of mortals was corrupted by the most foolish opinions, and that too in every department of life, and it was easier to pray than to hope for a cure. And so I thought I had found a way to insinuate myself in this fashion into minds which are hard to please, and not only cure them but amuse them too.' (W 3.115)

Erasmus' Lucianesque aims are quite explicit: 'curing' by amusing was his favourite device, inseparable from his most serious scholarship and works of piety in his personal mission to Christian Europe. The *Folly* does not come from the period of his mature thought; even when it was conceived it was only an occasional piece which grew into a fully developed satire, ending unexpectedly with a statement of his religious ideals. Despite its brilliance, it is imperfect in literary form, especially after the original text was altered by sometimes extensive additions, notably in 1514. Nevertheless, it is his best-known work, suffused with an energy which survives even today and in translation, cherished in part because of its very idiosyncrasy. If it does not epitomize his thought, in its elusive stance, captivating wit, impudence, and incisiveness, it seems to lead us more deeply than any other of his creations to the inner recesses of his mental world, to the resources of his demanding, erudite, and mercurial intelligence. For those reasons, although it appears here out of sequence, it will make a fitting conclusion to our survey.

In form the *Folly* is a rhetorical declamation, and it opens with a flourish: 'Folly speaks!' Its captivating, paradoxical tone is apparent from the very beginning—'I'm quite well aware that Folly is in poor repute even amongst the greatest fools . . .', and Folly plunges at once into an expansive account of her indispensable role in making life bearable: 'I am as you see me, the true bestower of good things . . .' (M 87).

Life itself owes its beginning to Folly. 'What man would be willing to offer his neck to the halter of matrimony if he applied the usual practice of the wise man and first weighed up its disadvantages as a way of life? Or what woman would ever agree to take a husband if she knew or thought about the pains and dangers of childbirth and the trouble of bringing up children? So if you owe your existence to wedlock, you owe the fact of wedlock to madness . . .' (M 90).

She warms to her theme: whatever advantages are offered throughout life are provided by Folly. It is not by accident that the happiest, universally enjoyable age of man is the first— that of infants, endowed with the charm of folly by a thought-ful Nature, 'so that they can offer some reward of pleasure to mitigate the hard work of bringing them up'. People on the brink of the grave are likewise recalled to childhood, for compassionate reasons. What is more, devotion to folly even postpones old age; the Hollanders are an example—'for why shouldn't I call them mine? They're my devoted followers, so much so that they've earned a popular epithet (that the older they are, the stupider they become).' Indeed, mother Nature has seen to it that some spice of folly is nowhere lacking, including the gift of woman to man in order to 'sweeten his harsh nature by her folly'. If this draws the wrath of the female sex, after all, this is folly speaking, 'and a woman myself'. The play of paradox intervenes: women are better off than men in many respects: their gift of beauty 'ensures their power to tyrannize over tyrants themselves' (M 95).

The chatter runs on—to parties, to friendship ('winking at your friend's faults, passing over them, turning a blind eye, building up illusions, treating obvious faults as virtues—isn't all that related to folly?'), to marriage ('Goodness me, what divorces or worse than divorces there would be everywhere if the domestic relations of man and wife were not propped up and sustained by the flattery, joking, complaisance, illusions, and deceptions provided by my followers!'), to self-esteem ('since for the most part happiness consists in being willing to be what you are, my Self-love has provided a short-cut to it by ensuring that no one is dissatisfied with his own looks, character, race, position, country, and way of life. And so no Irishman would want to change places with an Italian . . .'), even to great deeds ('no great deed was ever performed without my prompting and no new art discovered unless I was responsible') (M 99). And suddenly a familiar theme emerges. 'Of all deeds which win praise, isn't war the seed and source? But what is more foolish than to embark on a struggle of this kind for some reason or other when it does more harm than good to either side?' From this it is not far to statesmen and philosophers. Remarking that Plato is always quoted: 'Happy the states where either philosophers are kings or kings are philosophers', Folly observes, 'But if you look at history you'll find that no state has been so plagued by its rulers as when power has fallen into the hands of some dabbler in philosophy or literary addict. The two Catos are sufficient proof of this, I think, when one of them was a disturber of the peace of the republic with his crazy denunciations, and the other showed his wisdom by defending the liberty of the Roman people, and in doing so completely destroyed it.' (M 100)

From this happy beginning, Folly moves on to a sharper focus. Seeing learning and the professions as the discovery of a humanity which had lost the delicious pristine folly of the Golden Age, she turns her bantering discourse to the leaders of Church and State. The most highly valued amongst the learned disciplines are, after all, those 'which come closest to common sense, or rather, to folly'. These are led by medicine ('as it is practised now by so many it is really only one aspect of flattery, just as rhetoric is'), and the law. The philosophers are always laughing at lawyers but the profits of lawyers grow, 'while the theologian who has combed through his bookcases in order to master the whole of divinity nibbles at a dry bean and carries on a non-stop war with bugs and lice' (M 107).

As the declamation proceeds, the irony deepens. Among mortals, those who strive after wisdom are the furthest from happiness, simply because they ignore their humanity and try to adopt the life of the immortal gods. The least unhappy are those who come nearest to the instinctive folly of dumb animals, attempting nothing beyond the capacities of man. Such people have no fear of death; they suffer no pangs of conscience; they feel no shame, fear, ambition, envy, or love. 'Finally, if they come still closer to dumb animals in their lack of reasoning power, the theologians assure us they can't even sin'. (M 109)

Such people are the favourites of kings, and the reason is obvious enough. 'Wise men have nothing but misery to offer their prince; they are confident in their learning and sometimes aren't afraid to speak harsh truths which will grate on his delicate ear.' But the kaleidoscope of argument turns again, since we are next reminded that fools enjoy the peculiar privilege of speaking the truth to the mighty, where the truly wise man has to have two tongues, as Euripides says, 'one to speak the truth with, the other for saying what he thinks fits the occasion. . . . And so for all their good fortune princes seem to me to be particularly unfortunate in having no one to tell them the truth and being obliged to have flatterers for friends.' The fact is that fools can speak truth and be heard with pleasure; 'truth has a genuine power to please if it manages not to give offence, but this is something the gods have granted only to fools' (M 110). The reader is fairly put on notice.

Folly now introduces a theme with a great future in the *Moria* in a seemingly casual defence of her arts against the Stoics, who say that nothing is so pitiable as insanity, and that exceptional folly is near insanity. The place of madness, insanity, folly and its correlatives in human experience will be a recurring issue henceforth. It will allow Erasmus to introduce his surprising climax, and, along the way, to score against some of his favourite targets. Folly moves from gambling, to common superstition, to the superstitious abuse of religion, like indulgences. Scarcely any debased practice of popular religion escapes notice, until Folly despairs of her own catalogue; 'The ordinary life of Christians everywhere abounds in these varieties of silliness, and they are readily permitted and encouraged by priests who are not unaware of the profit to be made thereby. Meanwhile, if some disagreeable wiseacre were to get up and interrupt with a statement of the true facts: "You won't do badly when you die if you've been good in your lifetime.... The saint will protect you if you'll try to imitate his life"—if, I repeat your wise man starts blurting out these uncomfortable truths, you can see how he'll soon destroy the world's peace of mind and plunge it into confusion.' (M 115).

The discourse grows more ominous when Folly decides to demonstrate her universal sway, not by enumerating the common types of madness, but by looking at those with a reputation for wisdom: schoolmasters, for example ('by some sort of confidence trick they do remarkably well at persuading foolish mothers and ignorant fathers to accept them at their own valuation'). Grammarians, poets, rhetoricians, writers of books, lawyers ('the most self-satisfied class of people'), along with sophists and dialecticians, quarrelling about 'goat's wool' (an adage), and the philosophers, by which the scholastics are meant. 'Though ignorant even of themselves and sometimes not able to see the ditch or stone lying in their path [a reference to Horace]...they still boast that they can see ideas, universals, separate forms, prime matters, quiddities, ecceities, things which are all so insubstantial that I doubt if even Lynceus [an Argonaut whose eyesight could pierce the earth] could perceive them.' (M 126)

This, of course, is only a foretaste of Folly's discourse on the professionals who follow: the theologians, 'a remarkably supercilious and touchy lot'. None are so unwilling to recognize the services of Folly, yet they are under obligation to her on several accounts, 'notably for their happiness in their self-love, which enables them to dwell in a sort of third heaven, looking down from aloft, almost with pity, on all the rest of mankind as so many cattle crawling on the face of the earth'. The time was at hand for Folly to hold up to ridicule all the futility to which Erasmus had for years objected: the pursuit of theological niceties which owed more, in his view, to the refinements of philosophy than to the sources of Christian faith: 'how the world was created and designed; through what channels the stain of sin filtered down to posterity; by what means, in what measure, and how long Christ was formed in the Virgin's womb; how, in the Eucharist, accidents can subsist without a domicile? ... What was the moment of divine generation? Are there several filiations in Christ? Is it a possible proposition that God the Father could hate his Son? Could God have taken on the form of a woman, a devil, a donkey, a gourd, or a flintstone? If so, how could a gourd have preached sermons, performed miracles, and been nailed to the cross? And what would Peter have consecrated if he had consecrated when the body of Christ still hung on the cross?' (M 127)

It is clear by now that Folly's mood and tone changes constantly. As the assault on theologians and monks continues, the ways in which they abuse their vocations are contrasted with the religion of the New Testament, especially of Paul, and Folly's voice sounds often enough like that of Erasmus himself. The mask of Folly is always in place, however, teasing and protective. 'Now I think you must see how deeply this section of mankind is in my debt, when their petty ceremonies and silly absurdities and the noise they make in the world enable them to tyrannize over their fellow men, each one a Paul or an Anthony in his own eyes. For my part, I'm only too glad to leave these hypocrites, who are as ungrateful in their attempts to conceal what they owe to me as they're unscrupulous in their disgraceful affectations of piety.' (M 135)

Kings and courtiers are next ('nothing would be so dismal and as much to be shunned as the life they lead if they had even a grain of good sense'), where the issues are luxury, neglect of office, and corruption. Their familiar failings have been adopted by the princes of the Church, who 'think they do well when they're looking after themselves, and responsibility for their sheep they either trust to Christ himself or delegate to their vicars and those they call brothers'. The tone is bitter: 'wherever you turn, to pontiff or prince, judge or official, friend or foe, high or low, you'll find nothing can be achieved without money; and as the wise man despises money, it takes good care to keep out of his way' (M 141).

We are now at the final and most complex section of the *Moria*. Folly announces that, although there is literally no limit to her own praises, every speech must come to an end. First, however, she would like to assure her listeners that there are plenty of great authors who testify to her both in their writings and behaviour. After a brisk reference to some classical sources, Folly turns abruptly to authorities who will carry weight with Christians. For the most part, what follows to the conclusion is a discussion of the Pauline 'fools for Christ's sake'. Folly, with mock modesty, admits that she is venturing into theology ('it oughtn't to be so remarkable if I've acquired something from my long-standing association with the theologians, considering how close it has been'). She now expounds a straightforward account of the folly of the Cross, in which the praise of Christian ecstasy is the climactic theme. The influence of Plato is clear: the myth of the cave is cited directly. Erasmus' sources however are chiefly biblical and patristic. He is quite aware of and rejects any form of Dionysiac possession: his key example is Paul's rapture to the third heaven related in 2 Corinthians 12. M. A. Screech, noting that the myth of the cave was important also to Ficino, points out that while the realities behind the shadows which delude the ordinary carnal man are, for Erasmus, divine realities, figured in the truths of scripture, for Ficino, this doctrine is closely bound to the hermetic tradition, the 'ancient theology' which was held to antedate the Christian revelation and, to some extent, to supersede it.

It is apparent that Erasmus was strongly attracted (at least at this period of his life) by the Platonic view that the body is a prison house for the soul or mind, but even here he did not venture beyond the bounds of orthodoxy, although he left tempting traces for his critics. He was one with the many humanists both in Italy and in northern Europe who found in Plato the philosophical basis for a doctrine of the immortal soul which was lacking in Aristotle—another stick, incidentally, with which to beat the Aristotelian philosophers and theologians. But on the crucial question of the resurrection of the body Erasmus was unambiguous: it is the basis of Christian hope. When challenged, he also rejected a view found in the tradition of Eckhart and Tauler which his critics accused him of holding: that after death the soul loses its identity, swallowed up or annihilated in God. His main interest, it seems, was with the experience of Christian rapture which was the best clue in this life to the nature of life after death. He was fascinated by Paul's mystical experience, and longed for more information.

At the conclusion of the entire work, Folly explains that the supreme reward of human life is a kind of madness. Plato was on the right track when he wrote (in the *Phaedrus*) that the madness of lovers is the highest form of happiness: 'For anyone who loves intensely lives not in himself but in the object of his love.' An individual in a state of rapture is said to be 'beside himself'; this is a form of madness. When he has returned to his ordinary state, he 'is himself again'. In heaven, Folly continues, 'the spirit will itself be absorbed by the supreme Mind, which is more powerful than its infinite parts. And so when the whole man will be outside himself, and happy for no reason except that he is so outside himself, he will enjoy some ineffable share in the supreme good which draws everything into itself. Although this perfect happiness can only be experienced when the soul has recovered its former body and been granted immortality, since the life of the pious is no more than a contemplation and foreshadowing of that other life, at times they are able to feel some foretaste and savour of the reward to come. It is only the tiniest drop in comparison with the fount of eternal bliss, yet it far exceeds all pleasures of the body, even if all mortal delights were

105

rolled into one, so much does the spiritual surpass the physical, the invisible the visible. This is surely what the prophet [Isaiah, quoted in 1 Corinthians] promises: "Eye has not seen nor ear heard, nor have there entered into the heart of man the things which God has prepared for those that love him." And this is the part of Folly which is not taken away by the transformation of life but is made perfect.' (M 152)

This last is a deliberate allusion to the passage in Luke (10: 42) in which Mary, the contemplative, is praised as having chosen the 'best part' over that of the preoccupied Martha. There follows a description of the state of those experiencing religious ecstasy, 'something which is very like madness'— they speak incoherently, utter senseless sounds, and when they come to, say they do not know where they have been, or remember what they have heard or seen or said or done, 'except in a mist, like a dream'. All they know is that they wish to return to that state when they were happiest, in a bliss that is only the merest taste of the happiness to come.

Suddenly recalling herself, Folly concludes abruptly, apologizing for anything said which seems 'rather impudent or garrulous—you must remember it's Folly and a woman who's been speaking' (M 153). Whereupon appears the final paradox: Folly herself cannot remember what she has said. Are we to understand that what has gone before is to be taken as an image of ecstasy? The enigma is complete.

The foregoing provides only a shadow of the *Moria*, although the general structure and outline is clear enough. A comprehensive reading would have to take into account its classical antecedents, Erasmus' preoccupations at the time, the references to his critics and contemporaries, above all, the fluctuations in rhetorical form, and the richness of classical allusion. It was a work of intellectual virtuosity for the last reason alone.

The enigma remains. The aim of this brief epitome has been to present the leading ideas and concerns of its subject, and perhaps it is clear at least that his was a mind and personality of truly spectacular power, range, and complexity. Excepting only the New Testament, the whole of his vast editorial enterprise has had to be omitted from this account, as has voluminous writing on themes designed to further his enduring enterprise, the regeneration of Christendom. Most of this has by now been absorbed so long into the traditions of European religion and letters as to be invisible, a fate he would no doubt have regarded with satisfaction, although his dismay at the resistance to his most cherished ideals can only be imagined.

We have returned to the early years of this remarkable character with his *Praise of Folly*, whose verve and iconoclastic playfulness are at a far remove from the graver preoccupations of his last years. We are reminded of the slow evolution of his views with the accumulation of learning, the play of event, and, in his private life, the long search for security combined with independence. We know little in detail about his means of existence save that, after leaving the monastery, he lived always by his wits through the gifts of patrons, secular and ecclesiastical, his teaching in universities and in private, the income from ecclesiastical preferments and—least clear of all these—the earnings of his books. These last came not through royalties, the invention of which he did not live to see, but chiefly from the gifts of the influential people to whom he dedicated them.

Through all of his various activities and works the constant tenor of his ideas cannot be doubted, and the philosophy of Christ was always near the focus. In the brief compass of this essay it has been possible only to indicate the foundation of that ideal and some of its principal expressions in their importance for our own moral and intellectual culture. The task of compressing his vast achievement into so small a space inspires an adage for the occasion: 'to fold a featherbed into a matchbox'. Inevitably the effort bestows a heightened consistency on Erasmus' writings as the desire to present them sympathetically may confer an air of partiality which is unintended. A full account would run far beyond our prescribed limits, but it would expose, *inter alia*, a personality quite unlike the ideal Erasmus painted of the faithful Christian inspired solely by habits of charity and irenicism. The illegitimate orphan had little insulation on his nerve ends, and he flew sometimes even at the mildest of his critics with a pen that could stab and bite. He was charged by some, and not without reason, with vindictiveness, ingratitude, and duplicity. It is tempting to think that his preoccupation with the disparity between Christian ideals and the daily conduct of those who profess them was rooted in a deep awareness of his own shortcomings.

Despite those, he dominated his age through the sheer intellectual impact of his achievement combined with his wide-ranging evangelical concern. The whole was animated by his personal fervour, wit, and brilliant, insinuating style. He did not possess the most innovative mind of his generation; to look no farther than the immediate circle of northern colleagues, Vives, for example, was capable of more daring insight in his programme for the education of women and the care of the poor. No one, however, could approach the scale of Erasmus' personal contribution to the restoration of the sources of European learning and religion, nor rival his sweeping vision of a Christendom renewed by the propagation of a reformed educational programme and the elevation of the lay estate, this being the final consequence of Erasmus' insistence on the equal sanctity of vocations among the baptized.

His scepticism toward theological speculation—he declared that it was more pious to adore the unknown than to debate the unknowable—with his assaults on common pieties that seemed to him to distract from the proper focus of devotion, his insistence that most differences between Christians were of no final consequence and should be treated with mutual tolerance and respect—this attitude of mind, proclaimed in his restless outpouring of letters, satires, educational and devotional treatises, scholarly annotations and controversies, meant that even without the Lutheran convulsion, the Christian world could never have looked the same again. In the midst of all of this, however, he insisted that his sole aim was peace and spiritual unity, and that the tradition should be respected always; perhaps his scepticism about the attainment of final dogmatic truth in itself ensured that. Above all, he declared, those professing to be Christians should bend their every energy to live well.

To help toward that goal he assembled a programme that secured the pattern of liberal education for four hundred years. Whatever the ideal might become in the hands of generations of schoolmasters, it began with his belief in the power of wisdom, the tested moral experience of the race, to inform and renew our life together. Such wisdom, the generation of the Word, could be attained only with unremitting labour to comprehend the foundational texts, sacred and profane. To that task he brought unsurpassed industry and acumen. He forever raised the stakes of scholarship, and his personal skill was such that later generations, more practised in the science of philology, would pause before the sheer range of his erudition and his almost unerring instinct for a false attribution or forgery.

Never again would anyone be able to combine such learning with such unceasing devotion to the issues of the day. His correspondence is the best index of the daily activity of one who has come ironically to symbolize the withdrawn scholar. In his correspondence as in his printed works, he created a commonwealth of learning with access to the most influential persons, lay and ecclesiastical, in almost every corner of Europe.

In his own lifetime all of this seemed to come to nothing, and his final days were haunted by the seeming collapse of his cherished project for the peaceful renewal of a world of civility and understanding. Yet it left a legacy of common loyalties and ideals perhaps more durable than he dreamed, and wherever the cause of international peace and concord is admired, the name of Erasmus is still invoked.

Beyond all of this a unique voice remains, best discovered, no doubt, in the *Folly*. In the voice there lives on still the virtuoso personality and critical intelligence, audacious, paradoxical, elusive yet captivating, intimate yet forever alone. The motto of his personal seal was *Cedo nulli*—'I yield to no one.' The speaker was Death. It was also Erasmus.

109

Suggestions for further reading

The extensive modern literature on Erasmus in best approached through the bibliography of Jean-Claude Margolin, dealing in successive volumes with publications since 1936. These are: *Quatorze années de bibliographie érasmienne, 1936–1949* (Paris, 1969), *Douze années... 1950–1961* (Paris, 1963), and *Neuf années... 1962–1970* (Paris, 1977). Further volumes are promised.

Until recent years, the standard edition of Erasmus' letters and works was the folio *Opera omnia* published in Leiden in 1703–6 and known in the literature as LB. The critical edition of the correspondence is that by P. S. Allen, the *Opus epistolarum* in 11 volumes with an index volume added (Oxford, 1906–47). A new, critical edition of the works published in Amsterdam and known as ASD is sponsored by the Royal Dutch Academy and the International Union of Academies, and began to appear in 1969. A comprehensive English translation of Allen's edition of the correspondence (updated with respect to both texts and annotations) and of an extensive range of the works (excluding only Erasmus' editions and translations from the Greek) is being published at the same time by University of Toronto Press as *The Collected Works of Erasmus* (1974–   ). Of this series, known as CWE, 10 volumes of correspondence (to 1524) and 17 volumes of works have appeared to date. All of the citations in this book are taken from the relevant volumes of CWE with the exception of two. The *Paraclesis* is taken from the convenient, one-volume collection by John C. Olin, *Christian Humanism and the Reformation* (New York, 1987). The colloquies are quoted from the translation by Craig R. Thompson published in one volume in Chicago in 1965. This has been revised and Thompson's complete edition will appear soon in two volumes with full annotation in the CWE series. In addition, Toronto has published a three-volume biographical register of the correspondents of Erasmus and others mentioned in his works and letters, as *Contemporaries of Erasmus* (1985–7). The text of the *Praise of Folly* which appears in CWE is translated by Betty Radice, and appeared originally in Penguin Classics in 1971. The annotator of that translation, A. H. T. Levi, is editor of the volume (27) of CWE in which the *Praise of Folly* appears along with other of Erasmus' satires. His introduction will be useful in understanding the implication of the term 'satire'.

Among modern biographies those by Johan Huizinga, *Erasmus and the Age of Reformation* (New York, 1924) and Roland H. Bainton, *Erasmus of Christendom* (New York, 1969) are still available. The most recent biography, that by Cornelis Augustijn, has appeared in Dutch and German, and in English (1991). A favourite account of Erasmus' life and times remains that of Margaret Mann Phillips, *Erasmus and the Northern Renaissance*, first published in London in 1949, and revised and reissued after several reprintings in 1981.

With respect to individual works, Mrs Phillips was the author also of the most important monograph to be written to date on the subject of the *Adagia: The 'Adages' of Erasmus* (Cambridge, 1964). On the colloquies, apart from the work of Craig Thompson, the monograph of Pierre Bierlaire should be noted: *Les Colloques d'Erasme* (Paris, 1978). On the controversy with Luther, Ernest F. Winter translated and published an edited version of the debate as *Erasmus-Luther: Discourse on Free Will?* (New York, 1961). A helpful discussion referred to in the text is that of Gordon Rupp, 'Luther and Erasmus, 1525' in a collection of his studies on Luther, *The Righteousness of God* (London, 1953). Also of interest on the theological debate is Harry J. McSorley, *Luther Right or Wrong?* (New York, 1968). Recent accounts of the place of humanism in the establishment of the Reformation are those of James M. Estes, *Christian Magistrate and State Church: the Reforming Career of Johannes Brenz* (Toronto, 1982), and of James M. Kittelson, *Wolfgang Capito: from Humanist to Reformer* (Leiden, 1975). On the topic of Erasmus' political views, see James D. Tracy, *The Politics of Erasmus* (Toronto, 1978).

The most important single work dealing with the intellectual formation of Erasmus is the recent two-volume study of Jacques Chomarat, *Grammaire et rhétorique chez Erasme* (Paris, 1981). M. O'Rourke Boyle, *Erasmus on Language and Method in Theology* (Toronto, 1977) is valuable, as is James D. Tracy's *Erasmus: the Growth of a Mind* (Geneva, 1972). Some collections also contain suggestive essays on these and other themes, notably: J. Coppens, *Scrinium Erasmianum* (2 vols., Leiden, 1969); *Colloquium Erasmianum*, Actes du colloque international réuni à Mons (Mons, 1968); J.-C. Margolin, *Colloquia Erasmiana Turonensia* (2 vols., Paris, 1972). The second volume of the Coppens collection contains the essay by James McConica, 'Erasmus and the Grammar of Consent', which is cited in the text.

On the New Testament scholarship of Erasmus see, in particular, Jerry H. Bentley, *Humanists and Holy Writ* (Princeton, 1983), Erika Rummel, *Erasmus' Annotations on the New Testament* (Toronto, 1986), and Albert Rabil, Jr., *Erasmus and the New Testament* (San Antonio, 1972). A facsimile edition of Erasmus' annotations on the Gospels by Anne Reeve appeared in London in 1986, with an introduction by M. A. Screech, and a further facsimile edition of his annotations on Acts, Romans and 1 and 2 Corinthians, edited by Reeve and Screech was published in Leiden in 1990. The important article by Andrew Brown referred to in the text is 'The date of Erasmus' Latin translations of the New Testament', in *Transactions of the Cambridge Bibliographical Society*, vol. 8, pt. 4, '1984' (1985).

The literature on the *Praise of Folly* is immense. An important recent account of one aspect of the work is that by M. A. Screech, *Ecstasy and the Praise of Folly* (London, 1980). Further helpful information can be gathered from the introduction and annotations of A. H. T. Levi to the Penguin Classics edition mentioned above.

Francis Bacon

Anthony Quinton

Contents

Abbreviations

References in the text to Bacon's writings are given by an abbreviation of the title of the work in question, followed by a page-reference to *The Philosophical Works of Francis Bacon*, reprinted from the edition of Ellis and Spedding and edited by John M. Robertson, London, 1905.

The abbreviations are as follows:

A   The Advancement of Learning
G   The Great Instauration
D   De Augmentis (= De Dignitate et Augmentis Scientiarum)
E   Essays
N   Novum Organum
S   New Atlantis
L   Life, by Dr W. Rawley

For A and N references are first given to books and then, in A, to chapter and section, and in N to aphorism; the Ellis and Spedding page-reference follows after a full point.

1 Life

Francis Bacon was born on 22 January 1561 at York House, off the Strand in London. He was the second son of Sir Nicholas Bacon, Lord Keeper, and of his second wife, Ann Cooke. Nicholas Bacon had been born in 1509 in a comparatively modest social position: his father, according to the *Dictionary of National Biography*, being 'sheepreeve to the abbey of Bury St Edmunds'. But he got to Cambridge, became friends there with William Cecil, later Lord Burghley and Elizabeth's chief minister, and with Matthew Parker, later archbishop of Canterbury. In the 1540s he acquired a good deal of former monastic land and with the accession of Elizabeth was appointed Lord Keeper. Even if this was through the good offices of Cecil, Nicholas Bacon soon showed his capacity for a high post. Unlike his famous son, he was 'exceeding gross-bodied'.

Bacon's mother was a well-educated and doctrinally rigid Calvinist. It is possible to interpret her son's piously expressed insistence on the size of the gap that separates knowledge of nature, based on sense and reason, from supernatural knowledge, based on revelation, as a direct consequence of her severely Protestant teaching, on the assumption that the pious professions are sincere, or as an ironic rejection of that teaching, if they are not. Ann Bacon was the sister of the wife of William Cecil, her husband's Cambridge friend, the Lord Burghley who was to be the largely unresponsive object of constant pleas for preferment from her son, Francis.

Bacon accompanied his elder brother, Anthony, to Trinity College, Cambridge, in April 1573 at the seemingly rather unripe age of twelve years and three months. They stayed there for only two years. It has been speculated that Bacon must have been influenced by the philosophical currents running there at the time. In particular it has been suggested that he may have attended lectures at which the new logic of Ramus was expounded. Everard Digby, who was to defend the old logic against the Ramism of his former pupil, William

Temple, in the 1580s, became a fellow of St John's and began to lecture on logic in the year Bacon arrived in Cambridge. Much later in life Bacon said to his biographer, Rawley, that at Cambridge, 'he fell into the dislike of the philosophy of Aristotle; not for the worthlessness of the author, to whom he would ever ascribe all high attributes, but for the unfruitfulness of the way' (L2).

It is easy to understand why Bacon's biographers should seize on any possible clue to the development of his mind. From the time he left Cambridge when still less than sixteen until his disgrace in 1621 at the age of sixty he was continuously engaged in a busy public career: legal from the date of his father's death in 1579, frequently political or in the direct service of the crown. Where in all this and the extravagant glorification of his estate at Gorhambury was there time to acquire the stores of knowledge which made his gigantic philosophico-scientific project at least not ridiculously overweening, and enabled some substantial chunks of it to be realised?

The year after he left Cambridge Bacon accompanied Sir Amias Paulet on his embassy to France. He was still out of England in February 1579 when his father died. Bacon found himself in unexpectedly pinched circumstances and enrolled at Gray's Inn as a first step towards the repair of his fortunes. In 1582 he became a barrister, and two years later entered the House of Commons as member for Melcombe Regis, the first of a large number of places he was to represent. Before he was twenty he had begun the long-drawn-out process of badgering for favour, starting with his uncle Burghley, but going on in due course to other, sometimes more forthcoming patrons, such as Essex, Queen Elizabeth, Buckingham and King James I. It is naturally conjectured that Burghley's generally unenthusiastic response to his gifted nephew's solicitations was due to concern for the worldly fortunes of his own, rather less gifted, son Robert Cecil, later Earl of Salisbury, who despite his second-rate, if sturdy, abilities, succeeded his father as chief minister and remained in that position until his death in 1612.

Some time in 1591 Bacon made the friendship of the Earl of Essex, Elizabeth's last favourite, still in some disgrace for his marriage, not approved by the queen, to the widow of Sir Philip Sidney. Only twenty-three, Essex was six years younger than Bacon. His highest moment as a national hero after the expedition to Cadiz was still three years ahead. In 1592 Bacon wrote in a letter to Burghley the famous sentence, 'I have taken all knowledge for my province.' Perhaps the main outlines of 'The Great Instauration', the fabulous, grandiose programme of Bacon's intellectual career, were already worked out by this time. He was more visibly active in the world of public affairs. Essex's favour, often self-destructively impetuous, failed to secure for Bacon the post of Attorney-General. It went to the man who was to be throughout his life his most persistent enemy, Edward Coke, defender of the common law against absolutist tendencies in Elizabeth and James I. Even the lesser post of Solicitor-General was not forthcoming, since Bacon had aroused the queen's resentment by parliamentary opposition to her taxation policies.

During this comparative lull in his activities Bacon may have been engaged on writing the first of his *Essays*. The first collection of them, ten in number, came out in 1597. (They reached their final total of fifty-eight in the edition of 1625, a year before Bacon's death.) His financial affairs were in a bad state. In 1598 he was briefly arrested for debt. The disastrous failure of Essex's Irish expedition gave Bacon an opportunity to retrieve his position in the eyes of the queen, and to give evidence of somewhat reptilian qualities of character. Essex was informally tried for mismanagement and disobedience to the queen's commands. Enraged and affronted by his fall from the queen's favour, Essex planned an insurrection. The support on which he had counted failed to appear and he was soon a prisoner.

Both Bacon and Coke took part in the ensuing prosecution. Coke performed in a muddled and incompetent fashion and Bacon had to rescue the proceedings from his clumsiness. Essex was condemned and executed. Bacon has been much blamed for his betrayal of Essex, but, whatever responsibility he may bear for encouraging Essex to pursue his Irish mis-adventure, he does not seem to have had any knowledge of Essex's plot to seize the position of chief minister by a violent *coup d'état*.

These at least somewhat morally ambiguous services to the crown do not appear to have done anything to overcome Elizabeth's dislike for, or distrust of, Bacon. With her death in 1603 and the accession of James I Bacon's hopes of preferment once more came to life. He was indeed knighted four months after the new king came to the throne, but the lustre of that honour was dimmed by the fact that it was also conferred on three hundred other people. He was active in Parliament, par-ticularly in working on the consequences of the union of the English and Scottish crowns, but there was no preferment until in 1607 he finally achieved the Solicitor-Generalship, Coke being no longer an obstacle since his promotion to the bench in the previous year.

In 1606 Bacon married Alice Barnham, daughter of a sheriff of London and an heiress. The *Encyclopaedia Britannica* says that 'it seems that [this] marriage ... though childless, was not unhappy'. Aubrey takes a more colourful view of Bacon's domestic life, saying that he was a pederast and that 'his Ganimeds and favourites tooke bribes; but his lordship always gave judgement *secundum aequum et bonum*'. He goes on to suggest that Bacon's wife was not without consolation. 'His dowager', he writes, 'maried her gentleman-usher Sir (Thomas, I thinke) Underhill, whom she made deafe and blind with too much of Venus.'

In 1605 the first of Bacon's philosophical writings was published: *The Advancement of Learning*. The first book is a flowery panegyric to learning; the second, more than twice as long, is largely taken up with a highly elaborate classification of the varieties of knowledge that has exercised a profound influence on the arrangement of libraries and of encyclopedias ever since. Four years later Bacon's *De Sapientia Veterum* came out, an interpretation of the moral and prudential meaning of ancient myths that was, after the *Essays*, the most widely read of Bacon's books in his own lifetime.

The welcome death of the hated Salisbury in 1612 brought Bacon back to the public world. The other main human obstacle to his political advancement, Coke, was removed, not by death, but by promotion to the court of King's Bench at Bacon's suggestion. Now at last he achieved the post of Attorney-General he had pursued for such a long time. He addressed himself effectively to the king's new favourite, George Villiers, soon Earl, and eventually Duke, of Buckingham. He occupied himself with supporting the royal prerogative against the ancient rights and customs defended so doggedly by Coke, and developed his far-seeing ideas about the rationalisation of law.

In 1615 the case of Peacham took the long-standing hostility between Bacon and Coke a stage further and also supplied more material for assaults by Macaulay on Bacon's character. Peacham was a clergyman suspected of seditious conspiracy on account of notes for a sermon found among his papers. He was tortured, in Bacon's presence, to reveal his presumably non-existent accomplices, without success. In going on to prosecute Peacham for treason anyway, the government, advised by Bacon, sought the judges' opinions severally and not as a group. A series of collisions between Coke and the king about the jurisdiction of various courts, and, in the end, about the king's power to draw the boundaries between them, led to James's dismissal of Coke. In 1617 Villiers secured for him his father's post of Lord Keeper and, finally, in 1618 he achieved the highest legal position under the crown, that of Lord Chancellor.

Just as his fortunes seemed assured and his odious rival, Coke, irretrievably humiliated, Bacon slipped up again in the matter of the marriage contracted between the younger brother of his patron, Villiers, and the daughter of Coke. The young woman's mother was opposed to the marriage and Bacon thought to press Coke further down by obstructing it. His interference infuriated Buckingham and also the king. He apologised cringingly and in 1618 became Lord Verulam. In 1621 he was raised to the rank of Viscount St Albans. Less than three months later the greatest of all his misfortunes broke upon him in the form of petitions to the House of Commons charging him with bribery. The House of Lords took up the investigation, Bacon fell ill, thought of defending himself and, in the end, self-abasingly admitted the charges against him. The sentence delivered was severe: a fine of £40,000, imprisonment in the Tower during the king's pleasure, disqualification from Parliament and exclusion from the court and its neighbourhood. In fact the fine was, in effect, remitted; he remained only two or three days in the Tower. But he was unable to get released from his exclusion from within twelve miles of court until he had sold his birthplace and grand London dwelling, York House, to the greedy Buckingham, acting here with all the polished elegance of a looter scavenging at the scene of an air crash.

This reversal was the end of Bacon's public life. But he remained active and enterprising until his death five years later. *Novum Organum*, the second of his major philosophical works, had been published in 1620, a year before the catastrophe. Less than six months after sentence had been passed on him he had finished his monograph on King Henry VII. Two compilations of natural history, raw material arranged for investigation by the method he had worked out in *Novum Organum*, soon followed: *Historia Ventorum* in 1622, *Historia Vitae et Mortis* the year after. Also in 1623 he published *De Augmentis*, a considerably enlarged version of *The Advancement of Learning* of eighteen years earlier.

He did not give up his life-long habit of pestering the great for preferment. He sent a copy of *Novum Organum* to the king, who likened it, in a well-used formula, to the peace of God, since it passed all understanding. The story of his death, recounted by Aubrey, is well-known. It should be quoted in Aubrey's words.

He was taking the aire in a coache with Dr Witherborne (a Scotchman, Physitian to the King) towards High-gate, snow lay on the ground, and it came into my lord's thoughts, why flesh might not be preserved in snow, as in salt. They were resolved they would try the experiment presently. They alighted out of the coach, and went into a poore woman's howse at the bottome of Highgate hill, and bought a hen, and made the woman exenterate it, and then stuffed the bodie with snow, and my lord did help doe it himselfe. The snow so chilled him, that he immediately fell so extremely ill, that he could not then return to his lodgings (I suppose then at Graye's Inne), but went to the earle of Arundell's house at High-gate, where they putt him into a good bed warmed with a panne, but it was a damp bed that had not been layn-in in about a yeare before, which gave him such a cold that in two or three dayes, as I remember he [Hobbes, Aubrey's informant] told me, he dyed of suffocation.

Bacon's character has not been much admired. Pope's couplet is memorably concise:

> If parts allure thee, think how Bacon shined,
> The wisest, brightest, meanest of mankind.

It was a period when the more agreeable aspects of human nature were not much encouraged in English public life. Elizabeth and James I had some excuse in the dreadful fates of their respective mothers. The Cecils were devious and insincere: James I's catamites, Somerset and Buckingham, much worse. It is Bacon's special misfortune to have been the subject of a marvellously readable but rollickingly injudicious essay by Macaulay, in which the worst construction is put on his not unrepresentative fawning on the great, his betrayal of Essex and the malpractice that brought down on him the disaster of 1621.

He seems to have been a fairly cold fish. He said of himself, 'I have rather studied books than men', and ordinary private affections appear to have played little part in his life. If so it may help to explain how he managed to achieve as much as he did of his grand design while caught up, in Macaulay's phrase, with 'so much glory, so much shame'.

2 The intellectual background

In the history of English philosophy as it has usually been presented, Bacon stands out sharply, as a systematic thinker on a large scale, emerging in a wholly unanticipated way after a period of unrelieved stagnation. Careful reading of the small print of intellectual history often dissipates this kind of impression of absolute novelty. Bacon's case is not exceptional. All the same there is no doubt that the completed part of his giant project does add up to a system, even if the proportion of rhetoric to reasoning is much higher than in the work of his near-contemporary, Descartes, who is still to this day something of a model of philosophical professionality. It is also true that, even though much of what Bacon has to say can be traced in previous writers, these were, with one very important exception, not English. Rather like Bertrand Russell, Bacon served to bring to notice in this country tendencies on the other side of the Channel hitherto only dimly perceived.

The last great century of English (or British) philosophy had been the fourteenth. During its first half, ending with the Black Death, the most vigorous philosophical movement in Christendom was the group of Franciscan thinkers in Oxford whose most prominent members were Duns Scotus and William of Ockham. Very briefly put, their common, negative, achievement was to undermine the remarkable synthesis of Christian doctrine and the philosophy of Aristotle which had been constructed by Thomas Aquinas. He had tried with the greatest learning and ingenuity to provide rational arguments, Aristotelian in form and often in their foundations, for nearly all the main Christian dogmas (he had to admit that the doctrine of the Trinity depended on revelation).

Duns Scotus stood to Aquinas rather as Kierkegaard to Hegel, that is to say as one concerned to re-complicate what another had oversimplified. Ockham agreed that the human reason could achieve little in the supernatural domain of theology, but, on the positive side, went beyond Duns Scotus into a theory of natural knowledge as derived from the senses which was the first major presentation of the empiricism that has subsequently been the dominant British philosophy. It is Ockham, in particular, who is the exception to the principle that Bacon's main sources are not English. For in his development of the brief and nebulous account of induction given by Aristotle in various places in the logical writings that make up his *Organon* he explicitly sets out the main principles of the eliminative method that were systematised in Bacon's 'tables'.

Ockham himself died of the Black Death. His ideas were kept very much alive, but for the most part in France. To an increasing extent, furthermore, the school of Ockham became concentrated on physics. The scientific movement of the late fourteenth century was centred in Paris; its chief exponents, John Buridan, who anticipated the principle of inertia crucial to Galilean physics, and Nicholas of Oresme, who held, a century and a half before Copernicus, that the hypothesis of the earth's motion was, at any rate, consistent with the observed facts, were both French.

In his own country Ockham was succeeded by some able logicians but the fate of philosophy is represented, as it was (at least in part) caused, by the career of John Wycliffe. Wycliffe began as a traditionally-minded systematic philosopher. Subversive ideas about authority in Church and State supplanted his more abstract interests and brought him into disfavour. It was appropriate that he should work for a vernacular Bible, holding the prematurely Protestant ideas he did. The fierce suppression of his followers, the Lollards, after his death and into the next century, seems to have extinguished original thought in Oxford. The first signs of new life there were only marginally philosophical, the rise of a mild and respectably unpagan version of Italian humanism, imported in the first instance by such aristocratic patrons as Humphrey, Duke of Gloucester, and John Tiptoft, Earl of Worcester, coming to full flower with the circle round Erasmus: Colet, Grocyn and, most notably, Thomas More, a hundred years after Wycliffe's death. The intervening period in the intellectual life of the country remains obscure, most probably because there really was very little going on.

The sixteenth century was a dangerous one for theorists. Henry VIII's Reformation was a matter of Church government, not doctrine, but ideological Protestantism triumphed in the short reign of Edward VI. In the reaction under Mary the more zealous and obtrusive Protestant publicists were killed off. Finally in the reign of Elizabeth a moderate Church settlement was arrived at, and the chief thinker of the age, Richard Hooker, elaborated the theory of that settlement in a traditional, reasonable, eclectic spirit. The natural law content of his doctrine was as close to the scholastic rationalism of Aquinas as were his methods of argument. Anxious to repel the puritan conviction that divinely authoritative prescriptions for every detail of the conduct of life were to be found in scripture, Hooker reverted to the position that God's purposes for man are accessible to human reason without a particular revelation.

In thus rejecting the fideism, or theological irrationalism, of Scotus and Ockham (neither of whom was irrationalistic about *natural* knowledge), Hooker differed from most British thinkers until John Locke and the Cambridge Platonists in the second half of the seventeenth century, who agreed, in their distinct and often opposed ways, on the reasonableness of Christianity. The view that reason is limited to the natural world and incompetent to investigate God and the immortal soul can be shared by people of very different attitudes. It can be a stratagem of the devout for the protection of a faith they hold on authority. It can equally be a device for the preservation of natural inquiry from theological interference. Bacon firmly embraced it, according to most interpreters of his works, for the sake of disencumbering natural science. Some bold or hopeful commentators have claimed that his faith, firmly marked off from the sphere of rational knowledge, was sincere. Whether that is correct or not, there can be no doubt of his sincere concern for the autonomy of science.

There is a slightly suspicious resemblance between the views of Bacon about its being positively desirable that the dogmas of religion should be hard to accept, and a famous remark of Hobbes's: 'it is with the mysteries of our religion as with wholesome pills for the sick; which swallowed whole, have the virtue to cure; but chewed up, are for the most part cast up again without effect'. Bacon expresses himself a little more piously:

The prerogative of God extendeth as well to the reason as to the will of man; so that as we are to obey the law, though we find a reluctation in our will, so we are to believe his word, though we find a reluctation in our reason. For if we believe only that which is agreeable to our sense, we give consent to the matter, and not to the author; which is no more than we would do towards a suspected and discredited witness; but that faith which was accounted to Abraham for righteousness was of such a point as whereat Sarah laughed, who therein was an image of natural reason. (A II xxv 1.167–8)

But there are those who take even Hobbes to be a believing Christian.

The less cursory histories of English philosophy do manage to find a little activity in the mid-Elizabethan period in which Bacon grew up. They all depend on a pioneering study of 1892 by a German scholar, J. Freudenthal, who exhumed a violent controversy at Cambridge in the 1580s between Everard Digby, a conservative thinker in essentials who was nevertheless attracted towards the esoteric and mystical aspects of the revived neo-Platonism of Renaissance Italy, and William Temple, an enthusiast for the logical heresies of Ramus. For his Master of Arts degree Ramus had defended the thesis that everything affirmed by Aristotle is false. His considered view was less extreme, namely that the logic of Aristotle is artificial and intolerably and unnecessarily complicated. Logic should seek to follow the natural movement of thought, not to contort the intellect into the mechanical evolutions of the parade-ground. Thought as its best and most natural is to be found in the writings of the best, classical, authors, the proper object of humanistic study. In practice and in detail he departs surprisingly little from Aristotle, a testimony to the strength of that philosopher's grip on the European mind.

127

A convenient point of view for surveying the influences on Bacon and the intellectual atmosphere of his time from continental Europe is provided by his own threefold classification of unsatisfactory styles of learning which it is his ambition to replace, set out in the first book of *The Advancement of Learning*. The first of these is *contentious* or disputatious learning, in other words scholasticism, the orthodox Aristotelian tradition. This was still, and was to remain until the end of the century, the staple mode of thought in the English universities. Hobbes and Locke were to follow Bacon in attacking its vacant, repetitious, jargon-ridden character, but not until Locke's *Essay on Human Understanding* (published in 1689) had been available for some time were the writings of Aristotle and of his train of laborious commentators to any significant extent displaced. Bacon's only institutional acknowledgement was to be by the Royal Society through the encomiums of Robert Boyle and the Society's historian Bishop Thomas Sprat.

Bacon did not have to look abroad for exponents of the contentious learning of Aristotelian scholasticism. But its English representatives in the late sixteenth century were relatively humble authors of student texts. In Catholic Europe the Council of Trent in 1545 and the support of the Jesuits, founded shortly before, led to a scholastic revival in which Aquinas himself became the main authority. The most important of these counter-Reformation scholastics was the Spaniard Francesco Suarez. His *Disputationes Metaphysicae* of 1597 was highly learned, thorough and systematic. Luther's colleague Melanchthon preserved Aristotle in the learned world of German Protestantism, even if he was hostile to the traditional scholastic elaborations of Aristotle's ideas. In Italy too, the main source of new currents of thought, Aristotle had able disciples, notably Pietro Pomponazzi, but here too he was treated in a non-scholastic, naturalistic way, and therefore not one that Bacon would have seen as disputatious.

The second of Bacon's 'vanities of learning' is the *delicate* learning, the form of intellectual life of the humanistic scholars. They, too, opposed scholasticism, but rather for its barbarous, un-Ciceronian Latin than for its abstract and empty verbalism. Humanism as a general movement is far more than the kind of gentlemanly dilettantism and preoccupation with style rather than substance, decoration rather than content, that Bacon attacked. But the leading humanists—Erasmus, for example—were not interested in knowledge of nature, either for its own sake or, in Bacon's way, for the sake of power and the 'relief of man's estate'. At most it concerned them as an object of beauty, a setting for the free and comprehensive development of human powers which they saw as the great achievement of the ancient world and as obliterated by the gloom and self-denial of the Middle Ages.

Lorenzo Valla (1407–57) is perhaps a more representative figure than Erasmus or Petrarch, the greatest of humanist poets. He categorically asserted that pleasure is the sole end of man and attacked monasticism. A passionate enthusiast for the classical languages, he showed what expertise in them can achieve by his incontrovertible proof that the donation of Constantine, which purported to be an edict of that emperor according supreme power in the Church to the bishops of Rome, was a forgery. The classical emphasis of European education at its higher levels since the Renaissance is one consequence of humanism. Another, less obvious one is the distinction between the sciences and the humanities, the idea that a special method of inquiry must be applied to human beings and their achievements as distinct from the rest of the world. Humanistic scholarship is a matter of the interpretation of texts. In our own age it has been held by many that it is their possession of language, that of which texts are made, that makes human beings unamenable to the methods of the natural sciences. On this issue Bacon's position was clear. He praised Machiavelli, the unillusioned Florentine political theorist, for discussing men as they are rather than as they ought to be, and it is natural to suppose an affinity of sentiment between Machiavelli and Bacon. Furthermore, in his classification of the sciences Bacon put human philosophy beside natural philosophy and saw his inductive method as applicable both to man and to the rest of nature.

Bacon shared the humanists' hostility to the methods of scholastic reasoning. He did not follow them in their indifference to its object: knowledge of the world in which man is placed. The sceptical philosophies of the Renaissance may be seen as a more or less philosophical justification of humanist unconcern with philosophy and science and their confinement to the study of human nature, the arts and polite morality. The great sceptical encyclopedia compiled by the Hellenistic philosopher, Sextus Empiricus (second or third century AD), became generally available from 1562, the year after Bacon's birth. Cicero's account of the sceptical teachings of the 'Academy'—as the sceptical thinkers who derived rather tenuously from Plato, founder of the original Academy, were called—were accessible to Erasmus to support his attack on scholastic dogmatism in *In Praise of Folly* (1509). Montaigne wrote his extremely influential *Apologie pour Raimond Sebond* around 1576 in reaction to the violent disturbance to his beliefs brought about by reading the newly available Sextus Empiricus. Florio's translation of Montaigne's essays appeared in English in 1603. Bacon acknowledged indebtedness to Montaigne as an essayist. But he in no way shared the general intellectual pessimism of the sceptical philosophers; his scepticism about deductive metaphysics served to make the road clear for inductive science.

Renaissance critics of Aristotle often used Plato as a stick to beat their old enemy with. That is not surprising; Aristotle is to a considerable extent engaged in criticism of Plato. But the Plato of the Renaissance philosophers is not Plato himself, but two rather different individuals, different from him and from each other. In the Florentine Academy, a circle of philosophers sponsored by the Medici that met in the last third of the fifteenth century, and named after Plato's own philosophical school, an elevated Christian neo-Platonism, affirming the beauty and harmony of the world, was developed by Marsilio Ficino and Pico della Mirandola (admired by Thomas More, who translated his biography). This form of Platonism is not interested in science; its concern is with the enjoyment of beauty and the conduct of life.

But the name of Plato was widely invoked as their inspirer by a varied group of philosophers of nature: the German Nicholas of Cusa (1401–64), the Italians Francesco Patrizzi (1529–97), Tommaso Campanella (1568–1639) and Giordano Bruno (1548–1600). For them nature was a proper object of study in its own right. Some of them—Campanella, for example, and his teacher Bernardino Telesio (1509–88)—emphasised the role of observation with the senses. All speculated on a large scale about the form and nature of the cosmos, the physical world as a whole, terrestrial and stellar. The strongly Pythagorean, mathematical aspect of Platonism was revived by the new philosophers of nature, which in their rashly imaginative way can be seen as prefiguring the mathematically formulated systems of the cosmos of the first physicists proper: Copernicus, Kepler, Galileo.

Bacon took little account of this, more fruitful, side of naturalistic Platonism. What he did notice and identify as his third kind of defective philosophy, calling it fantastic learning, was its loosely associated underworld of believers in magic, alchemy, astrology, in the importance and availability of practical, and not simply contemplative, knowledge of nature. The most important and representative of these occult nature-philosophers was Paracelsus, whose real name was Theophrastus Bombastus von Hohenheim and who lived in the first half of the sixteenth century. Esoteric charlatanry, as well as an ultimately beneficial emphasis on experimentation, are mingled in the work of these believers in man as a microcosm of the universe, of nature as a great system of correspondences and analogies. The magical encyclopedia attributed to 'Hermes Trismegistus' (in other words the hermetic literature of the ancient world), the Jewish Cabbala and neo-Platonism were brought together in the idea of a world-spirit through which the forces of nature could be controlled for the advantage of man, as in the alchemical notions of a panacea, an elixir of life and the philosopher's stone.

Some commentators on Bacon have seen him, for all his overt hostility to the fantastic learning of the occultists, as himself ultimately one of them. This is not so much because

131

of endorsement of what he calls 'natural magic' but because of
his neglect of the mathematical mechanics and cosmology
that was the great scientific achievement of the seventeenth
century, for the sake of a merely observational and experimental study of nature, undertaken for use and not for the
sake of knowledge itself. This is to ignore his insistence
on methodical procedure, on the social nature of scientific
inquiry and on the capacity of anyone, going about it in the
right way, to secure useful scientific knowledge for himself.

The most notable English occult philosopher is Robert
Fludd, a younger contemporary of Bacon's, who produced a
defence of the Rosicrucians in 1616 and in subsequent years a
series of volumes about the universe as everywhere made of
the same two materials and thus permeated by sympathies
and antipathies whose perceptible signs can be interpreted by
the initiated.

Three of the four major currents of thought in Bacon's
time are, then, identified in his catalogue of philosophies that
deserve to be rejected. Aristotelian scholasticism was under
pressure from four directions: its logic was attacked as over-
complex and artificial; its rational theology as verbal sophisms
not needed by the faithful and not cogent enough to convince
the faithless; its physics as abstract and unempirical; its
system of values as ascetically self-mutilating. In his assault
on contentious learning Bacon associated himself with all
these criticisms.

The delicate learning of humanism had enjoyed a pathetically
short life in England. Henry VIII executed Thomas More;
Erasmus had left England by the time, with the death of Colet,
that the English humanist group was beginning to dissolve.
Erasmus and More, both apostles of tolerance, found their
ideas swept away in the torrent of bloodthirsty religious
frenzy initiated by Luther's Ninety-Five Theses of 1517. A
tenacious educational ideal survived, as did a habit or practice
of private cultivation. The scepticism derived from Sextus
Empiricus which was the expression of humanism in formal
philosophy did not take on at all as an elaborated doctrine
until William Chillingworth, of Falkland's Great Tew circle,

that civilised group of philosophically conversational friends meeting in the Oxfordshire countryside so much admired for their enlightened moderation by Matthew Arnold, just before the civil war, delighted in Sextus' arguments a number of years after Bacon's death. In Bacon's own time it was represented in England only in anti-astrological polemics.

The new nature-philosophy of his age was seriously underestimated by Bacon in being identified, under the label 'fantastic learning', with the esoteric occultism of Paracelsus and Fludd. Bacon is commonly criticised for a lack of response to the really significant natural science of his own period (see Chapter 9). It could just as well be argued that he failed to take account of the impressive body of philosophical theorising about nature between Nicholas of Cusa, who died a hundred years before Bacon was born, and Bruno, who died at the stake in 1600.

Bacon's map of his intellectual environment was, then, seriously incomplete in one respect. It was, all the same, comprehensive enough to be a reasonable guide and to reveal as unoccupied the region of ideas that Bacon was to make his own. That image of a map is appropriate to apply to the work of a thinker in, and very much of, the great age of discovery which inaugurated the spreading of the natural science of Europe to the rest of the world, and with it the technical and industrial transformation of traditional agricultural society. The Viennese historian of ideas Friedrich Heer writes that 'every English philosophy is a memorial to the political conditions of the time'. He goes on to say about Bacon that he 'was possessed by the hunger for power, possession, honour and influence. He wanted to hold the world in the palm of his hand. His drive to power made him the natural advocate of the inductive method and of an oppressive colonial and scientific policy. The inductive thought of Bacon was England's answer to Spain.' If there is anything to that, and the role of industrial primacy in England's historical mission as the final obstacle to continental European tyrants who go too far suggests that there is, there is more to Harvey's unkind remark that Bacon wrote science like a Lord Chancellor than its author intended.

3 The great instauration

It has usually seemed odd to those who have considered the matter that Kant should have dedicated his greatest work, the *Critique of Pure Reason*, to Bacon. Kant does claim to have been awoken from his dogmatic slumbers by an empiricist, by a philosopher who, like Bacon, saw sense-experience, and not reason, as the foundation of all real knowledge, namely Hume. But Kant is not, like Bacon, a partisan of inductive reasoning or, more generally, the propounder of a new method, except in philosophy itself. Where Bacon's aim was to revolutionise the scientific study of nature, Kant's was to consolidate the Newtonian system of the world which he saw as the crowning and completed achievement of science.

In the second edition of his *Critique*, Kant added a quotation to Bacon's name from the latter's preface to *The Great Instauration*, published in 1620 as a kind of grand ornamental approach to the *Novum Organum*, in which the formal details of Bacon's new method were set out.

Of myself I say nothing; but in behalf of the business which is in hand I entreat men to believe that it is not an opinion to be held, but a work to be done; and to be well assured that I am labouring to lay the foundation, not of a sect or doctrine, but of human utility and power. Next I ask them to deal fairly by their own interests ... join in consultation for the common good ... come forward themselves to take part in what remains to be done. Moreover, to be of good hope, nor to imagine that this Instauration of mine is a thing infinite and beyond the power of man, when it is in fact the true end and termination of infinite error ... (G 247)

It is not hard to see that part of the appeal of this to Kant is in its confident claim to have brought men at last into the light from long and seemingly interminable enslavement to confusion. But more significant is the fact that Kant's quotation is from *The Great Instauration*. This promissory fragment of about twenty pages is the most ambitious, if not the most detailed, of Bacon's displays of classificatory enthusiasm. Here there is a marked affinity with Kant, who divided his main philosophical project into three critiques, each themselves divided in an elaborately systematic way, and with gorgeous names for all the elements of the system.

Bacon's *Instauration*, or complete system of the sciences, was divided into six parts, actually carried out by him to very different extents and labelled in concrete Jacobean English where Kant relied on the utmost in professorial abstraction. The first part is the *division of the sciences*. In 1620 Bacon described this as 'wanting', although he admitted that some account of the matter would be found in the second book of *The Advancement of Learning*. In 1623 there appeared in Latin his *De Dignitate et Augmentis Scientiarum*, the revised and enlarged version of *The Advancement of Learning* that is usually referred to as the *De Augmentis*. It looks a little like the promised provision of a proper first part for the *Instauration*, but, as Bacon's great nineteenth-century editor James Spedding observes, if that is so it is odd that he did not call it something like 'Partitiones Scientiarum'. Perhaps it was still too like its English original of 1605 for his liking. For all his doubts it should be said that Bacon's classification of the sciences is one of the most thorough and without doubt the most influential things of its kind there has ever been. The intense devotion of the French *encyclopédistes* of the eighteenth century is not due only to his worldly concern with natural science and opposition to mystery. It owes something to their sense of him as a pioneer in the organisation of knowledge.

The second part of the project is the *Novum Organum* of 1620, further described as 'true directions concerning the interpretation of nature'. This is Bacon's principal work on what he saw, quite reasonably, as his most important achievement, his method for the acquisition of real knowledge of the natural world. Even here he shows some hesitation. He adds to the title phrase: 'not however in the form of a regular treatise, but only a summary digested into aphorisms'. It too, then, is in its author's eyes a second best, a series of notes for something more complete and worked-out. In this case nothing further was to appear. But the *Novum Organum* is a fair-sized work, only a little shorter than *The Advancement of Learning*, and it is generally agreed that Bacon took more trouble with it than with anything else he wrote. He seems to have begun to write it about 1608 and it was not published until twelve years later. Its defects are not those of sketchiness or incompleteness.

The third part of the system is the 'phaenomena universi' or natural history. Bacon's intention here was to accumulate particular items of information in a methodically ordered way, ready to be subjected to the inductive techniques of the *Novum Organum*. Bacon made some progress with this part of his scheme in the form of his 'histories' of the winds, of life and death and of the dense and the rare. There is also the *Sylva Sylvarum* ('wood of woods' or collection of collections), on which he was working at the time of his death and which contains some very dubious material, lending some colour to the conception of Bacon as not much more than a particularly bold and ambitious exponent of the magical and mystical lore of his age. A celebrated item in it is his remark that 'the heart of an ape, worn near the heart, comforteth the heart and increaseth audacity'.

Neither the fourth part, 'scala intellectus, or the ladder of the intellect', which was to consist of fully worked-out examples of Bacon's method in action, to serve as instructive paradigms, nor the fifth, 'prodromi, or forerunners or anticipations of the new philosophy', which he describes as conclusions arrived at, not by the new method, but by 'the ordinary use of the understanding' and so 'for temporary use only', seem to have taken on any solid literary form. As for the sixth and last, 'the new philosophy, or active science', this was conceived by Bacon as work not for his own hands but for the subsequent generations of scientific inquirers, brought up in his method, and spreading out into all the regions of knowledge whose boundaries had been established in *The Advancement of Learning*.

A number of smaller philosophical works by Bacon can be

regarded as preliminary to and sometimes as absorbed in the *Novum Organum*, such as his *Valerius Terminus*, his *Cogitata et Visa* and his *Temporis Parus Masculus*. The work of greatest philosophical or scientific interest that is not a part of the Instauration is the *New Atlantis* with its highly original conception of natural inquiry as an essentially co-operative undertaking.

In his own time Bacon was best known, as he is to students of literature today, for his *Essays*, of which several editions appeared between 1597 and the complete set of fifty-eight of 1625. The generalised, well-informed worldly prudence with which they abound is also a feature of *The Wisdom of the Ancients* of 1609 (translated into English in 1619), in which Bacon analyses the rational messages more or less hidden in the myths and fables of antiquity. Also worthy of consideration are his one substantial venture into history, the *History of Henry VII* of 1621/2, and various writings on legal subjects, notably *Maxims of the Law*.

My main concern in what follows will be with Bacon as a philosopher of science, and thus, above all, with *The Advancement of Learning* and *Novum Organum*. But some attention will be given to his ideas about law, politics and history and to his purely literary achievements and opinions.

4 The critique of false systems

Although the main business of *The Advancement of Learning* is the development of a classification of all the varieties of knowledge, that is only the topic of its second book, which is more than twice as long as the first. There are, as well, some preliminaries of varying degrees of importance. The first, and least, of these is an introductory passage in which the gifts and virtues of James I are praised with unappetising fulsomeness. There follows a more substantial defence of learning, or, more particularly, natural knowledge, against various sorts of detractors. In the course of this defence Bacon sets out his objections to the three kinds of fallacious learning mentioned already in the description of his intellectual environment. This criticism is briefly repeated in a somewhat different form in the consideration of the idols in *Novum Organum*, that is, the account of all the factors, innate, personal and social, which mislead men in the pursuit of truth. The fourth class of idols, the idols of the theatre, are the received systems of philosophy which get in the way of effective investigation of nature.

Bacon's defence first confronts the clergy with their frequent claim that the study of nature is impious. He relies here on his sharp anti-Thomist distinction between the study of nature and the study of the supernatural or divine. God, he says, 'worketh nothing in nature but by second causes', which is, in effect, to say that nature is a closed system from which nothing can be inferred, at any rate of a detailed sort, about God. 'We do not presume,' he says, 'by the contemplation of nature to attain to the mysteries of God.' 'Divers great learned men', he goes on a little later, 'have been heretical, whilst they have sought to fly up to the secrets of the Deity by the waxen wings of the senses.' Men cannot be 'too well studied in the book of God's word, or in the book of God's works, divinity or philosophy . . . only let men beware . . . that they do

not unwisely mingle or confound these learnings together'
(A I i 3.44–6).

After some pleasantly insubstantial material about the social
and political harmlessness of learning, in which he draws
comfort from the fact that Alexander the Great was Aristotle's
pupil, he arrives at more serious business, by way of an
amusing consideration of the mean employments and disagreeable manners of the learned.

The first to be examined of the false philosophies of the age
is the delicate learning with its 'vain affectations'. This, in
effect, is humanism and Bacon upbraids it for ornamental
vacuity, for concentration on style at the expense of substance. Obsession with eloquence and the worship of Cicero
are ridiculed but there is no very detailed account of what
is being proscribed nor any clear boundaries drawn to it.
Erasmus, for example, is cited as a witness against it, despite
his indifference to the kind of natural investigation Bacon
favoured.

What is overlooked, not surprisingly, in Bacon's critique is
the idea that has grown in strength increasingly since the
eighteenth century that the study of human affairs—the individual person, the intellectual and artistic products of man,
the various kinds of human society—must be carried on by
methods quite other than those applied in the study of non-
human nature. This thought was first presented in a thoroughly
worked-out way in the eighteenth century by Vico and in
the nineteenth was the common conviction of a series of
exponents of the autonomy of history. In our own age this
belief in the methodological uniqueness of the human world
has been applied to the social sciences, including psychology,
as well as to history. It has been generally admitted, perhaps,
that the humanities proper, the textual, literary disciplines
whose place in the educational scheme of things is a consequence of humanism, are not natural sciences, susceptible
of inductive treatment.

In Bacon's classification of the sciences 'history' is one of
the absolutely primary divisions, along with 'philosophy' and
'poesy'. But what he is talking about is not history in our

usual sense, although it includes it. For him it is that part of our mental activity concerned with the registering of particular, individual facts. By seeing it as the proper employment of memory (as philosophy is of reason and poesy of imagination) he seems to concentrate on the storage of particular items of knowledge to the exclusion of their discovery, but his associations of basic kinds of learning with faculties of the mind need not be taken very seriously.

Under history Bacon includes both natural and 'civil' history, regarding both as storehouses of data for the corresponding types of philosophy, in other words for natural and social science. It is clear that he believes that his methods apply to man and society, that human and civil philosophy (psychology and social science) are inductive disciplines. The point is enforced by his open admiration for Machiavelli as a great innovator who added to knowledge by studying what men are and not what they ought to be. In a memorable image Bacon ends his account of the delicate learning by comparing it to 'Pygmalion's frenzy'. 'Words are but the images of matter; and except they have a life of reason and invention, to fall in love with them is all one as to fall in love with a picture' (A I iv 3.54). The scientifically-minded still quite often feel like that about the humanities.

In my earlier consideration of the humanism of Bacon's age I claimed that the strictly philosophical expression of it was scepticism, most notably expounded for Bacon by Montaigne. Bacon mentions Montaigne approvingly in the first of his essays, the one on truth, and it is generally supposed that he chose to call his brief prudential writings 'essays' in polite imitation of Montaigne. Descartes's friend and impresario, Marin Mersenne, regarded Bacon as a sceptic himself because of his assault on the Aristotelian tradition.

Bacon criticised the contemporary admirers of the Pyrrhonians reported by Sextus Empiricus only in passing. He no doubt felt a sense of affinity with them, seeing them as engaged, as he was, in the destruction of scholastic orthodoxy. In the discussion of logic in *The Advancement of Learning* he mildly chides some 'academical' philosophers for going too far. In the *De Augmentis* version he says, 'their great error was, that they laid the blame upon the perceptions of the senses, and thereby pulled up the sciences by the very roots. Now the senses, though they often deceive us or fail us, may nevertheless, with diligent assistance, suffice for knowledge ... But they [the sceptics] ought rather to have charged the defect upon the mind ... and upon false forms of demonstration' (D 504).

A point to notice here is that the scepticism of the ancient world was much more concerned with the logical than with the perceptual sources of error and contradiction. In modern times, however, under the dominating impulse of the scepticism from which Descartes begins his philosophy, interest has fastened almost exclusively on the senses and memory. Bacon did not foresee this shift of focus, largely because he helped to create the conditions for it by insisting that the ultimate source of all real knowledge is sense-perception, not intuitions of self-evident truth. In his view the sceptics of his time were critics of deductive logic. Where he differed from them was in the attitude inspired by that criticism. They thought that if deductive logic was empty and formal no knowledge could be secured. He thought that he had a new logic with which to replace the old one. Thus he rejected their pessimism about the possibility of knowledge but did not blame them for it.

So although Bacon admits the fallibility of the senses—'the impressions of the senses,' he says, 'are erroneous, for they fail and deceive us'—he does not see this as a major difficulty of principle. For he goes on, 'we must supply defects by substitutions, and fallacies by their correction', which suggests that all that is needed is another look to make sure. That would not satisfy scepticism of Descartes's kind, which says that we can never be sure that we are not dreaming or the dupes of an evil demon. He prefers scepticism to dogmatism but maintains that 'when the human mind has once despaired of discovering truth, everything begins to languish ... But ... we are not to deny the authority of the human senses and understanding, although weak, but rather to furnish them with assistance' (N I 67.274).

The second, and most important, object of his criticism is the contentious or disputatious learning, which 'did chiefly reign among the schoolmen: who having sharp and strong wits, and abundance of leisure, and small variety of reading, but their wits being shut up in the cells of a few authors (chiefly Aristotle their dictator) as their persons were shut up in the cells of monasteries and colleges, and knowing little history, either of nature or time, did out of no great quantity of matter and infinite agitation of wit spin out unto us those laborious webs of learning which are extant in their books' (A I iv 5.55–6).

Bacon does not accuse the scholastics of deficient intelligence or motivation, allowing them 'great thirst of truth and unwearied travail of wit'. But to this they did not join 'variety and universality of reading and conversation'. So, 'as they are, they are great undertakers indeed, and fierce with dark keeping', neglecting 'the oracle of God's works', that is to say the natural world accessible to the senses, and adoring 'the deceiving and deformed images which the unequal mirror of their own minds, or a few received authors or principles, did represent unto them' (ibid.).

The obscure verbal splendour of this attack should not be allowed to conceal its argumentative limitations. It is, indeed, a largely rhetorical appeal to the age's mood of anti-traditional prejudice. In *The Advancement of Learning* Bacon does specifically instance the scholastic habit of attention to the subjects about which speculation and controversy are bound to be fruitless, namely supernatural ones, but that claim rests on a largely unargued if not unreasonable thesis about the effective limits of the human mind's operation. More crucial is his objection to scholastic method in which every thesis is at once subjected to refutations which are really only distinctions and which in turn excite further objections and distinctions in a kind of interminable to-and-fro of debate that amounts to 'monstrous altercations and barking questions' (ibid.).

There is a little more logical substance to Bacon's critique of scholastic disputatiousness in the first book of *Novum*

Organum when he is considering it as one of the idols of the theatre. Aristotle, he says, 'corrupted natural philosophy by logic', he 'imposed innumerable arbitrary distinctions upon the nature of things; being everywhere more anxious as to definitions in teaching and the accuracy of the wording of his propositions, than the internal truth of things'. In the course of this criticism he does give some particular examples of Aristotelian error but does not show that they are erroneous. In saying that Aristotle wrongly 'treated of density and rarity ... by the frigid distinctions of action and power' he does not produce an argument, only an abusive adjective (N I 63.271).

There is, of course, something seriously wrong with Aristotle's theory of the physical world, in its more common-sense terrestrial part as well as in the more obviously ridiculous celestial-cum-theological part. Very much more sensible ideas about the earth and the heavens were in circulation in Aristotle's time—those of Democritus, the great exponent of atomism, in particular—but they sank into oblivion and were not revived in any detail until shortly after Bacon's time by Gassendi, who somehow managed to reconcile being a priest with adhesion to the materialist philosophy of Democritus and Epicurus. On the other hand, if the term 'scholasticism' is interpreted with reasonable width to mean, not just Thomism, but medieval Christian philosophy in general, then it is not true that scholastic philosophy of nature was simply a reiteration of the physics of Aristotle. Ockham's insistence on the contingent nature of God's creation meant that we could not understand the natural world by scrutinising the purposes we could ascribe, by a priori reasoning, to God. It is necessary to observe what actually happens if we are to find out how God has arranged things. From this beginning the disciples of Ockham went on to develop a kind of mathematical physics that anticipated the form of the great seventeenth-century systems of the world from Galileo on.

An elementary criticism of Aristotle's philosophy needs to do two things: to produce an articulate account of the limitations of deduction and to fasten attention on the manner in which the axioms from which deduction proceeds are arrived at. Even if the logical theory available to Bacon was rudimentary, the idea that deduction does not provide genuinely new information but only extricates and renders explicit what is already contained in its premises was a familiar one. J. S. Mill's affronted objection that the syllogism (which is effectively all deduction in the Aristotelian tradition) is emptily question-begging was a standard Pyrrhonian manoeuvre, accessible to any student of Sextus Empiricus.

Aristotle did indeed maintain that a true science is a deductive system which must start from axioms or first principles that are both general and self-evident. The usual conviction of empiricist philosophers, modern or traditional, is that general propositions can be self-evident or irresistibly certain only if they are conceptual in nature and not substantial truths of fact. Bacon did not take this view and perhaps did not consider it a possibility. He called any process by which a general proposition is arrived at induction, and objected to the inductions of the scholastics on grounds of haste and over-eagerness, not because of any objection of principle.

Thus a standard empiricist would say that a science of natural fact must begin from reports of particular items of fact on which the science's general propositions or theories depend for their support. Since the theories always go far beyond the singular items of evidence they rest on, they can never, in a factual science, satisfy the Aristotelian requirement of self-evidence or certainty. Bacon, on the other hand, believed that certainty could be obtained by induction just as long as it was gradual and methodical. For him, then, the Aristotelians were doing the right sort of thing, but not enough of it. For other, later empiricists, they are doing the wrong sort of thing, namely relying on observation to supply or suggest general truths that are self-evident, certain and necessary.

One very important point Bacon does make in a slightly indirect way in his critique of disputatious, scholastic learning. In *Novum Organum* he attacks too much respect for the systems of antiquity, saying, 'nor must we omit the opinion, or rather prophecy, of an Egyptian priest with regard to the Greeks, that they would forever remain children, without any antiquity of knowledge or knowledge of antiquity; for they certainly have this in common with children, that they are prone to talking, and incapable of generation, their wisdom being loquacious and unproductive of effects' (N I 71.276). In *The Advancement of Learning* he says 'antiquity deserveth that reverence, that men should make a stand thereupon and discover what is the best way; but when the discovery is well taken, then to make progression.' He goes on, in the spirit of his observation that the ancients were really children, 'these times are the ancient times, when the world is ancient, and not those which we account ancient *ordine retrogrado*, by a computation backward from ourselves' (A I v 1.58).

This point of view is absolutely opposed to the governing conception of knowledge of the medieval philosophers. They saw themselves as orderers and preservers of knowledge, not as its creators. In the first place they took the knowledge that it is most important for human beings to have, that which concerns the divine governance of the world and human prospects of eternal life or damnation, to have been authoritatively revealed in the scriptures and authoritatively commented on in the writings of the fathers of the Church, particularly Augustine. Secondly, when the main bulk of Aristotle's work made its circuitous way to the West it was received with a generally submissive reverence. Aquinas regarded 'the Philosopher', as he called Aristotle, as an unquestionable authority in anything that did not directly conflict with the articles of faith.

Even if the humanistic philosophers of the Italian Renaissance rejected Aristotle, it was not to make room for fresh ideas of their own. They merely switched allegiances among the philosophers of the ancient world and came forward as the disciples of Plato. It is understandable, no doubt, that devout and orthodox Christian thinkers should see the past as superior to the future, or, at any rate, the terrestrial future. The idea of man's fall from initial perfection that is embodied in the story of Adam and the garden of Eden is a potent and concrete instance of the idea of a golden age in the past. Something like that idea is present in Plato with his account of the predestined stages of degeneration in the life of states and his belief that decay can at best be staved off by the rigid prevention of change.

Bacon is the most confident, explicit and influential of the first exponents of the idea of progress. J. B. Bury, the historian of that idea, could find only slight and soon obliterated traces of the belief in progress before Bacon: a momentary scintillation in Democritus that was not perceived by his Epicurean successors, a rather stronger hint in Bacon's medieval namesake, Roger. Bacon's progressivism is the outcome of two strains in his thought. The first of these is his more or less unprecedented notion of knowledge as cumulative. The second is his insistence that knowledge is for practical use, specifically for 'the relief of man's estate'.

In order for knowledge to be thought of in this way, as something to be constantly added to, a new conception of true, basic, paradigmatic knowledge has to be adopted. Bacon took that step by his clearly proclaimed diversion of interest from the divine to the natural. There is a parallel, attractive to some intellectual tastes, between Bacon's view of knowledge and the capitalist conception of wealth. Both replace the idea of a fixed, exhaustible stock, liable to decay and in need of careful preservation, with that of an interminable flow of human contrivance.

Bacon is often dismissed, with a measure of intellectual snobbery, as a mere propagandist for a natural science he did not understand. There is a point in that criticism. Bacon did not grasp the essential role of mathematics in the major scientific advances of his age. But in his belief in the possibility of large and continuous growth of knowledge, of finding new knowledge rather than retrieving old knowledge before it disappears irrecoverably, he played a crucial part in creating a mental atmosphere or environment in which the natural-science-centred conception of knowledge could flourish. This is the ultimate bearing of Bacon's attack on the disputatious learning of the scholastics and supports the claim that it is the most important of the three.

The third and last of the defective kinds of learning that

Bacon assails is the fantastic learning which is the uncritical acceptance and dissemination of marvels and fables, the most colourfully obvious form of the interest in the natural world of the thinkers of the Renaissance. Bacon's definition of what he has in mind under this head is not very precise. He gives as examples of 'admitting things weakly authorised and warranted', miracles 'wrought by martyrs, hermits, monks of the desert, and other holy men' in ecclesiastical history and 'fabulous matter, a great part not only untried, but notoriously untrue' in natural history. He also deplores giving too much credit to dubious sciences and authoritative persons, as well as to particular reports. 'The sciences themselves,' he says, 'which have had better intelligence and confederacy with the imagination of man than with his reason, are three in number: astrology, natural magic and alchemy.'

What Bacon has to say about these dubious sciences is more penetrating than his vaguely hostile gestures in the direction of reported marvels. He allows that the ends of these sciences are noble, namely the mastery of nature for human purposes, but holds them to be 'full of error and vanity', which their exponents seek to conceal by 'enigmatical writings... auricular traditions and such other impostures'. He neatly compares the alchemists' search for ways to turn base metal into gold with the story in Aesop of the father who told his sons gold was buried in the vineyard so that they dug it into unprecedented fertility in their pursuit of what was not literally there. 'The search and stir to make gold hath brought to light a great number of good and fruitful inventions and experiments' (A I iv 9–11.57).

An important point lies behind Bacon's not very argumentatively formulated distaste for the esotericism of the practitioners of the fantastic learning. This is that publicity is essential for valid scientific work, the exposure to the criticism of others of the evidence and reasoning on which the findings claimed are based. This is a different aspect of the conception of science as a social undertaking from that for which Bacon is best known. In his *New Atlantis* Bacon foresees the co-operative character of the scientific research of later ages, the type of institution in which the principle of the division of labour is applied to the work of natural investigation. But the pursuit of methodical economy and efficiency is a comparatively superficial proposal. The idea that criticism of scientific findings is indispensable if they are to be rationally acceptable is altogether more far-reaching.

The contention that science must be *critically*, and not just co-operatively, social is a central idea of the most influential of contemporary philosophies of science, that of K. R. Popper. 'If scientific objectivity were founded ... upon the individual scientist's impartiality or objectivity, then we should have to say good-bye to it ... science and scientific objectivity do not (and cannot) result from the attempts of an individual scientist to be "objective", but from the co-operation of many scientists ... First, there is something approaching free criticism. A scientist may offer his theory with the full conviction that it is unassailable. But this does not necessarily impress his fellow scientists; rather it challenges them. For they know that the scientific attitude means criticizing everything ... Secondly, scientists try to avoid talking at cross-purposes.'

Popper often refers to a traditional conception of science to which he is firmly opposed as 'Baconian'. But although this is not a misnomer, it does obscure some important matters of agreement between them. That science should ideally seek, or at least be institutionally constrained to undergo, external criticism is not the least of these.

As for Bacon's critique of the uncritical acceptance of individual reports of marvels or oddities, it does not, in itself, amount to much. But it points the way to a familiar requirement of scientific method as it has developed since his time, that experiments and, where possible, observations should be *repeatable*. In logic a general hypothesis of the form *All A are B* is proved false by the discovery of a single A which is not B. But that such a discovery has been actually made is not established by the occurrence of an honest report that some observer believes he has come upon an A which is not B. We are not infallible observers. Before an observation can be allowed to carry significant weight in relation to our theories it needs to be authenticated.

Bacon maintained that scientific inquiry ought to be co-operative in a methodical, institutional way. In so far as it rests on the individual observations of innumerable observers it is bound to be informally co-operative. Indeed, more generally, very much the greatest part of what each human being believes or claims to know rests on the authority of someone else. Testimony is the staple food of our cognitive diet, even if it needs to be supplemented with the salts or vitamins of our own direct acquisitions of knowledge. The problem of testimony, of the conditions under which it is rationally acceptable, has been little examined by philosophical theorists of knowledge. The most penetrating consideration it has received has been as a secondary aspect of Hume's inquiry into miracles. Bacon is no exception and is content to deplore rather than to investigate the credulity of the adherents of the fantastic learning.

No one would suppose that Bacon is a crypto-scholastic or that he is a humanist devoted to Cicero or Plato. But it is quite often said, despite his attacks on it, that he is really an exponent of the esoteric, magical lore of the Renaissance himself. J. H. Randall Jr says, 'in truth in his positive doctrine he belongs, not with the sciences—for he rejected mathematics and the new astronomy—but with these gropers after fantastic learning'. And, a little later, he repeats the charge: 'he merely organized and codified the crude experimentalism of the Renaissance fantastic learning'. According to Friedrich Heer, 'Bacon dreamed of an alchemistic universal science.'

This is too extreme. Of course there are pieces of fabulous and highly questionable matter floating about in the large body of Bacon's writings, such as the belief, mentioned earlier, in the therapeutic qualities of an ape's heart. But he is not blind to the merits of Aristotle and his scholastic followers and the influence of humanism is manifested both by his respect for Plato and by the conscious elegance of his writing. It is true that Bacon achieved nothing significant in the way of direct scientific inquiry and that he was a poor judge of the really important scientific developments of his own age. But, in the broadest sense, he understood the nature of modern natural science better and more explicitly than anyone in his epoch. The character of that method altogether removes him from the neighbourhood of Paracelsus and Fludd.

In his positive doctrine Bacon gives a central position to the views which conflict with the three erroneous systems he has criticised. Against the speculative deductions of scholasticism he argues for a cautiously gradual inductive procedure, based on systematic observation by the senses. Against the gentlemanly scholarship of the humanists he supports the co-operative mechanical experimentation of the scientific researcher. Against the secret and haphazard undertakings of the occultists he proclaims the need for publicly criticisable and methodical investigation of nature.

5 The idols

A more familiar part of the negative, critical preliminaries to Bacon's philosophy of science than his assault on received systems is the doctrine of idols, in the first book of *Novum Organum*. The idols of the mind are various widespread tendencies of the human intellect which explain its frequent lapses into error. He arranges them in four, colourfully named, classes as the idols of the tribe, the cave or den, the market and the theatre.

The idols of the tribe are mental weaknesses more or less universally typical of the human species. Those of the cave are individual peculiarities, which are nevertheless widely found, serving to distinguish one cast or style of mind from another. The idols of the market are the forms of error that can be traced to the influence of language, whose properties we are inclined to read into the world it is supposed to describe. The idols of the theatre are the received but erroneous systems of philosophy which have been considered in the previous chapter.

The idols of the tribe include the mind's tendency to suppose 'a greater degree of order and equality in things than it really finds' (N I 45.263), to ignore exceptions to principles that are generally accepted or pleasing to believe, to be over-influenced by what strikes it suddenly or excitingly, to carry on in a particular direction of thought even where there is no factual support for it and thus to end in such pseudo-explanations as those by final causes, to be swayed by emotions and, most important of all, to be led into falsehood by 'the dullness, incompetency and errors of the senses' (N I 50.267), as a result of which we are led to ignore the more subtle, delicate and invisible changes in the natural world.

The idols of the cave or den are, naturally, even more of a mixed bag. Men tend to apply the concepts and principles of their special interest to everything else. Some are apter at discerning differences; others, likenesses. Some revere antiquity; others love novelty. Some are obsessed by details; others by the whole.

The idols of the market are, in Bacon's view, the most troublesome. Words mark the most visibly obvious, not the most explanatorily significant, differences between things. As well as words that are 'confused, badly defined and hastily and irregularly abstracted from things' (N I 60.269) there are words that stand for nothing, like '*Fortune*, the primum mobile, the planetary orbits, the element of fire, and the like fictions' (ibid.), but these are the less obnoxious and easier to deal with of the two.

The idols of the theatre were described fifteen years after the forms of vain philosophy were discussed in *The Advancement of Learning*, and the two lists do not exactly coincide. The sophistic philosophers are Aristotle and his scholastic disciples, who rely too much on logic applied to uncriticised common assumptions. The 'empiric' philosophers make use of experiments, but too precipitately. Bacon gives the alchemists and William Gilbert, theorist of magnetism and first user of the word 'electricity', as examples, an unfortunate juxtaposition for his reputation as a student of form. Finally, there is the 'superstitious' school who corrupt philosophy by mixing it with superstition and theology. These are not the humanist exponents of the delicate learning. Who they positively are is not easy to determine. No clearly demarcated group of thinkers is identified by Bacon's formula.

The study of precisely definable formal errors in reasoning is as old as logic itself. Aristotle, who turned into a science what had previously been an unsystematic accumulation of rules, included a treatise on fallacies, *De Sophisticis Elenchis*, in his logical writings. Bacon's theory of idols inaugurates something of the same very general sort, but much more comprehensive. It is not simply an album of popular false beliefs and superstitions like Sir Thomas Browne's *Pseudodoxia Epidemica*, (1646) the initiator of a series of public enlighteners of a more or less 'rationalist' kind leading up to Ackermann's *Popular Fallacies* and Mackay's *Extraordinary Delusions*.

It is closer to such non-scientific books on the art of thought as Graham Wallas's book of that name, or to an aspect of them. It is, more exactly, a general pathology of thinking with not much more than an appearance of system and completeness. Its main utility cannot be preventative, except in the most diffuse fashion, as an inclusive warning to the incipient theoriser of all sorts of hazards ahead. It does supply a handy catalogue of explanations of why some piece of thinking has gone wrong. But it cannot by itself show that any bit of reasoning is defective. The weaknesses it enumerates are not guaranteed in all cases to lead to error. Much invalid reasoning rests on analogy, the favoured mental process of Bacon's devotees of resemblance. But so, also, do some discoveries of the greatest importance, such as the atomic theory of matter.

One particular analogy has been invoked to interpret Bacon's theory of idols in a suggestive manner. Bacon, it is said, retained from his puritan upbringing a sense of the fallen nature of man, but transposed it from the moral to the intellectual realm. We have certain very real and potentially fruitful intellectual capacities. But so far we have largely misused them, whether from greed, or idleness, or the intellectual pride that induces men to try to solve problems that are beyond them.

On this interpretation Bacon saw himself as an intellectual saviour, come to call sinners to the appropriate kind of repentance and, even more, to compensatory good works in the future. Like others with a saving message he is an optimist, not just in believing, truly, that he would have an effect, but that he would liberate men from the errors of the past and set them on a path in which the attainment of knowledge would be unobstructed by mistakes.

That idea represents him as more naïve than he was, as supposing that all the obstacles to knowledge are psychological. Bacon was, in fact, clear that nature is much more complicated than the human intellect that tries to decipher it. He did believe that if we are cautious, methodical and co-operative we can attain some certain knowledge of nature. But to suppose we can come to admit nothing but the truth is not to imagine we can ever get the whole truth.

In our own age there is something of a fashion for revelling in the non-rational or even superstitious sources of great scientific achievements, such as Kepler's painful move from the conviction that heavenly bodies must move in circles, in view of their perfection, to his laws of elliptical planetary motion. Less mischievous is the view that scientific hypotheses are imaginative constructions, as spontaneous as works of art at their best, and that their origins in general or particular deficiencies of the human mind are irrelevant to their validity. If that is so, there is no need to uproot the idols; the method of science is used not to replace them but to make a rational selection from the competing theories they induce us to put forward.

6 The classification of the sciences

Bacon's classification of the sciences is to be found in the second book of *The Advancement of Learning* and, in a considerably enlarged and elaborated form in books ii to ix of the *De Augmentis*. The main structure of the classification remains practically unaltered. It is as if a set of rooms had been provisionally furnished and then, over the years, more and more things had been disposed around the rooms, without any serious builder's work being carried out on them.

What Bacon says he is classifying is the varieties of learning, rather than sciences. Science proper, or philosophy as it is called in the earlier treatment, is only one of three main varieties recognised, but it receives ten times as much attention as history (a term Bacon uses pretty much in our sense). History, in turn, occupies nearly four times the space allotted to poesy. The basis of this ultimate threefold distinction is a distinction between three faculties of mind, conceived, presumably, as being specially relevant to learning. History relies on memory, poesy on imagination, and philosophy on reason.

Poesy, which he deals with second, seems to be an interloper here. It is not a primarily or obviously cognitive undertaking. We do not ordinarily go to it to add to our knowledge or modify our beliefs, although it may have such an effect tangentially. Furthermore, history and philosophy, in Bacon's sense, as knowledge of individual facts and of general laws, are necessary to each other. As Bacon so strongly insisted, the general laws of nature must be derived by inductive reasoning from individual facts of the kind that history, as he interprets it, records. Correspondingly, the laws of logic and of nature must be invoked in the critical examination of historical claims, where they are tested for consistency with each other and with the general run of things.

Bacon's general formula for poesy is 'feigned history', in prose as well as in verse. It gives men satisfaction by allowing them to contemplate what nature has failed to provide. It is a device for more or less edifying wish-fulfilment, for it submits 'the shows of things to the desires of the mind' (A II iv 2.88). Its subdivisions are into the narrative, the representative, and the allusive or parabolical. (In the *De Augmentis* the representative gives way to the dramatic, which, Bacon observes, is greatly fallen from its dignified position in the ancient world.) In the later book he spends most time on parabolical poesy, that in which some philosophical idea is concretely illustrated. It is this form of poetry which is most cognitive, closest to history and science.

The individuality and generality of their findings are a better basis for Bacon's distinction between the two essentially cognitive parts of the realm of learning than their respective assignment to memory and reason. To start with, the two mental faculties are not properly co-ordinate, since memory, unlike reason, is a store, not a source, of knowledge. The source of individual facts is perception or observation, conceived broadly enough to include our perception of our own states of mind. Furthermore scientific or philosophical reasoning relies on memory, both to supply its premises and as the preserver of the capacity of reasoning.

Besides this division in terms of individuality and generality there are two other forms of distinction which constantly recur in Bacon's system of classification. The first of these is that between the theoretical and the practical, between knowledge and action, or, in his terminology, between the speculative and the operative. This is applied through all the main branches of philosophy or science, but not to history, which he plainly conceives as a register of evidence for various sciences, theoretical and practical, but not as having any lessons to teach us on its own.

Secondly, there is a distinction between the divine and the non-divine, which itself divides, a little indefinitely, into the natural, the human and the civil (or social). The indefiniteness is due to the fact that, while he usually puts the natural and the human side by side (for example, as the two main kinds of non-divine philosophy), the civil is treated as a species of the human, and both spheres of investigation are held amenable to the same methods as non-human nature, except that the question of the nature and substance of the soul, as contrasted with its faculties, is remitted to revealed religion (which is divine knowledge or *scientia*, but not philosophy at all). It is probably correct to take these uncertainties as indicating a measure of embarrassment on Bacon's part at his removal of religious matters from the region of serious inquiry.

The major category of history in Bacon's system is not much more than a list. It is subdivided into natural, civil, ecclesiastical and literary kinds. The latter, understood widely as a history of learning, Bacon sees as wanting in his own time and much to be desired. It is calculated to 'make learned men wise in the use and administration of learning' (A II i 2.79–80). In the *De Augmentis* he says that it and ecclesiastical history are to be seen as parts of civil history (D 427).

Natural history is of 'creatures, marvels and arts' (A II i 3.80). The second is required, not for open-mouthed amazement of the sort once produced by Ripley's *Believe-It-Or-Not* or other such 'Mirabilaries', as Bacon calls them. It is, rather, to fasten attention on exceptions to common assumptions and as an aid to technological ingenuity: 'from the wonders of nature is the nearest intelligence and passage to the wonders of art' (A II i 4.80).

Civil history can be imperfect, that is, be the material of historical study in a raw state, whether it be as 'memorials', official documents and personal memoirs, or as 'antiquities', even rawer material, such as monuments, names, proverbs, tales. History proper, which he calls 'perfect history', is of three kinds: chronicles of epochs, lives of people, narrations of actions. In the course of this discussion he turns aside to address James I, to whom the books are dedicated, to suggest that a history of Great Britain, or at least of the Tudor period, is highly desirable now that the crowns are united. By the time these observations were repeated in the *De Augmentis* in 1623 his *History of the Reign of Henry VII* had come out.

Despite its title this is not simply the chronicle of an epoch, nor even the life of a particular monarchical person. It is

157

an instance of the type of history Bacon most favoured, an analytic and explanatory study of a connected sequence of actions and events: the establishing and centralising work of the Tudor dynasty. Bacon was led by his Machiavellian realism about politics to seek causes rather than to describe the ceremonial surface of public events. His own historical work, that is to say, was not a mere feat of memory or bald registration of the past. It undermined the distinction he himself drew between history and philosophical or scientific knowledge proper.

The study of this third and favoured category of learning is the main topic of the second book of *The Advancement of Learning* and it takes up all but one of the eight corresponding books of the *De Augmentis*. There is one slightly peculiar feature in this classification, testifying once again to Bacon's discomfort about religious knowledge. At the outset he divides knowledge (or *scientia*) into divinity and philosophy. But the divinity he has in mind here is 'inspired', or as we should say, revealed, theology and not natural or rational theology, the derivation of religious conclusions by rational argument, which Bacon calls 'divine philosophy' and sees as co-ordinate with 'natural philosophy' (for us, natural science) and 'human philosophy' (for us, the sciences, or study, of man and society).

On the whole Bacon allocates all the detail of religion to the domain of authoritatively revealed theology and remits it, from indifference or respect, perhaps both, to the end of his discussion, where it trails behind everything else a little forlornly. Of natural theology he says, 'it sufficeth to convince atheism, but not to inform religion'. He goes on, a little later, 'but ... out of the contemplation of nature, or ground of human knowledges, to induce any verity or persuasion concerning the points of faith, is in my judgement not safe ... we ought not to attempt to draw down or to submit the mysteries of God to our reason; but contrariwise to raise and advance our reason to the divine truth' (A II vi L.91–2). He ends his brief discussion of natural theology with the remark that far from there being too little of it there is far too much. Its entire business, in his view, is to infer from natural facts that

God exists. With a distinctly grudging admission that it is legitimate to inquire into the nature of angels and spirits, he moves on to the more agreeable topic of natural philosophy.

Just before this somewhat parenthetic treatment of natural theology there is a moderately turgid passage about *philosophia prima*, first philosophy, the main content of the *Metaphysics* of Aristotle. The branches of knowledge, he says, meet, like those of a tree, in a stem, not a point, and so we should acknowledge a universal science at the base of all the particular sciences. However, when he considers what goes by the name, he finds 'a certain rhapsody of natural theology, and of divers parts of logic; and of that part of natural philosophy which concerneth the principles, and of that other part of natural philosophy which concerneth the soul or the spirit; all these strangely commixed and confused' (A II v 2.90).

That anti-metaphysical, positivistic comment is not Bacon's final word on the subject. A tamed and humbled first philosophy is acceptable, one that confines itself to the role of 'a receptacle for all such profitable observations and axioms as fall not within the compass of any of the special parts of philosophy or sciences, but are more common and of a higher stage' (ibid.). The examples of its theses are something of a mixed bag: if equals be added to unequals the results will be unequal (seen as a maxim of arithmetic and of law); what God has made is perpetual, we cannot add to or subtract from it; 'is not the delight of the quavering upon a stop in music the same with the playing of light upon the water?' (A II v 3.90–1).

After this piece of musing and the bleak immuring of natural theology the serious business begins. Natural philosophy has a speculative or theoretical side, for Bacon, as for us, natural science, and an operative or practical side, which he asks leave to call by the provocatively alchemical name of natural magic. The first is 'the inquisition of causes'; the second 'the production of effects'. Each of these two sides of natural philosophy is further subdivided: natural science into physic and metaphysic; natural magic or natural prudence into 'experimental', 'philosophical' and 'magical' forms.

Physic is natural science proper, as it has been understood

159

since Bacon's time. It is concerned with material and efficient causes. Metaphysic, on the other hand, is concerned with formal and final causes. This reference to the traditional four causes of Aristotle is less than perfectly straightforward. The material cause of a thing is simply the matter of which it is made; the efficient cause is that which makes the thing in question out of the material. In so far as causal explanation is concerned with the making of things each of these kinds of causes is necessarily involved. But most interest in causes fastens on events that happen to things, changes in their characteristics and position, not on their coming into existence. In such cases there is an efficient cause, an antecedent event that brings about the change, but no clear or useful application for the idea of a material cause. In fact Bacon makes little use of the notion of material cause. Physic, for him, is essentially, the study of efficient causation in nature.

The final cause, part of the business allotted to metaphysic, is the purpose for which a thing is made (or, one could add, changed or moved). Bacon is rightly understood to have been an inveterate and influential enemy of the doctrine of final causation. 'The handling of final causes,' he says, 'mixed with the rest in physical inquiries, hath intercepted the severe and diligent inquiry of all real and physical causes, and given men the occasion to stay upon these satisfactory and specious causes, to the great arrest and prejudice of further discovery.' He does not here deny that natural events have final causes, that they are, in other words, the intentional outcome of the purposes of an intelligent being. Final causes are 'true and worthy to be inquired, being kept within their own province; but . . . their excursions into the limits of physical causes hath bred a vastness and solitude in that tract' (A II vii 7.96).

This does not, he protests, 'call in question, or derogate from divine providence', it highly confirms and exalts it. Nevertheless there is something badly adrift in Bacon's position. Metaphysic has been detached from the abstract universal science of *philosophia prima* and also from natural theology. All that can be rationally inferred from the contemplation of nature is *that* God exists, not what he is like, far less what his purposes are in minute detail. Yet final causes, the investigation of the intention of God as revealed in the natural world, is claimed to be a proper object of the rational discipline of metaphysic. Lack of candour, expressed as a desire to leave standing as much of the intellectual tradition, or its terminology, as possible, has led to a muddle. Whether Bacon believes that natural events in general have final causes or not, he cannot consistently maintain that they are a proper object for rational inquiry. The pursuit of final causes is just a proscribed form of that natural theology from which Bacon has been anxious to distinguish metaphysic, as a science or discipline wholly concerned with the natural world.

Here, with metaphysic as with physic, one of the alleged types of cause proprietary to it is redundant, the other essential. Metaphysic, for Bacon, is the science of formal causes. What he means by that traditional expression is a central problem of interpretation in his philosophy of science and will be the topic of Chapter 8. But it is at least clear that it does not mean what it initially meant for Aristotle.

For him everything consisted of matter and form, the marble of a sculpture and the human shape that makes it into a portrait. If that shape is considered on its own in a somewhat fanciful way it is possible to bring oneself to see it as somehow bringing about its own realisation in the statue of which it comes to be the shape. In the case in hand, which is insidious because of its combination of simplicity and untypicalness, the human shape can easily be thought of as somehow in the sculptor's mind, perhaps as a schematic visual image, before he externalises it in the statue. That is not possible with a child or a sapling, but people have got themselves to conceive that the adult human or arboreal form these things will come to have, if they develop fully to their perfect or completed state, is somehow lurking implicitly within them, perhaps as a 'programme', in the technological jargon of our day.

That is not Bacon's idea at all. To express his position briefly and dogmatically: the forms, for which it is the business of metaphysic to search, are the hidden states of the fine structure of things by reference to which their straight-forwardly observable properties can be explained. His theory of forms is at its most developed in the second book of *Novum Organum*. But already in *The Advancement of Learning* its importance is dimly discernible. He rejects the ordinary anti-Platonic view that 'the inquisition of man is not competent to find out essential forms' (A II vii 5.94). Plato was right in taking forms to 'the true object of knowledge', and mis-taken only in considering them as 'absolutely abstracted from matter'.

This way of putting his point is not illuminating. His real conviction is that there is an underlying simplicity in the order of nature, far from evident in the colourful and multi-form variety it exhibits to the senses. Just as the formation of words becomes readily intelligible when they are understood as made up of a modest handful of simple elements, the letters of the alphabet, so the vast array of different kinds of sub-stances in the world becomes intelligible when understood as the product of the action or working of a limited variety of forms.

Where metaphysic, then, finds out the simple, but hidden, formal causes of things, physic deals with their obvious, but complex, efficient causes. These last he sometimes calls the *variable* causes of given effects, because a cause of this sort, for example rubbing, will have one effect on one kind of substance, a different one on another, making glass shiny and suede matt. The complexity of physic is overcome in metaphysic by tracing all the various efficient causes of a given kind of effect to a single common, but unobvious, factor that is present in them all. His acceptance of this role for metaphysics is his answer to Mill's problem of the elimin-ability of a plurality of causes.

It is not necessary to linger over his subdivision of physics into three parts, concerned, in the *De Augmentis* version of the doctrine, with the 'principles', the 'fabric' and the 'variety' of things. What should be noticed is the operative or practical disciplines he takes to correspond to the two main branches of speculation or theory. To physic corresponds mechanic, to metaphysic, magic (in the *De Augmentis* at any rate, where there is no mention of a low-grade experimental kind of operative natural philosophy as there is in *The Advancement of Learning*). It is to natural magic, and not mechanic, that we must look for any major technical achievements, he believes. 'There can hardly be discovered any radical or fundamental alterations or innovations of nature, either by accidents or essays of experiments, or from the light and direction of physical causes; but only by the discovery of forms' (D 474).

There is still one more important component of natural philosophy, according to Bacon, namely mathematics. It is, he says, an 'appendix', not a substantive science. He has to insist on this 'by reason of the daintiness and pride of mathematicians, who will needs have this science almost domineer over physic' (D 476). He distinguishes between its pure and 'mixed', or applied forms: arithmetic and geometry on the one side, 'perspective, music, cosmography' and many more on the other.

It has long been a familiar, and well-founded, criticism of Bacon's philosophy of science that it does not adequately recognise the role in science of mathematics. It is in a strictly quantitative study of the properties of natural objects and events that natural science, in his own time as in ours, largely consists. Bacon has no real sense of this fact. He remains, in this respect at any rate, an unregenerate Aristotelian.

His view that mathematics is an auxiliary and not a substantive science is an early, and not very convincingly articulated, version of what was to become an empiricist orthodoxy. In modern times it is contrasted, as a formal or conceptual science, with factual sciences such as physics and biology. Along with his empiricist successors Bacon associates mathematics and logic, but gives no determinate account of the relation between them, where later thinkers have seen logic as the proto-science of which mathematics is the continuation, or as a part of mathematics, specifically as a sort of algebra.

Even if he is right about the dualism of the formal and the factual, which many well-informed critics would deny, that

163

does not overcome the criticism that he does not recognise the *indispensable* place of mathematics in science. An auxiliary can still be an essential auxiliary, and of that he shows no awareness.

Human and civil philosophy covers all the rest of Bacon's system of classification. It is a markedly mixed bag, suggestive here and there, but of much less depth, interest and influence than the non-human part of the system. He accepts the distinction of mind and body in a wholly unreflective and uncritical fashion, giving no account of what the basis or principle of the distinction is. He is in favour of the study of human nature, but mainly in the form of the study of the relations between mind and body, of how each works on the other and of how each reveals what is going on in the other. Physiognomy studies how body 'discloses' mind; 'exposition of natural dreams' shows what is revealed about the body by the 'imaginations of the mind', an even more reductive discipline than Freud's dream-interpretation.

The sciences of body are divided, fairly whimsically, into medicine, 'cosmetic' (which includes hygiene), 'athletic' (the old Greek gymnastics) and the 'voluptuary' arts (which in the *De Augmentis* primarily consist of a kind of psychological aesthetics, which is far from a purely bodily inquiry in Bacon's sense).

Turning to the sciences of the mind Bacon remits investigation of 'the substance or nature of the soul or mind', with a little reluctance, to religion. 'This knowledge,' he says, 'may be more really and soundly inquired, even in nature, than it hath been', but 'in the end, it must be bounded by religion' (A II xi 1.109). The soul was inspired by God into the body, not extracted from the general mass of the material world, and so is not subject to the laws of nature. Two disciplines associated with elevated conceptions of the soul are more or less swept under the carpet as discreditable in practice, even if not to be condemned absolutely because of religious support. One is divination, foretelling the future; the other is 'fascination', the exercise of influence on physical things by the soul without the use of its own body.

There are, however, some rational and respectable sciences of the mind. They deal with the soul or mind, not in itself, but through its operations, in particular with the faculties of understanding and will. The first of these is logic, very broadly conceived; the second is ethics, also taken comprehensively. In the *De Augmentis* he explicitly uses these terms and they are disquieting. For logic and ethics are not factual sciences, co-ordinate with physics and metaphysics as Bacon conceives them. He himself refers to the four logical disciplines he distinguishes as '*arts* intellectual', not as sciences.

What he actually offers, in place of the psychology of thought and will the reader has been led to expect, is a collection of rules for the right, proper and effective ordering of man's intellectual and volitional life. In terms of one of his own basic distinctions, these amount to operative or practical, rather than speculative or theoretical, disciplines. One could even call them *technologies*, of thinking and of conduct, with a little metaphorical licence. Now in the domain of non-human natural knowledge operative rules depend on speculative laws. It would be reasonable to expect a parallel speculative basis for the intellectual and moral 'arts' in the human domain, but nothing of the sort is provided.

In this failure to distinguish between the normative, rule-propounding arts of logic and ethics, on one side, and the factual science of psychology, cognitive and volitional, on the other, Bacon, it might be said, is doing something commonly objected to in later British empiricists, most notably Locke and Hume. Locke's *Essay concerning Human Understanding* sought to study the workings of the human intellect by the 'historical, plain method', the method of observation and inductive generalisation that would make the study of mind an empirical science. Hume described his *Treatise of Human Nature* as 'an attempt to introduce the experimental method of reasoning into moral subjects', which, in current English, means 'an attempt to apply empirical methods to the study of the mind'.

But Locke and Hume went about the task in a more resolute way and with a clear idea of what an empirical discovery

165

about the mind is. Both started from the factual generalisation that all our images are copies, whether directly or as a result of combination, of sensations we have previously experienced. They wrongly took this to be equivalent to the epistemological thesis that for a word to have meaning it must be connected to a type of sensation or experience, which is the criterion of its application. Underlying the belief that the generalisation and the epistemological thesis are equivalent is the mistaken conviction, endlessly seductive in its simplicity, that the meaning of a word, a concept, an element of our thoughts, is an image.

There is nothing of this in Bacon. He strides cheerfully forward into a discursive account of the traditional disciplines of logic and ethics, ornamenting them with many curious and frequently interesting additions, but without really doing anything to work them into a shape congruous with the requirements of his system. That he did not succeed in achieving a clear idea of the relation of logic and ethics, as usually understood, to the empirical psychology of the relevant aspects of mind is no disgrace. The only clear notions of the relation are plainly erroneous: that the two terms are identical, and its opposite extreme, that the two terms have nothing whatever to do with one another. But he should have done something to digest these borrowings from tradition. It was left to Hobbes, his sometime amanuensis, and to Locke and Hume to carry his governing idea forward.

Logic, as Bacon conceives it, is very closely similar to the trivium of logic, grammar and rhetoric that was the fundamental element of the medieval university course in arts. He divides the subject into four parts: invention, judgement, retention and the conveying (or 'tradition') of knowledge. The science of judgement is logic in the ordinary, comparatively narrow sense, that is, the discipline concerned with 'proofs and demonstrations' (A II xiv 1.117). Here the topic is only deductive inference, and specifically the syllogistic inference codified by Aristotle, where the premises necessitate the conclusion. Bacon attaches quite as much importance to the study of fallacies as to the systematisation of valid forms of reasoning. In the discussion of this subject in *The Advancement of Learning* (A II xiv 9–11.118–20), Bacon gives a first sketch of his theory of the idols of the mind that was considered in Chapter 5. That theory, it should be said, does have a reasonably factual character, being a kind of empirical pathology of the intellect.

Retention either is absorbed into 'tradition', the general study of language and expression, or consists of practical tricks which Bacon does not think much of, but believes could be greatly improved on. Tradition, the conveying of knowledge, covers a lot of interesting ground: linguistics in an embryonic state, grammar and rhetoric. Phonetics, cryptography, stylistics make brief, rudimentary appearances. Advice on the reading of books and the instruction of the young figures as appendices to the subject.

Bacon's central interest in the field of the 'arts intellectual' is in what he calls 'invention' and particularly in invention of arts and sciences, rather than of 'speech and arguments' (A II xiii 1.111–12). He sees it as hitherto largely deficient. Traditional, deductive logic 'doth not pretend to invent sciences, or the axioms of sciences' (ibid.). The induction of which the philosophers of the past spoke as the supplier of 'the principles of the sciences' is 'utterly vicious and incompetent' (A II xiii 3.113–14). What he here objects to is induction by simple enumeration, where the mere accumulation of favourable instances is taken to justify the corresponding general law, whereby from *This cow eats grass* and *That cow eats grass* and *The other cow eats grass* it is inferred that *All cows eat grass*. 'To conclude,' Bacon says, 'upon an enumeration of particulars, without instance contradictory, is no conclusion, but a conjecture' (ibid.).

In his discussion of 'that knowledge which considereth of the appetite and will of man' (A II xx 1.133). Bacon attacks what has previously been offered as being too grandiose and unpractical; it is 'a certain resplendent or lustrous mass of matter, chosen to give glory either to the subtility of disputations, or to the eloquence of discourses' (A II xx 2.133). What is needed are 'Georgics of the mind' so as to 'instruct and suborn action and active life' (A II xx 3.134).

Bacon considers that knowledge of what is good is to be found in adequate detail in the writings of past moralists. The question of how we come to know what is good does not trouble him. Yet he recognises a large measure of disagreement among proclaimed moral authorities, and judges the issues involved in a firm, confident way. Aristotle is wrong to prefer contemplative life to action. The Stoics and Socrates are right to value virtue for its own sake and not simply as a means to pleasure. Epictetus is reproved for neglecting the moral value of good intentions even where they do not succeed.

Bacon rests his criticism of Aristotle's contemplative ideal on a distinction between two kinds of goodness: 'the one, as everything is a total or substantive in itself; the other, as it is a part or member of a greater body' (A II xx 7.134). Applying this distinction to man, he concludes that 'the conservation of duty to the public ought to be much more precious than the conservation of life and being' (A II xx 7.135). This is a very commonplace observation. Bacon sees that there is a problem about inducing men to follow the moral course and pursue the common good. His great successor, Hobbes, took there to be no such problem about getting men to pursue their own interest or advantage, since it is impossible for them to do anything but what they believe will contribute to it. His task, then, is to argue that the path of social duty is, despite appearances, really in the best interests of necessarily self-regarding men.

The second part of Bacon's ethics, the 'regiment of the mind', a kind of technology of moral training or motivation, has no such theoretical basis. It simply rests on the fact that men do not act as virtuously as they should, even as virtuously as they admit that they should. Here, at least, empirical psychology makes a tentative appearance. 'The first article of this knowledge,' Bacon says, 'is to set down sound and true distributions and descriptions of the several characters and tempers of men's natures and dispositions (A II xxii 4.142). He sets out a programme of investigation into innate styles of personality, into the influence on character of age, sex and nationality, into the effects of good or bad fortune, into the sicknesses of personality and their cures. But he is content to illustrate this desirable science, without properly pursuing it.

The final part of human philosophy is 'civil knowledge'. Here, as in logic and, largely, in the individual part of ethics, practice is legislated for, without much attention to theory. Civil knowledge is more a technology than a science. Its first ingredient is 'conversation', essentially the technique of winning friends and influencing people, one which Bacon himself applied in a much too obviously technical way. Secondly, there is 'negotiation or business', a set of recipes for the prudent management of one's affairs. These can be culled from the proverbs of Solomon, the letters of Cicero, traditional fables, the writings of Machiavelli and aphorists generally. Bacon's *Essays* are his own, rather substantial, contribution to the subject, which he memorably labels 'the architecture of fortune' (A II xxiii 37.162).

The third constituent of civil knowledge is government, which is treated in an unrelievedly practical and manipulative fashion. Laws, he says, should be considered by statesmen; not by philosophers, whose 'discourses are as the stars, which give little light because they are so high', nor by lawyers, since 'the wisdom of a lawmaker is one and of a lawyer another' (A II xxiii 49.166). With this, apart from a section on sacred and inspired divinity, that is to say revealed, and not rational, religion, his survey is complete. 'I have been content,' he says, 'to tune the instruments of the Muses, that they may play that have better hands' (A II xxiv.167).

In a prouder image, at the very end of the book, he says, 'Thus have I made as it were a small globe of the intellectual world' (A II xxv 25.175). Bacon's system of the sciences is indeed a map of knowledge, full of the exploratory spirit of the age, the main masses outlined, but with large, unknown tracts within them awaiting investigation, while many fabulous

169

islands and continents have been obliterated. His 'human philosophy' is no more than a programme, with no real idea of what the empirical sciences of mind and society would turn out to be. Only with Hobbes are they recognisably inaugurated.

His account of natural philosophy is much more substantial. What he saw as its most important element, his theory of eliminative induction as the only valid method of arriving at the laws of nature, the next item in the catalogue of the 'Great Instauration', is worked out in detail in part II of *Novum Organum*. Before considering this, it is worth noticing that although his general scheme of classification suggests that human and natural philosophy are on the same footing, in their concrete description the two very greatly diverge. Human philosophy is almost wholly operative or technical, with only occasional recognition of the need of such disciplines for a speculative or theoretical basis. But it is only such theoretical sciences which can arise from Baconian induction. His account of the human sciences fails to connect them with the new method which alone makes what is claimed to be a science really scientific.

7 The new method

The most important element of the first book of *Novum Organum* is the theory of the idols of the mind which was considered in Chapter 5. That discussion is preceded by a rapid sequence of concise aphoristic paragraphs urging the need for a new method of investigating nature. Bacon's main point is the worthlessness and infertility of the axioms or first principles from which the sciences have hitherto been derived. They are defective in two main ways. The one which Bacon's new method is particularly calculated to overcome is the excessive precipitancy of the step of generalisation by which they are arrived at. The other is the habit of reliance on common, everyday notions, an insufficiently penetrating discernment of the important likenesses and differences between things.

Baconian induction will lead to the most general principles, not in one wild generalising swoop, but by gradual ascent. The suggestion is that the systematic way in which the evidence is acquired and set out by the new method will free its users from the paralysing dependence of previous students of nature on the rough and ready conceptual equipment of everyday observation. Its systematic nature is also calculated to 'level men's wits' (N I 122.297).

In a way the methodicalness of the method is almost as important as its precise formal structure. The proper and regular recording of observations will preserve us from all sorts of illusions and blind alleys. The deliberate, business-like nature of the whole undertaking will ensure that it is cumulative. The true philosopher, Bacon says, must resemble the bee, not the ant, who merely collects, or the spider, who merely spins frail constructions out of itself. He and the bee combine what the others do separately and fruitlessly: extracting matter, and working and fashioning it as well (N I 93.287).

In the course of these rather scattered preliminaries Bacon

171

makes an important point about the low esteem in which the physical, experimental study of nature is held. He rejects the 'opinion, or inveterate conceit, which is both vainglorious and prejudicial, namely, that the dignity of the human mind is lowered by long and frequent intercourse with experiments and particulars, which are the objects of sense, and confined to matter; especially since such matters generally require labour in investigation' (N I 83.281). This negative snobbery about getting the hands dirty is the counterpart of the positively snobbish over-valuation of the so-called ancients, who, of course, are really the children of the history of thought.

Bacon, in view of his public eminence, brought prestige as well as intellectual support to the study of the natural world. Thus began a process which was continued by Charles II's helpful patronage of the Royal Society and is comically symbolised by the description of Robert Boyle, leading figure in the early Royal Society and a great admirer of Bacon, as 'the father of chemistry and son of the Earl of Cork'. Something was thus done to loosen the hold on the European mind of the ideal of cultivated life expounded by the philosophers of a slave-owning society, an ideal which placed abstract intellectual contemplation at the summit of human activities, a kind of parallel to the moral asceticism which despised and condemned the pleasures of the body.

In book II the new method of induction is set out in detail. Bacon's claim is that his method of induction is a crucial innovation because it is *eliminative*. Behind that claim is his justly famous remark: *major est vis instantiae negativae* ('in establishing any true axiom the negative instance is the more powerful') (N I 46.266). G. H. von Wright, the most thorough and scrupulous of contemporary students of induction, says about this: 'Laws of Nature are not verifiable ... but they are falsifiable ... It is the immortal merit of Bacon to have fully appreciated the importance of this asymmetry in the logical structure of laws.'

What Bacon is opposing in his enthusiasm for eliminative induction is induction by simple enumeration, which he takes to be the kind of induction expounded by Aristotle and relied on by his disciples. Aristotle does indeed explicitly consider complete or perfect induction, in which a general statement is conclusively established by the verification of its particular instances. Perfect induction is possible only where the class of things referred to in the general statement is finite and accessible, as in *All George's wives had money of their own* or *All Minnesota towns with a population of more than 5,000 have a public library.*

Generalisations like these can be conclusively verified simply because they are no more than summaries of particular pieces of information. What happens in the more usual and interesting case where the general statement refers to an open and not a restricted class of things? Aristotle does not explicitly consider induction proper, the kind of inference which arrives at general conclusions about unrestricted classes, although he acknowledges something like it in a discussion of analogical reasoning.

The acceptance of a style of reasoning that has come to be called 'intuitive induction' has been ascribed to him on the basis of his views about the nature of science. He says that a science is a system in which conclusions are deductively inferred from axioms or first principles, which must themselves rest on something other than deductive reasoning. They must be general and they must be necessary, in that the predicate must mention an essential property of the subject. Each of these characteristics of axioms, as Aristotle understands them, rules out their being discovered by ordinary perception. The truths it establishes are contingent and singular.

It is concluded that there must be a non-inferential way of directly establishing truths that are necessary and general, and the name 'intellectual intuition' is introduced for it. Is there any such thing? There are alleged to be numerous examples of it: *Nothing can be red and green all over*; *Whatever has shape has size*; *Space has three dimensions*. It is said that we cannot discover such things without sense-experience, but that such experience alone is insufficient to establish them as necessarily true. For that we must rely on an intellectual grasp

173

of the necessary connection of the concepts involved, such as red and green, or shape and size.

That is not the conception of induction that Bacon ascribes to Aristotle and his scholastic followers. What he has in mind is simple enumeration, the derivation of an unrestrictedly general conclusion from a finite and perhaps very small collection of singular premises. These premises will report particular instances of the conjunction or connection asserted generally in the conclusion. Reliance on this highly untrustworthy procedure is abetted by one of the idols of the tribe. 'The human understanding,' he says, 'when any proposition has been once laid down . . . forces everything else to add fresh support and confirmation; and although most cogent and abundant instances may exist to the contrary, yet either does not observe or despises them, or gets rid of and rejects them by some distinction, with violent and injurious prejudice, rather than sacrifice the authority of its first conclusions' (N I 46.265).

His objection to enumerative induction is simply its rashness and notorious fallibility. He believed that by taking account of 'the greater force of the negative instance' with an eliminative method of induction he could make possible the discovery of laws that were *certain*. This is a residual echo of Aristotle's requirement that the 'first principles' of the sciences should be necessary, as is Bacon's dismissal of enumeration as 'not reason, but conjecture'. It would generally be agreed that this requirement cannot be satisfied. The most usual position in recent philosophy is that any sort of induction in which the conclusion does not deductively follow from the premises can allow only for the confirmation of the conclusion by the premises, for its acquisition of a degree of credibility from them that is inevitably incomplete.

The first stage of the new method is the preparation of 'a complete and accurate natural and experimental history' (N II 10.307). This material is then arranged in 'tables'. To start with there is the table of presence. In it, cases where the 'nature' or sensible characteristic being investigated is present are described, to supply an extensive and thoroughly reported account of its usual or typical accompaniments. Next, in the table of absence, cases where the accompaniments of the nature under investigation are present, but where the nature itself is not, are listed. Thirdly, in the table of degrees, cases are set out in which a greater or less amount of the nature in question is accompanied by a greater or less amount of some other variable characteristic. Matters are speeded up by including in the table of absence only cases which resemble (except, of course, in respect of the absence of the nature being studied) the cases listed in the table of presence.

The raw evidential material is now ready for the vital operation of elimination or exclusion to be carried out. Only that which is present in every case listed in the table of presence, and only that which is absent from every case listed in the table of absence can survive exclusions. What is absent in one of the cases of presence cannot be a necessary condition; what is present in one of the cases of absence cannot be a sufficient condition. Bacon sees it as the task of his method to reveal something that is both a necessary and a sufficient condition of any natural qualities it is applied to.

Bacon develops the method in *Novum Organum* in terms of an elaborately worked-out example, that of heat. The rays of the sun appear in the table of presence and, because of that, it follows that the 'form' or underlying cause of heat cannot be something exclusively terrestrial. The rays of the moon figure in the table of absence for they are not hot, or, he has to admit, do not appear to be hot. To settle that doubt he proposes passing them through the strongest possible burning-glass on to a thermometer. If the rays of the moon are properly in the table of absence, if, that is, they really are not hot, we may eliminate light as the form of heat we are looking for. The conclusion he comes to is that heat is 'an expansive motion restrained, and striving to exert itself in the smaller particles' (N II 20.326).

In view of the disparaging remarks that have been made about Bacon's capacities as a scientist from his own time to our own, it is worth noting that what he said about heat is a very reasonable approximation to the theory established by

Maxwell and Boltzmann in the nineteenth century that heat is molecular motion. The idea that heat was a stuff in itself, a subtle, weightless fluid called 'caloric', still had its defenders two hundred years after Bacon when Davy reported an experiment under the title 'Caloric does not exist'. (He also argued neatly for the view that the moon exerted an influence on the tides, and was one of the first to conceive the geological theory of continental drift). On the other hand, it should be admitted that he showed no appreciation whatever of the place of precise numerical measurement in the investigation of heat. As well as being qualitative where it should have been quantitative, his account of heat was static where it should have been dynamic. For all the comparative subtlety of his theory of heat, it still concerned itself with what heat essentially *is*, rather than with what it, or matter endowed with it, *does*. In Bacon's thoughts about heat there is really little inkling of thermodynamics.

Bacon's claim about his style of eliminative induction is that, by its utilisation of negative instances, it can arrive at certain and irrefutable laws, where enumerative induction is for ever at the mercy of a counter-example. In practice he is a bit less confident. He calls what is derived from a well-organised natural history of some nature by the 'exclusive' use of his tables a 'first vintage'. Its imperfection, in his view, derives from that of the concepts with which the natural world is described in the register of natural history. 'If we have not as yet good and just notions of simple natures, how can the exclusive table be made correct?' (N II 19.322).

His residual doubt about his method in practice, then, is that we are not in a position to apply it to adequate raw material. It is not that the available evidence may be unreliable. He admits that our senses are not to be trusted without any precautions, but believes that they can be used to correct themselves and be assisted by instruments. His point is that the likenesses and differences picked out by our sense-bound apparatus of description may well fail to discern the features of things that are really explanatory of what we perceive. This is a very direct consequence of his conception of the kind of cause that theoretical natural science proper, or 'metaphysic', should seek to discover. He does not, like Mill, see science as concerned to find observable antecedents for what we are interested in. Its aim, he supposes, is to unveil latent structures, which will inevitably be hard or impossible to observe.

Bacon's notion of forms or formal causes, to be considered shortly, is responsible for the imperfection in his method that he acknowledges. Before turning to it, other, more abstract and more inescapable difficulties must be noticed. As a host of critics has observed, Bacon assumes that there *is* a cause for every nature or natural property we can observe. To assume that is to assume that nature is causally orderly, is a deterministic system. Many philosophers have tried to prove that it is (though without much agreement that they have succeeded in doing so). Others, like Kant, have argued that it is a 'necessity of thought' that we should believe that it is (although orthodox quantum physicists seem to get away with denying it, as does anyone who believes that chance is an aspect of the nature of things and not simply a reflection of our ignorance). Bacon takes the determinacy of nature unquestioningly for granted.

A second difficulty is that even if the assumption of determinism, that every kind of thing or event does fall under an explanatory law, were correct, it does not follow that the causal factor, thus guaranteed to *exist* in every case, should be discoverable by us. It does not follow from the fact that every event has a cause that any such cause is sufficiently simple or near at hand or observable for us to record it in our register of evidence. The imperfection Bacon admits can be seen as a special case of this difficulty. It is a difficulty, furthermore, which stands in a close relation to the previous one about determinism. The more we restrict determinism by formulating it in terms of discoverable causes, the less plausible it becomes. It is not possible to come near to refuting conclusively the claim that every event has some cause or other, however obscure and complex it may be. But we could have very good reason to believe that something was not caused by any simple, observable factor, close to it in space and time.

There is a conflict in Bacon's idea of the relations between nature and the human understanding which has led commentators to say apparently contradictory things about it. Many have quoted his remark: 'the subtilty of nature is far beyond that of sense or of the understanding' (N I 10.260). But others have seen Bacon as assuming that nature is not all that complex, that, in particular, there is a manageably small variety of ultimate causes behind the complex multiformity of observable nature. In fact, both are correct. Nature is subtler than mind for Bacon. It is subtler than the senses since the forms that govern it are not obviously and straightforwardly observable. It is subtler than the understanding, which cannot work out on its own what the underlying order of nature is. But, he believes, if the mind is assisted by the right method certain knowledge of that underlying order can be achieved. There is nothing in Bacon of the idea, suggestively expressed in recent times by Chomsky, that the truth about the world might be of a level of difficulty that our minds, as practical contraptions hammered out in the process of evolution, are intrinsically unable to conceive.

Bacon's theory of forms led him to ignore all the respects in which causes, allowing that all or most events have them, might be hard or impossible for us to discover. The unobservable character of the forms, as has been mentioned, implies that they are calculated to escape description and registration. But he also fails to see that causes may be spatio-temporally remote from their effects, and complex in ways making them hard for us to grasp because of his conception of form. He sees the form of an observable characteristic as strictly contemporaneous with it. (Given the natural assumption that causal influence is conveyed by processes with a finite velocity, it follows from this that cause and effect must be in the same place as well). Finally, he always supposes that the true formal cause is an elementary, unconditional feature of the particles of which matter is composed.

In this last respect Bacon's position is less satisfactory than Mill's. Mill pointed out that causes could lack simplicity in two ways, by *plurality*, the case where many different factors can independently bring about a given effect, and by *complexity*, where a given effect can be brought about only by a conjunction of causal factors. Mill, indeed, thought the plurality of causes to be eliminable in principle, that further investigation would always reveal an underlying common element in apparently different independent causes. Bacon explicitly ruled out complex causes in Mill's sense, at any rate from 'metaphysic', in other words theoretical natural science. For him it was a defect of 'physic' that it typically gave the cause of an effect only relative to a given substance, as when whiteness is seen as the effect of heating in the case of egg-white, but of pulverising in the case of glass. In short, Bacon's theory of forms assumes away in advance the main difficulties that beset induction when it is conceived as a method of acquiring certain knowledge.

On the whole Bacon's interpreters in recent times have made unnecessarily heavy weather of his theory of forms. The distinguished historian of logic, W. C. Kneale, says, 'unfortunately this doctrine is extremely obscure'. W. R. Sorley says, 'he gives many answers to this question [viz. what 'form' means], and yet the meaning is not altogether easy to grasp'.

It is really quite clear that what is meant is a latent structural property of the particles of which matter, according to Bacon, is composed. (Bacon is not strictly an atomist; he rejected the idea of empty space, like Descartes). It is an arrangement or configuration of matter, not a thing in its own right. It is, as has been seen, a necessary and sufficient condition of the sense quality, or observable 'nature', that it is invoked to explain, and it is simultaneous with its effect. Forms are not observable, antecedent sufficient conditions like Mill's causes; nor antecedent necessary conditions as are the parts of the complex causes of events which we usually single out colloquially as the cause *simpliciter*. They are not events or processes, but states.

Bacon's forms are not, then, the causes that have been given most consideration by later philosophers, particularly in the empiricist tradition of Hume, Mill and Russell. They are, however, much more like the basic explanatory factors in modern physical science than the accessible, phenomenal causes of Hume and Mill are. Bacon anticipates an aspect of scientific development that empirically-minded philosophers from Hume to recent times have neglected: the preoccupation of natural science with fine structure. Locke's account of secondary qualities such as colour and taste in terms of the primary, largely spatial qualities of the microscopic parts of bodies is a less satisfactory, because more philosophically confused, recognition of the point that Bacon sees as central.

Nevertheless, Bacon's forms are different from the fine-structural explanations of natural science in being qualitatively conceived, and not as susceptible of numerical measurement, and as being static, persisting conditions of things, not events or processes in the history of their interactions with other things.

There are some aspects of Bacon's account of forms which make it easy to see why philosophers should have often so laboriously misunderstood him on this topic. By calling his underlying causes *forms* he puts some readers in mind of Plato, so that they think of them as abstract or mental. But his forms are physical, in that, like most of Aristotle's, they are embedded in matter. Secondly, he says at times that the form is identical with the quality or nature whose form it is, and he sometimes describes the search for form as a search for a definition. His prime example of heat is useful here. He can be seen in that discussion as working towards the discovery of *what heat really is*. That would succeed if something was found which is present when and only when objectively based experiences of heat took place. To do that is not to find what the word 'heat' really means, although it is to find a better meaning than the everyday one, a meaning that the word could come to be given.

Now and then Bacon says that the form of a nature or sense-quality is a *law*. In saying that the form of A is B he is propounding a law of a logically reciprocal form to the effect that everywhere and only where there is A there is also B. But the form B is not itself a law, only connected by law to the nature A whose form it is. Finally, he talks in a way calculated to mislead philosophers when he calls the form of something its *essence*. This at once suggests that it is an immaterial abstraction and that to give the form of a nature is to redefine it. But his positive account of form is really explicit enough to neutralise these misunderstandings.

There is a certain tension between Bacon's view that forms are the ultimate objects of scientific inquiry and his insistence on the practical usefulness of scientific knowledge, his anti-classical belief that knowledge is not for contemplative enjoyment but for the relief of man's estate. But that tension between theory and practice is not an inconsistency. It is, rather, to take the position that the best and most fruitful practice must be based on theory that penetrates deeply beneath the surface of things. The history of science supplies abundant instances of the way in which apparently purely theoretical speculations lead in time to practical consequences that are as good as inconceivable without them.

For nuclear weapons the physical theories of Einstein were needed, and for Einstein's physics the mathematical constructions of Riemann, a century earlier. A less sombre example is the dependence of radio and television on Maxwell's equations. To make the point in Bacon's verbally provocative but not altogether inappropriate phrase, there is such a thing as 'natural magic', that is to say, the production of effects not just by the modification of their observably regular antecedents, but by the exercise of influence on their hidden internal constitution.

The last pages of *Novum Organum* are taken up with a long discussion, almost as shapeless and digressive as that paradigm of Renaissance lore, Burton's *Anatomy of Melancholy*, of what he calls 'prerogative instances'. There are no less than twenty-seven of these, and at N II 21.327, where they are first introduced, they are only the first of nine enumerated 'helps of the understanding with regard to the interpretation of nature'. The book ends before any of the other eight are considered.

In a way the main importance of the doctrine of prerogative instances is negative, as an admission by Bacon that he recognises that the tables alone will not yield the certain knowledge of the laws of nature which he believes it to be somehow possible for us to obtain. In the light of the prerogative instances that possibility becomes very diaphanous. The pursuit of these in all their variety is represented as an open-ended business, an aid to the more rapid elimination of explanatorily irrelevant factors, indeed, but not as a systematic procedure that could be brought to completion. The doctrine, then, reveals Bacon's doubts about the certainty which he felt that a proper method for the investigation should be able to secure.

Those doubts are well-founded, and for many more reasons than Bacon recognised. He concentrated on our inadequate ideas of 'simple natures', namely those qualities of things that are really significant for scientific understanding. But, since his time, the most crucial objection to the idea that induction can certify its conclusions is the very same unverifiability of the unrestricted general statements in which the laws of nature are expressed which it was such a merit of Bacon to have stressed.

In fact, the prerogative instances are not particularly well-judged as devices for improving our conceptual apparatus. They are presented, as in the middle of the last paragraph but one, as aids to the more rapid elimination of erroneous explanations. Among them are 'solitary instances', where the property in question is present with none of its usual accompaniments. That, of course, will allow them all to be eliminated as necessary conditions. If there are any solitary instances of a property it can have no form in Bacon's very exigent sense. A *nearly* solitary instance, however, could do a great deal of eliminative work.

Others he lists are 'migrating' instances, where the property in question is observed to come into or go out of existence, that is, to be acquired or lost by something; 'conspicuous' instances, where the property in question is present in its most intense or purest form; 'instances of the cross', or what we call crucial experiments, in illustration of which he develops a very shrewd and elegant argument about the influence on the tides of the moon. Along with these are comparative odds and ends like the 'instances of the door or gate', which are mechanical aids to the senses like microscopes and telescopes. As the catalogue proceeds, any earlier intimations of a common principle are steadily eroded by the increasing miscellaneity of the items listed. The reader is left at the inconclusive end of the book with a series of more or less useful and perspicuous hints for the investigator of nature.

One of the most influential aspects of Bacon's thinking about science was the conception of a research establishment. This was set out, in a fanciful way, in the fragment of Utopian fantasy, *New Atlantis*, written a couple of years before his death and published a year after it in 1627 by his first biographer, William Rawley. The narrator is one of a ship's crew lost in the South Seas, without food and weakened by sickness. Very cautiously allowed to land on Bensalem, an unknown island (where quarantine regulations are in force), they find that the inhabitants, in the normal manner of Utopians, are remarkably chaste and do not accept tips.

What it all leads up to is the institution called Salomon's House, or the College of the Six Days' Works, set up by a Solon of the community long before, when he used its remoteness to hide it from the world's contagion. Bensalem trades only in light, that is knowledge, or, more precisely, it imports knowledge without paying for it, by means of a kind of industrial espionage.

More important is the cognitive home product of Salomon's house. Its purpose is 'the knowledge of causes, and secret motions of things; and the enlarging of the bounds of human empire, to the effecting of all things possible' (S 277). In pursuit of this end there is a large and varied array of appropriate structures and facilities: caves, towers, lakes, experimental laboratories and gardens, zoos, aquaria, kitchens, furnaces, enginehouses and everything else a fertile imagination could dream up for the object in question.

But the real interest of Salomon's house lies in the allocation of its personnel to particular tasks in a co-operative undertaking. Some travel, some extract material from books, some carry out experiments, some organise the findings of the experiments in tables, some work on technical applications, some devise new experiments, and some, finally—the interpreters of nature—develop the findings of the rest into organised theory.

A quainter and less fruitful anticipation of the future occurs in the very last pages of the fragment, a system of rites and ordinances not unlike the religion of humanity devised by Comte, but even more concentrated upon science and technology, the statues all being of inventors.

The seminal idea in Bacon's story about Salomon's House is that of the division of labour in science. It is sometimes said, indeed, that Bacon is the first exponent of the idea of the division of labour. A distinction needs to be drawn here between the view, central to Plato's social theory, that differences in natural aptitude require the division of labour, and Adam Smith's more sophisticated view that the complexity of production requires it, independently of differences in aptitude (with the recognition of which Smith's point is perfectly compatible). Smith made his version of the principle memorable with his example of the manufacture of pins. A group of men, each carrying out one of the constituent operations in pin-manufacture, could produce 48,000 pins a day. Working as individual pin-fabricators they would produce only 200. Bacon, it could be argued, anticipated Smith's version, not so much because he says nothing in *New Atlantis* about the qualifications of his various types of specialist, but because of his belief that his method would level men's wits.

It is generally agreed that the idea of Salomon's House was at work in the minds of those who founded the Royal Society and, generally, it can be seen as standing in much the same, more or less grandfatherly, relation to institutionally organised scientific research as Plato's *Republic* does to monasticism. But although its exposition of the virtues of co-operation in scientific work is agreed to have been beneficial, the associated neglect of, or indifference to, the solitary business of individual exercise of the imagination in science has come in for criticism, most notably from Popper. His view is that scientific discovery cannot be mechanised, turned into a straightforward methodical routine to be carried on by any trained scientific craftsman, because important scientific advances are made by the creation of novel theories, not the mere summarising of observations.

That is true and important as an objection to the idea that all science is a matter of craftsmanly co-operation. But Bacon does seem to have a special place in his system of scientific trades for the framers of hypotheses: those interpreters of nature who are mentioned last in his catalogue and in what seems to be a position of special honour. But nowhere in his detailed account of the proper scientific method they are to apply is there any explicit recognition of the irreducibly unregularisable work of the creator of hypotheses and theories.

The limitations of Bacon's theory of science will be considered shortly when his leading critics are surveyed. Looking back over it as a whole we may conclude that he maps the character and programme of a genuinely natural science of nature, independent of religion, unencumbered by the authority of past speculation, unified by a method of eliminative induction that is set out in fairly thorough formal detail, to be carried on in a co-operative fashion for the material benefit of mankind. As natural, it is free from theology and metaphysics; as social, it is untouched by occultism and fantasy; as methodical, it transcends the desultory accumulations of antiquarian scholarship. In these respects, at any rate, it constitutes as important a step forward as any towards the governing conception of the world of the modern epoch.

8 Human philosophy

It was pointed out in the discussion of Bacon's classification of the sciences that he did not effectively develop his professed principle that the same empirical and inductive method should be applied to man and society as to nature. The account he gives of logic, ethics and 'civil knowledge' in *The Advancement of Learning* represents them as arts, or even technologies, as operative or practical disciplines. There is no exposition of the theoretical sciences on which, for conformity with his doctrine about the two aspects of natural philosophy, they ought to rest.

He was, of course, quite right to see logic, ethics and 'policy', the art of prudent conduct in private life and politics, as practical or normative disciplines. Where his inventiveness failed him was in the matter of delineating in the abstract the theoretical correlates on which they should be based. The interesting thing is that he did better, from the point of view of his own principle of the comprehensiveness of the inductive method, in his practice as a student of human affairs than as a detached anatomist of the possible and desirable varieties of that practice.

Thus, when he was actually engaged in writing history or about politics and law or, again, in the worldly moralising of the *Essays*, a grimly realistic and empirical spirit prevails. Recommendations about how to deal with human beings are firmly founded on a thoroughly unsentimental conception of human motives and characters. He was, indeed, a distinguished practitioner of some of the social studies: history, politics and jurisprudence. He made a much more significant addition to the stock of first-order knowledge about the world in the human sphere than he did in the domain of non-human nature.

His chief historical work is his *Reign of the History of Henry VII*, written very quickly after his fall from glory in 1621, presumably from previously assembled materials. It has been established with the utmost Teutonic thoroughness, by the German historian of the early Tudors, Heinrich Busch, that Bacon's materials were not his own original discoveries, and that he relied for them almost entirely on the *English History* of Polydore Vergil, a protégé of Henry VII, published in 1533, nearly a quarter of a century after that monarch's death, and to a lesser extent on various Tudor chroniclers. More important is the fact that Bacon, for all his professions of scientific objectivity, used his materials very selectively and sometimes dishonestly.

Nevertheless, to suppose that if he is not an original source his sole importance as a historian derives from the excellence of his style betrays a pitiable kind of academic philistinism. What judgement would the egregious Busch have passed on Gibbon? In Bacon's time the writing of history in England was no longer the monopoly of monastic chroniclers. Their place had been taken by urban and lay chroniclers, culminating in Holinshed. Undigested material also accumulated in the work of a great generation of antiquaries. Thomas More's book on Richard III is a denigratory pamphlet. Bacon was the first analytic or explanatory English historian, since Polydore Vergil, the only possible earlier competitor for the description, was an Italian.

Bacon represents Henry VII as a cautious, suspicious and rational man, anxious to achieve his aims as cheaply and safely as possible. The reconstruction of the thinking that lay behind his manner of presenting himself to his new subjects after his victory in 1485 is nakedly and convincingly prudential. The prose of this book, incidentally, is much plainer and less ornamented than that of the *Advancement*, let alone that of the *Essays*. It is a working illustration of statecraft rather than an item of polite literature.

Bacon's political opinions are dispersed around various very different genres of writing. Half of the *Essays*, at their final count, deal with public affairs. There are also letters of advice to monarchs and ministers. He comes forward, not surprisingly, as the theorist of Tudor monarchy, but not as a supporter of the absolutism favoured by the Stuarts and above all by the first of them, James I. Bacon believed in a strong monarchy; advised but not in any way dominated by parliament; respectful of, but not exposed to the arbitrament of, the courts. Judges, as he said in a famous phrase, should be lions, 'but yet lions under the throne' (E 803).

He saw great accumulations of wealth as unfavourable to the stability of the nation. He wanted the king, in accordance with a traditional idea, to be rich enough 'to live of his own', reserving serious taxation for public emergencies. There is an echo of the Machiavelli of the *Discorsi* in his belief that the highest life for a citizen is military, that there should be a citizen army and never mercenaries. He saw war, in a moderately unattractive analogy, as the exercise of states, a kind of bodily exertion essential to their health.

His hostility to lawyers, at least in their more overweening, politically ambitious aspect, was more than a by-product of his long-drawn-out quarrel with Coke. It is entirely in keeping with his rational progressivism, his dismissal of the presumption of the greater wisdom of the past, that he should scorn the retrospective obsession of lawyers with precedent. In the same way his exclusion of religion from the serious life of the intellect is congruous with his Erastian attitude to the church. C. D. Broad described him as 'a sincere if unenthusiastic Christian of that sensible school which regards the church of England as a branch of the Civil Service'. He advised Queen Elizabeth to water down the oath of allegiance so as not to compel reasonable Roman Catholics into treason, while agreeing that they should be excluded from office.

Bacon's animus against lawyers was in no way the expression of a sense of personal inadequacy as a lawyer. He was proud of his own abilities in his pre-eminently professional sphere, predicted he would in due time be seen as a better lawyer than his enemy, Coke, and received, in the end, an endorsement of this claim from the great historian of English law, Sir William Holdsworth, who said of him that he was 'a more complete lawyer than any of his contemporaries'. Holdsworth goes on to say of chapter 3 of the eighth book of *De Augmentis*, which is the most articulate presentation of

Bacon's theory of law, that it was 'the first critical, the first jurisprudential, estimate of English law which had ever been made'.

Bacon lays characteristic stress on the need for certainty in law, seeing its absence as sometimes the result of there being no law in some area, sometimes of the obscurity of the law that there is. Obscure law leads to insecurity and to delay. The whole inherited mystery of the common law, with its immensely variegated constituents and its professional priesthood of devotional interpreters, suffered from what Bacon saw as the worst of vices in any human construction: inefficiency. He did not go so far as to recommend the complete codification of law. But he believed that English law should be digested, should have all obsolete, overruled and repetitive matter excised from it.

In his usual programmatic way this projected digest of the law should be accompanied by other works: a register of precedents, to be treated with respect, but not as binding authorities; a dictionary of legal terms; a volume of Institutes; and a volume, *De Regulis Juris*, listing fundamental legal principles, which he sketched himself in his *Maxims of the Law*, written in 1597 and published shortly after his death.

Bacon believed that the law should be efficient and cheap. He did not share the almost religious sentiments of many Englishmen towards their common law inheritance, and it was this attitude, incarnated in Coke, that was in the end to prevail, so that Bentham would react to the law of England in much the same way as Bacon two hundred years later. In the seventeenth century the common law was seen to be, and was, an obstacle to the arbitrary extension of the powers of the crown, something that was in part made inevitable by new circumstances, in part a matter of the Stuart dynasty's appetite for absolute power. Bacon, brought up under the more measured and cautious Elizabeth, did not see that danger, and was not minded to see absolutism as much of a danger anyway.

The historian Hugh Trevor-Roper regards Bacon as the clearest-sighted discerner of the critical problems of the monarchy in the early seventeenth century, above all the financial one of securing sufficient revenue to operate effectively. But his efforts to lead the crown to economic rationality, to curb its wastefulness, failed in face of the frivolous extravagance of James I and the jewelled catamites he ennobled. Bacon, Trevor-Roper writes, 'diagnosed the evil—no man perhaps so completely'. In law and in politics, then, his good advice was not taken: unthinking traditionalism prevailed in the one, foolish and wasteful arbitrariness in the other. But, as Trevor-Roper goes on to show, he still exerted an important social influence through his ideas about education.

Bacon did not have much to say about education directly. As regards schools he does little more in explicit terms than recommend imitation of the Jesuits. He has more to say about universities, the objects of some lively invective in *The Advancement of Learning*, where he disparages the ancient scholastic exercises of wordy disputation, and proposes a style of education fit to produce capable statesmen in which history and politics take the place of logic and Latin. It was not until a couple of decades after his death that a Baconian educational doctrine was colourfully propounded by the Bohemian John Comenius, a somewhat mystical version of Bacon's views, as it turned out, derived from *New Atlantis* more than less fanciful works, and associating apocalyptic prophecy with such Baconian ideas as the need to attend to things rather than words.

But if Bacon himself said little directly about education as an institution, much is obviously implied by his writings, above all the need for the perceptual study of natural objects instead of unmitigated book-learning. For all his own religious indifference, his opposition to contemplative, aristocratic use-lessness and his consequent concern with usefulness in the actual world were highly attractive to the growing spirit of moderate, non-fanatical Puritanism, for which sober pro-ductiveness and not millenial frenzy was the proper rule of life.

A general survey of Bacon's work cannot end without some reference to his more narrowly literary qualities and convictions. The contrast between the richness of his style and the plainness of his message is not by any means the largest paradox about Bacon, if it is a paradox at all. In his age to write well and to write strikingly were much the same; the self-effacingly 'natural' prose of Swift, the most perfect linguistic vehicle ever used for the conveyance of thought, was still far away. It should be remembered that Sir Thomas Browne was to some extent a Baconian chastener of superstitious error and an even more colourful and ornate writer.

It is not just their somewhat artificial air of being exemplary exercises that makes Bacon's *Essays* less attractive than other, more earnest-seeming works that he wrote in English. Their aphoristic style of construction, a string of epigrammatic felicities printed as continuous prose, is tiresome. The impersonality which is brought into vivid relief by the comparison with Montaigne is, we feel, inappropriate to the form: impersonality is for the treatise or paper; the essay proper should be more confessional and intimate. Douglas Bush memorably said of Bacon's *Essays*, 'everyone has read them, but no one is ever found reading them'.

Inevitably Bacon's are not the very first essays in English literature, but they are the first to have become famous, and they have always remained so. Most people, one may well suppose, know more of them than they realise. As a quarry for anthologists of memorable sayings Bacon's *Essays* cannot rank far behind *Hamlet*. The first ten, which were published in 1597, were simply sequences of aphorisms and might have benefited from being printed on separate lines in the familiar style of the proverbs and psalms of the Old Testament. In the final edition of 1625 the number of essays had risen to fifty-eight and the senior members of the collection had been often considerably enlarged. The staccato series of aphorisms had been modulated into a much more continuous discursive flow by the inclusion of illustrative anecdotes and citations from classical literature, by digressive embroideries on the original theme, and by the provision of simple verbal devices of connection.

The insistently aphoristic nature of the original essays tends to reveal itself, despite these changes, in their arrestingly memorable first sentences: 'What is truth? said jesting Pilate; and would not stay for an answer', 'Men fear death, as children fear to go in the dark', 'Revenge is a kind of wild justice', 'The joys of parents are secret; and so are their griefs and fears. They cannot utter the one; nor will they not utter the other. Children sweeten labours; but they make misfortunes more bitter', 'He that hath wife and children hath given hostages to fortune', 'It is a miserable state of mind to have few things to desire and many things to fear; and yet that commonly is the case of kings', 'Suspicions amongst thoughts are like bats amongst birds, they ever fly by twilight', 'God Almighty first planted a garden. And it is indeed the purest of human pleasures.'

Bacon's fondness for an aphoristic mode of expression is not just a bare idiosyncrasy of taste. He offers a defence of it in principle in *The Advancement of Learning* (A II xvii 6–7.125) as particularly suitable for the presentation of tentative opinions ('broken knowledges') and, in conformity with that idea, it is clear that he took the word *essay* in his first use of it in an etymologically primitive way, as meaning *attempt* or *experiment*. In later editions the more discursively expressed book was called *Essays or Counsels*.

The essays as a whole can be roughly divided into three main kinds: those which deal with public affairs, those which deal with particular aspects of private life, and those which deal with large abstract topics like truth and death, beauty and studies, revenge and the vicissitudes of things. The first group are comparatively practical and humdrum. At times, notably in the essay on usury, a lucid and competent piece of economic reasoning, they anticipate the impersonally rational style of exposition of the empirical social theorists of the eighteenth century. Bacon has sensible, only mildly unedifying views to communicate about the aristocratic order and social stability, the causes and cures of sedition, factions and negotiations, atheism and superstition, arrived at by careful and clear-sighted reflection on an ample experience of the matter in hand.

The cynical, reptilian side of Bacon is more evident, perhaps because less appropriate from the point of view of twentieth-century moral tastes, in the essays on such private topics as children and marriage (seen mainly as obstacles to worldly advancement), friendship and expense (friends are useful as receptacles for one's emotional overflow and as better critics of one's deeds than one is oneself), riches and ambition. An unusually sad experience of life is suggested by the remark, 'There is little friendship in the world and least of all between equals, which was wont to be magnified.'

It is the essays of the third group, dealing with large abstract ideas, that are deservedly the best-known. In them Bacon is freed from the fussy preoccupations of a high public official serving a third-rate despot, and from the obsession with advancement in the world that corrupts his thoughts about relations with other human beings. He said of himself that he had concerned himself more with studies than with men, and in these solitary, almost transcendental, meditations his prose is at its most free, rich and energetic. This is baroque prose, much closer to the language of Thomas Browne and Robert Burton, of John Aubrey, Jeremy Taylor and the Authorised Version, than it is to the plain expository style which the Royal Society, inspired by Bacon's *New Atlantis*, sought to make the vehicle of scientific thought.

Figures and conceits abound in these essays, resonant, mysterious, sometimes sinister. 'Truth may perhaps come to the price of a pearl, that sheweth best by day; but it will not rise to the price of a diamond or carbuncle, that sheweth best in varied lights.' 'Groans and convulsions, and a discoloured face, and friends weeping, and blacks, and obsequies, and the like, shew death terrible.' 'And at first let him practise with helps, as swimmers do with bladders or rushes; but after a time let him practise with disadvantages, as dancers do with thick shoes.' 'For the helmet of Pluto, which maketh the politic man go invisible, is secrecy in the counsel and celerity in the execution. For when things are once come to the execution, there is no secrecy comparable to celerity; like the motion of a bullet in the air, which flieth so swift as it outruns the eye.'

In a well-known essay on Bacon and the 'dissociation of sensibility' L. C. Knights has argued that the pervasively rich imagery of Bacon's prose is externally applied ornament, deliberately put on for illustrative purposes and not part of the actual fabric of his thought. He goes on to connect this with the new attitude to nature proclaimed in Bacon's writing, one in which nature is seen as a field of uses and manipulations, something alienated from the self, to be mastered, tricked, 'put to the question'. Certainly Bacon's view of nature would make such a stylistic consequence plausible. One may agree that there is not the same delight in the visible world in a Baconian view of it as in the attitude of the pagan Renaissance. But in the middle ages nature was from an orthodox point of view a snare, appropriately mentioned in the same breath as the flesh and the devil. It could well be that the dissociation of sensibility is rather to be attributed to the way in which people lived, to the change from a comparatively natural to a comparatively artificial environment, than to any formal doctrines about the character of the natural world.

The kind of specialised pursuit of inductive natural science with a view to its technological application that Bacon heralded has come to be culturally estranged from art and the imagination. Bacon himself, indeed, while allocating a dignified place to the imagination in the life of the mind as the basis of 'poesy', acknowledged that 'imagination hardly produces sciences' and that poesy is 'rather a pleasure or play of wit than a science'. In the same spirit is his mechanisation of scientific inquiry and the associated principle that no special gifts are needed to make profitable use of his method in that inquiry. Bacon, then, honoured art and the imagination but was emphatic about the difference between art and science.

In his own brief but significant remarks on beauty, above all in his one-page essay on the subject, Bacon adopts a more or less romantic view of the essential creativeness of the artist. Against the idea of there being canons of art he says, 'a painter may make a better face than ever was; but he must do it by a kind of felicity, . . . and not by rule' (E 788). The same attitude is expressed in his best-known aesthetic observation: 'there is no excellent beauty that hath not some strangeness in the proportions' (ibid.). These explicit remarks and the high position he accorded poesy and the imagination led such apparently un-Baconian figures as Shelley to admire him. The richness and colour of his own prose is, indeed, less in harmony with his main message about natural knowledge and the relief of man's estate than the plain style deliberately adopted by the members of the Royal Society in pursuit of his intellectual ends.

9 Followers and critics

It is a commonplace about Bacon that he was remarkably blind to the important scientific work that was going on in his own time. To start with things near at hand, he ignored the brilliant work of his own doctor, William Harvey, on the circulation of the blood. By interpreting the crucial aspect of human vitality in hydraulic terms as a pumping system, Harvey prepared the way for another of Bacon's associates, Thomas Hobbes, to develop an account of man as a wholly natural object. Bacon dismissed another instance of major scientific advance in his own immediate environment, Gilbert's theory of magnetism, as a kind of occultist fantasy. Going further afield, he disdained Copernicus and ignored Kepler and Galileo.

Nevertheless there is no question about the degree of respect in which he was held by British scientists of the succeeding generation. Robert Hooke and Robert Boyle praised him without qualification and he became the patron saint or presiding deity of the Royal Society. Hobbes, the great scientific philosopher of the period after Bacon's death, took an absolutely opposed view of the nature of science and made no acknowledgement of Bacon. But he was no scientist, only an incautious amateur mathematician, and an object of scorn to the Baconians of the Royal Society. On the other hand, the grand culmination of British science in the seventeenth century, the work of Newton, contains the puzzling, but highly Baconian, phrase *hypotheses non fingo*.

In the eighteenth century the glorification of British science of the immediately preceding period, first by Voltaire and, following him, by all the great figures of the French Enlightenment, unhesitatingly included Bacon, seen as the great originator of the whole process. The more specific detail of Bacon's work as a classifier of the sciences was the most admired and authoritative exemplar for the work of the creators of the *Encyclopédie*, the great collaborative work in which the leading thinkers of the French Enlightenment expressed their comprehensive liberal ideology in the light disguise of a reference book. Grateful praise is offered him in the *Discours préliminaire* by Jean d'Alembert, the great mathematician who was Diderot's co-editor.

The special regard of this particular party in the intellectual life of France explains two later, and directly opposed, attitudes to him. It is not surprising that Comte should have admired the most distinguished and unwavering prophet of positive science. On the other side, the most extreme and resonant of French conservatives, de Maistre, devoted a whole book of fierce criticism to Bacon and refers to him from time to time in more familiar works such as the *Soirées de Saint-Pétersbourg* as the initiator of the infidelity of the Enlightenment. For him Bacon is the first and most undisguised of those induced by satanic pride to reject the revealed knowledge judged by God to be sufficient for man and to turn from it to knowledge they have acquired on their own.

De Maistre's critique contains some knockabout philosophy of uncomplicatedly polemical intent. Bacon's belief that all causes are physical, he says, ignores the fact that laws of physical causation only describe. For explanation and real causes we must go behind nature to its transcendent source of motion. 'Full of an unconscious rancour, whose origin and nature he did not himself recognise, against all spiritual ideas, Bacon fastened the general attention with all his might upon the physical sciences in such a way as to turn men away from all other branches of learning. . . . In conformity with this system of philosophy, Bacon urges men to seek the cause of natural phenomena in the configuration of constituent atoms or molecules, the most false and gross idea ever to have stained the human understanding.'

If Bacon no longer elicits that sort of hostility, he does not excite the kind of enthusiasm among philosophers that he did from Comte and other nineteenth-century positivists such as G. H. Lewes, in whose *Biographical History of Philosophy* he occupies a position of honour. John Stuart Mill, indeed, pays Bacon the sincerest of compliments, that of rather exact imitation, encumbered with some muddle-headed complications. But he makes hardly any reference to him in the *System of Logic*. Macaulay admired the prophet of utility and progress, despised the man and cast some inept aspersions on the inductive logician. (Macaulay objects that the inductive procedure Bacon systematises is natural to men and does not need to be formulated. That is an irrelevant objection to start with. It may be 'natural' to reason in a certain way as a matter of habit or custom. It is quite another thing to give explicit verbal expression to the rules embedded in that practice. It is also a false objection. Many thinking men no doubt reasoned in an eliminatively inductive way before Bacon came on the scene. It is still a somewhat exceptional and sophisticated style of inductive thinking. Simple enumeration, the logical equivalent of the formation of conditioned reflexes, is vastly more usual).

The Scottish philosophers of common sense of the late eighteenth and early nineteenth centuries, exponents of the official academic philosophy of Britain and America until the 1850s and 60s, were the last professionals to be really devoted admirers of Bacon as a philosopher, apart from a couple of rather obscure figures swimming against the prevailing idealist tide of late Victorian Oxford: Thomas Fowler and Thomas Case. The greatest of the pragmatists, C. S. Peirce, wrote that 'superior as Lord Bacon's conception is to earlier notions, a modern reader who is not in awe of his grandiloquence is chiefly struck by the inadequacy of his view of scientific procedure'. He goes on to argue that any mechanical system, such as Bacon's tables of exclusion, cannot produce significant scientific knowledge.

Bacon has been almost wholly neglected by the analytic philosophers of the twentieth century. Von Wright, as we have seen, tried to do him justice in some brief historical asides in his writings on induction. But the major figures—Russell, Moore, Wittgenstein and Carnap—have next to nothing to say about him. This is partly because the treatment of induction by analytic philosophers has concentrated on the conception of it as *probable inference*, and the notion of probability has no place in Bacon's thinking, convinced as he was that his method was capable of yielding certain knowledge of the laws of nature. More generally, in their eyes Bacon lacks the right sort of rigour. Where his exposition is reasonably exact, as in his theory of elimination, it is the philosophically uncontroversial aspect of the field with which it is concerned and, where noticed at all, it is remitted to textbooks. But for the most part the admixture of rhetoric with argument is too strong for currently austere philosophical tastes.

The one important exception to this is the attention given to Bacon by Sir Karl Popper in his influential books on the philosophy of science. Popper sees the imaginative speculation, condemned by Bacon as the intellectual vice of scholasticism, as the nerve of scientific progress. Bacon's idea of scientific theorising as a mechanisable business, owing nothing to the special gifts of those who pursue it, is something it has been his main task to repudiate. It is interesting that he uses to undermine Bacon's position the very logical feature of general statements, the greater force of the negative instance, which Bacon relied on to demonstrate the weakness of simple enumeration. Popper would claim that by developing the full potential of the idea he has shown how little Bacon succeeded in making of it. Nevertheless he counts Bacon as an ally on the very broadest front, in opposition to the kind of purely verbal speculation which never puts its findings to the test of experience, recognising Bacon as a fellow-rationalist in the good, nineteenth-century sense of that word. On a particular point he suggests persuasively that there is less difference between what Bacon understood by true induction and what Aristotle did, the procedure now labelled 'intuitive induction' (cf. p. 57 above), than is usually supposed. Bacon himself thought that Aristotelian induction was simply enumerative, so he was in no position to acknowledge the identity of view, even if Popper is right about what he means by 'the interpretation of nature'.

Popper's, and for that matter Peirce's, criticisms are only particularly thorough and sophisticated versions of one of the two main and persistent objections to Bacon's theory of science, that it wholly fails to accord an adequate place to hypothesis, the imaginative construction of novel theories. As a result he neglected the importance of scientific creativity and, in his ideas about the levelling of men's wits, of the very marked inequality with which it is distributed. The other leading objection is that, unlike the Italian philosophers of nature who preceded him, he failed altogether to understand the importance of mathematics for the natural science of the new age.

This second deficiency—and it is, of course a real one— stemmed largely from the fact that he did not know much about mathematics anyway. But there is a more philosophical, or at any rate ideological, factor involved, namely the close association between mathematics and occultism, shown in numerology, astrology, the measuring of pyramids and the calculating of millennia. An analogous factor was at work in his attitude to imaginative speculation, namely his identification of it with the cobweb-spinning verbalism of the more dismally repetitive kind of academic Aristotelian.

A third weakness which is large enough to be mentioned alongside the two just considered is his dogmatism, his failure to conceive that the price of substantial general beliefs is uncertainty, that we cannot do more than confirm, render more or less rationally credible, the theories about the world in which science consists. It is not an objection of principle, but it is still an objection, that he made such an insensitive response to the real scientific advances of his own age.

He is sometimes defended on grounds of being too early on the scene, since, it is said, his methods, although not those of the great physicists of the seventeenth century, were very much those of the biologists of the nineteenth, as the greatest of them, Charles Darwin, explicitly testifies. If that is so, the same could be said of his ideas about the connection between science and technology. Science contributed negligibly to economic production before the nineteenth century and the emergence of industrially applicable chemistry. What it did do was help in the production of more science by making possible new scientific instruments.

Bacon's main claim to importance must rest on his role as a prophet and a critic. It remains a very large claim. His firm separation of science from religion and religious metaphysics; his transformation of the status of natural investigation from that of the forbidden, when seen as sorcery, or the despised, when seen as low drudgery; his intoxicating programme of a vast increase in human power and pleasure through inquiry in a great array of clearly and colourfully delineated fields—all these add up to a major turning-point in the history of the European mind. For it is the empirical natural science which Bacon called for and the technology that eventually sprang from it that have been the main contribution, an incalculably great and irrevocably ambiguous one, that Europe has made to the world, first by political mastery, now, more subtly, by mastery of thought. The completeness of his vision of a human future dominated by natural science was a speculative and wholly non-inductive leap of the mind which is none the less admirable for its uneasy conformity with his own ideas about the growth of knowledge.

Note on sources

The references for quotations from authors other than Bacon are as follows:

Page

120 John Aubrey, *Brief Lives*, edited by Anthony Powell, London, 1949, p. 190

122–123 ibid., pp. 192–3

127 Thomas Hobbes, *English Works*, ed. W. Molesworth, London, 1839, p. 360

148 K. R. Popper, *The Open Society and its Enemies*, Princeton, 1950, p. 203

149 J. H. Randall Jr, *The Career of Philosophy*, New York, 1962, vol. 1, p. 228

149 Friedrich Heer, *The Intellectual History of Europe*, New York, 1968, vol. 2, p. 150

172 G. H. Von Wright, *Treatise on Probability and Induction*, London, 1951, p. 152

179 W. C. Kneale, *Probability and Induction*, Oxford, 1949, p. 51

179 W. R. Sorley, *History of English Philosophy*, Cambridge, 1920, p. 27

188 C. D. Broad, *Ethics and the History of Philosophy*, London, 1952, p. 124

188 W. Holdsworth, *History of English Law*, London, 1924, vol. 5, p. 239

189 id., *Some Makers of English Law*, Cambridge, 1938, p. 108

190 H. R. Trevor-Roper, *Religion, Reformation and Social Change*, London, 1967, p. 84

191 Douglas Bush, *The Earlier Seventeenth Century*, Oxford, 1946, p. 186

194 L. C. Knights, *Explorations*, London, 1946

197 J. Lively (ed.), *The Works of Joseph de Maistre*, New York, 1965, pp. 228–9

198 J. Buchler (ed.), *The Philosophy of Peirce*, London, 1940, p. 5

199 K. R. Popper, *Conjectures and Refutations*, London, 1963, pp. 12–15

Further reading

The authoritative edition of Bacon's writings is the *Works* in 7 volumes, edited by James Spedding, R. L. Ellis and D. D. Heath (London, 1857–74). For all but the most refined purposes *Philosophical Works*, edited by J. M. Robertson (London, 1905) is entirely sufficient, being a one-volume selection of all the important items from the Spedding–Ellis–Heath compilation, together with W. Rawley's brief life of Bacon. Easier to get hold of is *Selected Writings of Francis Bacon*, edited for the Modern Library by Hugh C. Dick (New York, 1955). The *Essays* and *Advancement of Learning* are both available in Everyman's Library and World's Classics editions. For further detail see R. W. Gibson, *Bacon: A Bibliography of His Works and of Baconiana to the Year 1750* (Oxford, 1950).

The main biography of Bacon is *The Life and Letters of Bacon*, published in seven volumes between 1861 and 1874 by his editor, James Spedding. Much more manageable and very little damaged by the passage of time is the biography by R. W. Church: *Bacon* (London, 1884). Another nineteenth-century biography on a reasonable scale is the first and better of the two volumes of J. Nichol's *Bacon* (London and Edinburgh, 1888–9). Macaulay's lively piece can be found in any edition of Macaulay's literary essays (it was originally published in 1837).

One of the best books wholly devoted to Bacon's philosophy is nearly a century old: Thomas Fowler's brief, clear and sensible *Bacon* (London, 1881). There is a very good article by Robert Adamson in the 11th edition of the *Encyclopaedia Britannica* (Cambridge, 1911). Until the publication of P. M. Urbach's *Francis Bacon's Philosophy of Science* (Peru, Illinois, 1987), a most original and admirably argued book, the only substantial modern book was F. H. Anderson's *The Philosophy of Francis Bacon* (Chicago, 1948). This is a largely uncritical and unhistorical exposition and ordering of Bacon's views on the errors of his predecessors and the right method for the investigation of nature. A materialist line is taken about Bacon's emphatic separation of science and religion. Paolo Rossi's *Francis Bacon: From Magic to Science* (London, 1968) is more a usefully learned piece of intellectual history than a work of philosophy strictly so called.

There are good comprehensive essays on Bacon's philosophy by two well-known twentieth-century philosophers: one by A. E. Taylor in his *Philosophical Studies* (London, 1934), the other by C. D. Broad in his *Ethics and the History of Philosophy* (London, 1952). A more recent brief general account that can be recommended is the chapter on Bacon contributed by Mary Hesse to *A Critical History of Western Philosophy*, edited by D. J. O'Connor (London, 1964).

The most important essay on a crucial aspect of Bacon's philosophy is Tadeusz Kotarbiński's 'Development of the Main Problem in the Philosophy of Francis Bacon' in *Studia Philosophica I* (Lwow, 1935), where there are also abstracts of two other articles by him on Bacon. There are good treatments of Bacon's ideas about induction in chapter 12 of William Kneale's *Probability and Induction* (Oxford, 1948) and in chapter 4 of G. H. von Wright's *The Logical Problem of Induction* (2nd ed. (revised), Oxford, 1957).

A broad array of articles of largely extra-philosophical interest on Bacon has been edited by Brian Vickers: *Essential Articles for the Study of Francis Bacon* (Connecticut, 1968), in which the items by R. F. Jones and V. K. Whittaker are of particular interest.

The intellectual context of Bacon's philosophy can be studied in H. Höffding's *History of Modern Philosophy* (London, 1920) in books 1 and 2 of the first volume, or in book II of the first volume of *The Career of Philosophy* by J. H. Randall Jr (New York, 1962). See also Charles Webster's *The Great Instauration* (London, 1975).

Of interest about Bacon from a literary point of view are Lisa Jardine, *Francis Bacon: Discovery and the Art of Discourse* (Cambridge, 1974) and Brian Vickers, *Francis Bacon and Renaissance Prose* (Cambridge, 1968).

Thomas More

Anthony Kenny

Acknowledgements

I am indebted to Fr. J. McConica, Dr John Guy, Dr Maurice Keen, Mr G. Watson, Mr Keith Thomas and Dr Henry Hardy for assistance on various points in connection with the writing of this book.

Contents

Note on abbreviations

The following abbreviations are used in references given in the text:

D   *Dialogue of Comfort against Tribulation*, ed. Manley
E   *The Essential Thomas More*, ed. Greene and Dolan
H   Harpsfield's Life of More (Everyman)
L   *St Thomas More: Selected Letters*, ed. Rogers
R   Roper's Life of More (Everyman)
U   *Utopia*, ed. Surtz
W 1 and 2   *The English Works of Sir Thomas More*, ed. Campbell and Reed
Y   *The Yale Edition of the Complete Works of St Thomas More*.

Full bibliographical details of these and other works are given in the suggestions for further reading at the end of the book.

Introduction

Thomas More deserves a place in the intellectual history of Europe for three reasons. He wrote a Latin classic, *Utopia*, which is as widely read today as ever. In his life he set a particular pattern of scholarship, saintliness and public service which has continued to fascinate writers and historians of many different kinds, and which contributed to the standard English conception of the English character. His voluminous English writings occupy a significant place in the history of the language and of its controversial and devotional literature. These three claims on the historian of ideas are of unequal weight, and there would be no agreement among scholars about the order in which they should be placed. But the three claims must be considered together if More's significance is to be fairly assessed; and for this reason a Past Master on More must treat of his life and death as well as of the ideas he committed to paper.

Utopia can indeed be read and enjoyed even by those who know nothing of its author's life. It has given pleasure to many generations, whether it has been read as an account of a newly discovered continent (as it was by some of More's contemporaries), or as a light-hearted frolic of the imagination with no serious purpose other than satire (as it still is by some of More's Catholic co-religionists), or as a serious political and economic programme for setting up a communist society, written by a man of genius who 'championed the oppressed classes even when he stood alone' (as it was by the pioneer socialist Karl Kautsky). To begin to understand the book—ironic as it is in parts—it is enough to know that it is a product of the energetic drive for reform characteristic of the best Catholic scholars before the Protestant Reformation made their advocacy of change more qualified and more cautious.

But the reading of *Utopia* is enlightened by new insight, and darkened by new problems, when the reader realises that its author took an active part in the political life of the corrupt society he satirises, was prepared to die for doctrines flatly contradictory to those which the book seems to hold out for admiration, and helped put men to death for deviations from Catholic orthodoxy far less serious than those of the Utopians. An acquaintance with More's life and an understanding of his stance in controversy is not something extraneous to an intelligent reading of *Utopia*: it is essential to its correct interpretation.

Despite More's deep involvement in the religious battles of the age, he has often been admired as a pattern of erudition and integrity by the heirs of his opponents. No one has ever claimed him as a great statesman; but he is often held up, and not only by Catholics, as the pattern of an incorruptible judge and an unservile courtier. For Samuel Johnson he was 'the person of greatest virtue these islands ever produced'. Robert Southey, in *Colloquies on Society*, conjures his spirit from the grave as an embodiment of wisdom. For C. S. Lewis, More was 'a man before whom the best of us must stand uncovered'.

In the earliest biographies, and to a lesser extent in his own English writings, More appears as a man of uncommon wit and cheerfulness. His jokes, unlike most early Tudor jokes, are still pointed and amusing. More, indeed, is the first person to embody the peculiarly English ideal that the good man meets adversity and crisis not with silent resignation, nor with a sublime statement of principle, but with a joke. One of More's most recent biographers has very well said, 'More was never more witty than when he was least amused.' More was, I believe, the first person systematically to use wit to greet dangerous and desperate situations in a way that was later taken to express a characteristically English sang-froid throughout the country's history up to the Somme and the Battle of Britain. Something of the same style was to be observed in antiquity, from Socrates to Saint Laurence; but I know of no real-life Englishman to embody it so fully before More, though something of it is to be found in the fictional characters of Chaucer.

The charm and virtues of More naturally posed a conundrum

for those historians who regarded his stand in religious controversy as backward and perverse. Macaulay can serve as a spokesman for many: he offers the case of More as a proof that religion and theology are not progressive disciplines like the sciences.

We have no security for the future against the prevalence of any theological error that has prevailed in time past . . . When we reflect that Sir Thomas More was ready to die for the doctrine of transubstantiation, we cannot but feel some doubt whether the doctrine of transubstantiation may not triumph over all opposition. More was a man of eminent talents. He had all the information on the subject that we have, or that, while the world lasts, any human being will have . . . We are therefore unable to understand why what Sir Thomas More believed respecting transubstantiation may not be believed to the end of time by men equal in abilities and honesty to Sir Thomas More. But Sir Thomas More is one of the choice specimens of human wisdom and virtue; and the doctrine of transubstantiation is a kind of proof charge. A faith which stands that test will stand any test.

More's works of controversy are indeed the most equivocal of his legacies to the republic of letters. Even among Roman Catholics few read today, for the sake of their content, his defences of the doctrinal, sacramental and legal system of medieval Christendom. They would certainly never have been reprinted in recent years had they not been the work of the author of *Utopia* and the martyr of Tower Hill. Yet they cannot be entirely passed over by the historian of ideas. After all, the intellectual system of Western Christianity was one to which all the choicest minds had contributed for centuries: and More's defence of it is the fullest statement in English of the points of conflict between the traditional system and the Reformers who sought to break it. But More contributed little of his own to the system he defended; and so his English works have caught the attention less of historians of theology than of historians of the language.

Dr Johnson, in the 'History of the English Language' prefaced to his Dictionary, prints copious extracts from More's prose and verse, on the ground that 'it appears from Ben Jonson that his works were considered as models of pure and elegant style'. In the early part of the present century a grammarian wrote, 'whatever the language was when More found it, where he left it, there it remained until Dryden definitely civilized it'. Recent writers have been much more critical of his style and sceptical of his influence on the language. But C. S. Lewis, who is as severe on More the writer as he is in awe of More the man, repeatedly praises him as a comic writer and story-teller: his 'merry tales', he tells us, 'will bear comparison with anything of the same kind in Chaucer or Shakespeare'.

More's devotional writings have a much wider appeal than his controversial tracts. The noblest of these is the *Dialogue of Comfort*, written during his imprisonment at the end of his life. No one who shares the religious premisses on which the book is based can read it without admiration; and those who reject the premisses cannot remain unmoved by an encounter with the unblinking and cheerful manner in which More meditates on the prospect of pain and death.

In the present book I have tried to do justice, so far as its small compass allows, to the three aspects of More's impor-tance for the intellectual and moral history of our culture. I have set out the principal ideas of *Utopia* and offered an interpretation of its message; I have told the story of More's life so far as is necessary to indicate the impact of his personality on later admirers and to illustrate the wit of his spoken words; I have sketched the Catholic system that he was defending and given specimens of the energetic style in which he couched his defence. I have tried, finally, to show that the scholar, the martyred public servant, and the con-troversial prose writer are not three different, conflicting personalities, but a single, consistent human being.

1 The young humanist

Thomas More was born in the last years of the reign of Edward IV, a King of that Yorkish dynasty whose bloody feuds with the House of Lancaster are known as the Wars of the Roses. In 1483, when Thomas was about five, King Edward died, leaving the throne to his thirteen-year-old son, Edward V. Within the year young Edward was dead and his uncle, the Duke of Gloucester, became King as Richard III. Thirty years later More became Richard's first biographer: it was he who first told at length the story of the murder in the Tower of London of Edward and his young brother at the orders of their wicked uncle. Two years later Richard himself was slain, defeated in the final battle of the Wars of the Roses by the Lancastrian claimant, Henry Tudor, who succeeded as King Henry VII.

It was during the twenty-four year reign of Henry VII that More grew from boyhood to manhood. He was the son of John More, a barrister of Lincoln's Inn, whose family lived in the parish of St Lawrence Jewry in the City of London. After schooling at St Anthony's in Threadneedle Street, Thomas became a page to the Archbishop of Canterbury at Lambeth Palace. The Archbishop, John Morton, was Henry VII's Lord Chancellor and became a Cardinal: in his household the boy waited on the leading statesmen and ecclesiastics of the age. Visitors admired his precocious conversation, and remembered how wittily he improvised at Christmas stage-plays. 'This child here waiting at table,' the Cardinal is reported to have said, 'whosoever shall live to see it, will prove a marvellous man' (R 3).

On Morton's advice Thomas More was sent, in his early teens, to study at Oxford, perhaps to Canterbury College (now Christ Church), perhaps to Magdalen College School. The Master at Magdalen School was John Holt, tutor to the pages in Cardinal Morton's household; he published a textbook of grammar to which the adolescent More contributed a prologue and an epilogue in Latin verse. More was at Oxford less than two years altogether. He did not treasure his time there, and does not seem to have made many lifelong friends: the only one known to have been his Oxford contemporary is Cuthbert Tunstall of Balliol. In later years More recalls the poor fare of Oxford, and often mocks at the logic taught there. Most of his own scholarship he acquired after he went down from the University.

John More was anxious that his son should follow him in a legal career, and brought him back to London to qualify as soon as possible. Thomas entered one of the Inns of Chancery for preparatory training and went on to be admitted to Lincoln's Inn on 12 February 1496 (the first certain date of his career). He progressed steadily and was called to the Bar about 1502. In addition to his own legal studies he taught younger lawyers at Furnivall's Inn, and mastered ancient Latin literature so well that he was invited to give a course of lectures on St Augustine's *City of God* in the church of St Lawrence Jewry. The Rector there was William Grocyn, one of the very few scholars in England to know Greek. In 1501 More began to study the language with him and soon became competent enough to produce elegant Latin versions of difficult Greek epigrams. By the time that he was twenty-five he was, though a lawyer by profession, one of the most accomplished classical scholars of his generation.

The age in which More grew up was one of discovery and rediscovery. It was in the year that he first went to Oxford that Christopher Columbus discovered America. The study of the Greek and Latin literature of pagan antiquity had impassioned scholars in Italy for several decades; it had been given a fillip by the arrival of refugee Greek scholars when the Turks sacked Constantinople in 1453. This renaissance of classical learning was now spreading from Italy northwards through Europe: one of the greatest scholars of the age was a Dutch priest, Desiderius Erasmus, who met More on a visit to England in 1499 and soon became one of his closest friends.

Erasmus and his circle became known as 'humanists'. This did not mean that they desired to replace religious values with secular human ones: it meant that they believed in the educational value of the 'humane letters' or Greek and Latin classics. Humanists turned away from the technical, logical and philosophical studies which had preoccupied so many scholars during the later Middle Ages—the so-called 'scholastic' philosophy—and placed new emphasis on the study of grammar and rhetoric. They communicated with each other in Latin, and strove to write elegant prose on the model of the most admired authors of ancient Rome, instead of using the medieval lingua franca, which they condemned as barbaric. New philological methods were developed by them to establish sound and accurate texts of the ancient writers. These texts were published in handsome editions by the new printer-publishers who were exploiting the recently developed art of printing. Humanists believed that the tools of their scholarship, applied to the ancient pagan texts, would restore to Europe long-forgotten arts and sciences, and, applied to the texts of the Bible and of ancient Christian writers, would help Christendom to a purer and more authentic understanding of Christian truths.

The revival of letters was accompanied by a general flowering of culture. More lived at the climax of Renaissance art: Michelangelo was three years his senior, and Raphael five years his junior. The artistic renaissance, too, crossed the channel to England: it was a colleague of Michelangelo's who designed the tomb of Henry VII in Westminster.

In matters of religion, the Europe in which More grew up was a single whole. Britain, France, Germany, Spain, Italy and Austria alike consisted of Catholic States which acknowledged the central authority of the Pope, the Bishop of Rome. But the supremacy of the Papacy, and the unity of Christendom, had suffered a series of wounds which, in More's lifetime, were to prove fatal. For the greater part of the fourteenth century the Popes lived not at Rome but at Avignon in France. It was a scandal that the first bishop of Christendom should set an example of absenteeism, and in addition the Avignon Popes became notorious for extortionate taxation of the faithful. The return of the Papacy to Rome was followed in 1378 by the outbreak of the Great Schism: for nearly forty years the church had not one Pope but two, one in Rome and one in Avignon, each supported by half of Christendom, and each calling the other an impostor. The schism did not end until a General Council of the Church at Constance in 1417 elected Pope Martin V. The way in which the schism was ended left many Christians in doubt whether the supreme authority in the Church lay with Pope Martin and his successors, or with General Councils in succession to Constance. The Popes of the fifteenth century, moreover, acted less as universal pastors than as local Italian princes; in aggrandisement of their own families some of them did not shrink from bribery, warfare and assassination, and the ecclesiastical counterparts of these crimes, simony, interdict and excommunication. The Pope under whom Thomas More grew from boyhood to manhood was Alexander VI (1492–1503), the most villainous man ever to have occupied the Roman See.

More will have learnt as a child, of course, the lesson which he was later to repeat in controversy with Protestants, that the sacredness of an office is not destroyed by the unworthiness of its holder. Someone growing up in England, in any case, did not encounter ecclesiastical scandal on the gigantic scale found in the Church in Italy. English bishops, in the main, were worldly rather than wicked; English monasteries, for the most part, were comfortable rather than corrupt. Many of the high clergy were civil servants who derived their emoluments from church benefices; they paid impoverished substitutes to perform their pastoral duties. Dominican and Franciscan friars, whose vocation obliged them to live on alms, had once been admired for their zeal and poverty; they were now regarded by many, with greater or less justice, as idle parasites. But the parochial clergy remained popular enough, and the English people as a whole were reputed by foreigners to be devout. 'They attend Mass every day,' wrote a Venetian traveller in 1497, 'and say many Paternosters in public, the women carrying long rosaries in their hands.'

The profound importance of the Church to English people was manifest above all in the seven sacraments, or official ceremonies, which marked the main events, and catered for the spiritual needs, in the lives of the faithful from womb to tomb: baptism in infancy, confirmation in childhood, matrimony and holy orders to inaugurate a secular or clerical vocation, penance and eucharist to cleanse and feed the soul, the last anointing to comfort the sick and dying. The provision of the sacraments was the major function of the institutional Church, and the sacraments were essential if the believer was to achieve the holiness of life, or at the very least the holiness at the hour of death, which was needed to gain eternal life in heaven and avoid eternal punishment in hell. Such was the orthodoxy against which in England, since the time of the fourteenth-century Lollards, hardly any heretical voices had for long been raised.

England was devout, and free from overt heresy; but no Englishman had been canonised as a Saint since Thomas of Hereford, who died in 1282. Yet amid the easygoing, cosy Catholicism of the majority there were communities where holy men and women lived severe lives of poverty, of chastity and of obedience to a rigorous rule. One such was the London Charterhouse, where Carthusian monks lived in silent contemplation in solitary cells. More was attracted to this austere vocation; during his legal training he lived in or near the Charterhouse for four years, sharing in the monastic life of fasting and prayer. While writing his lectures on St Augustine, Erasmus tells us, More was almost resolved to become a priest, 'but, as he found he could not overcome his desire for a wife, he decided to be a faithful husband rather than an unfaithful priest'. But even after he married, More continued to practise monastic austerities, wearing a hair shirt beneath his clothes as a penitential garment. 'He used also,' his son-in-law records, 'sometimes to punish his body with whips, the cords knotted, which was known only to my wife, his eldest daughter, whom for her secrecy above all other he specially trusted, causing her, as need required, to wash the same shirt of hair' (R 25). Several of the London Carthusians were, like More, to meet a martyr's death: as he watched them going to their execution from his window in the Tower, More, talking to his daughter, compared the happy lot of these religious,

217

who after a life of penance went to their deaths like bride-grooms to their marriage, with 'such as have, in the world, like worldly wretches, as thy poor father have done, consumed all their time in pleasure and ease licentiously' (R 39).

At no time did More live in a way that a man of the world would have regarded as licentious. An epigram or two survives to tell of youthful love affairs. 'He showed no aversion to women, but he destroyed no one's good name,' Erasmus tells us. 'In fact he was always rather the tempted than the tempter and found more pleasure in the intercourse of mind than of body' (E 290). When More was about twenty-six he decided to marry. He was a regular visitor at the house of John Colt, a wealthy landowner living in Essex, who had three handsome daughters. More, according to his son-in-law, was most attracted by the second, as 'the fairest and best favoured'; 'yet when he considered that it would be both great grief and some shame also to the eldest to see her younger sister in marriage preferred before her, he then of a certain pity framed his fancy towards her and soon after married her' (R 4). More settled his wife Jane at a house called The Old Barge in Bucklersbury. He at once took her education in hand, doing his best to interest her in literature and music. Jane's progress was slow and tearful; she resented being catechised after the Sunday sermon. Besides, she had little time for learning, since in four years of marriage she bore four children, Margaret, Elizabeth, Cecily and John. But Erasmus, who was a regular visitor to the household in Bucklersbury, describes it as a happy and affectionate one. Jane, he tells us, was growing into an ideal intellectual companion for More when she died, still in her early twenties.

In the year of his marriage More was elected to Parliament. The Parliament was a brief one, summoned to grant a special feudal levy to King Henry VII. More denounced the King's demand as excessive, and the Parliament voted less than half the sum requested. The King was told that 'a beardless boy had disappointed all his purpose'. By his action, More forfeited all chance of royal favour and preferment for the rest of the reign; he would never again oppose a royal will so swiftly and incautiously. When, five years later, the King died and was succeeded by his eighteen-year-old son Henry VIII, More, like many other Englishmen, greeted the news with delight. He celebrated the coronation in Latin verse, contrasting the young King's virtues with the avarice and extortion that had characterised the previous reign:

> Now serfhood is fast bound, here's freedom's spring;
> Sadness is at an end, and joy's before.
> The youth today anointed England's king
> The age's splendour is for ever more. (E 120)

Henry was crowned on 24 June 1509 with Catherine of Aragon, his newly married Queen. Catherine had come to England in 1501 and married Henry's elder brother, Arthur Prince of Wales, but the Prince had died a year later. Henry, as her brother-in-law, was forbidden by church law to marry her: a dispensation to permit the marriage had to be obtained from Pope Julius II, who had succeeded Alexander VI in 1503.

A year after Henry's accession, in September 1510, More was appointed under-sheriff of London. His duties were to give legal advice to the sheriffs, and to sit as judge on Thursday mornings in the Guildhall. For these duties, and from fees for representing the City and his private clients in the courts at Westminster, the young lawyer was soon earning the substantial sum of £400 a year.

A number of literary works, both English and Latin, survive from these early years of More's life. At about the time of his marriage he translated a life of Giovanni Pico della Mirandola, an austere Florentine scholar and philosopher, now some ten years dead. More admired 'Picus' as a model for the life of a devout layman. He translated into English verse several of Pico's writings, including 'The twelve properties of a lover', of which the tenth runs as follows:

> The lover is of colour dead and pale;
> There will no sleep into his eyes stalk;
> He favoureth neither meat, wine, nor ale;

He mindeth not what men about him talk;
But eat he, drink he, sit, lie down or walk,
He burneth ever as it were with a fire
In the fervent heat of his desire.

Here should the lover of God ensample take
To have him continually in remembrance,
With him in prayer and meditation wake,
While other play, revel, sing and dance:
None earthly joy, disport, or vain pleasance
Should him delight, or anything remove
His ardent mind from God, his heavenly love.

(W 1.393)

More light-hearted were the verses entitled 'A merry jest how a sergeant would learn to play the friar', a jingling story, written perhaps for a lawyer's junket, about a sergeant who, to serve an arrest upon a bankrupt, disguised himself as a friar. Once admitted in his charitable disguise, the sergeant revealed himself

And out he took his mace
　　Thou shalt obey
　　Come on thy way
I have thee in my clutch
　　Thou goest not hence
　　For all the pence
The mayor hath in his pouch. (E 166)

There follows much boisterous description of knockabout farce. But the poem has a serious message: each man must stick to his trade. For

When a hatter
Will go smatter
In philosophy
Or a pedlar
Wax a medlar
In theology (E 159)

nothing will go well.

More wrote English verses also on the ages of man, and on the tricks of fortune. In collaboration with Erasmus, he

220

translated into Latin some of the works of the Greek satirist Lucian. These, published in 1506, sold in his lifetime best of all his works, being reprinted at least thirteen times.

Jane More died in the summer of 1511 shortly after giving birth to her fourth child. More married again within the month. His haste was not the fruit of any romantic passion: 'he rather married', we are told, 'for the ruling and governing of his children, house and family, than for any bodily pleasure' (H 105). His bride was Alice Middleton, a prosperous merchant's widow, who brought into the family a solid dowry. More's friends did not like Dame Alice; some called her 'aged, blunt and rude', and another could no longer bear to stay in the house because of her 'harpy's hooked nose'. More himself is said to have called her, ungallantly, 'neither a pearl nor a girl' (E 291). Most of the wives who figure in the 'merry tales' sprinkled through More's works are shrews; many biographers, no doubt rashly, have taken these figures as portraits of Dame Alice. It is clear from the earliest biographies that More habitually addressed his wife in a tone of affectionate teasing, rather than with the intellectual seriousness he used with his daughter Margaret. He did not try to interest his second wife, like his first, in literature: he contented himself with encouraging her to sing to the lute and zither. When More composed an epitaph for his first wife's tomb he praised Alice for being an affectionate stepmother to Jane's children; he could not tell, he said, which of his two wives was more greatly beloved: 'How fine it could have been if fate and religion had allowed us all three to live together.'

Besides More's children by Jane, his household now contained his new wife's daughter Alice (later Lady Alington), and his adopted daughter Margaret Gigs. It was soon extended by the addition of two infant wards, Anne Cresacre and Giles Heron. Wardships in Tudor times were often purchased as an investment, and these two wardships brought More a considerable income. But the two wards fitted happily into the family: Anne Cresacre married More's son John, and Giles married his daughter Cecily.

It was in the early years of his marriage that More wrote his first substantial prose work: a life of Richard III. He worked on two versions of it, one English and one Latin; neither was ever finished, and both were published, incomplete, after his death. The book has been described as the first serious historical biography in English; scholars are not agreed whether it gives an accurate portrait of the King. But the picture it draws of a monster of wickedness has taken an irrevocable hold on the popular historical imagination. This is because it lies, at one remove, behind Shakespeare's *Richard III*. Here is More's description of the killing of the princes in the Tower at the behest of the usurping King.

Sir James Tyrell devised that they should be murdered in their beds. To the execution whereof, he appointed Miles Forrest, one of the four that kept them, a fellow fleshed in murder beforetime. To him he joined one John Dighton, his own horsekeeper, a big, broad, square, strong knave. Then, all the others being removed from them, this Miles Forrest and John Dighton, about midnight (the silly children lying in their beds) came into the chamber and suddenly lapped them up among the clothes, so bewrapped them and entangled them, keeping down by force the feather bed and pillows hard into their mouths, that within a while, smothered and stifled, their breath failing, they gave up to God their innocent souls into the joys of heaven, leaving to their tormentors their bodies dead in the bed. Which after that the wretches perceived, first by the struggling with the pains of death, and after long lying still, to be thoroughly dead: they laid their bodies naked out upon the bed, and fetched Sir James to see them. Which, upon the sight of them, caused these murderers to bury them at the stair foot, meetly deep in the ground, under a great heap of stones. Then rode Sir James in great haste to King Richard, and showed him all the manner of the murder; who gave him great thanks, and, as some say, there made him knight. (W 1.450)

The Latin version of Richard III, it has been conjectured, may have been written for Erasmus. Certainly Erasmus continued as a regular guest in More's household after his second marriage, and a devoted correspondent throughout life. In 1511 he dedicated to More a light-hearted work, *The Praise of Folly*, with the punning Latin title *Encomium Moriae*. Some theologians pulled long faces at the mocking tone of the book: More took up his pen to defend Erasmus's underlying seriousness of purpose. This was shown abundantly when, in 1516, Erasmus published his pioneering edition of the Greek New Testament. The firsthand study of the Bible in the original languages, More and Erasmus believed, was worth much more than the textbook knowledge of contemporary theologians who parroted medieval commentators. But opposition to the new kind of scholarship was deeply felt. More, who was to become High Steward of the University of Oxford, had to write to the University in 1518 to defend the study of Greek against a series of attacks from lecturers and preachers. Of course, he wrote, a man might be saved without knowing Latin and Greek: but even worldly learning prepares the mind for virtue. Theology itself cannot be mastered without knowledge of Hebrew, Greek and Latin: it is vain to boast of a knowledge of Scripture and the Fathers if one is not master of the language in which they are written. More must have been gratified when a readership in Greek was set up at Corpus Christi College: doubly gratified when the reader chosen was John Clement, his children's tutor, who was later to marry his adopted daughter Margaret Gigs.

Among More's children, natural and adopted, girls outnumbered boys by six to two. All were given, at home, careful schooling in religion, classical literature and humanistic learning. More hired a series of tutors to teach his children and, in due course, his grandchildren. In a letter to one of these tutors, William Gonell, he urges the importance of training his daughters in virtues as well as in letters: 'for erudition in women is a new thing and a reproach to the idleness of men' so that, if a woman proves vicious, slanderers will attack female education 'and blame on letters the faults of nature, using the vices of the learned to make their ignorance count as virtue'. But if a woman combines virtue with letters, 'she will have more real benefit than if she added the riches of Croesus to the beauty of Helen' (L 103). More wrote his children Latin letters, of which a few have survived, some in prose and some in verse: he expected a letter in return from each of them, almost daily—quite a feat of Latin composition for young schoolchildren. Besides Latin the children learnt Greek, logic, philosophy, theology, mathematics and astronomy. The first textbook of arithmetic to be published in England—*On the art of Calculation*, by More's friend Tunstall—was dedicated to More 'to be passed on to your children'.

More's favourite and most accomplished daughter was his eldest, Margaret. He was proud of the beautiful Latin she wrote and would show off her letters to his learned friends; she and her sisters won praise even from the fastidious Erasmus. More's household was a paradigm of humanist enlightenment, and a pioneering venture in the higher education of women.

2 The commonwealth of Utopia

The year 1515 was a turning-point in More's life. In that year he was given by the King his first important commission, and he wrote the most famous of his works. With Tunstall, he was sent to Flanders to negotiate the interpretation of treaties of Henry VII governing the wool and cloth trade. Erasmus gave the ambassadors a letter of introduction to Peter Gilles, the town clerk of Antwerp. The months of negotiations left More the leisure to write the greater part of a work entitled *Utopia*. As we have it, the work is a dialogue between More, Gilles and a fictitious traveller named Raphael Hythlodaye, a companion of the navigator Amerigo Vespucci from whom the newly discovered continent of America took its name. The major part of the dialogue is a description by Hythlodaye of the distant commonwealth of Utopia, or Nowhereland. Like Plato's *Republic* before it, and the many Utopian constitutions devised since, More's *Utopia* uses the depiction of an imaginary nation as a vehicle for theories of political philosophy and criticism of contemporary political institutions. Like Plato, More often leaves his readers to guess how far the arrangements he describes are serious political proposals and how far they merely present a mocking mirror to reveal the distortions of real-life societies. The description of Utopia was complete when More returned to England in 1515; at home he added an introductory dialogue, which became book one of the final *Utopia*. But it is the second book which is the heart of the work.

Utopia is an island, shaped like a crescent moon, five hundred miles long and two hundred across at its broadest part. It contains fifty-four cities, each surrounded by twenty miles or so of agricultural land. Throughout the country there are farms, each containing, as well as a pair of serfs, a household of forty free men and women. These are city-dwellers who have been sent into the country for a two-year stint of farming. Twenty are sent each year by rota: they spend a year learning husbandry from their predecessors and another teaching it to their successors.

All the cities resemble each other in laws, customs and institutions. Each year three elders from each city meet in a Senate in the capital, Amaurot. In size, shape and situation Amaurot, as described by More, resembles the London of his day. But in one respect Amaurot is startlingly different: there is no such thing there as privacy or private property. The terraced houses back on to spacious gardens; the doors to the houses and through them to the gardens swing open easily and are never locked. 'Whoso will, may go in, for there is nothing within the houses that is private, or any man's own. And every tenth year they change their houses by lot' (U 65).

In each city, every group of thirty households elects annually a magistrate called a Syphogrant; there are altogether two hundred of these per city. Each group of ten Syphogrants, with their households, is ruled by a Tranibore, another elected annual magistrate. The Tranibores form the Council of the supreme magistrate or Prince, who is chosen for life by the Syphogrants from a panel elected by popular vote. Whenever the Council meets, two Syphogrants must be present, a different pair each day. Nothing can be decided until it has been debated for three days, and it is a capital offence to discuss State matters outside the Council. This is to prevent the princes and Tranibores from changing the republic into a tyranny. Matters of particular importance are laid before all the assembled Syphogrants, but nothing is decided until they have had time to consult their several households. On rare occasions matters may be laid before the Senate of the whole island.

Every citizen learns agriculture, first in school, and then during a turn of duty on the farm. In addition every citizen, male or female, is taught a particular craft, such as cloth-making, masonry, metalworking or carpentry. Utopia is unlike Europe, where differences of class and status are marked by elaborate distinctions in dress; people all wear the same clothes, except for a distinction between the sexes and between the married and the unmarried. All clothes are home-made in each household.

No one is allowed to be idle, and all must work every day at their crafts, overseen by a Syphogrant. Citizens can choose their crafts, but if they wish to specialise in a craft other than their father's, they must transfer to a household dedicated to that craft. The working day is brief: Utopians work for three hours before noon, rest for two hours after dinner, and then work a further three hours before supper. They go to bed at eight and sleep for eight hours: the hours of early morning and evening are thus leisure time to be spent as each pleases. In the morning there are public lectures, compulsory for those citizens who have been assigned as scholars, optional for others, male or female. The evening may be spent in music or in conversation, or in chess-like games in which numbers devour numbers, or virtues battle in panoply against vices.

How do the Utopians manage to satisfy all their needs while working so many fewer hours than Europeans? You can easily work this out, if you consider how many people in Europe live idly:

First, almost all women which be the half of the whole number: or else, if the women be somewhere occupied, there most commonly in their stead the men be idle. Besides this, how great and how idle a company is there of priests and religious men, as they call them; put thereto all rich men, specially all landed men, which commonly be called gentlemen and noblemen—take into this number also their servants: I mean all that flock of stout bragging swashbucklers. Join to them also sturdy and valiant beggars, cloaking their idle life under the colour of some disease or sickness. (U 71–2)

Even among the few real workers in Europe, many spend their time producing superfluous luxuries rather than the things which are necessary for survival, comfort or natural pleasures. No wonder, then, that in Utopia where no more than five hundred able-bodied persons in each city-state are dispensed from manual labour, a six-hour day suffices.

Dispensations are given, by the Syphogrants, on the advice of the priests, only to those who seem specially fitted for learning and scholarship. From this small class of scholars are chosen the Utopian priests, Tranibores and Princes. Syphogrants need not be scholars, but they too are exempted by law from labour; they take no advantage of this privilege, however, so as to set others an example of work.

The work in Utopia is made light, not only by the many hands, but by the simplicity of the needs they serve. The buildings, being all communal property, do not suffer from private neglect, nor are they being continually altered at the whim of new owners. The manufacture of clothes calls for no great labour, since Utopians prefer coarse and sturdy wear of undyed cloth.

Occasionally the citizens are summoned from their regular crafts to perform large-scale public works, such as the mending of highways. On other occasions, when the economy is thriving, a public proclamation will shorten the working day. The magistrates do not weary their citizens with superfluous labour; the keynote of their policy is this: 'What time may possibly be spared from the necessary occupations and affairs of the commonwealth, all that the citizens should withdraw from the bodily service to the free liberty of the mind, and garnishing of the same. For herein they suppose the felicity of this life to consist' (U 75).

In More's Utopia, unlike Plato's Republic, the primary social unit is the family or household. Girls, when they grow up, move to the household to which their husbands belong; but sons and grandsons remain in the same household under the rule of the oldest parent until he reaches his dotage and is succeeded by the next oldest. The size of the households is strictly controlled. The number of births is not regulated, nor the number of children under fourteen; but no household may include less than ten or more than sixteen children who have grown up. The excess children in the larger households are moved to households where there are less than the minimum. If the number of households in the whole city grows beyond the statutory limit of six thousand, families are transferred to smaller cities. If every city in the whole island is already fully manned a colony is planted in unoccupied land overseas. If the natives there are unwilling to join them, and resist their settlement, the Utopians will establish the colony by force of arms; 'for they count this the most just cause of war, when any people holdeth a piece of ground void and vacant to no good or profitable use, keeping others from the use and possession of it which, notwithstanding, by the law of nature, ought thereof to be nourished and relieved' (U 76). If any of the homeland cities become dangerously undermanned, as has sometimes happened in time of plague, the Utopian colonists are recalled from abroad to make up the lack.

Each household, as explained earlier, will be devoted to a single craft. The products of the household's labour are placed in storehouses in the market-place in the centre of the quarter to which the household belongs. Every householder can carry away from these storehouses, free of charge, anything which he and his family need. In their dealings with each other, the Utopians make no use at all of money.

For why should anything be denied unto anyone, seeing there is abundance of all things, and that it is not to be feared lest any man will ask more than he needeth? For why should it be thought that a man would ask more than enough, who is sure never to lack? Certainly, in all kinds of living creatures, either fear of lack doth cause covetousness and greed, or, in man only, pride, which counteth it a glorious thing to pass and excel others in the superfluous and vain ostentation of things. The which kind of vice among the Utopians can have no place. (U 77)

Food, likewise, is distributed freely to every household which needs it: but individual householders have to wait their turn until food has been allotted first of all to the hospitals, on the prescription of doctors, and secondly to the houses of the Syphogrants. These houses contain great halls large enough to contain the whole of the thirty households making up the Syphograncy. Here, at dinner-time and supper-time, a brazen trumpet summons all the households to a communal meal. No one is forbidden to eat at home, but it is frowned on and almost nobody does so. 'It were a folly to take the pain to dress a bad dinner at home, when they may be welcome to good and fine fare so nigh hand at the hall' (U 79).

229

The women of the households take turns to prepare the food and arrange the meals, but they leave the menial and dirty kitchen tasks to the serfs. The tables are set against the walls, as in European monasteries and colleges: the men sit with their backs to the walls, the women on the other side so that they can leave the table easily if they feel unwell or need to attend to a child. The nursing mothers—and Utopian women nurse their own children whenever possible—eat apart with the under-fives in a nursery, which is a 'certain parlour appointed and deputed to the same purpose never without fire and clean water, nor yet without cradles; that when they will, they may down the young infants, and at their pleasure take them out of their swathing clothes, and hold them to the fire, and refresh them with play' (U 80). The children over five wait at table, or if they are too young to do so 'they stand by with marvellous silence', having food passed to them from the tables. At every table the diners sit 'four to a mess', as they do to this day in the Inns of Court. The Syphogrant and his wife, and the most senior citizens, sit at a high table on a dais, just like the Benchers of an Inn. They are joined, if there is a church in the Syphograncy, by the priest and his wife.

Both dinner and supper begin with a brief reading from an edifying book; after that, conversation is allowed, and it is specially noted that the elderly are not allowed to monopolise the time with long and tedious talk, but must provoke the young to speak, 'that they may have a proof of every man's wit, and towardness, or disposition to virtue; which commonly in the liberty of feasting, doth shew and utter itself'. Supper lasts longer than dinner, because the working day is over.

No supper is passed without music. Nor their banquets want no conceits, nor junkets. They burn sweet gums and spices or perfumes, and pleasant smells, and sprinkle about sweet ointments and waters, yea, they have nothing undone that maketh for the cherishing of the company. For they be much inclined to this opinion: to think no kind of pleasure forbidden, whereof cometh no harm. (U 81)

230

Travelling in Utopia is carefully regulated. To go from one city-state to another a passport is needed from the Tranibores stating the duration of the absence, and no one is permitted to travel alone. A free ox-cart, with a serf to drive, is provided; but Utopians rarely take advantage of this. For they do not need to carry provisions, since on arriving in another city-state they stay with the members of their profession and work at their crafts just as if they were at home. Travel between city-states without a passport is severely punished, and for a second offence a citizen can be reduced to serfdom. Within the same city-state a man does not need a passport to travel in the country, only 'the good will of his father and the consent of his wife'. But wherever he is, he must do a morning's work before he is given dinner, and an afternoon's work if he is to be given supper. This all ensures that no one is idle, no one goes hungry, and no one needs to beg.

The Utopians travel overseas to trade with other nations: they will export grain, honey, wool, hides, livestock and the like once they have provided two years' supply of everything for themselves. When their ships arrive abroad, they distribute one-seventh of their cargoes to the poor of the country; the rest they sell at moderate prices. Though the Utopians do not use money among themselves, they need it for a number of international purposes. Iron, gold and silver are their main imports; they use exports principally to build up credit, to be drawn on to make loans to other people or to wage war. As a provision for time of war, they keep a large treasury at home to bribe enemy nationals or to hire mercenaries ('they had rather put strangers in jeopardy than their own countrymen').

Among the most astonishing things about Utopia are the arrangements for preserving the treasury of precious metals. The Utopians see, justly, that iron is of much greater real value than the precious metals. So they are careful not to set any artificial value on gold and silver. They do not lock them away, or work them into fine plate which they would be loath to part with in emergencies. Instead:

Whereas they eat and drink in earthen and glass vessels—which indeed be curiously and properly made, and yet be of very small

231

value—of gold and silver they make chamber pots and other vessels that serve for most vile uses; not only in their common halls, but in every man's private houses. Furthermore, of the same metals they make great chains, fetters, and gyves, wherein they tie their bondmen. Finally, whosoever for any offence be disgraced, by their ears they hang rings of gold: upon their fingers they wear rings of gold; and around their neck chains of gold: and, in conclusion their heads be tied with gold. (U 86)

Pearls, diamonds and rubies are cut and polished and given to children to keep with their rattles and dolls.

Hythlodaye recalls that during his visit to Utopia there arrived an embassy from the distant land of Anemolia. The Anemolian ambassadors, ignorant of Utopian customs, sought to impress their hosts by the gorgeousness of their apparel. They wore cloth of gold, and gold necklaces, finger-rings and ear-rings, and caps flashing with pearls and gems. The Utopians took the most simply attired servants to be the leaders of the embassy; the ambassadors they mistook for slaves because of the gold that weighted them down. 'Look, mother,' said one Utopian child, 'there is a great grown fool wearing pearls and jewels as if he were a little boy.' 'Hush, child,' said the mother, 'I think he is one of the ambassador's jesters.' After a few days in Utopia the ambassadors learnt their mistake, and laid aside their fine gear. 'We marvel', the Utopians explained, 'that any men be so foolish as to have delight and pleasure in the doubtful glistering of a little trifling stone, when they may behold any of the stars, and the sun itself' (U 88).

Just as the Utopians despise those who take pleasure in jewellery, so too they regard it as madness to take pride in courtly honours. 'What natural or true pleasure', they ask, 'does thou take of another man's bare head, or bowed knees? Will this ease the pain of thy knees, or remedy the frenzy in thine own head?' (U 96). Likewise, they cannot understand how men can find pleasure in casting dice upon a table, or hearing dogs bark and howl after a hare. What pleasure is there in seeing dogs run?

But if the hope of slaughter, and the expectation of tearing in pieces the beast, doth please thee, thou shouldest rather be moved with pity to see a silly innocent hare murdered of a dog: the weak of the stronger; the fearful of the fierce; the innocent of the cruel and unmerciful. (U 98)

So the Utopians regard the cruel sport of hunting as unworthy of free men. Even the slaughter of animals which is necessary for food is not permitted to citizens: only serfs are allowed to become butchers; because through the killing of beasts, they maintain, 'clemency, the gentlest affection of our nature' (U 98), decays and perishes little by little.

Though they despise cruel sports, the Utopians enjoy and delight in the pleasures of the body and of the senses, and take pride and joy in their unparalleled health and strength. They are no ascetics, and indeed regard as perverse bodily mortification for its own sake.

To despise the comeliness of beauty, to waste the bodily strength, to turn nimbleness into slothness, to consume and make feeble the body with fasting, to do injury to health, and to reject the pleasant motions of nature ... for a vain shadow of virtue, for the wealth and profit of no man, to punish himself, or to the intent he may be able courageously to suffer adversity, which perchance shall never come to him—this to do, they think it a point of extreme madness, and a token of a man cruelly minded towards himself, and unkind towards nature. (U 102)

But it is the pleasures of the mind, rather than of the body, which most delight the Utopians. Though only a few citizens are dispensed from labour to devote themselves entirely to study, all are taught letters (in their own vernacular) and most men and women devote their leisure throughout life to reading. Before Hythlodaye's visit they were ignorant of Greek and Latin literature, but had made as much progress in music, logic, arithmetic and geometry as any of the classical authors. They were ignorant of modern (that is, medieval) logic, and of astrology; and very much better so. But when they heard a description of Greek literature they were anxious to learn the language; and those who were chosen to do so mastered it within the space of three years. They were delighted to accept from Hythlodaye a fine library of classical texts in Renaissance editions. Indeed, printing and paper-making were the only two European arts which the Utopians envied. Here too they proved quick learners, and acquired both skills in a short time.

In describing the customs of Utopia mention has been made from time to time of serfs. Serfdom is not hereditary slavery: most serfs are Utopians or foreigners reduced to serfdom as punishment for the kind of crime which is elsewhere punishable by death. When Utopians take prisoners in war, they use them as serfs; but they do not buy the prisoners of others as slaves. Labourers from other countries, finding Utopian serfdom preferable to their own drudgery, sometimes become serfs voluntarily; these are given lighter work, and are allowed to return home if ever they please to do so.

The sick are well cared for by the Utopians, who pride themselves on the enlightened and sanitary design of their hospitals. They sit with the incurably diseased and comfort them by every possible means.

But if the disease be not only uncurable, but also full of continual pain and anguish, the priests and the magistrates exhort the man, seeing he is not able to do any duty of life, and by overliving his own death, is noisome and irksome to others and grievous to himself, that he will determine with himself no longer to cherish that pestilent and painful disease. And seeing his life is to him but a torment, that he will not be unwilling to die, but rather to take a good hope to him, and either dispatch himself out of that pain, as out of a prison, or a rack of torment, or else suffer himself willingly to be rid out of it by others. (U 108)

Such a suicide is regarded as a virtuous and noble action; but if a man kills himself without the advice of the priests and the magistrates, he is regarded as unworthy either to be buried or cremated; 'they cast him unburied into some stinking marsh' (U 109).

The marriage customs of the Utopians have attracted, or shocked, many of the book's readers. Men marry at twenty-two, and women at eighteen. Those convicted of premarital intercourse are forbidden to marry without a special pardon from the prince, and the heads of their household are disgraced. If promiscuity were allowed, the Utopians say, few would be willing to accept the burdens of monogamous matrimony.

Hythlodaye reports the custom observed by the Utopians in choosing wives and husbands.

A grave and honest matron sheweth the woman, be she maid or widow, naked to the wooer: and likewise a sage and discreet man exhibiteth the wooer naked to the woman. At this custom we laughed, and disallowed it as foolish. But they on the other part do greatly wonder at the folly of all other nations, which in buying a colt (whereas a little money is in hazard) be so chary and circumspect, that although he be almost all bare, yet they will not buy him, unless the saddle and all the harness be taken off; lest under those coverings be hid some gall or sore. And yet in choosing a wife, which shall be either pleasure or displeasure to them all their life after, they be so reckless that all the residue of the woman's body being covered with clothes, they esteem her scarcely by one hand breadth (for they can see no more but her face), and so do join her to them, not without great jeopardy of evil agreeing together if anything in her body afterward should chance to offend and mislike them. (U 110)

No doubt, after a marriage is consummated a body may wither or decay; in that case there is no remedy but patience. But before marriage no one should be allowed to conceal deformity beneath deceitful clothes.

Unlike most of their neighbours, the Utopians are monogamous, and marriage is in principle lifelong. However, adultery may break a marriage; the innocent, but not the adulterous, spouse is allowed to remarry. Besides adultery, 'the intolerable wayward manners of either party' provide grounds for divorce and the remarriage of the unoffending spouse. On rare occasions divorce by consent is permitted.

Now and then it chanceth, whereas the man and woman cannot well agree between themselves, both of them finding other with whom they hope to live more quietly and merrily, that they, by the full consent of them both, be divorced asunder and married again to others. But that not without the authority of the Council: which

235

agreeth to no divorces before they and their wives have diligently tried and examined the matter. Yea, and then also they be loth to consent to it; because they know this to be the next way to break love between man and wife—to be in easy hope of a new marriage! (U 111)

Adultery is punished with serfdom, and divorce follows automatically unless the guiltless spouse is prepared to share the bondage and drudgery. (Such selfless devotion sometimes wins pardon for the guilty party.) Death is the punishment for repeated adultery: the only crime so punished, other than rebellion by those already condemned to serfdom. Minor matrimonial offences of wives are punished by husbands; the use of cosmetics is regarded as wanton pride, for beauty is less esteemed than probity. 'As love is sometimes won with beauty, so it is not kept, preserved, and continued, but by virtue and obedience' (U 111).

Apart from the laws governing marriage, there is little to be told about Utopian municipal law, because of the lack of private property. Altogether, the Utopians have very few laws; they despise the massive tomes of laws and commentaries to be found in other countries. 'They think it against all right and justice, that men should be bound to laws which either be in number more than be able to be read, or else blinder and darker than that any man can well understand them' (U 114). Their own laws are simple, and always given the most obvious interpretation. This enables them to dispense altogether with lawyers: they think it better that a man should plead his own case, and tell the same story to the judge that he would tell to his attorney.

The Utopians' virtues have inspired their neighbours to invite Utopian proconsuls to govern them, ruling for a five-year period and then returning home. Such officials are untempted by bribes (for what good is money to them, since they will shortly be returning to a country where it is not used?) and undeflected by malice or partiality (since they are living among strangers). So the two vices which most corrupt commonwealths are absent from the Utopians' allies.

Though the Utopians have allies and friends among other nations, they make no treaties or leagues. If man and man will not league together by nature, the words of treaties will not make them do so, they argue.

They be brought into this opinion chiefly because, that, in these parts of the world leagues between princes be wont to be kept and observed very slenderly. For here in Europe, and especially in these parts where the faith and religion of Christ reigneth, the majesty of leagues is every where esteemed holy and inviolable: partly through the justice and goodness of princes, and partly at the reverence and motion of the Sovereign Pontiffs. Which, like as they make no promise themselves, but they do very religiously perform the same, so they exhort all princes in any wise to abide by their promises; and them that refuse or deny so to do, by their pontifical power and authority, they compel thereto. (U 116)

More's irony reveals the degree of contempt into which the pontifical government had been brought, even among loyal Catholics, by the perfidious behaviour of Alexander VI and Julius II. The readiness of rulers to break treaties, he goes on, makes men think that justice is a virtue which is far too plebeian for kings to practise; or at least

that there be two justices: the one meet for the inferior sort of the people; going a-foot and creeping low by the ground, and bound down on every side with many bands; the other, a princely virtue; which, like as it is of much higher majesty than the other poor justice, so also it is of much more liberty; as to the which, nothing is unlawful that it lusteth after. (U 117)

Unlike other nations, the Utopians do not regard war as anything glorious; but they are not pacifists either. Both men and women receive regular military training, and they regard war as justified to repel invaders from their own or friendly territory, to liberate peoples oppressed by tyranny, to avenge injustices done to their allies. Pecuniary losses abroad to their own citizens they do not regard as justifying war; but if a Utopian is wrongfully disabled or killed anywhere, they first send an embassy to inquire into the facts, and if the wrongdoers are not surrendered they forthwith declare war. They prefer to win wars by stratagem and cunning than by battle and bloodshed, glorying in victories won by gifts of intellect rather than by the strength and powers that men share with animals.

Their one aim in war is to secure the object which, if it had been granted beforehand, would have prevented the declaration of war; or else, if that is impossible, to punish those at fault so as to deter future wrongdoing. One of their methods of minimising bloodshed is this. When war is declared, they cause posters to be set up secretly throughout enemy territory offering great rewards for the assassination of the enemy king, and smaller but still considerable sums for the deaths of other named individuals, regarded as responsible for the hostilities. This spreads dissension and distrust among the enemy; but it also means that those most likely to be killed in a war are not the general guiltless mass of the enemy nation, but the few wrong-doers among their leaders. For they know that common people do not go to war of their own wills, but are driven to it by the madness of rulers.

When battles do have to be fought abroad, the Utopians employ mercenaries: the fierce, rough Zapoletans, who live in rugged mountains like the Swiss Alps, hardy people who have no trade but fighting and care about nothing but money. Since the Utopians have so much gold, they can outbid rivals in purchasing Zapoletans. Only a small contingent of their own citizens is sent abroad, to accompany the commander and his deputies; and no one is enlisted for foreign service unless he volunteers. If Utopia itself is invaded, however, then all are placed in the front line, on shipboard or on the ramparts, brave men and fainthearts together, men and women alongside each other.

In set field the wives do stand every one by their own husband's side; also every man is compassed next about with his own children and kinsfolk ... It is a great reproach and dishonesty for the husband to come home without his wife, or the wife without her husband, or the son without his father. (U 125)

This gives the Utopians unparalleled courage and spirit in battle.

In each battle, as in war generally, the main aim is to

destroy the leadership: a band of picked youths is bound by oath to seek out and kill or capture the opposing general. Once the battle is won there is no disordered pursuit or indiscriminate slaughter: the Utopians prefer to take prisoners than to kill the vanquished. They keep truces religiously, and they injure no non-combatants except spies; they never plunder captured cities, but the defeated are obliged to bear the expense of the war once it is over.

The final part of Hythlodaye's account of Utopia concerns religion. Some in Utopia worship heavenly bodies, or departed heroes; but the great majority there believe 'that there is a certain godly power, unknown, everlasting, incomprehensible, inexplicable, far above the capacity and reach of man's wit,' which they call 'the father of all' (U 130). The medley of Utopian superstitions is gradually giving way to the worship of this single supreme being; but the majority do not impose their religious beliefs on others. The founder of Utopia, seeing that religious divisions were a great source of discord,

> made a decree that it should be lawful for every man to favour and follow what religion he would; and that he might do the best he could to bring others to his opinion, so that he did it peaceably, gently, quietly and soberly; without hasty and contentious rebuking and inveighing against others. If he could not by fair and gentle speech induce them unto his opinions, yet he should use no kind of violence and refrain from displeasant and seditious words. To him that would vehemently and fervently in this cause strive and contend, was decreed banishment or bondage. (U 133)

There was one Utopian who became a convert to Christianity, and proselytised offensively with excessive zeal, consigning all non-Christians to everlasting fire. He was arrested, tried and banished, 'not as a despiser of religion, but as a seditious person and raiser up of dissension among the people' (U 133).

The tolerance proclaimed by the founder of Utopia was no mere device for keeping the peace: he thought it might well be true that God inspired different men with different beliefs so that he might be honoured with a varied and manifold worship. Even if only a single religion were true and the rest

239

superstitions, truth is best left to emerge by its own natural strength. But Utopian religious toleration has its limits. It is regarded as base and inhuman to believe that the soul perishes with the body; anyone who professes such an opinion is treated as untrustworthy, excluded from public office and forbidden to defend his belief in public. Those who err on the opposite side, and attribute immortal souls to non-human animals, are left in peace.

Utopians believe not only in immortality, but in a blissful afterlife. For this reason, though they lament illness, they do not regard death, in itself, as an evil. Reluctance to die they take as a sign of a guilty conscience; one who obeys the summons of death with reluctance is viewed with horror and carried out to burial in sorrowful silence. But those who die cheerfully are not buried but cremated amid songs of joy. 'And in the same place they set up a pillar of stone, with the dead man's titles therein graved. When they be come home, they rehearse his virtuous manners and his good deeds. But no part of his life is so oft or gladly talked of, as his merry death' (U 136).

The Utopians believe that the dead revisit their friends invisibly and move above the living as witnesses of all their words and deeds. Thus they feel protected as they go about their business, but also deterred from any secret misdoing.

We have seen that the Utopians despise asceticism for its own sake. None the less, there are groups among them who live selfless lives embracing tasks which are rejected as loathsome by others, giving up their leisure to tend the sick, or undertake public works on roads or in field or forest. Some of these people practise celibacy and vegetarianism; others eat flesh, live normal family lives and avoid no pleasure unless it gets in the way of their work. The Utopians regard the former sect as holier but the second sect as wiser.

The Utopians, we are told, have priests of extraordinary holiness 'and therefore very few'. There are thirteen in each city under a bishop, all elected by popular vote in secret ballot. They preside over worship and conduct services, but are also censors of morals: to be rebuked by the priests is a great disgrace. The clergy are not authorised to inflict any punishment other than exclusion from divine service; but this punishment is dreaded more than almost any other.

Women as well as men may become priests, but they are chosen only if they are widows of a certain age. The male priests marry the choicest wives. The priests, male and female, have charge of the education of children and young people. No Utopian court may punish them for any crime. In battle they kneel beside the fighting armies, 'praying first of all for peace, next for victory of their own part, but to neither part a bloody victory'. When victory comes they mingle with their own victorious armies, restraining the fury and cruelty of the soldiers. They have averted such slaughter that their reputation is high among all neighbouring nations. 'There was never any nation so fierce, so cruel and rude, but they had them in such reverence, that they counted their bodies hallowed and sanctified, and therefore not to be violently and unreverently touched' (U 142).

Hythlodaye's narrative of the Utopians concludes with a minute description of the feasts with which they keep holy the first and last days of the month and the year, to offer thanks for prosperity past and pray for prosperity future. All family quarrels are reconciled before the feasts; 'if they know themselves to bear any hatred or grudge towards any man, they presume not to come to the sacrifices before they have reconciled themselves and purged their consciences' (U 143). The priests wear vestments made of birds' feathers, like those of American Indian chiefs. The service ends with a solemn prayer in which the worshippers thank God that they belong to the happiest commonwealth and profess the truest of all religions. The worshipper adds that if he is in error in believing this, 'if there be any other better than either of them is, being more acceptable to God, he desireth him that he will of his goodness let him have knowledge thereof, as one that is ready to follow what way soever he will lead him' (U 145).

3 The King's councillor

The first book of *Utopia* was written after the second, and it is much less Utopian: instead of describing the constitution of an imaginary republic, it weighs the pros and cons of entering public service in real-life monarchies. It seems, indeed, to have been written to clear More's own mind when he was wondering whether he should become an official of Henry VIII. On the one hand, his own career hitherto pointed in that direction: the very embassy to Flanders out of which *Utopia* grew was an earnest of future royal employment. More's father and many of his humanist friends, including Tunstall, had already joined the Royal Council. On the other hand, Erasmus and some other humanists thought scholars had no business to enter public service, where the Court could corrupt them, and the needs of policy compromise their independent principles.

In *Utopia*, the case against royal service is made by Hythlodaye; the case in favour of it is made by the More of the dialogue. Service to kings, Hythlodaye suggests, is little better than slavery: why should a scholar give up his ease for it, when kings are only interested in war-making? Hythlodaye recalls his own firsthand experience of the English Court in the time of Cardinal Morton. He relates a long and spirited denunciation of the rapacity of the English upper classes, whose unscrupulous greed and passion for luxury destroy the livelihood of the poor and make them first starve, and then steal, and then hang for stealing. No one took any serious notice of that: they all just watched to see the Cardinal's reaction. More too can recall Morton's court from his days as a page there, but he reminds Hythlodaye that Plato believed that commonwealths could only be happy if either philosophers become kings, or kings turn to philosophy. How far off happiness is if philosophers will not even condescend to give advice to kings!

Plato was no doubt right, Hythlodaye says, to think that

kings would never take philosophers' advice unless they
became philosophers themselves. Plato himself, at the court of
Sicily, found how useless it was for a philosopher to offer
advice to an unphilosophical king. If Hythlodaye were to offer
good advice to contemporary monarchs, it would fall on ears
as deaf as Plato's did. There is no room for philosophy with
rulers.

That may be true of scholastic philosophy, More says: but it
is possible to adapt philosophy for statesmen. 'If evil opinions
and naughty persuasions cannot be utterly and quite plucked
out of their heart, if you cannot even as you would, remedy
vices which use and custom have confirmed; yet for this cause
you must not leave and forsake the commonwealth: you must
not forsake the ship in a tempest, because you cannot rule and
keep down the winds' (U 50). It is fruitless to try to convert
rulers to a wholly new way of thinking;

but you must with a crafty wile and subtle train study and endeavour
yourself, as much as in you lieth, to handle the matter wittily and
handsomely for the purpose, and that which you cannot turn to good,
so to order it that it be not very bad: for it is not possible for all things
to be well, unless all men were good; which I think will not be yet
these good many years. (U 50)

Such dissembling is dishonourable, says Hythlodaye; only
radical change will do any good. Where there is money and
private property there can be no justice or true prosperity in
the commonwealth. More doubts whether if the profit motive
were altogether removed there could be enough goods produced. That, says Hythlodaye, is because More has never seen
Utopia; which he proceeds to describe in the second book
which was summarised in our previous chapter.

In the dialogue, Hythlodaye is given the last word: but in
the event, More seems to have been more convinced by the
arguments he puts in his own mouth. By August 1517 he had
accepted an invitation to join the King's Council, though he
did not dare to tell Erasmus until nearly a year later. He
allowed Erasmus to believe, rightly or wrongly, that he had
accepted the invitation with great reluctance. King Henry

could not rest, Erasmus wrote, until he dragged More to court —literally dragged 'because no one has ever been as eager to get into court as More was to stay out of it' (E 292).

More's first employment as councillor was a modest embassy to Calais in 1517 to settle a commercial dispute between English and French merchants. His effective superior was Thomas Wolsey, Archbishop of York and Cardinal, who for the next twelve years was Henry VIII's Lord Chancellor and the leading figure in English politics. Wolsey controlled the Council, which the King rarely attended; only a handful of councillors accompanied the King as the Court moved around the country. More took part in the work of the Council at Westminster, but much of his time in the royal service was spent in the King's household as it travelled. The King often sent for him, to discuss astronomy, geometry or divinity with him, as well as public affairs; at night time he would invite him on to the roof 'to consider with him the diversities, courses, motions and operations of the stars and planets'. More was called so frequently to entertain the King and Queen that he could not get away from court more than two days together in a month: he had 'to dissemble his nature' and to 'disuse himself of his former accustomed mirth' until they let him go home to his wife and children (R 7).

More's household was now growing. In 1521 Margaret More married William Roper, twelve years her senior, son of a family friend of the Mores and now a student of Lincoln's Inn. John Aubrey, in his *Brief Life* of More, tells the story of Roper's wooing thus:

He came one morning, pretty early, to my Lord, with a proposal to marry one of his daughters. My Lord's daughters were then both together abed in a truckle-bed in their father's chamber asleep. He carries Sir William into the chamber and takes the sheete by the corner and suddenly whippes it off. They lay on their Backs, and their smocks up as high as their armepitts. This awakened them, and immediately they turned on their bellies. Quoth Roper, I have seen both sides, and so gave a patt on the buttock he made choice of sayeing, Thou art mine. Here was all the trouble of the wooing.

Aubrey says he had the tale from the granddaughter of one of Roper's cronies, but it is more likely derived from the provisions in *Utopia* for premarital inspection.

Roper came to live in More's household, and later became his first (and still his best) biographer. Margaret Roper was soon pregnant, and More wrote happily to her in the expectation of his first grandchild:

> May God and our Blessed Lady grant you happily and safely an addition to your family like to his mother in everything except sex. Let it indeed be a girl, if she will make up for the disadvantage of her sex by her zeal to imitate her mother's virtue and learning. I would most certainly prefer such a girl to three boys. (L 155)

Even an intimate note of this kind was written in Latin, and Margaret was not to let her family duties interrupt her studies. Writing in the early days of her marriage More said, 'I earnestly hope that you will devote the rest of your life to medical science and sacred literature' (L 149), and he concluded by urging her to overtake her husband in the study of astronomy.

A year or two after the Ropers' marriage More moved his household from the City centre to a thirty-four-acre farm on the river at Chelsea, where now Battersea Bridge joins Cheyne Walk. He constructed a mansion there with a separate building in the garden containing a chapel, and a library as a hideaway for himself. In 1526 the painter Hans Holbein visited Chelsea: he described the house as 'dignified without being magnificent'. He was commissioned to paint a series of family portraits and a family group. Sketches for the portraits are now at Windsor Castle and a draft of the family group is at Basle. The painting itself survives only in copies, but they and the sketches give a picture of the Chelsea household which is familiar to millions.

Among the many visitors to Chelsea was the King himself. An admirer of learning who shared More's enthusiasm for the education of women, Henry was impressed when More's three daughters engaged each other in formal philosophical disputation. Roper recalls the King's visits: there was one in particular which dwelt in his mind.

For the pleasure he took in his company, would His Grace suddenly sometimes come home to his house in Chelsea, to be merry with him; whither on a time, unlooked for, he came to dinner to him, and after dinner, in a fair garden of his, walked with him by the space of an hour, holding his arm about his neck. As soon as His Grace was gone I, rejoicing thereat, told Sir Thomas More how happy he was whom the King had so familiarly entertained... 'I thank our Lord, son,' quoth he, 'I find His Grace my very good lord indeed, and I believe he doth as singularly favour me as any subject within this Realm. Howbeit, son Roper, I may tell thee I have no cause to be proud thereof, for if my head could win him a castle in France (for then was there war between us) it should not fail to go.' (R 12)

More was at this time in constant service on the King as Royal Secretary. He was a valuable intermediary between Henry and Wolsey because he was almost the only man they both trusted. Wolsey was anxious to bring impartial justice within the reach of poor as well as rich in England, and he professed himself a lover of international peace. The author of *Utopia* was attracted by both these goals: as things turned out, he was able to contribute much more to the former than to the latter. On his travels with the King he dealt with bills of complaint brought to the itinerant court; in Westminster he sat as judge in the Star Chamber, Wolsey's chosen means to expedite and simplify litigation. At discussions of foreign policy in the council he was forced to observe that Wolsey's projects for peace took second place to Henry's ambition for military glory.

The shifts and turns of Wolsey's foreign policy involved More in a number of diplomatic ventures. In 1520 he accompanied Henry to meet Francis I of France at the Field of the Cloth of Gold, a sumptuous pageant at which the two kings swore eternal friendship; a year later he accompanied Wolsey to Calais on a mission which led to an alliance against Francis with the Emperor Charles V. He found his work in England more useful and congenial than a diplomatic career, and he later refused to undertake an embassy to Spain.

In 1523, when war broke out with France, a Parliament was summoned to raise the necessary taxes: More, by now a Knight, and Under-Treasurer of the Exchequer, was chosen Speaker. Wolsey demanded a tax of four shillings in the pound, but the Commons resisted this heavy imposition. Wolsey appeared in person to press the demand, and asked each member in turn his opinion. None would reply: the custom was for the Speaker to be their mouthpiece in dealing with the King or his representative.

'And thereupon he required an answer of Master Speaker, who first reverently upon his knees excusing the silence of the House, abashed at the presence of so noble a personage, able to amaze the wisest and best learned in a Realm', went on to defend the custom that 'for them to make answer was it neither expedient nor agreeable with the ancient liberty of the House'. Nor could he reply himself: true, they had all trusted him to be their voice; 'yet except everyone of them could put into his one head all their several wits, he alone in so weighty a matter was unmeet to make His Grace answer' (R 10). Four months later the Commons voted three shillings in the pound instead of four, over a period of years instead of a lump sum.

Wolsey was not pleased with More. ' "Would God" ', he said to him one day in his Whitehall gallery, ' "you had been at Rome, Master More, when I made you Speaker." "Your Grace is not offended, so would I too, my Lord," quoth he' (R 11).

More's career as Speaker had not been undignified; but the raising of heavy taxes to support war between Christian princes was not the kind of royal service for which the author of *Utopia* had left the leisure of the scholar.

Publicly, however, More's relations with Wolsey remained cordial as long as Wolsey remained in power. When peace was made in 1525 More was one of the signatories of the Treaty, which brought the French, the English and Pope Clement VII into league with each other against the Emperor. The Pope gained little from this alliance: Rome was twice sacked by the Emperor's armies. Henry was unwilling to spend more than words in support of the Pope. It fell to More, as Secretary, to write the letters of consolation: 'I trust I have so couched and

247

qualified them,' he wrote to Wolsey, 'that they shall be to the satisfaction of the Pope's holiness and such other as shall hear and read the same, without binding the King to anything that might redound to his charge.' The King did, however, send More and Wolsey to France in 1527 to encourage the French to mount an expedition to rescue the Pope. For Henry now had a reason of his own for wanting the goodwill of Clement.

By 1527 Henry had grown tired of his marriage with Catherine of Aragon. He had, it will be recalled, married her as his brother's widow, with a dispensation from Pope Julius II. After eighteen years of marriage he had still no male heir: Princess Mary was the only survivor of a series of miscarriages, still births and cot deaths. If he died without a male heir the kingdom might return to the chaos of the Wars of the Roses. His attention was drawn by someone to the words of Leviticus: 'He that marrieth his brother's wife doth an unlawful thing... they shall be without children.' Beside these reasons of State and conscience, more pressing reasons of the heart made Henry anxious to terminate his marriage. Some time in 1527 he had fallen in love with a maid-of-honour, Anne Boleyn, the younger sister of a former mistress. Unlike her sister, Ann was unwilling to admit the King to her favours without at least the prospect of becoming Queen.

Could it be claimed that Pope Julius's dispensation was invalid, *ultra vires* because against the text of Leviticus? If so, the marriage with Catherine was no marriage, and Henry was free to marry Anne. But the matter was complicated. Was it certain that the marriage between Catherine and Arthur had ever been consummated? Was there not a text of Deuteronomy to set against that of Leviticus? Was it likely that Clement VII would overrule his predecessor's decision, thus calling in question the dispensing power of the Papacy? Moreover, Catherine was aunt to the Emperor Charles V: and in the year after the sack of Rome Clement knew well the price of incurring the Emperor's displeasure.

The King decided, however, that it was worth while to seek an annulment of the marriage. He caused himself to be cited before Cardinal Wolsey's court for having lived in incest for eighteen years. He sought the advice of his bishops, including the poorest and holiest of them, John Fisher of Rochester. Fisher replied, guardedly, that he saw no reason to believe that the dispensation granted by Pope Julius was beyond the Papal powers.

When More returned from his French embassy he too was asked for advice. At Hampton Court the King showed him the text of Leviticus and told him that he believed the marriage with Catherine was so far against the laws of nature as to be beyond dispensation by the Church. More looked up the comments of Church Fathers upon the King's biblical text: he found them unfavourable to the royal wishes. He showed them to Henry, but expressed no opinion on the validity of the bull of dispensation: he was, he said, no canon lawyer.

Wolsey's Anglo-French-Papal alliance collapsed shortly after, on the defeat of the French. It was now necessary to make peace with the Emperor: a conference was called at Cambrai. But Wolsey was unable to attend: he and an Italian Cardinal had been appointed by the Pope to try Henry and Catherine's divorce case in London. In his stead, More and Tunstall were sent to the peace conference. It was More's last diplomatic mission, and the only one in which he took enough pride to record it on his epitaph. The peace that was made lasted fourteen years, and was still in force at the time of his death.

On their return More and Tunstall found that the divorce proceedings had been interrupted by an appeal from Queen Catherine to the Pope. More had hopes that he would not be troubled further about the matter. He turned to the less disagreeable task of combating the increasing force of heresy.

4 A defender of the faith

In the year in which Thomas More joined the King's Council, a Professor of Theology at Wittenberg, Martin Luther, threw down a challenge to the Pope's pretensions that was to lead half Europe to reject Papal authority. The occasion of his protest was the proclamation of an indulgence in return for contributions to the building of the great new church of St Peter's in Rome. The offer of an indulgence—that is, of remission of punishment due to sin—was and is a normal part of Roman Catholic practice; but this particular indulgence was promoted in such an irregular and catchpenny manner as to be a scandal even by the lax Catholic standards of the period. But Luther's attack on Catholic practices soon went much further than indulgences. By 1520 he had questioned the status of four of the Church's seven sacraments, arguing that only baptism, eucharist, and penance were authorised in the Gospels. In his book *The Liberty of the Christian Man* he stated his cardinal doctrine that the one thing needful for the justification of the sinner is faith, or trust in the merits of Christ; without this faith nothing avails, with it everything is possible.

Henry VIII viewed Luther's writings with horror, and his officials burned several of his books at St Paul's Cross. Aided no doubt by a number of English scholars, the King published an *Assertion of the Seven Sacraments* in confutation of Lutheran doctrine. More was among those who assisted, though only, by his own account, in a minor editorial capacity. The book took a very exalted view of the authority of the Pope, and More felt it necessary to utter a word of caution.

'I must put your Highness in remembrance of one thing, and that is this. The Pope, as Your Grace knoweth, is a Prince as you are, and in league with all the other Christian Princes. It may hereafter so fall out that Your Grace and he may vary upon some points of the league, whereupon may grow breach of amity and war between you both. I think it best, therefore, that that place be amended, and his authority more slenderly touched.'

'Nay,' quoth His Grace, 'that shall it not. We are so much bounden unto the See of Rome that we cannot do too much honour to it.' (R 34)

Certainly, Pope Leo X was highly pleased by the book. In gratitude he designated Henry *Fidei Defensor* ('Defender of the Faith'): a title which is still borne on the coins of Henry's successors.

Martin Luther replied in a contemptuous and vituperative pamphlet. To reply in person would have been beneath Henry's dignity, and More was commissioned to write a riposte under an alias. More couched his reply in verbose and truculent Latin; it is only slightly better mannered than Luther's. The tone of the work at its worst can be illustrated from the following sample, in which Sister Scholastica Mandeville's translation has well preserved the flavour of the original.

Since he has written that he already has a prior right to bespatter and besmirch the royal crown with shit, will we not have the posterior right to proclaim the beshitted tongue of this practitioner of posterioristics most fit to lick with his anterior the very posterior of a pissing she-mule until he shall have learned more correctly to infer posterior conclusions from prior premises? (Y 5.123)

Erasmus, like More, was prevailed upon to write in the defence of the traditional teaching: his work *On Free Will* attacked Luther's claim that man of himself is not free to choose between good and evil. Luther replied with a substantial treatise, *On the Bondage of the Will*. More wrote a Latin letter in 1526 on similar topics in reply to a Lutheran pamphleteer's *Letter to the English*.

Lutheran ideas began to find favour in some quarters in England. None knew this better than More, for his son-in-law Roper, as we learn from Harpsfield, was one of the first to follow the new fashion. Reading Luther's works convinced him 'that faith only did justify, that the works of man did nothing profit, and that, if man could once believe that our

Saviour Christ shed his precious blood and died on the cross for our sins, the same only belief should be sufficient for our salvation'. He began to think that all the ceremonies and sacraments used by the Church were vain. Such was his enthusiasm for heresy, we are told, that 'neither was he content to whisper it in hugger-mugger, but thirsted very sore to publish his new doctrine and divulge it, and thought himself very able to do so, and it were even at Paul's Cross' (H 100).

More argued with Roper, but in vain; he told Margaret,

'Meg, I have borne a long time with thy husband; I have reasoned and argued with him in those points of religion, and still given to him my poor fatherly counsel, but I perceive none of all this able to call him home, and therefore, Meg, I will no longer argue and dispute with him, but will clear give him over, and get me another while to God and pray for him.' (H 102)

Lutheran books were imported to London by traders from overseas; More, in 1526, ordered a search for heretical works in the German quarter. Four merchants, as a result of this search, were forced to abjure their errors at St Paul's Cross. Roper was cautioned along with them; then or later he returned to Catholic belief.

One of the most energetic English admirers of Luther was William Tyndale, who in 1526 completed an English version of the New Testament and wrote a heretical pamphlet with the title *The Obedience of a Christian Man*. Tunstall, now Bishop of London, tried to prevent the circulation of this New Testament in his diocese; he regarded the translation as tendentious, and there was no mistaking the anti-Catholic and anti-Papal nature of some of the notes. The Bishop tried to buy up copies for destruction, but this, of course, financed further printings. More sagely, Tunstall invited More to write against Luther and Tyndale in English, so that arguments for the traditional doctrines could be read not only by scholars but by the public, who were eager readers of the new vernacular testament.

The first outcome of this was *A Dialogue concerning*

Heresies, which was printed in 1529 and, slightly revised, in 1531. As it is the best written of More's anti-heretical works, we may give it consideration as a fair sample of the whole. It is cast in the form of a dialogue in the garden at Chelsea between More and a messenger sent to him by a 'right worshipful' friend to report how ignorant people are calling in doubt traditional doctrines, and murmuring about the clergy's suppression of heretics. The dialogue considers in particular the heretics' allegations that the worship of images is idolatrous, and that prayer and pilgrimages to saints are vain. It contains an interesting defence by More of vernacular versions of the Bible (which were suspect to many conservative churchmen). The fourth book may be considered in detail as a sample of the work.

At the opening of the fourth book the messenger voices the opinion that the only reason the clergy ban Luther's books is that 'they are afraid that in them laymen may read the priests' faults'. More will have none of this.

If it were now doubtful and ambiguous whether the church of Christ were in the right rule of doctrine or not, then were it very necessary to give them all good audience that could and would anything dispute on either part for or against it, to the end that, if we were now in a wrong way, we might leave it and walk in some better. But now on the other side, if it so be (as indeed it is) that Christ's church hath the true doctrine already, and the selfsame that St Paul would not give an angel of heaven audience to the contrary, what wisdom were it now therein to shew ourself so mistrustful and wavering that for to search, whether our faith were false or true, we should give hearing, not to an angel of heaven, but to a fond friar, to an apostate, to an open incestuous lecher, a plain limb of the devil, and a manifest messenger of hell? (W 2.255)

Rebuking sinful clergy is not enough to get a book banned: the writings of many holy fathers of the past are full of such stuff. It is enough to rehearse Luther's doctrines to see that they are abominable heresies. 'He began with pardons and with the Pope's power, denying, finally, any of both to be of any effect at all. And soon after, to show what good spirit moved him, he denied all the seven sacraments, except baptism, penance and the sacrament of the altar, saying plainly that all the remnant be but fained things, and of none effect' (W 2.257). Even those sacraments he retains, Luther handles ill. The value of baptism is degraded by the doctrine that faith is all-sufficient. In the eucharist, Luther teaches, against the Catholic doctrine of transubstantiation, that bread and wine remain in the sacrament of the altar joined with the body and blood of Christ. In penance, he removed the need for a priest; every man and woman can hear confession and absolve. 'Marry,' says the messenger, 'this were an easy way.' He dislikes most confessors at sight; 'but if I might, after Luther's way, be confessed to a fair woman, I would not let to be confessed weekly' (W 2.257).

More itemises Luther's 'other wild heresies':

He teacheth against scripture and all reason, that no Christian man is or can be bounden by any law made among men, nor is not bounden to observe or keep any. Item, he teacheth that there is no purgatory. Item, that all men's souls lie still and sleep till the day of doom. Item, that no man should pray to saints nor set by any holy relics nor pilgrimage, nor do any reverence to any images. (W 2.261)

Item, he teacheth that no man hath no free will, nor can anything do therewith, not though the help of grace be joined thereunto; but that everything that we do, good and bad, we do nothing at all there in ourself, but only suffer God to do all thing in us, good and bad, as wax is wrought into an image or a candle by the man's hand without anything doing thereto itself. (W 2.260)

More, in his *Dialogue*, does not offer many theological arguments against Luther's doctrine. Rather, he attacks the motives and conduct of Luther and his disciples. Luther looks at the Church 'through a pair of evil spectacles of ire and envy'; he is goaded by the 'itch and tickling of vanity and vainglory' which 'cast him clean beside his mind and memory' (W 2.267–9). He is forever inconsistent, at one moment appealing to a general council and at another utterly rejecting conciliar authority; at one time saying that no man nor angel is able to dispense with a vow made to God, and at another that no vow could bind any man at all. 'But it well appeareth that he wrote the first of anger and malice toward the pope, and then changed to the second of a lecherous lust to the nun that he minded to marry' (W 2.270).

If Luther's doctrines are suspect because of his base motives, they are manifested as wicked by their effects. Look at the Peasants' War and the massacres in its train! Look what happened when Lutheran soldiers in the service of Charles V captured Rome in 1527! More tells the horrors of the sack, the robberies, mutilations, rapes and murders, and as a climax tells how

Some failed not to take a child and bind it to a spit and lay it to the fire to roast, the father and mother looking on. And then began to bargain of a price for the sparing of the child, after first an hundred ducats, then fifty, then forty, then twenty, then ten, then five, then twain, when the poor father had not one left but these tyrants had all already. Then would they let the child roast to death. And yet in derision, as though they pitied the child, they would say to the father and mother, 'Ah, fie, fie for shame, what a marvel is it though God send a vengeance on you. What unnatural people be you that can find in your hearts to see your own child roasted afore your face, rather than ye would out with one ducat to deliver it from death.' (W 2.275)

To be sure, there are cruel and wicked men in every sect. But other Christian men's cruelty cannot be attributed to their Christianity, since their evil living is contrary to the doctrine of Christ. The wickedness of Lutherans, however, arises directly from Luther's teaching.

For what good deed shall he study or labour to do that believeth Luther that he hath no free will of his own by which he can, with help of grace, either work or pray? Shall he not say to himself that he may sit still and let God alone? What harm shall they care to forbear, that believe Luther, that God alone without their will worketh all the mischief that they do themself? (W 2.276)

It is by licensing voluptuous living and violence that Luther makes converts: a license symbolised by his own marriage with a nun. What shame, 'to see such a rabble spring up among us, as professing the faith and religion of Christ, let not to set at nought all the doctors of Christ's church, and lean to the only authority of Friar Tuck and Maid Marion' (W 2.278).

The German Lutherans, the messenger concedes, may deserve all that More says of them. But the English Lutherans seem honest and godly men; and they explain Luther's doctrines in ways that make them seem 'not much discrepant from the true faith of Christ's church'. The doctrine of justification by faith merely means that men should put their trust in God's promises rather than take pride in their own deeds. More denies this flatly. 'When Luther saith that nothing can damn any Christian man but only lack of belief, he sheweth manifestly that we not only need no good works with our faith, but also that so we have faith, none evil works can hurt us' (W 2.289). But More is more courteous with the English Lutherans than he is with Luther, and at this point he gives a lucid, though unsympathetic, theological evaluation of the doctrine of justification by faith. He agrees with the Lutherans that our works, in themselves, are of no value to God.

But as we see that one ounce of gold whereof ten pound weight were not of his own nature toward man worth one ounce of wheat, nor one hundred pound weight thereof, of the nature self, worth one silly sheep, is yet among men, by a price appointed and agreed, worth many whole sheep, and many a pound weight of bread: so hath it liked the liberal goodness of God to set as well our faith, as our deeds, which were else both twain of their nature right little in value, at so high a price, as none is able to buy them and pay for them but himself, because we should work them only to him, and have none other paymaster. (W 2.295)

The most abominable of all the Lutheran heresies, More says, is the belief that God predestines people to damnation, when they have no liberty to choose good: 'so that God, whose goodness is inestimable, doth damn so huge a number of people to intolerable and interminable torments only for his pleasure, and for his own deeds wrought in them only by himself'. Besides being blasphemous in itself, this doctrine takes away any motive, whether threats or promises, for striving after good.

If we be of the chosen sort, none evil deed can damn us. And if we be of the unchosen sort, no good deed can avail us. He that thus believeth, what careth he what he doth, except for the fear of temporal laws of this world? And yet if his false faith be strong, he careth little of them also. For he shall think dying in his bed or on the gallows cometh not after his deserving but hangeth all upon destiny. (W 2.299)

But no one can hold this fatalism for long consistently.

If free will serve for nought, and every man's deed is his destiny, why do these men complain upon any man, except they will say they do it because it is their destiny to do so? And why will they be angry with them that punish heretics, except they will say because it is their destiny to be so? For if they will hold them to their own sect, and say men do them wrong to burn them for their heresies, because it was their destiny to be heretics, they may be then well answered with their own words, as one of their sect was served in a good town in Almayn, which when he had robbed a man and was brought before the judges, he could not deny the deed, but he said that it was his destiny to do it, and therefore they might not blame him; they answered him, after his own doctrine, that if it were his destiny to steal, and that therefore they must hold him excused, then it was also their destiny to hang him, and therefore he must as well hold them excused again. (W 2.300)

The rest of the dialogue is taken up with the justification of the practice of punishing heretics. 'The fear of these outrages and mischiefs to follow upon such sects and heresies, with the proof that men have had in some countries thereof, have been the cause that princes and people have been constrained to punish heresies by terrible death, whereas else more easy ways had been taken with them' (W 2.301).

The messenger says, 'I would all the world were agreed to take all violence and compulsion away on all sides, Christian and heathen, and that no man were constrained to believe but as he could be by grace, wisdom, and good works induced, and then he that would go to God, go on in God's name, and he that will go to the devil, the devil go with him' (W 2.302).

This is correct, More says, as between Christians and non-Christians: if Christ's teaching and Mahomet's are each peacefully preached, no doubt Christianity will gain many more souls than it will lose. 'But heretics rising among ourself, and springing of ourself, be in no wise to be suffered, but to be oppressed and overwhelmed in the beginning. For by any covenant with them Christendom can nothing win' (W 2.303).

Parliament, then, did well to make an Act in King Henry IV's time for the punishment of heretics. At the first fault, if a man forswears his heresy and does penance, he is received back into favour; if he is taken in the same crime again he is excommunicated, and handed over by the clergy to the secular power. It is the lay magistrate, not the bishop, who puts to death: but 'the bishop should surely not have such pity that rather than other men should punish the heretic's body he should be allowed to infect other men's souls' (W 2.305)

To punish internal heretics is as lawful as to resist the infidel by force. But some say that the present victories of the Turks against Christendom are due to the use by Christians of violence against their enemies. This is like the reasoning of an old fool in Kent at an assembly to inquire why Sandwich haven was silted up.

Some laid the fault to Goodwin Sands, others to the lands inned [enclosed] by divers owners in the Isle of Thanet. Then started up one good old father, and said he knew the cause well enough, for he had marked it going on and getting worse. 'And what hath hurt it good father?', quoth the gentlemen. 'By my faith, masters,' quod he, 'yonder same Tenterden steeple, and nothing else, that, by the mass, cholde twere a fair fish pole.' 'Why hath the steeple hurt the haven, good father?', quod they. 'Nay, by our Lady masters,' quod he, 'I cannot tell you why, but chote well it hath. For, by God, I knew it a good haven till that steeple was builded, and by the Mary mass that marked it well, it never throve since.' (W 2.307)

Bishops and magistrates could lawfully use much stricter means than they do to chastise heretics.

Surely as the princes be bounded that they shall not suffer their people by infidels to be invaded, so be they as deeply bounded that they shall not suffer their people to be seduced and corrupted by heretics, since the peril shall in short while grow to be as great, both with men's souls withdrawn to God, and their goods lost, and their bodies; destroyed by common sedition, insurrection and open war within the bowels of their own land. (W 2.309)

More ends the *Dialogue* with a prayer that God will

send these seditious sects the grace to cease, and the favourers of these factions the grace to amend, and us the grace that stopping our ears from the false enchantments of all these heretics we may, by the very faith of Christ's catholic church, so walk with charity in the way of good works in this wretched world, that we may be partners of the heavenly bliss. (W 2.324)

In answer to More's dialogue, Tyndale wrote a treatise of about ninety thousand words, printed in Antwerp in 1530. More replied in the massive *Confutacyon of Tyndales answere*—some half a million words, published as a serial: three books in 1532, five books in 1533, and a ninth volume left unfinished at his death. None but the most scholarly admirer of More could derive any pleasure or profit from reading through these increasingly crabbed polemics.

It was not only with his pen that More fought for orthodoxy: as a judge he was active in enforcing the laws against heresy, especially when he later became Lord Chancellor. During his Chancellorship six heretics were executed. Not a large number, say some of his apologists; but then, in Wolsey's much longer Chancellorship, none were executed at all. More was personally involved in detecting three of these six cases. He would not have thanked those modern biographers who have sought to play down his zeal against heresy. In answer to an anti-clerical pamphlet entitled 'A Treatise concerning the Division between the Spirituality and the Temporality', More wrote an *Apologye* in which he defended his record. He could show that there had been nothing irregular in his treatment of heretics: no brutality or cruelty in their examination; no injustice in the verdicts or sentences which had eventually been given on them. But of his part in the enforcement of the law he was not ashamed, but proud. He regarded heresy in the same way as a modern liberal magistrate regards racist propaganda: something disgusting and corrupting in itself, likely to lead to civil discord and violence, and therefore needing to be firmly stamped out. When he came to write his epitaph More described himself as a judge 'relentless towards thieves, murderers, and heretics'.

5 The troubles of the Chancellor

The Peace of Cambrai in 1527, which was so greatly welcomed by More, was a humiliation for Henry, who had hoped for a glorious victory over the Emperor. For this, and for the slow progress of his divorce, he blamed Wolsey. Suddenly he stripped the Cardinal of the office of Chancellor and most of his rich possessions. He charged him with an offence under the old statute called *Praemunire* which forbade the acceptance of Papal appointments: this although Wolsey's power as Papal Legate had been conferred at the King's own request. Many were glad to see Wolsey fall but the Council did not find it easy to elect an acceptable successor to the Chancellorship: after long discussion the choice fell on More. The appointment was in several ways a surprising one. Neither before nor after his appointment did More exhibit or show any wish to acquire the arts by which political power is exercised; and he was the first layman to hold the Chancellorship since men could remember. Still, he had a long experience of the law which would enable him to preside in the Courts of Chancery without exasperating the courts of common law in which his own career had hitherto lain. On accepting the Chancellorship, More received an assurance from the King that he would not be expected to take any part against his conscience in proceedings about the 'great matter of the divorce'.

One of More's duties as Chancellor was to preside, commoner though he was, over the House of Lords. In November 1529 the Parliament met that was to go down in history as 'the Reformation Parliament'. More's speech at its inception was a bitter attack on Wolsey, a 'great wether' among the King's flock of sheep who 'so craftily, so scabbedly, yea, and so untruly juggled with the King' that the good shepherd Henry had been forced to separate him from the sheep and give him his just deserts.

Partly because of his detachment from the divorce proceedings, More as Chancellor did not succeed to Wolsey's enormous political power. That went rather to the bluff and haughty Duke of Norfolk and the shrewd and unscrupulous Secretary, Thomas Cromwell. It was not as a politician, but as a judge, that he made his mark as Lord Chancellor. In an age when a blind eye was turned if judges enriched themselves by gifts from litigants, he avoided taking anything which even malice could represent as a bribe. At a time when family partiality often affected the course of justice, he was remembered for a 'flat decree' he gave against one son-in-law, and the stiff advice he gave to another: 'I assure thee on my faith that if the parties will at my hands call for justice, then, all were it my father stood on the one side, and the Devil on the other, his cause being good, the Devil should have right' (R 21). In an age when, as in all ages, litigants were exasperated by the law's delays More was legendary for clearing away long backlogs of cases.

More carried forward the reforms which Wolsey had introduced to bring justice within the reach of the poor, and worked hard to overcome the hostility which Wolsey's innovations had aroused among the more traditional common lawyers.

More could be proud of his work in the courts: he could look only with sorrow on the laws which went through Parliament during his Chancellorship. In 1529 the Commons passed a series of bills reducing the privileges of the clergy; 'a violent heap of mischief', said Bishop Fisher in the Lords, 'whereupon will ensue the utter ruin and danger of the Christian faith'.

Meanwhile, King Henry became more and more impatient at the slow progress of his divorce. Peers and bishops were invited to sign a memorial to the Pope in its favour: neither Fisher nor More did so. Universities at home and abroad were invited to express opinions about the divorce. The King began to toy with the idea of rejecting papal jurisdiction altogether.

Wolsey died in November 1530. A few weeks later the King accused the whole clergy, as he had formerly accused Wolsey, of violating the statute of *Praemunire* by exercising jurisdiction in Church courts. The clergy in the Canterbury Convocation sued for pardon, offering to pay a fine of £100,000.

But this was not enough for Henry: they must also accept him as 'only Supreme Head of the English Church'. Despite Fisher's opposition, this was eventually accepted by the clergy, but with the qualification 'as far as the law of Christ allows'.

More's position became more and more difficult. On 30 March 1531 it was his duty to present to Parliament the opinions of the universities which had been collected in favour of the King's divorce. His speech to the Commons on this occasion was reported by a witness, the chronicler Hall:

You of this worshipful House I am sure be not so ignorant but you know well that the King our sovereign lord hath married his brother's wife, for she was both wedded and bedded with his brother Prince Arthur, and therefore you may surely say that he hath married his brother's wife, if this marriage be good or no, many clerks do doubt.

More went on to report the judgements of the universities, so that 'all men shall openly perceive that the King hath not attempted this matter of his will or pleasure, as some strangers report, but only for the discharge of his conscience and surety of the succession of his realm'.

More was a man to choose each word with care: he expressed no opinion of his own about the divorce. But even reporting the favourable opinions of others went against the grain for a man who, in private, encouraged the defenders of Queen Catherine. He begged the Duke of Norfolk to ask the King to discharge him 'of that burdensome office of the Chancellorship, wherein, for certain infirmities of his body, he announced himself unable to serve' (R 26).

The infirmities of the body were real enough: but before release from office More was made to swallow further toads. In March 1532 the Commons presented a Supplication setting out their grievances against the clergy. In May the King demanded that all future clerical legislation in Convocation should receive the royal assent. When the bishops resisted this the King exploded. 'We thought the clergy of our realm had been our subjects wholly, but now we have well perceived they be but half our subjects, yea, and scarce our subjects: for all the Prelates at their consecration make an oath to the Pope clean contrary to the oath they make to us.' On 15 May Convocation abandoned its resistance, and yielded to all the King's demands. On the following day Thomas More gave up the Great Seal to the King.

On giving up the Chancellorship, More lost most of his income. He explained to his family that he could no longer maintain his household, and retrenchment would be necessary:

'I have been brought up', quoth he, 'at Oxford, at an Inn of Chancery, at Lincoln's Inn, and also in the King's Court, and so forth from the lowest degree to the highest, and yet have I in yearly revenue at this present little above an hundred pounds by the year, so that now must we hereafter, if we like to live together, be contented to become contributaries together. But, by my counsel, it shall not be best for us to fall to the lowest fare first; we will not therefore descend to Oxford fare, nor to the fare of New Inn, but we will begin with Lincoln's Inn diet, where many right worshipful and of good years do live full well; which, if we find not ourselves the first year able to maintain, then will we next year go one step down to New Inn fare, wherewith many an honest man is well contented. If that exceed our ability too, then will we the next year after descend to Oxford fare, where many grave, learned and ancient fathers be continually conversant; which, if our power stretch not to maintain neither, then may we yet, with bags and wallets, go a-begging together and hoping that for pity some good folk will give us their charity.' (R 27)

More was forced to pay off his staff: he found places for most of them with other bishops and noblemen, and he passed on his eight watermen, with his official barge, to Thomas Audley, who succeeded him as Lord Chancellor. His family, and particularly his wife, found it hard to adjust to the diminished state. But he had long warned them, 'We may not look at our pleasure to go to heaven in feather-beds; it is not the way' (R 95). For himself, office lost was leisure gained. 'I have longed', he wrote to Erasmus, 'that I might have some time to devote to God and myself, and that, by the grace of a great and good God, and by the favour of an indulgent prince, I have at last obtained' (L 173).

The indulgent prince, however, was unwilling to leave More

at peace. It irked him that his most honest and most famous councillor should be at odds with him upon his great matter. Henry married Anne Boleyn in January 1533; the marriage was made public four months later when the new Archbishop of Canterbury, Thomas Cranmer, annulled the marriage with Catherine. King and Archbishop had tired of waiting for the Pope's verdict: it was not until March 1534 that Pope Clement declared Catherine's marriage valid, seven years after the issue had first been raised. The Pope did not take so long to declare void the marriage with Anne and to excommunicate Henry.

In June 1533 Anne was to be crowned in Westminster Abbey. Tunstall and two other episcopal friends of More urged him to attend the coronation, and sent him twenty pounds to buy a new gown to do so. More accepted the twenty pounds but declined the invitation to the coronation. 'My lords,' he said, 'you required two things of me, the one whereof, since I was so well content to grant you, the other therefore I thought I might be the bolder to deny you.' Roper puts in his mouth a story of a Roman emperor who prescribed that the penalty for a certain offence should be death, unless the offender were a virgin. Unfortunately, the first offender was a virgin, which cast the Emperor's council into great perplexity. They were relieved of their doubt by a good plain man who said, 'Why make so much ado, my lords, about so small a matter? Let her first be deflowered and then after may she be devoured.' So too, More implied, the bishops might be deflowered by countenancing the King's new marriage; 'and when they have deflowered you, then will they not fail soon after to devour you' (R 29).

From the moment when More absented himself from Queen Anne's coronation, his friends believed, she and her friends began to seek to devour him. Her father, the Earl of Wiltshire, accused him of taking bribes while Lord Chancellor. More dealt with the accusations case by case. He had indeed been given a gilt cup by the wife of the successful litigant in *Vaughan* v. *Parnell*. But having filled it with wine, and drunk her health, he had handed it back as a New Year's gift to her husband. Another cup he had accepted from a litigant, but given a more precious one in return. The accusations of bribery all fell flat. But the affair of the Maid of Kent was a more serious matter.

Elizabeth Barton was a maidservant who began to believe, in 1525, that she was in receipt of divine visions and messages. Word of her mystical experiences reached the King. More told him that there was nothing in her utterances other than 'a right simple woman might, in my mind, speak it of her own wit well enough'. But the nun began to speak against the King's plans for marriage: if he married anyone other than Queen Catherine, one month later he would cease to rule, and die a villain's death. By the spring of 1533 the prophecy had already been falsified: in the summer she was arrested and questioned and confessed to a degree of fraudulence. Under interrogation she mentioned, among her supporters, Bishop Fisher and Thomas More. In fact, More had behaved with impeccable discretion, as he made clear in letters to Cromwell and the King: he had been careful, in conversation with her, to avoid any discussion of the King's matters, and he had indeed written to her urging her to keep from talking with any persons, specially with lay persons, 'of any such manner of things as pertain to princes' affairs or the state of the realm'. This did not prevent his name from being included, with that of the nun, her friends and John Fisher, in a Bill of Attainder brought before Parliament in February 1534. More wrote to Henry in March, reminding him that he had cleared himself, in his letter to Cromwell, of all untoward dealings with 'the wicked woman of Canterbury'.

Our Lord for his mercy send you I should once meet with your Grace again in heaven, and there be merry with you, where among mine other pleasures this should yet be one, that your Grace should surely see there then that (howsoever you take me) I am your true beadman now and ever have been, and will be till I die, howsoever your pleasure be to do by me. (L 203)

It was More's last letter to the King.

When the Bill came to the House of Lords, the peers insisted that More be given a chance to defend himself. He was invited before a commission of Cranmer, Audley, Norfolk and Cromwell. No word was said about the Maid of Kent. Instead, he was invited 'to add his consent' to the King's marriage to that of Parliament, bishops and universities. More replied: 'I verily hoped that I should never have heard of this matter more, considering that I have, from time to time, always from the beginning, so plainly and truly declared my mind unto His Grace, which His Highness to me ever seemed, like a most gracious Prince, very well to accept, never minding, as he said, to molest me more therewith.' They taunted him with the part he had played in the King's response to Luther, alleging that he had incited the King to overvalue the Papal power. More, who knew the exact opposite to be the truth, replied: 'These are threats for children.'

As he went home, Roper tells us, 'by the way he was very merry'. ' "Are you then put out of the Parliament Bill?", said I. "By my troth, son Roper," quoth he, "I never remembered it." ' The reason he was merry was that, as he said, 'I had given the devil a foul fall, and that with those lords I had gone so far as without shame I could never go back again' (R 34). But his name was in fact put out of the Act of Attainder: the King vented his anger by stopping his salary as Councillor. It was Cromwell who gave the good news to Roper that More's name had been excluded. But when Margaret told her father, he merely murmured that postponement was not the same thing as prevention.

6 'To lose one's head and have no harm'

The Parliament which met in January 1534 passed an Act to regulate the succession to the throne. It declared that the marriage between Henry and Catherine was against God's law, and was utterly void notwithstanding any licence, or dispensation. It fixed the succession on the offspring of the marriage with Queen Anne; on the eldest surviving son, if there should be one, or if not on the Princess Elizabeth. Catherine's daughter Mary was passed over.

Severe penalties were attached to the Act. Any who slandered the marriage with Queen Anne, or the heirs established, were guilty of treason, which carried the death penalty and forfeiture of all possessions. All the King's adult subjects were to take a public oath to observe and maintain 'the whole effects and contents of this present Act'. Those who refused to do so were guilty of misprision of treason, that is, treason in the second degree; the penalty was life imprisonment and confiscation of goods.

After the passing of the Act More was not left long at liberty. On the Sunday after Easter, he went with Roper to hear the sermon at St Paul's. After Mass More went to see his adopted daughter, now living in his old home in Bucklersbury. There he was summoned to appear the next day at Lambeth palace to take the oath prescribed in the Act. He at once returned to Chelsea to take leave of his family. Roper records how he bade farewell the following day, after attending Mass.

Whereas he evermore used before at his departure from his wife and children, whom he tenderly loved, to have them bring him to his boat, and there to kiss them all, and bid them farewell, then would he suffer none of them forth of the gate to follow him, but pulled the wicket after him, and shut them all from him, and with an heavy heart, as by his countenance it appeared, with me and our four servants there took he his boat towards Lambeth. Wherein sitting still sadly a while, at last he suddenly rounded me in the ear, and said 'Son Roper, I thank Our Lord, the field is won.' (R 36)

267

At Lambeth More found himself the only layman among a group of clergy who had been summoned to swear the oath. More was the first to be called before the Commissioners. He was shown the oath, under the great seal; he asked for the text of the Act of Succession, and read through the printed roll. He compared the two carefully together, and then gave his answer. As he wrote to Margaret a few days later:

I showed unto them that my purpose was not to put any fault either in the act or any man that made it, or in the oath or any man that swore it, nor to condemn the conscience of any other man. But as for myself in good faith my conscience so moved me in the matter that, though I would not deny to swear to the succession, yet unto the oath that there was offered me I could not swear without the jeopardizing of my soul to perpetual damnation. (L 217)

Historians have sometimes been puzzled why, if More was willing to swear to the succession established by the Act, he refused to take the proffered oath. Was it the implicit rejection of Papal authority in the Act's incidental remarks about dispensations from marriage impediments? Perhaps: but the matter is really quite simple. More was willing to swear to the succession, because it was within the competence of Parliament to fix that upon anyone; but to swear to the invalidity of a marriage which he was convinced was perfectly sound would be to invite God to endorse a falsehood.

The Commissioners told him that he was the first person to refuse to take the oath; they showed him the list of all the members of the Lords and Commons who had sworn at the last session of Parliament, and then they sent him out of the room in the hope that he would think better of his refusal. Through a window he watched the London clergy passing through the garden to take the oath; most were cheerful enough, slapping each other on the back and calling for beer at the Archbishop's buttery. Recalled before the Commissioners, he was asked why he was so obstinate that he not only refused to swear, but even to say what part of the oath went against his conscience.

More replied that he feared he had greatly displeased the

King by refusing the oath. 'If I should open and disclose the causes why, I should further exasperate his Highness, which I would in no wise do, but rather would I abide all the danger and harm that might come toward me, than give his Highness any occasion of further displeasure.' The words were carefully chosen. By refusing the oath, More was making himself liable to imprisonment and forfeiture; to say that he refused it because he regarded the marriage with Catherine as valid would be treason in terms of the Act and would invite the death penalty. He would willingly, he offered, put the ground of his refusal in writing if the King would promise that this would not give offence nor bring him in danger of any Statute. The Commissioners replied that even letters patent from the King could not exempt him from the Act of Parliament. 'Well,' said More, 'if I may not declare the causes without peril, then to leave them undeclared is no obstinacy' (L 220).

The chief Commissioner, Archbishop Cranmer, then argued that since More had said he condemned nobody who swore, he could not regard it as a matter of certainty that it was wrong to swear. 'But then', he went on, 'you know for a certainty and a thing without doubt that you be bound to obey your sovereign lord your king.' More was taken aback to hear this argument from the Archbishop of Canterbury, and hesitated how to reply. But he insisted that he was not bound to obey the King in a matter which went against his conscience, provided that he had taken sufficient pains to see that his conscience was rightly informed. Indeed, if Cranmer's argument was conclusive, 'then we have a ready way to avoid all perplexities. For in whatsoever matters the doctors stand in great doubt the king's commandment given upon whither side he list solveth all the doubts' (L 221).

Secretary Cromwell was another of the Commissioners. He 'swore a great oath', More tells us, 'that he had liefer his own only son had lost his head than that I should thus have refused the oath. For surely the King's Highness would now conceive a great suspicion against me, and think that the matter of the nun of Canterbury was all conceived by my drift.' More's refusal was put in writing to be reported to the King. He asked it to be recorded that though he did not swear the oath, 'I never withdrew any man from it, nor never advised any to refuse it, nor never put, nor will, any scruple in any man's head, but leave every man to his own conscience. And me thinketh, in good faith, that so were it good reason that every man should leave me to mine' (L 222).

For four days More was kept in the custody of the Abbot of Westminster while the Commissioners considered whether he might be permitted to swear simply to the succession. But the King insisted on the full oath. It was tendered to him again on 17 April, and was again refused. On the same day Bishop Fisher likewise refused: he too was willing to swear to the succession, but not to 'the whole effects and contents of this present Act'.

More and Fisher were forthwith committed to the Tower. Roper recalls his wife's first visit to her father, after he had been a prisoner for about a month.

'I believe, Meg,' said Sir Thomas, 'that they that put me here, ween they have done me a high displeasure. But I assure thee, on my faith, my own good daughter, if it had not been for my wife and you that be my children, whom I account the chief part of my charge, I would not have failed long ere this to have closed myself in as strait a room and straiter too. I find no cause, I thank God, Meg, to reckon myself in worse case here than in my own house. For me thinketh God maketh me a wanton, and setteth me upon his lap and dandleth me.' (R 37)

One cause of grief to More in prison was that none of his family joined, or fully understood, his stand against the oath. Nor could he explain his reasons, even to them, without risking his words bringing him within the scope of the newly made treasons. Roper and Margaret took the oath, following the example of Bishop Tunstall. Margaret even wrote a letter to her father urging him to give in and take the oath. More, wounded, wrote back:

If I had not been, my dearly beloved daughter, at a firm and fast point (I trust in God's mercy) this good great while before, your lamentable letter had not a little abashed me, surely far above all other things, of which I hear divers times not a few terrible toward me. But surely they all touched me never so near, nor were so grievous unto me, as to see you, my well-beloved child, in such vehement piteous manner labour to persuade unto me, that thing wherein I have of pure necessity for respect unto mine own soul, so often given you so precise answer before. (L 224)

After this Margaret ceased trying to dissuade her father from his course. 'But we live in hope', she ended her next letter, 'that we shall shortly receive you again. I pray God heartily we may, if it be his holy will.'

Her stepmother, Dame Alice, found it difficult to keep patience with her husband. In an unforgettable passage Roper describes her first visit to the prisoner in the Tower.

'What the good year, Master More,' quoth she, 'I marvel that you, that have been always hitherto taken for so wise a man, will now so play the fool to lie here in this close, filthy prison, and be content thus to be shut up amongst mice and rats, when you might be abroad at your liberty, and with the favour and good will both of the King and his Council, if you would but do as all the Bishops and best learned of this realm have done. And seeing you have at Chelsea a right fair house, your library, your books, your gallery, your garden, your orchard and all other necessaries so handsome about you, where you might in the company of me your wife, your children and household be merry, I muse what a God's name you mean here still thus fondly to tarry.'

After he had a while quietly heard her, with a cheerful countenance he said unto her, 'I pray thee, good Mistress Alice, tell me one thing.'

'What is that?', quoth she.

'Is not this house', quoth he, 'as nigh heaven as my own?'

To whom she, after her accustomed homely fashion, not liking such talk, answered 'Tilly-vally, tilly-vally'.

'How say you, Mistress Alice,' quoth he, 'is it not so?'

'*Bone deus, bone deus*, man, will this gear never be left?', quoth she.

'Well then, Mistress Alice, if it be so,' quoth he, 'it is very well. For I see no great cause why I should much joy either of my gay house or of anything belonging thereunto, when, if I should but seven years lie buried under the ground, and then arise and come thither again, I should not fail to find some therein that would bid me get out of

271

doors, and tell me it were none of mine. What cause have I then to like such an house as would so soon forget his master?' (R 41)

While in the Tower More wrote the most popular of all his devotional works, the *Dialogue of Comfort against Tribulation*. It is an imaginary conversation between two Hungarians, Antony and his nephew Vincent, about the threat of martyrdom arising from the advance of the Turk Suleiman the Magnificent into Hungary. It is a meditation on the prospect of painful death, filled with biblical allusions and drawing on Catholic doctrine for topics of comfort. It is written in a much simpler and homelier style than the works of controversy. Thus, meditating on Christ's tears over Jerusalem, More writes:

We may see with how tender affection God in his great goodness longeth to gather under the protection of his wings, and how often like a loving hen he clucketh home unto him, even those chickens of his that willfully walk abroad into the kite's danger, and will not come at his clucking, but ever the more he clucketh for them, the farther they go from him. (D 108)

In spite of the solemn theme of the book, it is not lacking in the 'merry tales' which adorn all More's works and illustrate his gifts as a raconteur. 'There is no tale so foolish', said More, 'but that to some purpose it may hap to serve'; and with that he starts upon the fable of the ass and the wolf that went to confession to a fox: a magnificently told story, too long to quote. Vivid domestic similes are used to point a moral: chaplains who flatter a man in power are thus rebuked:

In such wise deal they with him as the mother doth sometime with her child, which when the little boy would not rise for her in time but lie still abed and slug, and when he is up weepeth because he hath lain so long, fearing to be beaten at school for his late coming thither, she telleth him it is but early days, and he shall come time enough, and biddeth, 'Go, good son, I warrant thee I have sent to thy master myself. Take thy bread and butter with thee. Thou shalt not be beaten at all.' And so thus she may send him merry forth at door, that he weep not in her sight at home; she studieth not much upon the matter, though he be taken tardy and beaten when he cometh to school. (D 48)

To illustrate that some tribulations are sent by God to prevent us from falling into sin, More makes use of his gift for the concrete presentation of detail and exhibits his fondness for jingle and alliteration:

Some young lovely lady, lo, that is yet good enough, God seeth a storm coming toward her that would (if her health and fat feeding should a little longer last) strike her into some lecherous love, and instead of her old-acquainted knight, lay her abed with a new-acquainted knave. But God, loving her more tenderly than to suffer her fall into such shameful beastly sin, sendeth her in season a goodly fair fervent fever, that maketh her bones to rattle, and wasteth away her wanton flesh, and beautifieth her fair skin with the colour of the kite's claw, and maketh her look so lovely that her lover would have little lust to look upon her, and maketh her also so lusty that if her lover lay in her lap, she should so sore long to break unto him the very bottom of her stomach that she should not be able to refrain it from him, but suddenly lay it all in his neck. (D 30)

It is possible to follow More's thought as he composed the work by comparing the *Dialogue* with the letters he wrote to his family and the conversations he had with visitors during his imprisonment: the same themes and some of the illustrations occur in both. Of particular interest is a letter which Margaret Roper wrote to her stepsister Alice Alington, describing a visit to the Tower. (The letter was included in the 1557 Edition of More's *Works*.)

Margaret told More that some suspected he was unduly influenced by the example of Bishop Fisher. He replied that he had informed his own conscience; he was unable blindly to follow the judgement of another, even of a man of the wisdom, learning and virtue of Bishop Fisher.

'Verily, daughter, I never intend (God being my good lord) to pin my soul at another man's back, not even the best man that I know this day living; for I know not whither he may hap to carry it. There is no man living, of whom while he liveth, I may make myself sure. Some may do for favour, and some may do for fear, and so might they carry my soul a wrong way.'

More told a story of a jury which tried a London bailiff for wrongful seizure of goods. Eleven of the jurors were northerners, who were keen to give judgement against the defendant, since the plaintiff too was a northern man. The twelfth juror, an honest man, stood out; they urged him to side with them for the sake of fellowship or good company. He asked:

'What will happen when we shall go hence and come before God, and he shall send you to heaven for doing according to your conscience and me to the devil for doing against mine? If I shall then say to all you again, masters, I went once for good company with you, which is the cause that I go now to hell, play you the good fellows now again with me, as I went then for good company with you, so some of you go now for good company with me: would you go?'

Similarly, More said to Margaret, if he were to swear the oath out of good fellowship with his old companions, what should he say when he stands in judgement at the bar before the divine Judge?

'If he judge them to heaven and me to the devil, because I did as they did, not thinking as they thought, if I should then say, "Mine old good lords and friends, naming such a lord and such, yea and some bishops peradventure of such as I love best, I sware because you sware, and went that way that you went, do likewise for me now, let me not go alone, if there be any fellowship with you, some of you come with me."'

More doubted that he would find one who would be willing for good fellowship to go to the devil with him.

Margaret replied that she was not asking him to swear for good fellowship, but to be swayed by the authority of learned men and the commandment of Parliament. More answered:

'As for the law of the land, though every man being born and inhabiting therein, is bound to the keeping in every case upon such temporal pain, and in many cases upon pain of God's displeasure too, yet is there no man bound to swear that every law is well made, nor bound upon the pain of God's displeasure to perform any such point of the law as were indeed unlawful. Of which manner kind, that there may such hap to be made in any part of Christendom, I suppose no man doubteth, the General Council of the whole body of Christendom excepted.'

Margaret was at her wits' end and said that she could offer no further argument, except the one made by Henry Patenson, her father's jester. He, told that More was in the Tower, had said: 'What aileth him that he will not swear? Wherefore should he stick to swear? I have sworn the oath myself.' So Margaret, after offering in vain the example of so many wise men, could only say, 'Why should you refuse to swear, father, for I have sworn myself?' At this More laughed and said, 'That word was like Eve too, for she offered Adam no worse fruit than she had eaten herself.'

Before leaving, Margaret passed on to More a warning she had received from Cromwell. 'Master Secretary sent you word as your very friend, to remember, that Parliament lasteth yet.' Further legislation might bring More yet again within danger of the death penalty. More replied that he had long considered this possibility: but no law could be made which could justly bring him into further danger, and in such a case 'a man may lose his head and have no harm'.

The seventh session of the Reformation Parliament opened in November 1534. More had now been imprisoned for seven months and had still not been brought to trial. He could have been charged with misprision of treason for refusing to take the oath to the Succession Act, and it is uncertain why proceedings were not brought. More himself told Margaret that his detention was irregular because the oath administered to him was of a form not specified in the Statute. If this was the defect, it was to be remedied in the new session of Parliament.

Four Acts of this session affected More's fate. The first was the Act of Supremacy, which declared that the King was supreme head of the English Church, and rejected all foreign authority in ecclesiastical matters. A second Act of Succession regularised the oath which had been exacted under the previous Act. A new Act of Treasons was passed which made it treasonous to attempt to deprive the King of any of his titles, including the title conferred by the Act of Supremacy. To be guilty of treason in this way it was not necessary to proceed from words to deeds: it was enough if a person did 'maliciously wish, will, or desire, by words or writing,' so to do. Finally, at the end of the session, Acts of Attainder were passed against More, Fisher and five other non-juring clergy.

The Act of Attainder denounced More for his obstinate refusal to take the oath: it condemned him, without the need for further trial, to imprisonment for life, and confiscation of goods. But the new treason act went further: it would bring him to the scaffold if he was ever incautious enough to deny the Royal Supremacy before witnesses. Four months after the Parliament was prorogued, on 30 April 1535, More was interrogated in the Tower by Cromwell and other members of the Council, including the Solicitor-General, Sir Richard Rich. More described the scene a few days later in a letter to Margaret.

Cromwell asked whether he had seen the new Statutes. More said that he had, but that he had looked only briefly at the book and had not studied their effect. Had he not then read the first, of the King being Head of the Church? The members of the Council present had been instructed by the King to ask his opinion of it. More answered that the King well knew his mind on the matter. 'I neither will dispute King's title nor Pope's, but the King's true faithful subject I am and will be, and daily pray for him and all his, and for you all that are of his honourable Council, and for all the realm, and otherwise than this I never intend to meddle.' Cromwell told him that this manner of answer would not content the King. Even though a life prisoner, he was still bound to obey the Statutes, and the King would let the laws take their course against those who were obstinate. More replied, 'I do nobody harm, I say none harm, I think none harm, but wish everybody good. If this be not enough to keep a man alive in good faith, I long not to live.' Two days before, as More knew, a group of Carthusians had been condemned to be hanged, drawn and quartered for denying the Supremacy. On Margaret's next visit, on 4 May, he watched with her as the three set off on the way to Tyburn to be executed. The sight did not weaken his resolution: he expressed only envy of the priests going cheerfully to the vision of God.

King Henry played cat and mouse with him. A few days later Cromwell brought him a comforting message: the King, he reported, had decided to trouble his conscience no further. More was not deceived; when Cromwell departed he wrote with a piece of charcoal the following verses:

> Eye-flattering fortune, look thou never so fair
> Nor never so pleasantly begin to smile
> As though thou wouldst my ruin all repair,
> During my life thou shalt not me beguile.
> Trust I shall God, to enter, in a while,
> His haven of heaven, sure and uniform;
> Ever after thy calm look I for a storm.

The storm came when news reached England that the Pope had made Bishop Fisher a Cardinal. The King was enraged. 'Let the Pope send him a hat when he will,' he raged; 'I will so provide that whenever it cometh he shall wear it on his shoulders, for head shall he have none to set it on.' The Council redoubled their efforts to trap More and Fisher into an explicit denial of the Supremacy.

On 3 June Audley, Cranmer and Cromwell examined More again in the Tower. The King commanded him, Cromwell reported, to make a plain answer whether the statute was lawful, and either to acknowledge the King as Supreme Head or else 'to utter plainly his malignity'. More replied that he had no malignity to utter: he was a loyal servant of the King. 'I have always from the beginning truly used myself to looking first upon God and next upon the King according to the lesson that His Highness taught me at my first coming to his noble service, the most virtuous lesson that ever prince taught his servant.' It was hard to be compelled to make a plain answer. 'For if it were so that my conscience gave me against the statutes (wherein how my mind giveth me I make no declaration), then I nothing doing nor nothing saying against the statute it were a very hard thing to compel me to say either precisely with it against my conscience to the loss of my soul, or precisely against it to the destruction of my body.'

Cromwell asked if More had not examined heretics, when

Lord Chancellor, and compelled them to answer precisely whether they believed the Pope to be head of the Church? There was a difference between the cases, More replied, 'because at that time as well here as elsewhere through the corps of Christendom the Pope's power was recognised for an undoubted thing which seemeth not like a thing agreed in this realm, and the contrary taken for truth in other realms'.

'They were as well burned for the denying of that as they be beheaded for denying of this,' said Cromwell, 'and therefore as good reason to compel them to make precise answer to the one as to the other.' The difference that mattered, More insisted, was the difference between a conscience which conflicted with a local law, and one which conflicted with a law 'of the whole corps of Christendom'. 'The reasonableness or the unreasonableness in binding a man to precise answer standeth not in the difference between beheading or burning, but because of the difference in charge of conscience, the difference standeth between beheading and hell.'

The commissioners failed to trap the prisoner into any direct denial of the Supremacy. As he was dismissed More was asked why, if he was, as he said, ready to die, did he not speak out plain against the statute? The reply was characteristic of him. 'I have not been a man of such holy living as I might be bold to offer myself to death, lest God for my presumption might suffer me to fall.'

Servants in the Tower were interrogated about letters which had passed between Fisher and More. Each had naturally been anxious to know how the other was faring: but nothing in the correspondence could be made out to be a conspiracy to deny the Supremacy. Fisher had argued that since the Statute made it an offence only to deny the royal title 'maliciously', a man would be safe from its penalties if he spoke nothing in malice. More replied that he feared that the statute would not be so interpreted.

The conditions of More's imprisonment had been, up to this point, comparatively humane: he had been allowed to employ a servant and to keep papers and books. The Council now decided to employ greater rigour. Two servants of Cromwell were sent to remove his books; with them came Sir Richard Rich. Unknown to More, a few days earlier Rich had succeeded, by pretending to seek confidential advice, in entrapping Fisher into an explicit denial of the Supremacy. He clearly hoped to do the like with More. After a flattering allusion to More's legal learning, he put to him a case.

'Admit there were, Sir, an Act of Parliament that all the Realm should take me for King. Would not you, Master More, take me for King?

'Yes, sir,' quoth Sir Thomas More, 'that would I.'

'I put case further', quoth Master Rich, 'that there were an Act of Parliament that all the Realm should take me for Pope. Would not you then, Master More, take me for Pope?'

More gave no direct reply; instead he put another case in turn. 'Suppose the Parliament would make a law that God should not be God. Would you then, Master Rich, say that God were not God?' 'No Parliament,' replied Rich, 'may make any such law.' More, in silence, left the moral to be drawn, and Rich departed saying, 'Well, Sir, God comfort you, for I see your mind will not change, which I fear will be very dangerous for you.'

This visit did indeed prove dangerous: it was decided to make the exchange with Rich the basis of an indictment. Fisher was tried and convicted on 17 June and beheaded on Tower Hill five days later. On the first day of July it was More's turn to face trial in Westminster Hall.

The charge in the indictment was that More had 'traitorously and maliciously, by craft imagined, invented, practised, and attempted, wholly to deprive our sovereign lord the King of his dignity, title and name of Supreme Head in earth of the Church of England'. It was based on three counts: the accused's silence at the interrogation of 7 May, his correspondence with Fisher, and his conversation with Rich.

More replied to the first count, 'Your statute cannot condemn me to death for such silence, for neither your statute nor any laws in the world punish people except for words or deeds.' The King's proctor said that silence was proof of malice. 'Surely,' replied More, 'if what the common law says is true, that he who is silent seems to consent, my silence should rather be taken as approval.'

In his correspondence with Fisher More denied that he had said, as alleged, that the statute was 'like a sword with two edges, for if a man answer one way, it will confound his soul, and if he answer the other way, it will confound his body'. He had only written conditionally: '*If* the statute cut both ways like a two-edged sword, how could a man behave so as not to incur either danger?'

Rich now gave evidence on the final count. He told the story of the exchange, and attributed to More a damning additional remark: 'No more than Parliament could make a law that God were not God could Parliament make the King Supreme Head of the Church'.

Against whom thus sworn, Sir Thomas More began in this wise to say, 'If I were a man, my lords, that did not regard an oath, I needed not, as it is well known, in this place, at this time, nor in this case, to stand here as an accused person. And if this oath of yours, Master Rich, be true, then pray I that I never see God in the face, which I would not say, were it otherwise to win the whole world.'

He then gave the true version of the conversation, and said: 'In good faith, Master Rich, I am sorrier for your perjury than for my peril.' He listed matters which undermined Rich's credit, then, turning to the bench, he said:

'Can it therefore seem likely unto your honourable lordships that I would, in so weighty a cause, so unadvisedly overshoot myself as to trust Master Rich, a man of me always reputed for one of so little truth, as your lordships have heard, so far above my sovereign lord the King, or any of his noble Councillors, that I would unto him utter the secrets of my conscience touching the King's Supremacy, the special point and only mark at my hands so long sought for, a thing which I never did, nor never would, after the statute thereof made reveal either to the King's Highness himself, or any of his honourable Councillors?'

Two witnesses were called who had been present during the exchange. Neither of them would confirm either Rich's or

More's account: they had been too busy, they said, trussing More's books in a sack to give ear to the talk.

Despite the weakness of the evidence, the jury took less than a quarter of an hour to find More guilty. Lord Chancellor Audley began to pronounce sentence, but he was interrupted by the prisoner. 'My lord,' said More, 'when I was toward the law the manner in such case was to ask the prisoner before judgement, why judgement should not be given against him.' The Chancellor gave way, and More, liberated by the verdict from his long silence, at last spoke his mind about the Act of Supremacy:

'Seeing that I see ye are determined to condemn me (God knoweth how) I will now in discharge of my conscience speak my mind plain and freely touching my Indictment and your Statute withal. And forasmuch as this Indictment is grounded upon an Act of Parliament directly repugnant to the laws of God and his Holy Church, the supreme Government of which, or of any part whereof, may no temporal Prince presume by any law to take upon him, as rightfully belonging to the See of Rome, a spiritual pre-eminence by the mouth of our Saviour himself, personally present upon earth, only to St Peter and his successors, Bishops of the same See, by special prerogative granted; it is therefore in law, amongst Christian men, insufficient to charge any Christian man.'

The English Parliament could no more make a law against the law of the Universal Church than the City of London could make a law against an Act of Parliament. The Supremacy Act was contrary to the very first article of Magna Charta and to the coronation oath to uphold the rights of the Church.

The Lord Chancellor reminded More that the universities, the bishops and all the most learned men in the kingdom had agreed to the Act. More replied:

'If the number of Bishops and Universities be so material as your Lordship seemeth to take it then I see little cause, my lord, why that thing in my conscience should make any change. For I nothing doubt but that, though not in this Realm, yet in Christendom about, of these well learned Bishops and virtuous men that are yet alive, they be not the fewer part that be of my mind therein. But if I should speak of those which already be dead, of whom many be now Holy Saints in

281

heaven, I am very sure it is the far greater part of them that, all the while they lived, thought in this case that way that I think now. And therefore am I not bound, my lord, to conform my conscience to the Council of one Realm against the General Council of Christendom.'

The Lord Chancellor now invited the opinion of Lord Fitz-James, the Lord Chief Justice of the King's Bench, on the sufficiency of the indictment. 'By St Just,' he said, a little lamely, 'I must needs confess that if the Act of Parliament be not unlawful, then is not the Indictment in my conscience insufficient.' Whereupon the Lord Chancellor passed sentence. More was allowed a final word:

'Like the Blessed Apostle St Paul, as we read in the Acts of the Apostles, was present, and consented to the death of St Stephen, and kept their clothes that stoned him to death, and yet be they now both twain Holy Saints in heaven, and shall continue there friends for ever, so I verily trust and shall therefore right heartily pray, that though your lordships have now here in earth been judges to my condemnation, we may yet hereafter in heaven merrily all meet together, to our everlasting salvation.'

More was led out of Westminster Hall and taken back to the Tower. At Tower Wharf Margaret Roper was waiting.

As soon as she saw him, after his blessing on her knees reverently received, she, hasting towards him and, without consideration or care of herself, pressing in among the midst of the throng and company of the guard that with halberds and bills went round about him, hastily ran to him, and there openly in the sight of them all, embraced him, took him about the neck and kissed him. Who, well liking her most natural and daughterly affection towards him, gave her his fatherly blessing and many godly words of comfort besides.

The penalty for treason was to be hanged, drawn and quartered; the King graciously permitted More to be executed with an axe, the privilege of a peer. Four days elapsed between trial and execution. Margaret's maid visited the Tower each day; she brought back More's hair shirt and his last letter to his daughter, with keepsakes for the members of his family.

Our Lord bless you good daughter and your good husband and your little boy and all yours and all my children and all my godchildren and all our friends . . . I cumber you good Margaret much, but I would be sorry, if it should be any longer than tomorrow, for it is St Thomas Eve and the octave of St Peter, and therefore tomorrow long I to go to God, it were a day very meet and convenient for me. I never liked your manner toward me better than when you kissed me last for I love when daughterly love and dear charity hath no leisure to look to worldly courtesy. Farewell my dear child and pray for me, and I shall for you and all your friends that we may merrily meet in heaven.

On the day after this letter was written, Sir Thomas Pope brought word that More was to be executed before nine o'clock; the King's wish was that at his execution he should not use many words. More asked that Margaret be allowed to be present at his burial, and was told that permission had already been given for all the family to be there.

More intended to be beheaded in his best gown, but was persuaded by the Lieutenant of the Tower that cloth-of-gold would be wasted on the executioner, so he went to the scaffold in front of the Tower in his servant's coarse grey gown. 'Going up the scaffold, which was so weak that it was ready to fall, he said merrily to Master Lieutenant, "I pray you, Master Lieutenant, see me safe up, and for my coming down let me shift for myself." ' In obedience to the King's command he said little before execution, merely asking the people's prayers and protesting that he died in and for the Catholic faith. 'Afterwards, he exhorted them and earnestly beseeched them to pray God for the King, so that He would give him good counsel, protesting that he died his good servant, but God's first.'

7 The man for all seasons

Since his death Thomas More has continued to fascinate and attract later generations, and to be admired by people of different religions or of none. His influence on later ages has been less through his writings than through the story of his life. Just as Samuel Johnson is remembered less for his *Dictionary* and for his *Lives of the Poets* than for his conversation in the pages of Boswell's *Life*, so the sayings of More that have echoed in the minds of succeeding generations have not been quotations from his own works so much as the remarks, merry or sober or both at once, that have been preserved in his son-in-law's biography. Apart from *Utopia* and the *Dialogue of Comfort*, More's writings would have been quickly forgotten had it not been for the remarkable life and death of their author.

It is not easy, however, to identify precisely the source of More's appeal to the wide circle of his admirers. It is not to be wondered at, of course, that he has been admired and venerated by Roman Catholics and canonised as a saint of the Church of Rome. He was executed, after all, because he refused to consent to Acts of Parliament which negated Papal supremacy. But it would be wrong to think of him as a martyr for that exalted concept of the Papacy, typical of devout Catholics in the late nineteenth and early twentieth centuries, which found its most triumphal expression in the definition of the primacy and infallibility of the Pope at the first Vatican Council in 1870.

For the first Vatican Council the authority of the Pope was supreme over all General Councils of the Church; More never placed the Pope above Councils. The Vatican Council proclaimed that all Christians must believe that the supremacy of the Pope was directly instituted by Christ; for much of his life More believed that the Papacy was an ecclesiastical institution of gradual growth, and never ceased to regard the matter as one on which good Christians might reasonably differ. Devout Catholics at the time of First Vatican regarded the Italian dominions of the Church as essential to the Papal office: More realised very well how the temporal sovereignty of the Popes could interfere with their pastoral mission. In recent decades it has been characteristic of loyal Catholics to admire and venerate not only the office but the person of a Pope; More, living in the most worldly period of the Vatican's history, writes of the Pontiffs at best in a tone of embarrassed apologetic, at times with an irony verging on contempt. Indeed, the Popes and the Papacy are mentioned astonishingly rarely in his voluminous anti-Protestant writings. It has been well said that if More had been told in advance that he was to die a Christian martyr, and had been told that he could die for the doctrine of his choice, the Supremacy of the Pope would have been the very last article of faith which he would have selected.

Yet, in the end, it was the Papal Supremacy for which he died, and not for the seven sacraments or for the traditional practices of Catholic piety which he defended with so much greater enthusiasm in his writings. And there was in this, after all, something entirely fitting. For even in its worst times the universal authority of the Papacy had been a symbol, however obscured by the local dynastic ambitions of vicious Popes, of the essential unity of Christian peoples in a single commonwealth of Christendom. And this was something about which More cared throughout his life. He entered public life in the service of Wolsey's plan for universal comity between Christian nations: the proudest moment of his diplomatic career was his part in the Peace of Cambrai. He fought the heresy of Luther and withstood the autocracy of Henry because both worked to split the unity of the Christian commonwealth; in the Tower and at his trial his appeal was from the nationalist usurpation of the English Parliament to the supreme judgement of the larger body of Christendom.

Many who do not share More's beliefs have admired him as a prisoner and martyr of conscience. This indeed he was, but it is important not to misunderstand the operation of his conscience. More is best known to many of the present

285

generation as the hero of Robert Bolt's play *A Man for All Seasons*. Bolt conceives More as 'a man with an adamantine sense of his own self'—a man who knew how far he would yield to love and to fear, but who became rigorous and unyielding when at last 'he was asked to retreat from that final area where he located his self'.

At many points in his play Bolt stresses More's sense of self. When Margaret urges him to take the oath of succession More says, 'When a man takes an oath he's holding his own self in his own hands. Like water; and if he opens his fingers then, he needn't hope to find himself again.' In the trial scene More tells Cromwell, 'In matters of conscience the loyal subject is more bounden to be loyal to his conscience than to any other thing.' 'And so provide a noble motive', retorts Cromwell, 'for his frivolous self-conceit!' 'It is not so, Master Cromwell— very and pure necessity for respect of my own soul.' 'Your own self, you mean!', says Cromwell. 'Yes', replies More, 'a man's soul is his self.' And a stage direction underlines the importance of this confrontation: 'They hate each other and each other's standpoint.'

Bolt's play is vividly written, accurate often in detail, and uses many of More's own words: none the less, the man it portrays is very different from the real More, who would not have agreed that a man's soul is a self of the kind described by Bolt. It is true that More said, when accused of being influenced by Fisher in refusing the oath, 'I never intend to pin my soul at another man's back.' It is true that he refused to condemn those who did take the oath. Thus he can be made to appear as a forerunner of modern ideas of toleration and respect for sincerity, and the contemporary notion that each man must make his own moral decisions for himself. In these respects his attitude seems to contrast with the intolerance and authoritarianism of the medieval Church and the Renaissance state.

Set in their context, however, More's remarks take on a different appearance. For him, as for Thomas Aquinas before him, the human conscience was not an autonomous lawgiver. Rather, a man's conscience was his belief, true or false, about the law made by God. To act against conscience was always wrong, because it was acting against what one believed to be God's law. But to act in accordance with conscience was not necessarily right; for one's conscience might be an erroneous opinion. One had a duty to inform one's conscience correctly; perhaps by consulting the Scriptures, or the writings of the Saints, or the authoritative documents of the Church. It was thus that More tried to inform his own and the King's conscience in the difficult matter of the divorce. The only case where a mistaken conscience would excuse from wrongdoing would be where the moral issue in question was a debatable one, where there was a division of opinion among the saints and sacred writers.

On this theory, it was not enough to act in accord with one's conscience: one's conscience must be rightly informed. Thus More, when he told Cranmer that it was against his conscience to swear, added: 'I have not informed my conscience either suddenly or slightly, but by long leisure and diligent search for the matter.' But for the More in Bolt's play what matters is not whether the Pope's supremacy is true, but the fact that More has committed his inmost self to it. As he says to Norfolk, 'What matters to me is not whether it's true or not, but that I believe it to be true, or rather not that I believe it, but that *I* believe it.'

The reason why More would not pin his soul to another man's back was not that each man must be his own lawgiver in morals: it was simply that no man could be trusted to persevere in correct conscience. When More refused to condemn others' consciences, it was not that he did not think their judgements were incorrect. He thought so, and said so, to both Cromwell and Henry, before ever he was imprisoned in the Tower. But he did not meddle with others' consciences, in the sense that he did not try to convert others to his way of thinking. Nor did he censure them, or set himself as judge over them: 'I will not misjudge any other man's conscience', he said, 'which lyeth in their own heart far out of my sight.' But this was because the particular matters at issue—the legitimacy of the Act of Succession and the oath thereto—

were disputable matters, matters in that restricted area where a man might have an erroneous conscience without moral fault. It is quite clear that More had no general theory that conscience is a sufficient justification for action. He never suggested that Luther and Tyndale were excusable because they were acting according to their consciences in denying Catholic doctrine.

The comparison was made by Cromwell when More refused to give a precise answer about the lawfulness of the Act of Supremacy. Had not More forced heretics to answer precisely whether the Pope were Head of the Church? There was a difference between the cases, More replied: the Pope's power was recognised throughout Christendom, which was not like a matter which was agreed in England while the contrary was taken for truth in other realms. Whenever the real More appealed against the laws of England, it was never to some private soul or self within, but to 'the whole corps of Christendom' without. And what he feared to incur, by taking the oath, was not a metaphysical spilling of self, but the everlasting loss of God.

Naturally, a playwright is at liberty to adapt history to his purpose. No doubt, when so few people share More's beliefs in the damnation of perjurors or in the unique authority of the Roman Catholic Church, the hero of the play can be made more comprehensible if these beliefs are taken metaphorically and interpreted as a sense of selfhood or a concern for society's protection against the terrifying cosmos. None the less, the More of Bolt's play turns out to be a less consistent character than the real More.

In the play, it is difficult to make out the difference between the loyalty to self which is admirable in More and the obstinacy which Cromwell blames him for. The More of the play seems to combine a tender respect for his private conscience with an exaggerated deference to public law. Conscience and law, as the play represents them, seem to be irreconcilable values: conscience the expression of the individual will, and law the invention of the communal reason. Above all, it is hard to see why the More of the play sticks where he does.

Why does he both refuse to take the oath and refuse to tell anyone why he refuses? Why should his conscience make him so unbending against one of the King's laws, so anxious to comply with another?

In the More of history there was no real conflict between conscience and law, for true conscience is simply the right appreciation of God's law. Human laws must be obeyed, in general, provided that they do not conflict with God's laws. To show that the Act of Succession was a law which should not be obeyed, More did not appeal to any metaphysical self. 'If there were no one but my self upon my side, and the whole Parlement upon the other,' he said, 'I would be sore afraid,' but 'I am not bounden to change my conscience and conform it to the council of our realm against the general council of Christendom.' Yet, so far as he could, he would obey the King's law, including the law against positively speaking against the Act; for he did not wish presumptuously to expose himself to the death penalty. More's appeal against the courts of the realm of England is not to the narrow, interior, metaphysical court of his own self, but to the wider, public, universal court of the community of Christian nations.

The More of Bolt's play is not only very different from the martyr on Tower Hill: he is unrecognisable as the same person as the author of *Utopia*. The constitution of Utopia is designed, as scholars have emphasised, for the purpose of excluding Pride. This purpose governs even the economic arrangements, the absence of money and the lack of a market. Pride is the canker of the commonwealth, the peculiarly human vice which makes men more greedy than the beasts. The author of *Utopia* would surely view the hero of Bolt's play as puffed up with pride. In this point the Cromwell of the play is closer to the true More when he condemns its hero's fiendish self-conceit. A man's soul is his self, says Bolt's More. Not so, says the real More. In Utopia as in Christendom, a man's soul is never more healthy than when it is at its most selfless.

But if Bolt's More contrasts with the More of real life, is there not an equally great contrast between the Catholic

289

martyr and the author of *Utopia*? How can we—people ask—reconcile the tolerant humanist who wrote the dialogue with the bigoted Chancellor who fought heretics with his pen and through the courts? Wherever we turn in *Utopia*, it seems, we find something which is contradicted in More's life. More has attracted admirers in every generation above all as a man of integrity. But integrity means wholeness: how can we speak of More's integrity when there seems to be a mass of inconsistencies between his life and death on the one hand and the contents of his best-known work on the other?

Let us list some of the inconsistencies which have been detected between the practices of Utopia and More's own conduct. First, the Utopians have few laws and small regard for lawyers: More devoted most of his life to the law and became England's chief law officer. Secondly, Utopians despise the precious metals, while regarding ascetic practices as a mark of folly; More, in and out of office, wore a golden chain, and beneath it a shirt of hair to tame his flesh. In Utopia, thirdly, it is lawful to follow, peaceably, any religion one chooses; More prided himself on his reputation as a severe castigator of heretics. Fourthly, in *Utopia* the clergy are allowed to marry, and indeed to select the choicest partners; More, in controversy with Luther, harps beyond the bounds of taste on his marriage with a nun as nullifying all his doctrinal claims. Fifthly, divorce is permitted in Utopia on comparatively easy terms; in life More went to prison rather than consent to a divorce which half the divines of Christendom thought was allowable according to Scripture and canon law. Sixthly, suicide in Utopia, in appropriate circumstances, is regarded as permissible and even laudable; More, however weary of life in the Tower, was scrupulously careful not to utter a word that would bring him within the death penalty and thus create a risk that he would face God before God had called him. Seventhly, the constitution of Utopia is radically egalitarian; More, right up to his death, behaved to the tyrant Henry with an obsequiousness bordering on servility which could not, as it could in the case of others less brave, be attributed to fear. Finally, in *Utopia* the Papacy is spoken of with contemptuous irony; it was, in the end, for the prerogatives of the Pope that More gave his life.

It would not be difficult to prolong such a list of paradoxes. How are they to be resolved?

Some of the contrasts we have listed are doubtless overdrawn. The Utopians regard unprofitable asceticism as perverse, but they do admire those who choose austerity in the service of others. Though they do not imprison heretics, Utopians debar from office those who hold particularly obnoxious religious beliefs. But even when the emphasis has been rectified, the conflicts remain: More's austerities went beyond those approved by the Utopians, and Tyndale's heresies were well within the bounds of Utopian toleration. The inconsistencies are still in need of reconciliation.

Some despair of reconciliation, and write off either the Catholic More or the Utopian More. Socialists have admired the anti-market communism of the early work, and regretted the gradual corruption of More into a persecuting zealot obsessed with death and an imaginary afterlife. Catholics have invited us to regard *Utopia* as a joke, or as a youthful indiscretion for which More was later to make ample amends in his sufferings for orthodoxy.

Both approaches are mistaken. One cannot make a contrast between cheerful, far-sighted humanism in More's youth and morbid bigotry in his later days. Contemporary with *Utopia* there survive meditations on death, as full of Christian pessimism about the ways of the world as anything which More wrote in the Tower. Nor can *Utopia* be dismissed as a joke. It is More's most careful piece of writing; and the constitution of the imaginary Republic is attached to a dialogue discussing a question which More took deeply seriously, the pros and cons of a humanist entering the public service. Of course it is full of wit; but More's wit is never a sign of frivolous purpose.

Utopia is undoubtedly meant seriously: but in what way are we to take it seriously? It is not intended, any more than Plato's *Republic*, as a model constitution for an actual state, such as was drawn up by the founding fathers of the United States. Nor is it meant as a description of an ideal, though

291

unfortunately unattainable, society. The word 'Utopian' suggests to us the notion of unpractical idealism. But when More coined the word, it carried no suggestion that the constitution it referred to was ideal. If to us 'Utopian' suggests 'desirable', that is because many readers of More's work have found the conditions he describes attractive and inspiring. The treatise does indeed inquire into the best form of commonwealth; but the Utopian constitution is not presented as the simple answer to the inquiry.

To a modern, secular reader many of the provisions of the Utopian constitution seem humane and far-sighted. Not all find enticing the money-free communism and the absence of privacy; but the ideal of secular, bisexual, quasi-monastic communities sharing the fruits of their labours has been influential in our own time in capitalist no less than in socialist countries. Had the Utopian rules about colonisation and the conduct of war been adopted by Christian countries in the centuries after More's death, the world's history would have been far happier. The provisions concerning suicide, divorce and penal practice in Utopia may well seem to the reader preferable to the code enforced in Christian countries in More's time, or to the mores prevailing in Western countries in our own.

But did More himself mean the reader to find the Utopians' practices admirable? Some of them, such as the permission of divorce and suicide, went clean against Christian teaching: members of societies which tolerated such things should have been, according to the orthodox teaching, condemned or pitied rather than admired. Did More think that a society such as Utopia was even possible? According to a Christian tradition which claimed Augustine as its spokesman, human nature was so corrupt after the Fall that without grace no one could long keep the most basic precepts of the natural law. Could a society like Utopia, ignorant of Christ and out of touch with the means of grace, uphold such a rewarding life and provide an environment for so many virtues to flourish?

I believe that More did mean us to admire many things in Utopia, and that he may well have thought a society such as he described was possible, though naturally he was amused when some of his contemporaries took the work at face value as a description of an actual civilisation in a distant land. Augustinian pessimism about the possibilities of nature unaided by grace was soon to be restated and dramatically heightened by reformed theologians, and was affirmed by the Council of Trent in tones only slightly less stark. But at the time when More wrote, the Augustinian tradition was partly in eclipse, as Luther was loudly to complain. It seems possible that More combined a deep pessimism about the society in which he lived with optimism about what might have happened in societies with a different history.

One message which *Utopia* is meant to carry to the reader is clear. The Utopians are pagans, who lack the privileges of Christians who have received divine revelation through Christ and the Church. See how well they manage to behave, what peaceful and rewarding lives they live on the basis of their lesser light! We Christians, who have incomparably greater advantages, behave far worse than they do in such matters as the treatment of the poor, faithfulness to our wives, the keeping of treaties, the making of war, the exploitation of subject peoples.

This does not mean that the Utopians are better off without Christianity. Had they accepted Christianity they would have had to abandon some of their practices; to have adopted tighter rules about marriage and against euthanasia, for instance. In exchange they would have learnt many truths about man and God, and have received the promise of a more glorious immortality. Perhaps among the things they would have had to give up would have been their hardy equality, having accepted a hierarchical Church and maybe a quasi-sacramental monarchy. There is no reason, though, why they should have had to give up their familial communism; and as Christians they would have been able to appreciate better the selflessness of those who choose celibate and vegetarian lives to care for the sick and perform unpopular labour. Utopians converted to Christianity would put European Christians to shame even more than did the unconverted pagans described in the dialogue. And once converted, they would no longer find rational that toleration of error which was appropriate when they were uncertain seekers after religious truth.

The lack of an unambiguous and explicit political or theological message is, of course, part of the fascination of *Utopia*; in its ironic temper, as in other things, it resembles the *Republic* of Plato. In style and in form *Utopia* is very much a work of the Renaissance: one cannot imagine a medieval political treatise susceptible of such varied and contradictory interpretations.

Utopia indeed shows Christian humanism's most attractive face. When we turn from it to More's controversial writings we see a more repellent product of humanist education. Many of the matters which More debated with Luther and Tyndale had been subjects of controversy among scholastic theologians over several centuries. The scholastic debate had been conducted in a manner which, though it might seem arid and technical, was almost always sober and courteous. But humanist education replaced the study of formal patterns of argument with a systematic quest for rhetorical effect. The model of Latin style was Cicero, who had made his name as an attorney anxious to make the most persuasive case for his client or the most damning indictment of his opponent. Humanist scholars practised their wits, as More himself did, in the composition of diatribe and invective. It was not a training which was likely to make for fairness and moderation in controversy. More, writing against the Protestants, is always a barrister hectoring a hostile witness; he is far removed from a scholastic like Thomas Aquinas, always anxious to put the best possible interpretation on the position of those he disagrees with.

More, to be sure, was replying in kind to the invective of Luther. Both Luther and More shared a disdain for recent scholastic theology; both of them shared the humanistic desire to cut through systematic theological speculation to the closer study of the Scriptures and early Christian texts; both of them shared an enthusiasm for elaborate and rhetorical abuse on the classical model. The pugnacious conventions of humanist debate were one of a number of factors which led to the hardening of positions on each side. If More and Luther had been able and willing to bring to such issues as the doctrine of justification that patient willingness to understand rival positions which characterised scholastic debate, the theological gap between them might well have narrowed. Had they been less suspicious of the apparatus of logical distinctions developed in the Middle Ages, they might have been able to see ways of reconciling theological opinions which on the surface clashed. It was in part the scholarly climate of the Renaissance which made the Reformation so divisive.

More's polemical works are now read only by historians; *Utopia* continues to entertain and instruct. Indeed, for those who do not share More's religious premises, *Utopia* stands out among his works much more than it has ever done for his co-religionists. But even the most secular reader of *Utopia* cannot help, as he reads the book, reminding himself constantly of its author's eventual martyrdom.

It is not fanciful to link the ideals of *Utopia* with More's final constancy. If only More's fellow Catholics can fully enter into what More died *for*, all too many people in the present age have had experience of what he died *against*. The imposition of a novel ideology by fear and force is hateful in itself, whether its consequences be good or evil; few can refuse to admire the courage of those who like More die rather than submit to such an imposition. The ideal of a supranational community to which the individual can appeal from the oppression of local tyranny is one which in both its religious and secular forms has a pressing appeal to the present age.

The English Reformation and Counter-Reformation produced many martyrs both Catholic and Protestant. More remains one of the most attractive of all. Some men, of admirable constancy, almost repel by the way in which they seem to have cultivated martyrdom as a profession; others, however unjust and brutal their sufferings, give the impression that they would have been misfits even in the most humane and tolerant society. More is that rare figure, an Establishment martyr: a man to whom the world and all its promises were open, who had riches and power to hand, which he could have kept if he had been willing to bend to the wind, and who went to his death without bitterness and with a jest. The Utopians would have been proud of him: when a good man dies 'No part of his life is so oft or gladly talked of, as his merry death.'

Suggestions for further reading

(Abbreviations used in references to the works given here are listed at the beginning of the book.)

The standard scholarly edition of More is *The Yale Edition of the Complete Works of St Thomas More* (1963 ff.). Eight volumes of this have appeared, and when it is complete it will include all of More's extant works. Its price puts it beyond the reach of most individual scholars, but fortunately the Yale University Press is also publishing a series of selected works in economic format and modernised spelling. Three of these have been used to provide references in the present work:

St Thomas More: Selected Letters, edited by Elizabeth Frances Rogers (1961)

Utopia, edited by Edward Surtz, SJ (1964)

A Dialogue of Comfort against Tribulation, edited by Frank Manley (1977).

Though I have given page references to Surtz's edition of *Utopia*, I have preferred to quote the earliest translation of Ralph Robinson (1551).

English works of More which have not appeared in these Yale editions are quoted from the unfinished edition of More's works, *The English Works of Sir Thomas More*, of which the first two volumes appeared in 1931 edited by W. E. Campbell and A. W. Reed.

A handy selection of More's writings, including the whole of *Utopia* in translation, is *The Essential Thomas More*, edited by J. J. Greene and John P. Dolan (Mentor-Omega, 1967). I have referred to this from time to time, but have preferred to give my own translations from Latin.

Roper's Life of More is a classic in its own right. It is quoted from the most accessible edition, the Everyman volume edited by E. E. Reynolds, in which it appears accompanied by Harpsfield's fuller but less vivid Life.

The best modern life of More is still *Thomas More* by R. W. Chambers (Cape, 1935). E. E. Reynolds has written a number of works on More from an explicitly Catholic viewpoint: the fullest is *The Life and Death of St Thomas More* (Burnes and Oates, 1978). Those who find these works excessively hagiographical may discover something more to their taste in the lively but hostile narrative of Jasper Ridley, *The Statesman and the Fanatic* (Constable, 1982).

On *Utopia* there are three books of particular importance: J. H. Hexter, *More's Utopia: The Biography of an Idea* (Princeton, 1952); Edward L. Surtz, *The Praise of Pleasure: Philosophy, Education and Communism in More's Utopia*, and *The Praise of Wisdom: A Commentary on the Religious and Moral Problems and Backgrounds of St Thomas More's Utopia* (both Chicago, 1957).

The most scholarly account of More's judicial and political career is J. A. Guy, *The Public Life of Sir Thomas More* (Harvester, 1980). The best general account of the reign in which his career was set is J. J. Scarisbrick's *Henry VIII* (London, 1968).

An interesting account of More's intellectual career is Alistair Fox's *Thomas More: History and Providence* (Oxford, 1982). This pays particular attention to the controversial writings. A detailed account of both sides of the controversies in which More was engaged is given in R. Pineas, *Thomas More and Tudor Polemics* (Bloomington, Indiana, 1968).

On More's place in the history of English language and literature, see C. S. Lewis, *English Literature in the Sixteenth Century Excluding Drama* (Oxford, 1954). On his place in the humanist movement, see James K. McConica, *English Humanists and Reformation Politics* (Oxford, 1963).

On individual works the valuable introductions to the Yale edition should be consulted; the introductions to *Utopia* by Hexter and Surtz are particularly useful.

A number of the most influential articles of recent years is collected in the anthology edited by R. S. Sylvester and G. Marc'hadour, *Essential Articles for the Study of Thomas More* (Hamden, Connecticut, 1977). This contains pieces on different aspects of More's life and work by Coulton, Derrett, Elton, McConica and others.

A mine of interesting information about More is to be found in *The King's Good Servant*, by J. B. Trapp and H. S. Herbrüggen, published by the National Portrait Gallery as a catalogue of the exhibition held in 1977 to mark the quincentenary of More's birth.

Montaigne

Peter Burke

Preface

As an intellectual historian let loose in a field traditionally grazed by students of literature, I am particularly grateful to Dorothy Coleman, Margaret McGowan, and Ruth Morse for their comments on earlier drafts. I should also like to thank Henry Hardy, Quentin Skinner and Keith Thomas for their criticisms and suggestions, and Riccardo Steiner for drawing my attention to Freud's interest in Montaigne, and Montaigne's fortune in Italy.

All translations of Montaigne are my own. References in parentheses to quotations from the *Essays* are to book and chapter respectively.

P.B.

Contents

For Sue

1 Montaigne in his time

Like Shakespeare, Montaigne is, in a sense, our contemporary. Few writers of the sixteenth century are easier to read today, or speak to us as directly and immediately as he does. It is difficult not to like Montaigne, and almost equally difficult not to treat him as one of ourselves. He was a critic of intellectual authority before the Enlightenment, a cool observer of human sexuality before psychoanalysis, and a dispassionate student of other cultures before the rise of social anthropology. It is easy to see him as a modern born out of his time.

However, Montaigne is not as modern as he looks. His interest in autobiographical details may seem reminiscent of the Romantics, but his self-analysis was undertaken for different reasons. Although he was a sceptic, he was not an agnostic in the modern sense. To call him a 'liberal' or a 'conservative' in the sense in which we use these terms today is equally to misunderstand his position. Montaigne shared interests, attitudes, values and assumptions—in other words, a whole mentality—with his contemporaries, more particularly with those who belonged to the same social group and the same generation as he did. Other Frenchmen of his time, besides Montaigne, had doubts about the power of human reason to reach the truth, condemned both parties in the civil wars, and published short discourses on various subjects. Indeed, some of the topics on which he chose to write were commonplaces of the day; it is what he made of them that distinguishes him from his contemporaries. He was a true, if not a typical, sixteenth-century man. This does not mean that he has nothing to say to us. He challenges our assumptions as he did those of his own generation.

Montaigne was not a systematic thinker. Indeed, he presented his ideas in a deliberately unsystematic way. As a result there are serious dangers awaiting anyone who attempts to give a systematic account of his thought. Such an account naturally takes the form of quotations with a commentary elucidating them. These quotations have to be taken out of their original context. To treat Montaigne's work in this way is peculiarly dangerous because he relied on context to an unusual extent. He liked to be ambiguous and ironic. He liked to quote other writers, but also to play the quotations off against their new context to give them another meaning. One of the pleasures in reading Montaigne is that one constantly finds fresh possible meanings in his writings; the difficulty is to decide whether a given meaning was intended or not. There is no infallible way of doing this, and all firm assertions about Montaigne's beliefs should be treated with scepticism. However, we will have no chance at all of understanding him if we do not replace him in his social and cultural milieu.

Michel Eyquem de Montaigne was born in 1533. He belonged to what might be called the 'generation of the 1530s'. Generations cannot be calculated exactly; they are definable in social and cultural terms as much as by dates of birth, held together as they are by a sense of community deriving from common experience. The generation of the 1530s, in France, was the first group which had no memory of the world before the Reformation. This group includes the lawyer-historian Etienne Pasquier (born in 1529), an acquaintance of Montaigne and a great admirer of the *Essays*; Montaigne's best friend, Etienne de La Boétie (1530); Jean Bodin (*c.* 1530), the leading intellectual of later sixteenth-century France, a man whom Montaigne greatly esteemed, although he rejected his views on witchcraft; the scholar-printer Henri Etienne (1531), and the gentleman-soldier François de La Noue (1531), both Calvinists (Calvin himself, born in 1509, belonged to an older generation). It is perhaps worth stretching this notion of a 'generation of the 1530s' to include at one end Pierre Charron (1540), who was an intellectual disciple of Montaigne's, and at the other Pierre Ronsard (1524) and Marc-Antoine Muret (1526), who was one of Montaigne's teachers.

Whether they opted for Catholicism, Calvinism, or something more unusual (Bodin is believed to have turned Jew), this generation had to come to terms with an unprecedented division of opinion over issues generally considered to be absolutely fundamental. Montaigne's experience of religious divisions within his family (his sister Jeanne became a Calvinist, and so, for a time, did his brother Thomas, while his father remained a staunch Catholic), was far from untypical. A preoccupation with the problem of religious diversity was characteristic of the time, although Montaigne's attitude was very much his own.

As important as a knowledge of his generation for understanding the ideas of Montaigne is a knowledge of the social group to which he belonged. He was the eldest son and heir of a Gascon gentleman, Pierre Eyquem. However, his mother, Antoinette de Loupes, was of Spanish origin, and probably Jewish (though her family had lived in France for centuries), and his father's nobility was of relatively recent vintage. 'Vintage' is the appropriate word, for there were wine merchants in the recent past of his family, which lived and owned land not far from Bordeaux. One might say that Château d'Yquem flowed in Montaigne's veins, but it should be added that he was not proud of his origins. A fourth-generation nobleman, he was the first of his line to drop the surname 'Eyquem' and call himself by the name of the estate he inherited, Montaigne. He described his family, not quite accurately, as famous for 'valour' (*preud'homie*, the characteristic virtue of the medieval knight). He liked to refer to himself as a soldier, the basic role of the traditional nobility, although his principal occupation, between university and early retirement, was in fact that of magistrate (*conseiller*) in the court (*parlement*) of Bordeaux, a post he held from 1557 to 1570. In practice he was closer to the new legal nobility (*noblesse de robe*), into which he married, than to the older military nobility (*noblesse d'épée*).

These military nobles were traditionally no lovers of learning, and Montaigne's frequent protestations that he was not a scholar should not be understood in terms of personal modesty, true or false, but as commonplaces expected from the social group with which he identified. His reflections on the education of children (1.26) are explicitly concerned with the training of a gentleman, and they emphasise the need to avoid what he calls pedantry. The ideal is that of the amateur, the dilettante. In similar fashion Montaigne liked to give the impression that he did not study, but simply browsed through his books from time to time 'without order, without method'; that he did not polish what he wrote, but simply put down whatever came into his head; and that his aim in writing, as he declared in the preface to the *Essays*, was purely 'domestic and private', for the sake of his family and friends, not for the general public. This was the only form of writing of which a French gentleman of the time had no need to be ashamed.

The extent to which Montaigne held the views contemporaries expected from a member of the French nobility should not be exaggerated. If he had been typical, we would not remember him at all. To come a little closer to appreciating the blend of the distinctive and the conventional in his attitudes, it may be useful to look at one of the major decisions in his life: retirement. In 1570 he sold his post as magistrate—the sale of such offices was normal at the time—and retired to the country estate which he had inherited on his father's death two years earlier. He withdrew to his library on the third floor of a round tower, a room which he decorated with inscriptions in Greek and Latin. There, he told his readers, he spent 'most of his days, and most hours of the day' (3.3).

Why did he retire? The most obvious explanation is political. Montaigne later described his estate as 'my retreat, to rest myself from wars' (2.15). By 1570 the civil wars had been raging for eight years. Michel de L'Hôpital, chancellor of France, who had tried in vain to prevent Catholics and Protestants from killing one another, had given up the struggle in 1568 and retired to his estate at Vignay. In any case, Montaigne was thirty-seven in 1570. A few years later, he would describe himself as 'well on the way to old age, having long since crossed the threshold of forty' (2.17). It seems that he thought of his retirement more or less like a modern sixty-year-old. This idea was not a morbid peculiarity of his. In the sixteenth century, it was perfectly normal for people to consider themselves old at forty. What we perceive as the mid-life crisis, leading to awareness that the future is circumscribed and to what one psychiatrist calls 'constructive resignation' was perceived in the sixteenth century as the end-of-life crisis, and often with good reason. Although Montaigne had in reality twenty-two years to go in 1570, his great friend Etienne de La Boétie had died in 1563 at the age of thirty-two, and the poet Joachim du Bellay had died in 1560 at the age of thirty-seven. That Montaigne retired to prepare for death is suggested by the fact that a major theme of his essays is what contemporaries called the 'art of dying well'.

Montaigne saw his retirement as the beginning of his end, although it turned out to be no more than the end of his beginning. He was to leave his tower to visit Germany, Switzerland and Italy in 1580–1, and to serve two terms as mayor of Bordeaux on his return (1581–5). In 1588, he was involved in the negotiations between the king, Henri III, and the Protestant leader, Henri de Navarre (later Henri IV). In the intervals between these activities, he wrote the *Essays*.

As for the decision to bury himself in the country, which may seem odd in a man who disliked cultivating his garden, let alone hunting and estate management, this too was conventional. For the élites of Renaissance Europe, as of ancient Rome, the countryside was associated with learned leisure (*otium*), just as the city was associated with business, in the sense of political affairs (*negotium*). An inscription in Montaigne's library, dating from 1571, dedicates it to liberty, tranquillity and leisure, and describes its owner as 'quite weary of service to the court and of public office'. Montaigne thus situated himself in a long and distinguished tradition of the rejection of public life, more particularly life at the courts of princes, a rejection expressed by many ancient and modern writers, such as Horace (one of his favourite authors), the Spanish bishop Antonio de Guevara, whose *Contempt for the Court and Praise of the Country* (1539) was also well known to him, and the *Pleasures of Rural Life* of the Gascon gentleman Guy du Faur de Pibrac (1529–84), whom he admired as 'a noble spirit'.

Montaigne's retirement was an escape from society, but it was a mode of escape which was structured by society and reflected the contemporary ideal of studious leisure. The former chancellor, Michel de L'Hôpital, spent his retirement composing Latin verse, where his modern equivalent would settle down to write his memoirs. L'Hôpital conformed to the ideal of the Renaissance humanist. There is a good case for regarding Montaigne too as a humanist.

2 Montaigne's humanism

Since Jacob Burckhardt's famous study of *The Civilisation of the Renaissance in Italy* (1860), the concept 'humanism' has been popular with historians, but they have not all used it in the same way. Some of them use the term in a fairly vague sense to mean concern with the dignity of man, and contrast a man-centred Renaissance—at times rather too simply—with a God-centred Middle Ages. Other historians prefer to use the term 'humanist' in the way in which contemporaries employed the term *umanista*, which was part of student slang in Italian universities about 1500. A humanist in this sense was a professional teacher of the 'humanities' (*studia humanitatis*), that is, of history, ethics, poetry and rhetoric. These four subjects were considered particularly 'humane' by Cicero and other Roman intellectuals, and again at the Renaissance, because it was believed that man's essential characteristics were his ability to speak and to tell right from wrong.

Renaissance humanists in this sense of the term stood out from their academic colleagues by their rejection of the 'schoolmen' (*scholastici*), that is, medieval philosophers such as Thomas Aquinas, Duns Scotus and William of Ockham, and their master Aristotle. The humanists disliked both the language of scholastic philosophy, which was unclassical (and therefore, in their eyes, barbarous), and its concentration on logic, which they considered arid and lacking in relevance compared to the study of ethics. They rejected the culture of what they were the first to call the 'Middle Ages' in favour of classical models for both language and behaviour. Cicero showed them how to write; Socrates, Cato and Scipio showed them how to die and how to live.

The humanist movement, which flourished in the fifteenth and sixteenth centuries, lasted too long and involved too many people to be uniform or unchanging. Some humanists admired Julius Caesar; others preferred Brutus, his assassin.

311

Some humanists, now often described as 'civic', thought the life of action superior to that of contemplation. They would have considered that Montaigne was fulfilling himself administering Bordeaux rather than sitting in his tower. Other humanists believed exactly the opposite. Some concerned themselves with rhetoric, others with philosophy, and there were many conflicts between the two groups. Some humanists followed Plato, others Aristotle (though unlike the schoolmen, they read him in Greek), and yet others the stoics, especially the Roman philosopher Seneca (4 BC–AD 65), and the ideal of 'constancy' expressed in his *Letters to Lucilius*. The constant man, according to Seneca, travels light through life. He knows how to limit his desires and for this reason he stands as unmoved by the buffetings of inconstant fortune as an oak tree in the wind. This is a good philosophy for bad times, and it is scarcely surprising that it seemed particularly attractive to European intellectuals during the religious wars of the later sixteenth century. In France, Montaigne's brother-in-law Pressac (1574) and the Calvinist nobleman Mornay (1576) both translated Seneca's letters. In the Netherlands, which also suffered what he called 'the tempest of civil wars', the great scholar Justus Lipsius, an admirer of Montaigne, edited Seneca and wrote his own treatise *On Constancy* (1585). Around 1590 the French lawyer Guillaume Du Vair wrote a book on the same subject, which became quite popular.

Diverse as they were (or became), the humanists shared an admiration for classical antiquity, a belief that the wisdom of the ancients could be reconciled with Christianity, and a central concern with man. Like Socrates, they thought self-knowledge the important thing, not the knowledge of nature. They liked to quote a saying of the Greek philosopher Protagoras (c. 485–c. 415 BC), the somewhat cryptic remark that 'of all things the measure is man, of the things that are, that they are, and of the things that are not, that they are not'.

Montaigne was no humanist in the strict professional sense, like (say) Adrien Turnèbe, professor of Greek at the Collège royal in Paris, who, he wrote, 'knew everything', and was the greatest scholar for 'a thousand years'. However, he did share

humanist interests and attitudes. Although he may have had
little Greek, his Latin was excellent. Thanks to his father's
taste for educational experiment, Latin was literally Montaigne's first language. Nothing else was spoken to him, he
tells us, until he was six (1.26). As a result, he was reading
Ovid for fun at an age when other boys were reading romances
of chivalry—the westerns of the sixteenth century—if they
were reading at all. Montaigne went on to receive a thorough
humanist education at the newly-founded Collège de Guyenne
at Bordeaux, which, besides being conveniently near at hand,
was one of the best schools of the new kind to be found
in Europe at that time. He was taught by humanists who
later became famous, notably Marc-Antoine Muret and the
Scotsman George Buchanan, and acted in the Latin tragedies
they composed. It is likely, though it cannot be proved, that
he went on to study with Turnèbe and others at the University of Paris.

This education left its mark. We have already seen how
Montaigne regarded his retirement from public life in classical
or humanist terms. About five years later, he had fifty-seven
maxims painted on the beams of his library, just as the
humanist Marsilio Ficino had had maxims painted on the
study walls of his villa at Careggi in Tuscany. Twenty-five of
Montaigne's maxims were quotations from Greek, and thirty-
two from Latin, including one from the Roman playwright
Terence (c. 195–159 BC) which might stand as a motto for
humanism in its wide sense: 'I am a man, I consider nothing
human to be alien to me' (*Homo sum, humani a me nihil
alienum puto*).

It is a rare essay which is not stuffed with Latin quotations
(1,264 of them altogether). Montaigne often got his quotations
at second hand, as he frankly admits, but it is clear from his
references and borrowings that his favourite authors were all
ancients. Nine Romans and two Greeks are quoted more often
than any post-classical writers. His favourites are, in ascend-
ing order of importance, Ovid, Tacitus, Herodotus, Caesar,
Virgil, Diogenes Laertius (author of *Lives of the Philosophers*,
and used for what the philosophers said rather than for what

he said about them), Horace, Lucretius, Cicero, Seneca and Plutarch. Montaigne shared the admiration of his contemporaries for Seneca, and especially for the *Letters to Lucilius*. Some of the earliest essays are little more than mosaics of quotations from the Roman philosopher (Montaigne himself speaks of 'inlay'), and the informal, un-Ciceronian prose of the *Essays* also owes a great deal to Seneca. As for the works of Plutarch (*c.* 46–*c.* 127 AD), Montaigne studied them carefully in the new French translation by the bishop Jacques Amyot, and he refers to them or borrows from the moral discourses and the lives of famous Greeks and Romans nearly four hundred times in the course of his *Essays*. Like Henri IV, he might have called Plutarch his 'conscience'. His favourite poets, like his favourite philosophers, were classical; not only Ovid and Horace, but Catullus, Martial and Juvenal.

Montaigne's heroes are all ancients as well. The discussion of 'the most excellent men' (2.36) centres on Homer, Alexander the Great, and, in the highest place of all, the Theban general Epaminondas (died 362 BC). Later, it was Socrates who became Montaigne's hero, 'this incomparable man', 'the wisest man who ever existed', 'the most perfect who ever came to my knowledge'. Montaigne thought his own age mediocre compared to the glories of antiquity, and the ancients were his point of reference for judging the present, just as they were for the humanists.

Like the humanists, Montaigne had little time for the schoolmen, or for 'the god of scholastic learning' Aristotle, at least not for his *Logic* or *Metaphysics*. When, relatively late, Montaigne discovered the *Ethics* and the *Politics*, he appreciated them much more, and in this respect too he was a man of his time. Like Socrates, Cicero, and the humanists, he believed that the proper study of mankind is man: the human condition, not the physical universe. The first thing a child had to learn, he wrote, was 'to know himself, to know how to die well and how to live well' (1.26). Montaigne was not ignorant of the physical sciences. He was aware of the heliocentric theory of Copernicus as he was aware of 'the atoms of Epicurus, or the fullness and emptiness of Leucippus and

Democritus, or the water of Thales' (2.12), but these abstract ideas did not awaken his curiosity. He did not care whether Copernicus or Ptolemy was right, whether the sun revolved around the earth or the earth around the sun. Montaigne was rather more interested in contemporary technology, in ingenious machines, as is revealed by the journal of his foreign travels, with its careful descriptions of the automatic gates at Nuremberg and the 'miraculous' grotto at Pratolino in Tuscany, where water power caused statues to move and music to play. However, when he reached Rome, his enthusiasms were those of any humanist. He went to the Vatican Library and admired the manuscripts of his favourite authors, Plutarch and Seneca, and he spent days in the study of the physical remains of the classical city. He praised ancient and modern works of art, but had little to say about them.

Montaigne has sometimes been presented as a critic of humanism, as part of a 'Counter-Renaissance'. It is not altogether clear what he thought of the major humanists of his century. He owed a good deal to Erasmus, but rarely referred to him, perhaps because the Church had come to associate Erasmus with Luther. He disliked pedantry and made fun in a somewhat Erasmian way of the scholar burning the midnight oil: 'do you think he is searching in his books for a way to become better, happier or wiser? Nothing of the kind. He will teach posterity the metre of Plautus's verses, and the correct spelling of a Latin word, or he will die in the attempt' (1.39). On occasion, like Erasmus again, Montaigne criticised the stoic ideal of the constant man, 'an immobile and impassive Colossus', as unnatural, perhaps inhuman (1.44). If the humanists were uncritical believers in the value of classical philology, rhetoric, the dignity of man and the power of human reason, then there can be no doubt of Montaigne's detachment from their attitudes; but, as the example of Erasmus indicates, this is to simplify the movement unduly. There were humanists who criticised rhetoric or wrote against the stoics just as there were ancient writers who did so, Plutarch for example, showing himself once again a man after Montaigne's heart.

As for the dignity of man, it would be a mistake to draw too strong a contrast between Pico della Mirandola's famous *Oration on the Dignity of Man* and Montaigne's no less famous puncturing of human pretensions in his 'Apologia for Raymond Sebond' (2.12). It is true that Montaigne is turning Pico on his head, and arguing for the littleness of man, 'this miserable and wretched creature, who is not even master of himself ... and yet dares to call himself lord and emperor of this universe.' The disagreements of the philosophers, the wisdom of animals—like the dog who 'deduces' with his nose which way his master has gone—the unreliability of sense-data, and many other arguments are pressed into service to combat human vanity and presumption, and especially the idea that it is the use of reason which distinguishes man from beast. Montaigne brings out the stock humanist quotation from Protagoras only to pour scorn on it: 'Truly Protagoras told us a tall story, making man the measure of all things, when he had never taken his own' (2.12).

However, the humanists were not unaware of human weaknesses. Their rhetorical set-pieces on the dignity of man often went with companion-pieces on his misery, laying out the arguments for and against, as the French writer Pierre Boaystuau did in his *Theatre of the World* (1559), a book which was in Montaigne's library. Pico was putting a case for one side, and Montaigne for the other. The apologia is a set-piece, very different in tone from the other essays. Despite his claim to distrust rhetoric, what Montaigne has given us here is a brilliant oration on man's misery. It was not the whole story, and he knew it. Elsewhere he suggested that 'There is nothing so fine and so legitimate as to play the man well and properly, nor is there any science so difficult as to know how to live this life well and according to nature; and of all our infirmities the most serious is to despise our being' (3.13).

Montaigne was not a 'typical' humanist—if there is such a thing. He was too much the individualist for that. He was certainly no neoplatonist, as many humanists were. He thought Plato's dialogues were boring, and no doubt enjoyed what he called his 'sacrilegious boldness' in saying so in public. He considered it better to know one's own language well, and perhaps the language of a neighbouring country into the bargain, than to know Latin and Greek; in this respect he had certainly reacted against the education given him by his father. He did not think that the ancients were authoritative. Unlike most of his contemporaries, Montaigne did not believe in authorities (apart from the Church). As we have seen, he thought much classical learning useless pedantry. He declared that he would rather understand himself than understand Cicero. He had little faith in human reason. An eccentric humanist, without doubt. If, after all these qualifications, the term still seems appropriate, it is on account of Montaigne's constant use of classical antiquity as a point of reference, and of his admiration for certain individual ancients, such as Socrates and Plutarch.

It is not difficult to see why Montaigne admired Socrates, whose awareness of his own ignorance, insistence on self-knowledge, contempt for the professional sophists, informality and irony all remind us of Montaigne himself. In the case of Plutarch too there was a marriage of true minds. Plutarch was a philosopher, but also a practical man, a patrician who had held public office both at Delphi and in his native Chaeronea. His concern with how to live is revealed in his parallel lives of famous Greeks and Romans as well as in his ethical discourses, which were translated into French in 1572, just in time for Montaigne to make use of them. He has one discourse on the rationality of animals, from which Montaigne borrowed for his apologia, another on the affection of parents for their children, echoed by Montaigne's essay on that subject, and others, from which Montaigne also learned a good deal, on the decline of oracles and on 'superstition'. More generally, the self-revelation, the humour and the colloquial tone of these discourses remind us of Montaigne, as do the frequent digressions and the still more frequent quotations (Erasmus referred to Plutarch's 'mosaic'). It is clear that Plutarch, even more than Seneca, helped Montaigne to find his own voice.

This was, of course, the great function of the classical

317

writers for Renaissance humanists. They were 'past masters'. To call Montaigne a humanist is to place him in a cultural tradition without which it would be difficult to understand the *Essays*. But we have seen that Montaigne was a humanist of a particular generation, which faced intellectual problems rather different from those of its predecessors. One of the most serious of these problems is the subject of the next chapter.

3 Montaigne's scepticism

Que sais-je? What do I know? is the phrase which posterity has associated most closely with Montaigne. With reason: it was quite literally his motto, which appeared on one side of a medal which he had struck, in true Renaissance style, in the middle of the 1570s. On the other side there was a pair of scales in suspense, making the same point in visual terms. On the beams of Montaigne's study was painted 'all that is certain is that nothing is certain', and 'I suspend judgement'. The last phrase was one of eight quotations, all to the same effect, from the late classical philosopher Sextus Empiricus.

Sextus, who flourished around AD 200, was the author of the *Hypotyposes* or 'outlines' of scepticism, an introduction to the subject which survived when the writings of the philosophers on whom it was based (such as Pyrrho of Elis, after whom scepticism is sometimes called 'pyrrhonism'), were lost. He defines the basic principle of scepticism as that of 'opposing to every proposition an equal proposition', and of suspending judgement between the two, on the grounds that we do not and cannot know which is correct. Sextus argues the case for scepticism on a number of grounds. One is the unreliability of our senses. 'The same impressions are not produced by the same objects', for, to take a commonly repeated example, 'sufferers from jaundice declare that objects which seem to us white are yellow.' Again, our reaction to a particular kind of occurrence, such as the appearance of a meteor in the sky, varies with its frequency or rarity; so the same occurrence seems normal at one time and amazing at another. Another argument for scepticism is the diversity of human judgements and customs. 'Indians enjoy some things, our people other things . . . Some of the Ethiopians tattoo their children, but we do not . . . and whereas the Indians have intercourse with their women in public, most other races regard this as shameful.' It seems impossible to avoid relativism, that is, the conclusion that all customs are as good as one another. Once again, judgement is suspended. Of course one cannot live in a state of permanent suspense and Sextus recommends in practice that we live 'a life conformable with the customs of our country and its laws and institutions'. What he opposes is dogmatism, the confidence that our own customs and attitudes are right and those of others wrong. Sextus even criticised the Greek philosopher Protagoras, as Montaigne was to do, for making man 'the measure of all things', in other words for ethnocentrism at the level of the whole human race.

Sextus's position is an elaboration of that of Socrates, who was reported as saying that he knew nothing except that he knew nothing. Another classic statement of the sceptical position comes in Cicero's *Academica* (written about 45 BC), a dialogue which discusses the views of Arcesilas, a philosopher of the 'New Academy' who went even further than Socrates and declared that we could not even be certain that nothing was certain; a reflexive, self-critical scepticism.

In the Middle Ages, Sextus's book was lost and little interest seems to have been taken in epistemological debates of this kind until the fourteenth century, when the English philosopher William of Ockham (c. 1300–49) argued that it was impossible to prove by human reason that God is infinite or omniscient or even that there is one God rather than many. Unlike the classical sceptics, he did not doubt our knowledge of this world; what Ockham did was to separate the realms of faith and reason, as the philosophers of the Muslim world had been doing. In the fifteenth century, Nicholas of Cusa's *On Learned Ignorance*—a book known to Montaigne—explored the converse of Ockham, in other words the possibility of knowing God by non-rational means.

Ockham's ideas were well known in the sixteenth century; they were taught in many universities. It is likely that they made ancient scepticism somewhat easier to accept when it was rediscovered, that they diminished intellectual resistance to Pyrrhonist ideas. It is also likely that the ancient sceptics were viewed through Ockhamist spectacles. A synthesis of the two intellectual traditions was sketched by Erasmus. In his *Praise of Folly* (1509)—another book in Montaigne's library—

Erasmus exploited to the full the paradoxical possibilities of a mock oration in praise of folly delivered by Folly herself, used scepticism to undermine what he regarded as the dogmatism of the scholastic philosophers, and ended in the manner of Nicholas of Cusa (and St Paul) by presenting Christianity as a form of folly which is superior to wisdom. Erasmus thus joined together themes from the classical and Christian traditions.

So did Gianfrancesco Pico della Mirandola, the nephew of the Pico who had written on the dignity of man. His *Examination of the Vanity of the Doctrine of the Pagans* (1520) uses Sextus (although it was not yet in print), to attack both classical philosophy and divination, chiromancy, geomancy and so on, which were taken seriously by many of the educated as well as by ordinary people at this time. For Gianfrancesco Pico, the true sources of knowledge are prophecy and revelation. More like Erasmus's book in its air of wilful paradox, the German humanist Agrippa of Nettesheim's *On the Uncertainty and Vanity of the Sciences* (1526) takes each branch of knowledge in turn and demolishes its claims to truth. Sceptical of rational roads to knowledge and power, Agrippa seems to have believed in the efficacy of non-rational roads to the same destination, for he was a practising magician. His work too was known to Montaigne.

Around the middle of the sixteenth century, when Montaigne was a student, a group of Paris intellectuals was taking considerable interest in these epistemological issues. Petrus Ramus, one of the most controversial figures at the university, was attacking Aristotle and being denounced by the Aristotelians as a sceptic. A young lawyer, Guy de Bruès, published *Dialogues against the New Academics* (1558), a creative imitation of Cicero's *Academica* which discussed not only the problem of knowledge but also that of legal relativism. In the 1560s, two Latin versions of Sextus's *Hypotyposes* were published in Paris. In 1576, the philosopher Francisco Sanchez wrote a critique of Aristotle and of medieval logicians entitled 'Nothing is known' (*Quod Nihil Scitur*). Sanchez was an old boy of Montaigne's school, the Collège de Guyenne. Whether

Montaigne knew his work or not—and it was not published till 1581, a year after the *Essays*—it is another illustration of the appeal of scepticism to Montaigne's generation.

The point of this account of the development of scepticism in western culture is to stop anyone thinking that Montaigne went into his tower to go through what has been called his 'sceptical crisis' in isolation. He had retired from public life, but he was not isolated intellectually. He read Sextus, Cicero, Erasmus, Agrippa, de Bruès and others. In France in his day, the problem of knowledge might even be described as topical.

The problem certainly fascinated Montaigne. From the first essays to the last, he stresses the variety and consequently the unreliability of human opinions. 'No two men ever had the same opinion of the same thing' (3.13). He pours scorn alike on the predictions of the palm-readers and the diagnoses of the physicians, noting the disagreements among the practitioners of both arts over the ways in which the 'signs' are to be read. Individually, Montaigne's sceptical ideas are reminiscent of his predecessors, but the combination is his own. Like Erasmus, he exploits his opportunities for irony to the full. Like Gianfrancesco Pico, he makes a point of attacking diviners; unlike him, Montaigne is also critical of prophecy. Like Sextus, and more recently, de Bruès, he makes the diversity of customs and laws one of the most important arguments for scepticism. Like Sanchez, he also stresses changes in opinions over time, and interprets change as evidence of unreliability.

How seriously did Montaigne take his sceptical arguments? The answer is far from clear. We cannot be sure whether he passed through a personal 'crisis' or just employed doubt as a rhetorical device, though the recurrence of sceptical themes in the essays makes the first conclusion appear the more likely. It is difficult, in any case, to consider these epistemological questions for any length of time without a strong and unpleasant sensation of intellectual vertigo. Again, we cannot be sure whether Montaigne was opposed to reason or simply to dogmatism. He seems to use the term *raison* in a variety of ways, to accept *raison universelle* (the principles underlying nature and culture), while rejecting *raison humaine*; but here too it is necessary to distinguish a hostile attitude to theorising from a favourable attitude to what might be called 'practical reason'. He praised the sceptics because 'they use their reason to enquire and debate', though not to choose (2.12). This was precisely the procedure he followed in his essays. In any case, whether he was wilfully or unconsciously inconsistent, his scepticism did not prevent Montaigne from making all sorts of grand general statements like 'every movement reveals us', or 'the world is in a state of incessant change'.

The question of Montaigne's doubts and how far he went with them is obviously a crucial one to any interpretation of his thought. On our answer to this question, our interpretation of his religious or political attitudes necessarily depends. The reader is invited to bear this point in mind and also to suspend judgement—at least for a time—while reading the chapters which follow.

4 Montaigne's religion

It is scarcely surprising that Montaigne found scepticism attractive, for his generation, the generation of the 1530s, had to face a problem which was new, acute and urgent. Which form of Christianity should they choose—Catholic or Protestant? What is more, the theologians of each party had been undermining the foundations of the beliefs of the other. The Protestants had questioned the authority of tradition, and the Catholics had in turn cast doubt on the authority of the Bible. The results of this 'shaking of the foundations' were serious, according to Montaigne, and such as neither party intended:

for the vulgar ... once they are emboldened to criticise and condemn the opinions they had previously held sacred (like matters of salvation), and once they see that some articles of their religion have been called into question, will soon come to regard their other beliefs as equally uncertain and to accept nothing at all on authority. (2.12)

In this crisis, Montaigne was requested to translate the *Natural Theology* (or *Book of Creatures*) of the fifteenth-century Catalan writer Raymond Sebond. The translation, which was published in 1569, was Montaigne's literary apprenticeship. The *Natural Theology*, a stout volume of nearly a thousand pages, describes Nature as a book, given us, like the Bible, to reveal the existence of God. Nature is described as a hierarchical society with man at the top, the most noble and perfect part of God's creation. Sebond's book is a 'natural theology' in the sense of a theology based on reason, without the aid of faith or revelation. It echoes the ideas of contemporary humanists concerning the dignity of man.

Whether or not it was of use to his father, who commissioned the translation, the *Natural Theology* does not seem to have done very much for Montaigne, who was, as we have seen, plagued by doubts in the middle 1570s. It was at this time that he wrote one of the most famous of his essays, the

'Apologia for Raymond Sebond' (2.12). Couched as a defence of Sebond's natural theology, it is in fact precisely the opposite, a sceptic's demolition of the pretensions of human reason. It argues that man is presumptuous to think himself the most noble creature in the universe, since the animals have as much practical reason as we do, while our theoretical reason is unreliable, and its conclusions uncertain.

To a twentieth-century reader, Montaigne may well appear to be an agnostic; but appearances are misleading. His scepticism is very different from modern agnosticism. The term 'agnosticism' was coined in 1869 by the scientist T. H. Huxley to describe the belief that we cannot know God or any alleged reality beyond phenomena. That is, Huxley had his doubts about the 'supernatural', but trusted phenomena and human reason. Montaigne's view was more or less the opposite. He did not trust phenomena (more exactly, he did not trust human perceptions of phenomena), and he did not trust human reason, but he seems to have had faith in faith. The apologia concludes that faith alone can embrace the mysteries of Christianity and that man can only raise himself above humanity if God lends him a helping hand.

This view is known nowadays as 'fideism', a term coined in the nineteenth century to describe a rejection of natural theology on somewhat different grounds. Montaigne's drily sceptical obedience is distinct from Kierkegaard's more emotional leap of faith. It was not an unusual view for a sixteenth-century Christian to hold. There was a strong tradition of natural theology, exemplified by greater men than Sebond, such as Thomas Aquinas, who tried to demonstrate the existence of God by five separate arguments all based on human reason alone. This is what Montaigne was rejecting. However, there was also a strong anti-rational tradition within Christianity (or at least, anti-rational tendencies), running from St Paul (four quotations from whom were painted on Montaigne's ceiling), through St Augustine and William of Ockham (who declared it impossible to prove God's existence by 'natural reason'), to the sixteenth century. Luther, for example, was a fideist who mocked 'Lady Reason' for judging divine things by a human measure. Montaigne's father took Raymond Sebond as an antidote to Lutheranism, but Montaigne's apologia sounds more like Luther. However, there were Catholic fideists as well as Protestant ones. Gianfrancesco Pico della Mirandola, whose attack on pagan learning has been discussed already, was one of them. For a Catholic to express scepticism about the validity of natural theology was not unorthodox in the middle of the sixteenth century. Indeed, Sebond's prologue had been condemned by the Church in 1559 precisely because it claimed too much for reason.

The middle of the sixteenth century was a time when the Church was changing. The Council of Trent, which first met in the 1540s but issued its main decrees in 1562–3, was a watershed in the history of Catholicism because it defined orthodoxy on a number of questions which had previously been open, or at least half-open. This was the moment when justification by faith was declared heretical; when the Vulgate, the traditional Latin version of the Bible, was declared official, at the expense of both Greek and Hebrew texts and of translations into the vernacular; and that the much-criticised cult of saints and their relics was reaffirmed. Orthodoxy was reinforced more thoroughly than before, by means of the Inquisition and the Index of Prohibited Books. The result of these decrees was to divide Europe into two camps, Catholic and Protestant, where there had been a wider, vaguer spectrum of religious opinion.

Where exactly did Montaigne stand? He seems to have behaved like an orthodox Catholic of the period following the Council of Trent. On his visit to Rome, so his journal informs us, he listened with pleasure to the Lenten sermons, and he went, like any other pilgrim, to see the relics, like the Veronica in St Peter's and the heads of Saints Peter and Paul in St John Lateran. He also made a visit to the Holy House of Loreto, one of the most popular Catholic shrines of the day, and spent fifty *écus*, no mean sum, on images and candles. Whenever he wrote about the French religious wars, he called the Catholic party 'us'. He also expressed some sympathy for the new-style Catholicism associated with Trent. He had words of admiration for the austerities of San Carlo Borromeo, the ascetic, militant archbishop of Milan. He believed that there was 'much more danger than profit' in the translation of the Bible into the vernacular; who would be competent to check the accuracy of the translations into Basque or Breton? In any case, he wrote, the Bible 'is not for everyone to study'. In the same essay he went out of his way to declare his intention to write nothing contrary to the doctrines of 'the Catholic, Apostolic and Roman Church in which I was born and in which I shall die', adding that he submitted his ideas to 'the judgement of those to whom it belongs to direct not only my actions and my writings, but my thoughts as well' (1.56). Montaigne here gave his public assent to the Church's right to thought control, and to the attitude of mind recommended by St Ignatius in his *Spiritual Exercises* (1548): 'I will believe that the white object I see is black if that should be the decision of the hierarchical Church.' After all, sceptics knew that the senses could not be trusted.

However, Montaigne was no ordinary Catholic. No ordinary Catholic layman published his ideas on religious matters, still less such unusual ideas as Montaigne's were for their period. His ideas on miracles, for example. The conventional Catholic view was that miracles are suspensions of the law of nature, specially permitted by God. Montaigne's view was that 'miracles depend on our ignorance of nature, not on nature itself'. It is the strange event which is called miraculous, and ideas of what is strange are necessarily ethnocentric. 'The barbarians are no more strange to us, than we are to them' (1.23). Montaigne was echoing Cicero and Sextus Empiricus on the relativity of 'wonders', and the word he uses, *miracle*, was the ordinary word for 'wonder'. However, the circumstances of the day, not so long after the Church had reaffirmed the importance of miracle-working saints and relics, gave his remark a significance rather different from anything that Cicero or Sextus said. To make the same point in a different situation is to say something different. Montaigne's epigram is opaque, perhaps deliberately so. He seems to be saying that although miracles do occur, we cannot know, in any given instance, whether a miracle has occurred or not. The Church did claim to know, but Montaigne's 'we' may well refer to unaided human reason. On the other hand, it is possible that Montaigne intended to make a much more radical suggestion, and that is that the very concept of a miracle (or any other wonder) is meaningless because it is ethnocentric. Montaigne's belief in the variety of nature inclined him not to take its 'laws' very seriously, and if there are no laws, there is nothing to suspend.

In similar fashion, Montaigne thought conventional Christian views of Providence should be dismissed as ethnocentric.

If the frost nips the vines in my village, my priest concludes that the wrath of God is hanging over the human race ... To see our civil wars, who does not exclaim that the world is turned upside down and that Judgement Day is upon us, without thinking that many worse things have been seen, and that times are good in ten thousand other parts of the world. (1.26)

This remark may be no more than a Christian critique of human presumption for claiming to understand the ways of God. 'Thy judgements are a great deep' (Psalms 36.6, a sentence Montaigne had painted in his study). Alternatively, Montaigne could be denying Providence altogether, along the lines suggested by Lucretius, a Roman poet of the first century BC whose *Nature of the Universe* presents it as a meaningless dance of atoms. We know that Lucretius was one of Montaigne's favourite authors. On the other hand, he may have enjoyed the poem as fiction, without sharing the author's ideas. Once again, Montaigne is opaque. It is easy to see what he is against but difficult to decide what he is for.

Montaigne's defence of witches in one of the best-known of his essays proceeds on similar lines to his discussions of miracles and of Providence. 'The witches of my part of the world are in danger of their life', he wrote, every time anyone takes it into his head to accuse them. Yet, as he drily observed, 'to kill people one needs evidence which is clear and does not admit of doubt' (*A tuer les gens, il faut une clarté lumineuse et nette*) (3.11). This 'luminous' clarity is simply not to be found in the witch-trials, which are full of contradictory evidence. The confessions of the witches are not good enough evidence to condemn them, for, like the accusations, these confessions can sometimes be shown to be inaccurate. Human testimony is to be believed in purely human affairs, but not in cases involving the supernatural. The accused should have been given 'hellebore, not hemlock'. That is, they are sick, not criminals, and in need of a purge to take away the melancholy humour which had made them imagine crimes they had probably not committed. After all, 'It is taking one's conjectures rather seriously to roast someone alive for them' (*c'est mettre ses conjectures à bien haut pris que d'en faire cuire un homme tout vif*) (3.11).

Once again, human presumption is under attack. Montaigne is not necessarily denying the existence of witches, any more than he denies the existence of miracles. What he is calling into doubt is the power of human reason and its 'conjectures' to detect witches. Yet it is hard for the modern reader (at least) not to entertain the idea that witches (and miracles, and even Providence), may not exist at all, and hard not to think that Montaigne, in true Socratic fashion, was not encouraging the reader to do this. Here as elsewhere in the *Essays*, Montaigne gives the impression of wanting readers to draw conclusions which are never explicit in the text. The difficulty for us, four hundred years later, lies in deciding what he expected contemporaries to read between his lines.

The point Montaigne was making openly about witches would have been shocking enough to many people. It was a view close to that of the Italian humanist Andrea Alciati (who had made the crack about hellebore some seventy years earlier), not to mention Montaigne's former colleagues in the parlement of Bordeaux, who had been treating cases of witchcraft as 'false imagination'. However, this view was in complete contradiction to the conventional attitude that witches were a real threat, an attitude expressed by Montaigne's distinguished contemporary Jean Bodin, an almost universal scholar (best known today as a political theorist), in

329

a book published in the same year as the *Essays*, called the *Demonomania*.

Miracles, Providence and witchcraft were not the only religious issues on which Montaigne expressed unconventional opinions. He also compared prayers to spells or charms used for 'magical effects', on the grounds that most people prayed without real devotion; a bold remark at a time when Protestants were criticising the magic of the Catholic Church (1.56). He rehearsed the arguments in favour of suicide, although suicide was forbidden (2.3). He was interested in comparative religion, and pointed out that the ideas of the Flood, the Incarnation and the Virgin Birth are all known outside the Jewish-Christian tradition, together with practices such as the celibacy of the priesthood, fasting and circumcision (2.12).

The last point might seem particularly subversive, but Montaigne turns it to Christian use and explains similarities between Christianity and the religions of the American Indians by 'supernatural inspiration'. Did he mean what he wrote? What, more generally, was his religious position? We have seen that the *Essays* are both informative and opaque. Montaigne gives us a good deal of information, while making that information difficult to interpret. The problem of interpretation may be posed, for the sake of simplicity, in the form of a dilemma.

The first possibility is that Montaigne was more of a Catholic than a sceptic, a man who entertained all sorts of unorthodox opinions but did not really take them seriously. All he was doing in his book, he claimed more than once, was putting forward his 'fancies' (*fantasies*), in the same way that theses were put forward for disputation in the universities in his day, provisionally, tentatively, 'not to declare the truth but to look for it'. These fancies were, he wrote, 'matters of opinion, not matters of faith: what I think to myself, not what I believe according to God.' They were simply thought-experiments, offered for correction 'as children offer their exercises', and it was for this reason that he gave them the title, then unusual, of his 'essays' (1.56). Montaigne here seems close to the view of 'double truth' put forward by the sixteenth-century Italian philosopher Pietro Pomponazzi. Pomponazzi argued that there were cases where a given proposition, for example, 'the soul is immortal', is known to be true according to faith but cannot be demonstrated by reason, while its converse is supported by equally strong, or even stronger, rational arguments. Montaigne knew that some of the views he advanced were 'temerarious' (to use the theological term for doctrines which are unorthodox but have not been condemned as heretical), but he declared his willingness to submit to the authority of the Church. When he was in Rome, he did in fact submit the *Essays*, which had just been published, to the papal censor. They were passed with six objections, which cannot have been serious, since Montaigne was told it was up to him whether he corrected them or not, and in fact he did not. The censor found nothing worse than the frequent references to 'fortune' (rather than Providence), the naming of poets who were heretics (like the leading Calvinist Theodore Beza), and the defence of a convert from Christianity, the fourth-century emperor Julian the Apostate. Does the censor's reaction show that we are anachronistic to find Montaigne subversive? It would be a rash historian who claimed to have a sharper nose for heresy than a sixteenth-century papal censor, yet it is difficult not to wonder whether this censor was aware of all the implications of Montaigne's ideas. One reason for his mildness was no doubt the fact that in the 1580s the most serious threat to the Church came from the Protestants. Montaigne was not particularly sympathetic to Protestantism, while scepticism seemed more an ally than an enemy in the fight against heresy. The protestations about mere 'fancies', and the comparison with children's exercises, were no doubt taken quite literally by the censor. But suppose that (like the off-hand remarks about his 'scribblings' elsewhere), they were intended ironically?

The obvious alternative view is that Montaigne was more of a sceptic than a Catholic, and that he never abandoned the principle of suspension of judgement. He once declared that of human opinions on religion (those unsupported by faith), the one with most plausibility (*vraysemblance*) was that which 'recognised God as an incomprehensible power, origin and conserver of all things ... taking in good part the honour and reverence which humans rendered unto him by whatever name and in whatever form' (2.12). Sextus Empiricus recommended the sceptic to follow the customs of his own society, and Montaigne's behaviour is consistent with this advice. When in Rome, he did as the pope did. The statements of his submissiveness to ecclesiastical authority can be seen as part of this exterior conformity, practised for purely prudential reasons.

One is reminded of Montaigne's acquaintance the scholar Justus Lipsius, who behaved as a Calvinist when he taught in Leiden, in the Dutch Republic, but as a Catholic when he taught in Louvain, in the Spanish Netherlands. In fact, as we now know, he was a member of a small sect, the Family of Love, which recommended this exterior conformity to all its members. I am not suggesting that Montaigne was a 'Familist'—he may never even have heard of this group—but simply pointing out that there were sixteenth-century Europeans who practised exterior conformity to one form of religion while believing that another was better.

According to this second interpretation of his position, Montaigne was being prudent and insincere when he wrote that it belonged to the Church to tell him what to think, but revealing his true attitude when he declared that 'Society has nothing to do with our thoughts' (*la société publique n'a que faire de nos pensées*), that we all need a 'room at the back of the shop' (*une arrière boutique*), where we can be ourselves, and that 'the wise man ought to retire into himself, and allow himself to judge freely of everything, but outwardly he ought completely to follow the established order' (1.23). Where the 'Catholic' view of Montaigne takes this statement, from the essay 'On custom', as referring to secular matters alone, the 'sceptical' view takes him to be referring to religion as well as politics. This second view seems to make better sense of Montaigne's literary tactics of preferring hints to open statements and of hiding unconventional opinions in essays which appear to be concerned with something quite different.

It implies that Montaigne's protestations of frankness were a mask, and that he was one man in public but another in private. The public and the private Montaignes will be discussed in the next two chapters.

5 Montaigne's politics

We have seen that Montaigne's religion is not easy to characterise. His political position does not fit neatly into modern categories either. Some writers have called him a liberal, others have reacted against this and labelled him a conservative. Both terms are anachronistic. The word 'liberal' generally refers to a package of modern attitudes—approval of democracy, toleration, the rights of minorities, freedom of speech, and so on—attitudes which Montaigne did not share. His famous defence of witches is based not on liberal but on sceptical grounds, on the fact that the identification of a witch is pure conjecture. He did not advocate freedom of worship for the French Calvinists of his day. He opposed the Protestant theory of the Christian's duty to disobey unjust commands by the ruler: 'It should not be left to the judgement of the individual to decide where his duty lies. He must be told what to do' (2.12). Like Socrates and Sextus Empiricus, he advocated outward conformity to the customs of one's own country.

His support of outward conformity may suggest that Montaigne was a conservative. The difficulty here is that if we want to use the term in a precise sense, we have to say that a conservative is someone who opposes the liberals. In this sense, no one was a conservative in the sixteenth century. Right and Left, as names of specific parties, were born together at the French Revolution. If we resolve to use the term 'conservative' in a vaguer sense, we are faced with the opposite problem. In the weak sense of the word, everyone was a conservative in the sixteenth century, for everyone, Luther no less than the pope, defended his views by appealing to tradition.

What we can say is that Montaigne disliked change, whether or not it was justified by an appeal to the past. He was well aware that there was much that was wrong with the society in which he lived. The sale of the office of judge was something which struck him as particularly absurd (1.23). The 'corruption' or 'sickness' of his age is a recurrent theme in his essays. However, he argued that change was always to be feared. 'In public affairs, there is no course so bad, provided that it is stable and traditional, that is not better than change and alteration ... It is easy enough to criticise a political system (*une police*) ... But to establish a better regime in place of the one which has been destroyed, there is the problem' (2.17). His scepticism cut both ways. It condemned revolution no less than repression, and for the same reason. 'It demands a great deal of self-love and presumption, to take one's own opinions so seriously as to disrupt the peace in order to establish them, introducing so many inevitable evils, and so terrible a corruption of manners as civil wars and political revolutions (*mutations d'estat*) bring with them' (1.23).

There we have it. Montaigne was not simply drawing the consequences of scepticism, but thinking about the civil wars, which were at the centre of his reflections on politics, as they had to be for a Frenchman of his generation. Historians often distinguish four civil wars in France in the second half of the sixteenth century, but in practice the whole period from 1562 (the date of the massacre of Vassy and the battle of Dreux), to 1595 (when the pope absolved Henri IV), was one of continual war. 'Religious' wars they are called, with Catholics on one side and Calvinists, known as 'Huguenots', on the other. The Huguenots, who included noblemen (and noblewomen), lawyers, merchants and craftsmen, were particularly strong in the towns of the south, including Bordeaux. The government, or more precisely the regent, Catherine de'Medici, and the chancellor, Michel de L'Hôpital, began by making concessions to the Huguenots who were given freedom of worship in 1562. As the Huguenots grew stronger, the government's attitude changed. The notorious Massacre of St Bartholomew of 1572 began as an attempt by Catherine de'Medici to have the Huguenot leader, Admiral Coligny, assassinated, but it quickly developed into a massacre of the Protestants in Paris, an example soon imitated at Lyons, Toulouse, Bordeaux and elsewhere. When Catherine returned to a policy of concessions to the Huguenots, she provoked a Catholic reaction.

It was at local, popular level that intolerance could be found. The formation of a 'Catholic League' on a nation-wide scale, in 1576, to defend the interests of the Catholics, who felt themselves betrayed by the government, followed the establishment of local leagues of the same kind.

Why did the Catholic majority hate the Protestant minority with such violence? People were not yet used to religious diversity in this period, and they felt threatened by it. Most French Catholics (though not Montaigne) hated and feared Huguenots as they hated and feared Jews, Turks and witches (and as English Protestants hated and feared 'Papists'). The Massacre of St Bartholomew was an attempt to appease God and purify the community by destroying nonconformists. Such attitudes were not universal—Montaigne was on good terms with the Protestant gentry of his neighbourhood—but they were common, and this was one of the main reasons for the civil wars.

These wars also had a political dimension. The great nobles, like the Guises and the Bourbons, did not create the situation, but they did exploit it, in their natural conflict of interest with a monarchy which had recently been pursuing policies of centralisation at their expense. The Guises put themselves at the head of the Catholic League, while the Bourbons supported the Huguenots, who created a federal state of their own, in the Swiss style, in Languedoc. These great nobles made religion a 'cloak' to cover their ambition, according to the *politiques*, a third force which emerged in the course of the civil wars and tried to put an end to them. Jean Bodin was one member of this group; Montaigne was another. He once remarked that both Henri Duke of Guise and the Bourbon Henri of Navarre (later Henri IV), advocated in public, for political reasons, the exact opposite of their true religious beliefs: 'For Navarre, if he did not fear to be deserted by his followers, would be ready to return of his own accord to the religion of his forefathers; and Guise, if there were no danger, would not be averse to the Augsburg Confession.' He doubted whether all those who fought for nothing but religious or patriotic motives would together make 'a complete company of armed men', let alone an army. High motives concealed low ones. 'Our zeal works wonders, whenever it supports our inclination toward hatred, cruelty, ambition' (2.12). He thought the better party 'that which maintains the ancient religion and constitution of the country' (*la religion et la police ancienne du pays*) (2.19), but he tried to pursue a middle course in the wars, with all the 'inconveniences', as he put it, 'that moderation brings in such illnesses'. With a wry reference to the faction-fighting of medieval Italy he added 'To the Ghibellines I was a Guelph, to the Guelphs a Ghibelline' (3.12).

The French civil wars encouraged men to rethink their political theory, as civil wars often do. It concentrates the mind wonderfully on the question where power lies (or ought to lie), when that power is being used to destroy something that one values. From the point of view of the political theorist, the wars were a conflict between two views of kingship. The first was the view that the power of the king comes from the people, that this power is limited, and that in certain circumstances rebellion against the 'tyrant' is justified. This was the view of the Huguenots after the Massacre of St Bartholomew, as expressed, for example, in the pseudonymous *Defence of Liberty against Tyrants* (1579). A similar position was taken up in *The Law of the Kingdom in Scotland*, a treatise by Montaigne's old teacher George Buchanan, written about the year 1570 to justify the deposition of Mary Queen of Scots (1568), but published in 1579 because of its relevance to the situation in France. In the 1580s, a similar view of the right of resistance to tyrants was put forward by supporters of the Catholic League. Extremes met.

The alternative was the theory that the power of the king comes from God, not from the people; that this power is not shared or limited but 'absolute' (*puissance absolue*); and consequently that rebellion is never justified. This was the view of Adam Blackwood, a Scot living in France who answered his compatriot Buchanan with an *Apologia for Kings* (1581). The idea that sovereignty is indivisible received powerful support from Jean Bodin.

Montaigne never put forward anything as systematic as a political theory. Despite the description of the essays by their first English translator, Florio (following the Italian version), as 'Moralle, Politike and Millitarie Discourses', few of them deal directly with political questions. All the same, Montaigne was well aware of contemporary controversies over the nature and limits of monarchy. The latest books were clearly reaching him in his tower. He commented with amused detachment on Buchanan and Blackwood: 'Less than a month ago, I was leafing through two Scottish books which took up opposite positions on this subject. The democrat (*le populaire*) puts the king lower than a carter; the monarchist places him well above God in power and sovereignty' (3.7).

Montaigne found the two Scotsmen amusing because he thought disputes about the best form of government or society to be of no practical value, conjectures 'fit for nothing but the exercise of our wit' (3.9). He was no utopian. In politics as in religion he had an acute sense of the limits of human reason. Like Machiavelli, he was well aware of the importance of the incalculable in human affairs, a force they both described as 'Fortune'. Like Machiavelli, he thought it necessary, on occasion, for princes 'to use bad means to a good end'. However, he had his reservations about Machiavelli. The *Discourses* he described as 'very solid', so far as the subject allowed; 'but it has been extremely easy to criticise them, and those who have done so have been equally open to criticism.' Machiavelli's belief in general rules 'which rarely or never fail' did not appeal to Montaigne, who considered political forecasts to be about as unreliable as weather forecasts—he was thinking of the almanacs and prognostications of his day; to do the exact opposite of what they recommend, he declared, is no more imprudent than to trust them (2.17). By different means one may arrive at the same result, and by the same means, at different results. The Emperor Julian the Apostate used 'the same recipe of liberty of conscience, to kindle civil war, which our kings have just employed to extinguish it' (2.19). That particular remark may be a covert critique of the rulers of his day, but Montaigne's acute awareness of diversity always made him extremely sceptical of generalisations.

In principle, therefore, Montaigne was no supporter of monarchy, aristocracy or democracy. His views were pragmatic and relativist. Unlike many of his contemporaries he did not believe in an eternal immutable 'law of nature' underlying actual law; the diversity of human customs was too great for that. He thought that monarchy was best for France, but that different political regimes were appropriate to different societies, precisely because of the power of custom. 'Peoples who are brought up in liberty and self-government regard all other regimes as monstrous and unnatural. Those who are accustomed to monarchy do the same' (1.23). This is a view not far from that of Machiavelli, who recognised the difficulty for a prince to become master of a city which had been accustomed to freedom, but Montaigne's conclusions about human diversity are taken much further than Machiavelli wanted to take them.

The most excellent and best regime for any nation is that under which it has maintained itself. Its essential form and utility depends on usage. We are easily displeased with the system we have, but all the same I hold that it is wicked and stupid to wish for the rule of the few in a democracy, or in a monarchy, another kind of regime. (3.9)

Or again, with the simplicity and immediacy of a proverb, 'Let every foot have its own shoe' (3.13).

In short, Montaigne wanted to maintain the traditional political order, but for untraditional reasons, reasons which he expresses on occasion with an unusual and brutal (not to say cynical) frankness, which may remind the modern reader of Hobbes. 'The laws are maintained in credit, not because they are just, but because they are laws. That is the mystical foundation of their authority; they have no other' (3.13). For Montaigne, the study of other cultures and the 'legitimation crisis', the conflict over authority through which France was passing during the civil wars (and through which England would pass in Hobbes's day), demystified the law. It was clear to Montaigne both that specific laws were arbitrary, not natural, and that these laws must not be questioned, but obeyed.

The civil wars also demystified the monarchy. Many Frenchmen of the day believed in their king's power to work miracles, more particularly to cure sufferers from scrofula by the virtue of the royal touch. Even members of the *politique* group, like the lawyer Etienne Pasquier, argued that it was necessary to regard the monarch as 'sacrosanct, inviolable and holy'. Like his friend La Boétie, Montaigne seems to have thought otherwise. La Boétie wrote a treatise which was critical of monarchy in general and the 'miracles' of the French kings in particular. He described public rituals as 'drugs' to make the people submissive (an idea which is not far removed from Marx's description of religion as the opium of the people). Unlike La Boétie, Montaigne was, as we have seen, no enemy of the institution of monarchy, but like him he seems to have felt the need to strip away illusions from it, to show that the emperor has no clothes, or rather, that it is only his clothes which make him different from the rest of us. 'Why do people respect the package rather than the man?' (*Pourquoy, estimant un homme, l'estimez vous tout enveloppé et empaqueté?*) 'the Emperor, whose pomp dazzles you in public ... look at him behind the curtain, and you see nothing but an ordinary man' (1.42). Elsewhere he points out that 'the souls of emperors and cobblers are all cast in the same mould' (2.12), and that 'even if we sit on the highest throne in the world, we are still sitting on our own bottom' (*au plus eslevé throne du monde, si ne sommes assis que sus nostre cul*: 3.13). Montaigne was of course well aware that kings are not the only people to play social roles. Clothes, custom and ceremony support not only the monarchy but the whole social hierarchy. It is much easier for us to imagine a craftsman 'upon his close stool or upon his wife' than a president of a parlement in the same position, because he appears in public dressed in splendid robes (3.2). Unlike some of his contemporaries, Montaigne did not want to overturn the social and political order. However, he did not want people to have illusions about it either.

In his wish to strip public life bare of pretence, Montaigne was, like La Boétie, a moralist in the stoic tradition. Marcus

Aurelius (AD 121–80), although an emperor himself, had a view of the profession which was not far from Montaigne's. In his *Meditations*, he wrote that 'where there are things which appear most worthy of our approbation, we ought to lay them bare and look at their worthlessness and strip them of all the words with which they are exalted. For outward show is a wonderful perverter of the reason.' The unmasking of public life is the reverse of Montaigne's praise of private life, to which we must now turn.

6 Montaigne as psychologist

Montaigne retired to his tower because he was tired of public office and public life. He wanted solitude and tranquillity of mind. Marcus Aurelius had written that there was no need for seekers of tranquillity to retreat to a house in the country, 'for it is in your power to retire into yourself whenever you choose'. Montaigne, who was aware of this objection, admitted that 'true solitude' was a state of mind, and that it might be enjoyed 'even in the midst of towns or courts', but, he added, 'it may be enjoyed more conveniently away from them'. The important thing was not to give oneself up completely to public affairs (or, indeed, to domestic affairs), but to have a back room for ourselves alone (*une arrière boutique toute nostre*); 'wholly ours, and wholly free, for the sake of our true liberty, as if we lacked wife, children, goods, followers and servants' (1.39).

Montaigne's taste for privacy is not difficult to appreciate today. For a sixteenth-century French gentleman, however, it was unusual in its intensity. Admitting, at least on occasion, that the most honourable occupation is 'to serve the common-wealth, and be profitable to many', he declared his own intention to live a life which was simply 'pardonable', 'burdensome neither to myself nor to anyone else'. After all, he had no head for business, and in any case, he was old (3.9). After living for others it was time to live 'these remains of life' for himself (1.39). So far Montaigne was expressing a relatively conventional rejection of *negotium* for *otium*, but he went further. On two occasions in the essays, he makes clear his distaste for the public death-bed scene which was conventional at the time, complete with 'the wailing of mothers, wives and children ... a dark room; tapers burning; our bed beset by physicians and preachers' (1.20). 'I have seen a number of dying men, most pitiably beset by all this throng; it stifles them ... I am content with a death ... quiet and solitary, wholly mine, appropriate to my retiring and private life ...

there is no role for society in this scene; it is an act for one character alone' (3.9). For many of his contemporaries, on the contrary, what was pitiable was to die alone. Here as elsewhere in his essays, Montaigne shows his preoccupation with death and how to meet it. Preoccupation, not obsession; a concern with the 'art of dying well' was no personal peculiarity but a characteristic of his age. Death was not yet taboo.

Montaigne's preference for solitude was more personal. Yet it was not a preference of the same order as his taste for fish, which he tells us was his favourite food. Montaigne believed in private life while he did not believe in public life, at least not in his own troubled times. He was no civic humanist. Quoting the saying that 'we are not born for our private good, but for the public', he went on to suggest that this sentiment was no more than a cover for 'ambition and avarice', and that men really sought public office for private profit (1.39). The more fools they, for 'Of all the follies of the world, the most widely accepted and most universal is the care for reputation and glory' (1.41). There can be no doubt what Montaigne would have thought of Louis XIV or Napoleon. It is true that he did admire Alexander the Great, but not in an unqualified way. He thought Socrates the greater man.

I can easily imagine Socrates in Alexander's place, but not Alexander in that of Socrates. If anyone asks Alexander what he can do, he will reply, 'Conquer the world'. Socrates will answer the same question, 'Lead my life in a manner befitting its natural condition'; a form of knowledge more general, more important, and more legitimate. (3.2)

It seems, then, that Montaigne was being ironic when he made his excuses for retiring to his ivory tower. He did not really see withdrawal from public life as escapism. On the contrary, he thought private life more challenging. He equated the private realm with the natural, and the public realm with the artificial, as his recurrent use of imagery from the theatre reveals.

Anyone may . . . represent an honourable man upon the stage; but to follow a rule within oneself, where everything is possible, and everything hidden, that's the real problem . . . we who live a private life not exposed to any gaze but our own need to have a touch-stone in our hearts to determine the quality of our actions . . . I have my own laws and my own court to judge myself. (3.2)

Like Socrates, whose famous 'demon' was a kind of interior oracle, Montaigne was advocating what an American sociologist has called 'inner-direction', as opposed to the uncritical acceptance of traditional norms of behaviour or the standards of one's peers. He was undermining the dominant noble ethic of the time, the ethic of honour, based on 'the approbation of others . . . a much too uncertain and unstable foundation' (3.2). To follow the 'inner light' in this way was not an odd claim to make in sixteenth-century Europe (not in Protestant circles, at least), but it was unusual to make this claim in secular terms and in a secular context, as Montaigne was doing here.

If the true man is the man off-stage, behind the curtain, it follows that we need to study the private life of the heroes of antiquity. Unfortunately, classical and Renaissance notions of the 'dignity of history' excluded intimate details from the record. Montaigne has some sharp and penetrating criticisms of historians, ancient and modern, who all too often 'select the matters which they consider most worthy to be known and conceal a word or a private action which would reveal much more'. Montaigne would rather have known what Brutus talked about 'in his tent with some of his close friends, the night before a battle, than the speech he made to his army the next day; and what he did in his chamber, or closet, than in the Forum or the Senate' (2.10).

For this reason Montaigne preferred biography to history. As the French bishop Amyot put it in the preface to his translation of Plutarch's *Lives*, one of Montaigne's favourite books, 'the one [history] is more concerned with things, the other [biography] with persons; the one is more public, the other more private; the one more concerned with what is outside, the other with what comes from within; the one with events, the other with the reasons for actions.' Montaigne does not seem to have known the *Lives of Illustrious Men* by the sixteenth-century humanist bishop Paolo Giovio, or Vasari's lives of Italian artists, published in 1550. However, he did know his Plutarch, he did read the *Lives of the Caesars* by Suetonius (*c.* 69–*c.* 140 AD), and he did appreciate the *Lives of the Philosophers* by the third-century Greek writer Diogenes Laertius, who tells us, for example, not only that Zeno was the founder of the Stoics, but also that he came from Cyprus and was fond of fresh figs.

Trivia? Not for Montaigne, who believed that a man's character was expressed in such apparently unimportant details, just as it was made manifest, to those who had eyes to see, by the habitual and unconscious movements of the body. 'Every movement reveals us (*tout mouvement nous descouvre*). The very same mind of Caesar, which we see in the order and direction of the battle of Pharsalia, is also visible in the planning of his leisure and his love affairs' (1.50). And again: 'Our body easily retains some impression of our natural inclinations, involuntarily and unconsciously (*sans nostre sceu et consentement*)... Julius Caesar used to scratch his head with his finger, which is the gesture of a man oppressed by painful thoughts; and Cicero, as I recall, had a tic of wrinkling his nose, which is the sign of a scoffing nature' (2.17). Their body language spoke volumes. Montaigne also believed that dreams revealed the dreamer's wishes. In his essay 'on the force of the imagination', he also discussed the possibility of a psychological explanation for the stigmata of St Francis and for the cures effected by the royal touch (1.21). He rejected the claims of the diviners, but he did not reject the possibility of reading signs. What he did was to interpret these signs in a naturalistic manner.

It is not difficult to see why Sigmund Freud should have read Montaigne with attention. They agreed about dreams and about the importance of the earliest years, when habits are formed: 'our greatest vices take root in our most tender infancy and the most important part of our education is in the hands of nurses' (1.23). Like Freud, Montaigne saw himself as a lone explorer of the self, a pioneer in the 'thorny enterprise (more difficult than it looks), of following a path as wandering as that of the mind and of penetrating the dark depths of its inner folds' (2.6).

However, we should not take the self-image of the lone explorer too seriously in either case. Original as they both were, neither man really cut himself loose from the traditions of his culture. What Montaigne did was to create a personal synthesis from the insights expressed in medical, philosophical, rhetorical and theological traditions which went back to the ancient Greeks. Hippocrates (*c.* 460–380 BC) formulated rules for diagnosing illness from symptoms. Aristotle's *Rhetoric* discusses the symptoms of emotion. To diagnose personality from symptoms was the next step, taken, at the latest, by Theophrastus (*c.* 372–*c.* 288 BC), a pupil of Aristotle's and the author of the *Characters*, a set of vivid vignettes of 'the boor', 'the superstitious man', and so on. These ideas were part of the cultural context of the biographies by Plutarch and Diogenes Laertius, on whom Montaigne drew so freely. In his own day, artists, playwrights and actors were all well aware of the symptoms of emotion and character, and some physicians, notably in their studies of melancholy, were formulating the laws of what we call 'psychology'. The term 'psychology' was in fact coined in the sixteenth century, but had no success till the eighteenth. In his discussion of the outward signs of personality, as in other parts of his essays, Montaigne was not making a suggestion which was completely unthinkable by his contemporaries, but rather picking up an idea which, though current, ran counter to the conventional belief in the dignity of history, taking it more seriously, exploring its implications more thoroughly and developing it further than anyone else.

A similar point might be made about Montaigne's analysis of what Freud called 'rationalisation', our propensity to credit ourselves with better motives than true self-knowledge would allow. *Piperie*, 'cheating', is his favourite word for it. Where Calvin, for example, had discussed self-deception in religious terms, Montaigne's analysis is essentially secular. We have seen that the *politiques* argued that religion was a rationalisation, or in their more vivid phrase, a 'cloak' for many selfish designs. Montaigne, however, went much further in his analysis of *piperie*, and his essays have a place between the

Confessions of St Augustine (a book he seems not to have known), and the *Maxims* of La Rochefoucauld (who knew the *Essays* well), as a classic exposure of the workings of self-love and hypocrisy. He was well aware that zeal for the public good may conceal ambition (1.39); that a man may be humble out of pride (2.17); that the public profession of virtue may mask a vicious private life (3.5), and, more generally, that there is often a gap between a man's individual weaknesses and his public 'role' (*role* is a term which occurs several times in the *Essays* in this sense). It is scarcely surprising that no man is a hero to his valet, or more exactly, in Montaigne's version of the epigram, that *peu d'hommes ont esté admirez par leurs domestiques* (3.2).

Given his desire for total honesty and his awareness of the masks which others wear, Montaigne could deal with some of his central themes only by discussing himself. 'Other people do not see you at all, but guess at you by uncertain conjectures' (3.2). The apparent digressions into the details of his private life, his health, his colic, his idiosyncrasies in food and clothes, digressions which irritated contemporary readers, are there for epistemological reasons, on the grounds that 'every man embodies the whole pattern of the human condition' (*chaque homme porte la forme entiere de l'humaine condition*) (3.2). *Forme* seems to be used in this passage in the Aristotelian sense of the design embedded in matter. Montaigne in his tower has something important in common with Descartes in his stove, or with Proust observing himself on his death-bed. His detailed description of his sensations after falling from his horse reads like the account of an experiment designed to discover what it feels like to die (2.6). This crucial epistemological point is partly disguised by Montaigne's characteristic presentation of the autobiographical passages as nothing but harmless self-indulgence. He noted that King René of Anjou had painted a self-portrait: 'Why is it not as legitimate' (he added), 'for every man to portray himself with his pen, as it was for him to do it with a crayon?' (2.17).

Montaigne knew that autobiography had been tried before, though, curiously enough, he cannot have been aware of

347

its development in Renaissance Italy. The autobiographies of Pope Pius II (writing in the 1460s), Benvenuto Cellini (writing in the 1560s), and the Milanese physician Girolamo Cardano (writing in 1575), ran parallel to the rise of the self-portrait in the same region and the same period (Pinturicchio, Vasari and Titian, for example). The affinities between Cardano's presentation of himself and Montaigne's are particularly striking. Cardano's book includes chapters on his health, his appearance ('a rather too shrill voice . . . a fixed gaze, as if in meditation'), and 'those things in which I take pleasure', including fishing, solitude and reading history. However, none of the three Italian autobiographies was in print at the time that Montaigne was writing. The coincidence in time between Cellini, Cardano and Montaigne suggests that awareness of individuality is a social phenomenon.

Of a piece with his frankness in other respects was Montaigne's attitude to sex, *l'action genitale* as he called it. One of his essays, 'On the force of the imagination', is essentially concerned with impotence, which he interpreted in psychological terms and not, like so many of his contemporaries, as the result of sorcery. Montaigne explained impotence by anxiety and consequent self-consciousness which inhibits action, noting, here as in his discussion of nervous tics, the independence of our bodies from our will (1.21).

His most extended discussion of sexuality occurs in the essay 'On some verses of Virgil' (highly explicit verses from the eighth book of the *Aeneid*, describing Venus and Vulcan making love). The essay raised the problem of the sex taboo in Montaigne's own culture, a taboo which he found extremely odd:

Why was the act of generation made so natural, so necessary and so right, if we dare not speak of it without embarrassment, and exclude it from serious conversation? We are bold enough to pronounce words like kill, rob, betray; but this word we only speak under our breath . . . Are we not brutes to call 'brutish' the act which engenders us? (3.5)

How recent the taboo was in Montaigne's day is difficult to say. There are some grounds for suggesting that it was growing stronger in the later sixteenth century than it had been in the age of Rabelais. In Montaigne's day, as he pointed out in this essay, a pope could be shocked by the nudity of Rome's population of classical statues.

What is striking about this particular essay is, first, Montaigne's determination to discuss, coolly and publicly, what had become the most private of subjects (many of his contemporaries broke the taboo, but no one else, to my knowledge, discussed it), and second, his comparative approach. He discusses attitudes to sexuality in different cultures; parts of the world where nudity is the norm, where there is a cult of the phallus, or where eating is an activity with the same associations of shame and privacy that sex has for us. Montaigne views this panorama of human diversity with a serene and ironic curiosity. His general attitude to other cultures is the subject of the next chapter.

7 Montaigne as ethnographer

One of the most striking characteristics of Montaigne—for us late-twentieth-century readers at least—is the breadth and depth of his interest in other cultures, his freedom from ethnocentrism combined with an acute awareness of the ethnocentrism of others. His essay on custom lists society after society where what Europeans would consider odd, funny, or shocking is treated as normal: 'where virgins show their private parts openly ... where there are male prostitutes ... where women go to war ... where women piss standing up, and men squat', and he concludes that 'The laws of conscience, which we say derive from nature, derive from custom ... whatever is beyond the compass of custom is thought to be beyond the compass of reason' (1.23).

Still more famous is his essay on cannibals, which gives a detailed description of some of the newly-discovered Indians of Brazil; their food, their long-houses, their songs and dances. Montaigne notes that these Brazilians had 'no trade, no knowledge of writing, no arithmetic, no magistrate, no political subordination ... no riches or poverty, no contracts, no inheritance ... no clothes, no agriculture, no metal.' However, he refuses to call them barbarians or savages. They are 'wild' (*sauvages*) only in the sense that we call certain fruits 'wild'—because they are natural, not domesticated (1.31).

After reading passages like these, one is tempted to describe Montaigne as an anthropologist, or at least as a 'precursor' of modern social anthropology. The danger in doing this is that of failing to discriminate between the cultural context in which the discipline of social anthropology was founded, at the end of the nineteenth century, and that of Montaigne's day. He was writing as a moralist; modern anthropologists, generally speaking, do not. For this reason the word 'anthropologist' will be replaced, throughout this chapter, by the vaguer term 'ethnographer'.

Ethnography, in the sense of curiosity about exotic customs, was certainly flourishing in Montaigne's day. Such curiosity had not been unusual in the later Middle Ages, as Marco Polo's account of China will remind us, or the travels of 'Mandeville', which were fictional but taken as factual and were apparently widely read. In the sixteenth century, the interest in the exotic seems to have become still stronger, witness the popularity of the *Customs of Different Nations* (1520), compiled by Johann Boehm, canon of Ulm.

There are two obvious reasons for the trend. The first is the revival of classical antiquity. The ancient Greeks had shown great interest in other cultures. Socrates, as Montaigne reminds us, treated the whole world as his native city, and the stoics had similar cosmopolitan ideals. Herodotus, who was much studied in the sixteenth century, had a keen eye for ethnographic detail; it was he who recorded the fact that in Egypt, unlike Greece, it was the women who carried loads on their heads and passed water standing up. Besides details of exotic customs, the classics offered conceptual schemata for interpreting them. Sixteenth-century writers who discussed whether the American Indians were 'slaves by nature', or whether they were still living in the golden age, before the introduction of private property, were looking at the Indians through classical eyes.

The interest in alien customs was also encouraged, naturally enough, by the discovery of America. Books about the discovery often devote chapters to the way of life of the Indians, whether the attitude of the author is sympathetic, hostile, or neutral. A well-known example is the *General History of the Indies* (1552), by the Spanish cleric Francisco López de Gómara. The dedication of the history to the emperor Charles V sums up Gómara's attitude. Before the Spaniards arrived, he declares, the Indians were idolaters, cannibals and sodomites. He interprets the conquest of the New World and the conversion of its inhabitants to Christianity and the Spanish way of life as the work of God. It should be added that the author was in the service of Hernán Cortés, the conqueror of Mexico.

Gómara was an apologist for Spanish conquest in general and that of Cortés in particular. A very different account of

351

Indian customs emerges from the *History of the New World* (1565) by Girolamo Benzoni. A Milanese, hence himself subject to Spanish rule, Benzoni, who had spent fourteen years in the New World, condemns the cruelty of the Spaniards and gives a detailed and sympathetic description of the Indian way of life.

Montaigne's Brazilians had been studied in particular detail in the twenty years or so before he wrote. A German, Hans Staden, had been captured by the Tupinamba and learned their language while waiting to be eaten, but escaped to publish a curiously detached account of their customs in 1557. Montaigne does not seem to have known about Staden's book, but he did know accounts of Brazil by two French visitors, André Thevet and Jean de Léry. Thevet was a Franciscan. His *Singularities of Antarctic France* (1558) showed considerable interest in the 'way of life' (*manière de vivre*) of the inhabitants of Brazil. He thought that they lived 'like beasts' (*brutalement*). All the same, the comparison between Brazil and 'our Europe', as Thevet calls it, is not altogether to our advantage. Idolatrous as they are, the Brazilians are better than the 'damnable atheists of our time'. A similar point was made by the French Protestant Jean de Léry in his *Story of a Voyage to Brazil* (1578). Léry thought the Brazilians barbarians who illustrated the corruption of human nature after the Fall. At the same time, he emphasised what he called their 'humanity', and declared that their peace, harmony and charity put Christians to shame at a time when innocent people were being massacred in France.

In his *Germania*, the great Roman historian Tacitus (first century AD) had described the courage and the simple manly life of the German barbarians as a reproach to his effeminate contemporaries. In a similar way, Léry used the Brazilians to condemn the St Bartholomew's Day massacre and other atrocities of the French religious wars. We might call this technique the 'Germania syndrome'. It can also be found in Ronsard, who declared his wish to leave France and its troubles for the Antarctic, 'where savages live and happily follow the law of nature', and in La Boétie, who wrote a Latin poem lamenting the civil wars and expressing a desire to start life afresh in the New World.

At this point we may return to Montaigne, to whom La Boétie's poem was addressed, and ask how he differed from these contemporaries. Montaigne read Gómara, Benzoni, Thevet and Léry. What he took from Gómara was information, not ideas. Where Gómara had celebrated the Spanish conquest of America, Montaigne, in his essay on coaches, denounced it: 'So many cities razed to the ground; so many nations exterminated; so many millions of people put to the sword; and the richest and fairest part of the world turned upside down for the sake of the trade in pearls and pepper: Base victories.' (3.6). The Spaniards had sometimes pointed to the Indians' cannibalism as a justification for enslaving them. Montaigne's apologia for the cannibals is in part a critique of Spanish policy. He is closer to his compatriots Thevet and Léry than he is to Gómara. Like Léry, he exemplifies the 'Germania syndrome' and uses the Brazilians as a stick to beat his own society as well as to beat Spain. He treats cannibalism on the level of the mote in the neighbour's eye. 'I am not sorry that we note the horrid barbarity of such an action, but I am sorry that, judging their faults correctly, we should be so blind to our own. I think that there is more barbarity in eating a man alive, than in eating him when he is dead.' Like Léry, Montaigne goes on to comment on the cruelty of the French wars of religion (1.31).

Montaigne wrote as a moralist, not a social scientist. He wanted to influence his readers' behaviour and he used nations as his *exempla*. He recommended travel as one of the best methods of education—moral education. 'So many humours, sects, judgements, opinions, laws and customs teach us to judge sensibly of our own', to see beyond the end of our noses and recognise the limitations of our reason (1.26).

Shortly after the publication of books one and two of the *Essays*, in 1580, Montaigne went travelling himself, in Germany, Switzerland and Italy. It is interesting to see him practising what he preached. His journal shows the trouble he took to enquire, everywhere he went, into the local customs and beliefs. In Germany, he questioned the Lutherans about their theology; in Switzerland, the Zwinglians and the Calvinists. In Verona, he visited a synagogue and asked the Jews about their rituals. He also went to High Mass in the cathedral there and noted—for once with surprise—how the Italian men stood talking with their backs to the altar and their hats on their heads during the service. In Tuscany, he questioned a peasant woman who had a reputation as a poet, and asked her to compose verses for him. In Rome, he went to a circumcision, an exorcism and a procession of flagellants, noting—from the condition of their footwear—that the flagellants were poor people who probably whipped themselves for money. His ethnographical eye also observed the crowds. 'Walking in the streets,' he commented, 'is one of the most common activities of the Romans.' In France he had once interviewed a Brazilian (through an interpreter), and, on another occasion, a dozen witches; but it was Italy which gave Montaigne his best opportunities for fieldwork. In these enquiries we see the practical sceptic, who wants to investigate everything for himself, rather than the metaphysical sceptic, who doubts the evidence of his own senses.

Montaigne did not simply observe, he participated, eating in the local style wherever he went, 'to experience to the full the diversity of manners and customs' (*pour essayer tout à fait la diversité des moeurs et façons*). He uses the word *essayer* in the same sense as his *Essays*. Other travellers of the period paid attention to the local customs, thanks to the growing interest in the exotic. What was distinctive about Montaigne was that his ethnography was reflexive. He made fun of the parochialism of people who took laws to be universal which were no more than 'municipal' (2.12). He approached all customs in the same way, whether they were Brazilian, Roman or Gascon. 'Everyone calls barbarous whatever is not customary with him' (*Chacun appelle barbarie ce qui n'est pas de son usage*) (1.31). Yet 'every custom has its function' (*chaque usage a sa raison*) (3.9). Here Montaigne sounds not unlike a modern functionalist sociologist or anthropologist. This is not really surprising, since, consciously or unconsciously, both he and they draw on an Aristotelian tradition. Everything, according to Aristotle, seeks its own conservation, and everything has a function or 'final cause'. This belief of Montaigne's underlies his opposition to change in the law. He thought it better to trust custom than fallible human reason.

It is in this sense that Montaigne was a relativist. He explored relativism most fully in his 'Apologia for Raymond Sebond'. There he pointed out that there are no universal standards of human beauty. 'The Indians think of it as black, with thick lips and a flat nose . . . In Peru, the biggest ears are the most beautiful, and they stretch them as far as they can.' He made a similar point about religion: 'we are Christians by the same title that we are either Perigordins or Germans', though we cheerfully assume that the views we hold as a result of this accident must be the right ones (2.12). Elsewhere in his essays, Montaigne made a similar point about the position of women. As we have seen, he was aware that societies existed where men were prostitutes and women went to war. He concluded that 'Males and females are cast in the same mould: there is little difference between them except by education and custom.' The authority of men over women derived not from nature but from 'usurpation' (3.5).

Almost equally bold were his scattered remarks about ordinary people. He had, for a French noble of his day, an unusual capacity for admiring ordinary people, as well as for sympathising with their sufferings in that age of witch-trials and civil wars. Ordinary people (*le vulgaire*) were, he thought, ignorant and easily misled by appearances, but also spontaneous, close to nature, and so, on occasion, fine examples of patience, constancy and wisdom, without benefit of Aristotle or Cicero. 'I have seen in my time a hundred crafts-men, a hundred peasants who were wiser and happier than rectors of the university, and whom I would rather have resembled' (2.12). They had, by instinct, the right attitude to death. 'I have never seen one of my peasant neighbours worrying about how he would pass his last hour. Nature teaches him not to think about death until he dies' (3.12). Montaigne's ethnography began at home.

Montaigne went further still and criticised ethnocentrism at the level of the whole human race. 'Man creates his image of divinity according to its relation to himself (*selon la relation à soy*) . . . man can only imagine according to his capacity.' He questioned the smug assumption of human superiority to animals. 'When I play with my cat, who knows whether she is amusing herself with me, rather than I with her?' (2.12). Of course this remark has to be taken in context. As we have seen (p. 12 above), Montaigne was using Plutarch's stories about the wisdom of animals as a way of attacking complacent assumptions about the dignity and rationality of man. However, this view of animals as a group with as much right to judge us as we have to judge them follows from his general relativist views. One might say that he regarded animals as another culture, if his admiration for them were not part of his admiration for nature.

It has already been pointed out that Montaigne was not the first person to be aware of the variety of human customs, beliefs and norms. Nor was he the first to draw relativist conclusions from this observation. The presocratic philosopher Xenophanes, who flourished *c*. 530 BC, noted that 'Ethiopians have gods with snub noses and black hair, Thracians have gods with grey eyes and red hair', and he concluded (in a passage quoted by Montaigne), that 'if oxen and horses could draw . . . horses would draw pictures of gods like horses, and oxen of gods like oxen.' Sextus Empiricus opposed custom to custom as he opposed statement to statement, and suspended judgement. Boccaccio told the story of the three rings, symbolising the three laws given by God to the Jews, the Christians and the Muslims, each people thinking it had the true one, 'but the question remains, which of them is right' (*Decameron*, 1.3). In late-sixteenth-century France, the ideological wars encouraged relativism, as they encouraged admiration for other, happier cultures.

Montaigne reacted in both ways on different occasions, for he was not a thoroughgoing relativist. Sometimes he wrote from the point of view of his own culture, declaring, for example, that 'the most useful and honourable skill and occupation for a woman is that of household management', as if unaware of differences in the sexual division of labour (3.9). At times he tried to arbitrate between cultures, as in his suggestion that the Italians gave women too little freedom but the French too much (3.5). At other times he treated different cultures as equally good. On other occasions he criticised culture itself from the standpoint of nature, arguing that the Indians were better than the Europeans because 'we have abandoned nature' while they lived close to her (3.12).

Such inconsistencies would be worrying if Montaigne claimed to be a systematic philosopher. He did not. Like his admired Socrates, his function was to be a gadfly, and to sow doubt where there had been complacency. We may say that he was less tightly laced into his own culture than most of his contemporaries—and most of us—and drew more far-reaching consequences than most from his reflections on human variety. With his remarkable gift for seeing the other's point of view—even the cat's—he took pains to record the impression made by French culture on three Brazilians; their surprise that armed men 'would submit to obeying a child' (Charles IX), and also that the poor begged at the gates of the rich 'and did not take the others by the throat, or set fire to their houses' (1.31). Montaigne drew the subversive consequences of the insight that the Brazilians found the French at least as odd as the French found them. In a period when many artists believed in an ideal beauty which could be calculated mathematically, he observed that this ideal was a purely local one, and he was prepared to make a similar point about Christianity. At a time when Europeans were congratulating themselves on their discovery of printing and gunpowder, he reminded them that 'other men, at the other end of the world, in China, had enjoyed them a thousand years earlier' (3.6). Lacking the customary ethnocentrism, Montaigne's attitude to history could scarcely be conventional either.

8 Montaigne as historian

Montaigne's awareness of human diversity extended over time as well as over space. Among his favourite books were the histories of Herodotus, Livy and Tacitus, Caesar's *Commentaries* (in other words, his memoirs), and Plutarch's *Lives*. He also appreciated Froissart's chronicle of the Hundred Years' War, and that of Commynes on the wars of Louis XI and Charles the Bold, just as he admired the *History of Italy* by Francesco Guicciardini, one of the historical masterpieces of the Renaissance. His interests extended from local history to world history, from Bouchet's *Annals of Aquitaine* to the *History of the Great Kingdom of China* by González de Mendoza.

Montaigne believed that the study of history was an essential ingredient in the education of children (he was thinking of noble boys), because reading history allows one to frequent the company of 'the worthiest minds, who lived in the best ages' (1.26). By the 'best ages' he meant ancient Greece and Rome, as his examples show. Cato the younger was 'a model chosen by nature to show how far human virtue and constancy can reach' (1.37). The essay on 'three good women' is concerned with three Roman matrons, and followed by one on the 'most excellent men' who have ever existed—Homer, Alexander the Great, and the Theban general Epaminondas (2.35, 2.36). The point of this reading is to learn virtue, not to learn dates. A good teacher will 'imprint in his pupils's minds not so much the date of the ruin of Carthage, as the morals of Hannibal and Scipio' (1.26). In suggesting that history taught virtue through the careers of exemplary individuals, Montaigne was very much a man of his time. His cultural relativism was overcome by his admiration for classical antiquity. Only the late essay on coaches suggests that the courage and constancy shown by the Mexicans and Peruvians in their resistance to the Spaniards was equal to 'the most famous ancient examples' (3.6).

The choice of Alexander, Cato and Scipio as heroes was also conventional enough in Montaigne's day. More unusual was his placing of Homer and Socrates in the same class as the political leaders (above, p. 37). So was the suggestion—anodyne as it may seem today—that the main reason for reading history books was that in them could be found the general knowledge of man, 'the variety and truth of his inner conditions, more lively and complete than anywhere else' (2.10). In other words, Montaigne was suggesting that history taught not only virtue but also psychology, revealing, for example, 'how we weep and laugh at the same thing', for Duke René of Lorraine wept for the death of his enemy Charles the Bold (1.38). Although he found the author's comments too cynical, Montaigne was delighted by Guicciardini's *History of Italy* because it was full of maxims about human nature and motivation.

History taught psychology because human nature was, despite the diversity of customs and the difference between one individual and another, essentially the same. This was the justification of Montaigne's study of himself: 'each man bears the whole form of the human condition', form in its Aristotelian sense of pattern, of potential (3.2). 'It is one and the same nature rolling by (*qui roule son cours*). Anyone who has judged the present accurately may draw valid conclusions about the future and the past' (2.12).

At the same time, Montaigne was aware of change, almost to the point of obsession. It was appropriate that his favourite childhood reading should have been Ovid's *Metamorphoses*, for change, together with other forms of diversity, is a central theme of his essays. What an extraordinary variety of terms he uses to describe it: Among the adjectives, *caduque, coulant, roulant, labile, mobile, fluant, remuant, vagabonde, ondoyant.* Among the nouns, *alteration, agitation, branle* ('dance'), *corruption, decadence, declinaison, decrepitude, fluxion, inclination, instabilité, mouvement, mutation, passage, remuement, revolution* (but not in the political sense), *variation,* and *vicissitude.* In this dance of words it may be useful to attempt to pick out some of the different movements, and to formulate

359

distinctions which are implicit in Montaigne, though never formally expressed.

To begin with the author himself, and what he calls his own 'instability'. 'What pleases me now, will soon be painful . . . my judgement floats, it wanders' (2.12). This sounds like an apologetic description of an individual quirk of personality, but other passages show that Montaigne was making a point about the human condition. It is always difficult to follow 'a path as wandering as that of the mind'. The self will not remain still for its portrait. Whenever one focuses on it, it dissolves. Hence what is needed is a moving picture, a story. 'I am not describing the essence but the passage . . . from day to day, from minute to minute' (3.2).

It is not only the individual who changes. Societies do the same. 'Instability is the worst thing I find in our state; our laws can no more take a stable form than our clothes' (2.17). Ideas change too: sometimes one opinion flourishes, sometimes another. 'The beliefs, judgements and opinions of men . . . have their revolutions, their seasons, their births and deaths, like cabbages' (2.12). Morality changes. Montaigne thought that the men of his day were less honest than they used to be, full of simulation and dissimulation. 'Our morals are extremely corrupt, with an extraordinary tendency towards deterioration' (2.17). Montaigne often returned to the theme of the corruption of his own age, as revealed, for example, in the civil wars. However, he made it clear that he believed the trend to be purely local. 'It is absurd of us today to argue the decline and decrepitude of the world from the evidence of our own weakness and decadence.' This is mere ethnocentrism, belied by the discovery of the New World, which is still young at a time when we are old (3.6). Montaigne took the adjectives 'old' and 'young' literally, not metaphorically. 'The infirmities and other conditions of our bodies are also seen in states and governments: kingdoms and commonwealths, like us, are born, flourish and fade with age' (2.23).

From his Olympian viewpoint it was clear to Montaigne that the corruption of manners in France, like his own old age, was no more than a tiny part of the universal flux. 'All things are in continual movement, change and variation' (2.12). 'The world is in perpetual motion (*le monde n'est qu'une branloire perenne*). Everything in it moves incessantly: the earth, the rocks of the Caucasus, the pyramids of Egypt... Constancy itself is nothing but a dance in slower time (*un branle plus languissant*)' (3.2). Some changes can be resisted, at least for a time. Individuals form habits and societies form customs. The laws, he once remarked, 'like our rivers, grow larger and grander as they go (*grossissent et s'ennoblissent en roulant*)' (2.12). He also saw them as a rock of relative stability amid the universal flux, not to be improved by fallible human reason. However, most changes are as sadly inevitable as old age.

How unusual was Montaigne's sense of change? The idea of universal mutability was a classical commonplace. The Greek philosopher Heraclitus, who flourished about 500 BC, argued, as Montaigne himself reminds us, that 'no man ever stepped twice into the same river'. The stoics stressed the inconstancy of worldly affairs, to which the ideal man would respond by his inner constancy, and Seneca in particular expressed an acute sense of the passing of time. It was Seneca too who drew the analogy, later commonplace, between changes in the human body, from infancy to old age, and changes in the 'body politic', the state. Other classical writers, such as Sallust and Juvenal, had a good deal to say about the corruption of morals, the change from primitive simplicity to decadent luxury. All these points were frequently reiterated in the sixteenth century. Many Frenchmen agreed with Montaigne that they lived in an age of decline, though some would have added, unlike him, that this was the old age of the whole world.

Some of Montaigne's contemporaries showed particular sensitivity to particular kinds of change. Protestants were aware of changes in the Church, more especially the gradual decline from 'primitive' poverty and simplicity into wealth and corruption, a decline which they believed it possible to reverse. A group of French lawyers were particularly interested in changes in laws and customs. At the Renaissance there had been a movement to study ancient Roman law in order to revive it, but the more they studied Roman law, the more this group of men became aware that Roman law was not appropriate to their own society because times had changed. In this sense they were relativists. 'The diversity of laws is due to the diversity of manners which arises in people according to the diversity of regions and environment', wrote one of the group, Montaigne's friend Etienne Pasquier. In his *Method for the Easy Understanding of History* (1566), Jean Bodin, another member of this group, declared 'the absurdity of attempting to establish principles of universal jurisprudence from the Roman decrees, which were subject to change within a brief period'. He recommended the study of world history in a systematically comparative way in order to explain 'the beginnings, growth, conditions, change and decline of all states'. Widening out still further, the classical scholar Louis Le Roy devoted a whole treatise to the problem of change, his *Vicissitude, or Variety of Things in the Universe* (1575), a book which dealt with languages and the arts as well as with laws and empires, and with other cultures, including the Arabs, as well as the Greeks and Romans. Le Roy's basic conceptual scheme was that of the cycle of change from roughness to polish and from polish to corruption.

In Le Roy's interpretation of history, the rise and fall of arms and letters, empires and civilisations usually occurred simultaneously. Pasquier, on the other hand, believed that 'common-wealths rise by arms and decline with letters', a view which seems to have been shared by Montaigne. 'Writing seems to be a symptom of an unbalanced age. When did we ever write so much as we have done since our troubles? Or the Romans, as in the time of their decline?' (3.9). Le Roy saw a providential pattern in the 'vicissitudes' of history; in that sense he believed in progress, a spiral rather than a cycle. Bodin, for his part, saw numerological patterns in world history, which he thought influenced by the stars. Montaigne was more modest and more sceptical. It was enough for him to describe change. He did not presume to offer any explanation.

It should be clear that Montaigne's historical and geographical relativism was not unique to him. It was an attitude shared with a group of scholars, mainly lawyers, of more or less his generation, a group to which he belonged by training, early career and personal acquaintance. His reflections on the history of law, language and other institutions were based on less learning than those of Pasquier and possibly some other scholars. His ideas were not developed into a fully-fledged theory like those of Bodin and Le Roy.

On the other hand, Montaigne's vision was broader than theirs, and perhaps deeper as well. He combined the relatively precise sense of institutional change characteristic of the lawyer-antiquarians with the more general sense of flux expressed by philosophers such as Seneca and poets such as Ronsard, and, a little later, by the Italian Marino, the Spaniard Quevedo, and a number of minor French writers. Unlike the stoic and neostoic philosophers, he saw the self, as well as the world, as in flux, and constancy itself as change in slower motion. Of his contemporaries, only the Italian physician Girolamo Cardano (above, p. 41) approached him in his sense of the elusiveness of the ever-changing self. Although parallels can be found for virtually every one of the ideas about change to be found in Montaigne, the combination, together with the deep concern with time, is distinctively his own.

This concern with process, with decay, with becoming is reflected as well as expressed in his essays, their apparent inconsistencies and digressions being so many ways to catch the movement of a mind in pursuit of truth. The extent to which Montaigne was a conscious stylist, matching his originality of content with originality of form, will be discussed in the next chapter.

9 Montaigne's aesthetics

Montaigne made no claim to be a literary artist; quite the reverse. He did not want people to discuss the language of the essays, but their content. He declared that he simply wrote down his thoughts as they occurred to him. 'I generally begin without a plan: the first word begets the second' (1.40). 'I speak to the paper, as I speak to the first person I meet' (3.1). He would no doubt have lifted an eyebrow at the suggestion that he had an 'aesthetic', a term which was not used in the sixteenth century. However, he did express forceful and relatively unconventional views about the language of others. In the light of these comments, his own essays look more and more like words of conscious literary art.

'The language I love', Montaigne declared, 'is a simple language, the same for writing as for speaking, rich, vigorous, laconic and pithy (*un parler succulent et nerveux, court et serré*), not delicate and affected, but vehement and brusque . . . free, loose and bold (*desreglé, descousu et hardy*) . . . not in the style of schoolmasters, or friars, or lawyers, but in that of soldiers (*non pedantesque, non fratesque, non pleideresque, mais plutost soldatesque*)' (1.26).

In other words, Montaigne was against jargon, against strict rules, against magniloquence, and against affectation, such as the 'fantastic Spanish Petrarchist elevations' of some poets of his day, and what he called 'vain subtleties', such as writing poems in the shape of wings or hatchets, as had been done by certain late classical and Renaissance poets—and was to be done again by English 'metaphysical' poets and French 'baroque' ones.

The poetry Montaigne enjoyed was the poetry of his contemporaries Ronsard and Du Bellay, and also what he called 'popular poetry' (*la poësie populaire*), thinking, for example, of the *villanelles* of his native Gascony, or the songs of peoples without writing—he owned transcriptions of some love-songs and war-songs of the Indians of Brazil. As for prose style,

364

he was bold enough to reject Cicero, the model of literary Latin for so many of his contemporaries, as 'boring' (*sa façon d'escrire me semble ennuyeuse*), and to praise the medieval chroniclers Froissart and Commynes for their simplicity, their *franche naïveté* as he calls it. In a similar manner he praised Amyot, the French translator of Plutarch, for the simplicity (*naïveté*) and purity of his language. (The term *naïveté* does not seem to have had the patronising overtones it has since acquired.)

Montaigne's praise of simplicity and of writing as one speaks is not as easy to interpret as it may look. He was opposing rhetorical extravagance but he was not opposing rhetoric. He did not reject all classical models along with Cicero, and still less did he reject literary models altogether. In praising *un parler succulent et nerveux, court et serré*, he was in fact following a literary model and echoing Erasmus's recommendation of a 'weighty, concise and muscular style' (*dicendi genus solidius, astrictius, nervosius*). There was more than one classical model to follow. 'My inclination', Montaigne confessed, 'is to imitate the style of Seneca' (2.17). This was not purely a matter of personal inclination. In the later sixteenth century, Seneca was becoming fashionable as a stylist, just as he was becoming fashionable as a moralist. The so-called 'Senecan amble', the relatively loose and informal construction of his sentences, appealed to Muret, Lipsius and others besides Montaigne. It is true that Seneca does not write like Froissart, but in a more mannered style. However, what was important for Montaigne was what the style of these two writers had in common. They did not write complex sentences with many subordinate clauses in the manner of Cicero, but strung their points together with 'ands' rather than 'therefores', and gave an impression of greater informality.

Informality was appropriate for what Montaigne was trying to do. Since he was more concerned with Brutus at home than with Brutus on the battlefield, it was right for his prose to put off dress uniform for something unbuttoned (*descousu*, one of Montaigne's adjectives for his own style, literally means 'unstitched'). He rejected elaborate rhetoric as he rejected

365

elaborate ceremony. He described his own style on one occasion as 'comic and domestic' (*un stile comique et privé*). By 'comic' he did not mean that he was trying to make the reader laugh; the word had a technical meaning. Classical dramatists wrote in a 'high' or artificial style in their tragedies, devoted to the public lives of the great, but in a 'low' or ordinary style (*sermo humilis*), in their comedies, which were concerned with the private lives of ordinary people. Montaigne was following classical standards of appropriateness ('decorum') by writing in a conversational tone about 'an ordinary life, without distinction', as he described his own.

In any case, the low style had considerable advantages for what Montaigne was trying to do. The loose sentence construction was appropriate for his method of juxtaposing ideas and deliberately suspending judgement. The low style had a word for everything, whereas the high style had a much more restricted vocabulary. One of Montaigne's criticisms of ancient and modern historians was that they left out relevant material because they thought it undignified and because they were unable to express it in the high style (*pour ne la scavoir dire en bon Latin ou François*). Froissart and Commynes scored because they did not aim so high.

Another advantage of the low style is that a well-placed colloquialism is an appropriate instrument for one of Montaigne's favourite literary activities, deflating human pretensions. It brings the reader down to earth with a bump. Man may think he lives in the centre of the universe, but earth is merely 'the ground floor of the house' (*dernier estage du logis*). Empires grow and decay 'like cabbages' (*comme des choux*). Montaigne is of course prepared to turn this weapon on himself. His literary efforts are his 'scribblings', his 'bundle' (*fagotage*), or his 'stew' (*fricassée*). But a term like 'stew' should not be taken to mean that Montaigne had no interest in the cooking.

This is not to suggest that he sat down in his tower one day with the idea of writing 'essays'. Since a number of early essays are not much more than a patchwork or mosaic of quotations from Seneca and other writers, it looks as if they grew out of the common sixteenth-century practice of keeping a 'commonplace book' of memorable sayings and useful pieces of information. It would not be the only book which was created in this fashion. Erasmus published a collection of classical adages together with his comments on them, and the comments grew longer from edition to edition, so that his remarks on a three-word Latin proverb, *Dulce bellum inexpertis* ('Sweet is war to those who have not experienced it'), ended up as what we would call an 'essay' in praise of peace. In a similar way Montaigne gave less and less attention to the quotations he had assembled, and more and more to his own reactions and reflections.

The idea of publishing a discursive treatment of a number of different subjects within the covers of a single volume was not new in Montaigne's day. For example, in the late fifteenth century the Italian humanist-poet Angelo Poliziano had published his 'Miscellanies'. A common name for this genre was 'discourses', as in the case of Machiavelli's *Discorsi* on, or more exactly around, the first ten books of Livy's history of Rome, or the *Discours politiques et militaires* published in 1587 by the Huguenot gentleman and military leader François de la Noue. In their Italian translation of 1590, Montaigne's essays were entitled 'Moral, Political and Military Discourses'. The genre of discourses was a revival of the Greek *diatribe*, which may be defined as a short treatment of a moral theme, written in a vivid immediate and humorous way, so that the reader has the sense of listening to the author. Plutarch's *Moralia*, one of Montaigne's favourite books, was a collection of 'diatribes' in this sense. So was the *Silva* ('wood', another term for 'miscellany') of the Spanish gentleman Pedro Mexia, whose 120 discourses deal with much the same historical and moral topics as Montaigne; with Heraclitus and Democritus, with cruelty, with the continence of Alexander and Scipio, and so on. Mexia's book was translated into French in 1557 and Montaigne knew it.

The form of the essays owes something to other classical literary genres besides the diatribe. It has a good deal in common with the soliloquy, as exemplified by that of the emperor Marcus Aurelius, and also with the open letter. An example Montaigne knew well was that of Seneca's *Letters to Lucilius* (which were, as Bacon remarked, 'dispersed meditations' or essays), and he was also familiar with some sixteenth-century Italian letter collections. Some of his essays were, like letters, addressed to individuals of his acquaintance; *On the education of children* to Diane de Foix, and *On the resemblance of children to their parents*, to Madame de Duras. Another genre which has left its mark on the essays is the paradox, such as the praise of ignorance, which can be found in Plutarch and also in some sixteenth-century writers known to Montaigne, such as Agrippa, Gelli and Landi, not to mention Erasmus's *Praise of Folly*.

Out of the diatribe, the letter, the soliloquy and the paradox Montaigne gradually developed a form of his own, which is most distinctive not in its length or subject-matter but rather in its author's attempt to catch himself in the act of thinking, to present the process of thought, *le progrez de mes humeurs*, rather than the conclusions. This was the point of giving the collection the title, then unusual, of *essais*: 'attempts', 'trials', or even, perhaps, 'experiments'. It is in this sense that Montaigne was the creator of a new literary genre.

The essay in his own individual sense was a shoe of exactly the shape for Montaigne's foot, a genre which would allow him to talk about himself, to question what others took for granted without committing himself one way or the other, and to digress. Digression was a standard rhetorical device, but not on this scale. His book is in some ways remarkably open, frank and immediate, and it speaks to us across the centuries as few sixteenth-century books do.

In other ways, however, the book is extremely opaque, reticent, paradoxical and ambiguous. The labels on certain essays seem to have nothing to do with the contents. 'Custom of the island of Cea' is largely devoted to the problem of suicide; 'On some verses of Virgil', with attitudes to sex; 'On coaches', with the New World; 'On the lame', with witchcraft. It is always possible that the digression ran away with the essay on these occasions, but it is more likely that Montaigne was planning to give the reader a surprise. He may also have been making things difficult for the censor, and making sure that he was not condemned by anyone who did not take the trouble to read more than the chapter headings.

Another paradox is that Montaigne's book is stuffed with quotations (1,264 from the Latin classics, about 800 from proverbs and similar material), yet suggests that generalisations are impossible and even that 'there were never two identical opinions in the world, any more than two hairs, or two grains' (2.37). As unlike as two peas, one might say. It is characteristic of Montaigne to turn a proverb upside down in this way, just as it is characteristic of him to place quotations in such a context that they convey a different meaning from that of the original author. Again, he claims to compose by a kind of free association ('the first word begets the second') whereas his essays do in fact have a formal structure, often that of a circular tour at the end of which we are led to glimpse familiar notions and customs from an unfamiliar angle. As in a symphony, themes recur and apparent digressions and parentheses often suggest conclusions which are never stated openly. At one point he warned the reader to expect this. 'I express my opinions here so far as custom allows me; I point with my finger to what I cannot say openly' (3.9).

Like Socrates, Montaigne seems to have no opinions but is in fact sometimes manipulative. Like Castiglione's ideal courtier, Montaigne put considerable effort into achieving the effect of spontaneity. For a declared enemy of rhetoric as 'vanity of words' he made a remarkably full use of the figures of speech, notably irony. At times he produced brilliant rhetorical setpieces, notably in the apologia for Sebond, which is at once an oration on the misery of man (an anti-Pico), and a philippic against the uncertainty and vanity of learning, in the manner of the 'declamation' on the same subject written earlier in the century by the German humanist Agrippa von Nettesheim.

It is hard to resist the conclusion that Montaigne's critique of rhetoric functions, at least on occasion, as a form of rhetoric, a technique of persuasion. It lessens the reader's resistance to disturbing ideas. So does the image of the author as a 'plain man', a persona which is projected too skilfully for Montaigne to have been anything of the kind. The 'I' of the essays—one might call him 'Michel'—is as much a literary device as Proust's 'Marcel'. It is scarcely surprising to find that—as the next chapter will suggest—Montaigne has often been misunderstood.

10 The development of the *Essays*

'I add, but I correct nothing ... my book is altogether one' (3.9), Montaigne claimed in one of the last essays. He certainly added a good deal. The 1588 edition contained numerous interpolations in books one and two of the *Essays*, as well as a new book three; scholars call this the 'B-text' to distinguish it from the 1580 version. Montaigne annotated his own copy of this 1588 edition (the 'Bordeaux copy', as it is called), and added about a thousand more passages, thus creating a third version, the 'C-text'. But did he really alter nothing? So acutely aware of his changes from minute to minute, as we have seen, Montaigne seems to have been virtually unconscious of his intellectual development from 1572 to 1592, from the time he began writing till his death. In this respect he differs markedly from Rousseau, Goethe, and the many autobiographers who have followed in their wake, writers whose main theme was precisely their intellectual or spiritual development.

If Montaigne was not aware of his own development, what can posterity hope to know about it? We can in fact know something, thanks to the careful detective work of one of the greatest of Montaigne scholars, Pierre Villey—although his conclusions are not accepted by all the specialists. Villey worked out when Montaigne read a number of his favourite books; Caesar in 1578, López de Gómara between 1584 and 1588, Herodotus and Plato after 1588, and so on. Villey also dated the composition of forty-five essays to the period 1572–4, and of forty-nine more to the period 1575–80. For the years 1580–1, there is a record of Montaigne's thoughts in the journal he kept while travelling in Italy and elsewhere. For the period 1580–8, we have the third book of the *Essays* and the B-text of books one and two, and for 1588–92, the after-thoughts of the Bordeaux copy. On this evidence, together with some letters, Villey based his famous study of 'the evolution of Montaigne', published in 1908.

What was this 'evolution'? Villey divided Montaigne's intellectual life into three. There was the stoic period of his youth;
a sceptical period, following a crisis in the middle of the
1570s; and a final mature period in which Montaigne expressed
his faith in the essential goodness of man. These three periods
correspond more or less with the three books of the *Essays*.

It is always somewhat artificial and misleading to carve
people up into periods, as if the young Marx, to take a much-
debated example, was not the same person as the author of
Capital, and as if we were not—as Montaigne saw so clearly—
changing all the time. Whatever we think of the three periods,
however, it is difficult to disagree with Villey about the
general direction of Montaigne's development. The evidence
for his early stoicism includes the letter he wrote in 1563,
on the death of his friend La Boétie, praising him for his
tranquillity of mind and for the 'invincible courage' with
which he met death's assaults. The first group of essays are
thoroughly impregnated with stoic values. An obvious example
is the argument that good and evil largely depend on our
attitudes towards them (1.14). The early essays are rather
short, and they indulge their author's taste for moral maxims.
It is in these essays that Montaigne is most typical of his age.

Then came what Villey calls Montaigne's 'sceptical crisis',
when he was in his early forties. The change can be dated to
1575–6 because Montaigne had his 'que sais-je?' medal struck
at this time, when he was writing his apologia for Sebond.
Whether 'crisis' is the best description of Montaigne's change
of mind is less clear. It is a strong term, implying psychological
shock as well as a clean break with the past. It can obviously
be a shock to find oneself doubting what one had previously
taken for granted, but we have no concrete evidence of
Montaigne's emotional reactions at this time, and in any case
the author of the apologia of Sebond does not give the impression of a man in a state of shock. On the contrary, he is
very much in control of his argument.

As for the essays in the third book, they are different from
the rest in a number of ways, and especially different from the
ones composed in the early 1570s. They are much longer; on

average, as Villey pointed out, an essay in book three is six times the length of an essay in book one. The later essays rely less on quotations to make their points, but draw on autobiography instead, a sign of the emancipation from intellectual authorities which is recommended in the remarks on the education of children (1.26). The later essays are more critical of the stoics, and much bolder altogether; Montaigne is, for example, more and more outspoken in his opposition to torture. His opinions became less and less like those of other men of his generation. He gained control of the essay form, or rather, he developed it into something which was distinctively his own. In short, one has a much stronger impression from the third book than from the others that Montaigne had found both what he wanted to say and how to say it.

To say that Montaigne had found himself at last implies that he had changed, but also implies a fundamental constancy; not so much a case of 'evolution' (Villey's rather dated term) as 'development' in its original sense of unfolding, unrolling, in other words of revealing what had really been there all the time. It has to be added that on certain questions Montaigne did change his mind altogether. He had once been rather contemptuous of ordinary people, 'the vulgar', as the upper classes generally were, but he came to have a more positive attitude towards them, to attribute to them some of the virtues he admired in the savages of Brazil. He came to place private values above public ones, to admire Alexander the Great less and Socrates more. He had once believed, with the stoics, that philosophy taught us how to die. He ended by thinking that what it taught was how to live (3.2). In his late forties, Montaigne came to accept himself as never before. He concluded that it is 'an absolute perfection, and virtually divine, to know how truly to enjoy one's own nature' (*scavoyr jouyr loiallement de son estre*) (3.13). He had achieved that serenity which he once defined as the distinguishing mark of wisdom.

If we can rely on Montaigne's own account of his former beliefs, referring (presumably) to the period before 1572, then another important change comes into view. He had 'once', so he tells us, 'taken the liberty of making my own choice and of ignoring certain points in the practice of our Church which seemed somewhat misguided or odd' (*qui semblent avoir un visage ou plus vain ou plus estrange*). Once, he continues, 'if I heard someone talking of ghosts, or prophecies, magic or sorcery . . . I would feel pity for the poor people who were taken in by these follies.' Now, he was no longer so confident (1.27). Scepticism cuts both ways; to suspend judgement is as different from disbelieving in witches as from believing in them. In other words—modern words—he believed that he had gone beyond rationalism.

Montaigne once criticised biographers who made their subjects too consistent, 'arranging and interpreting all the actions of a certain person' according to their fixed idea or image of that person, and so doing violence to reality (2.1). This would be a fatal mistake to make in Montaigne's own case. He was not a systematic thinker, but a man full of insights, some of which are not consistent with others. His attitudes in later life are most easy to understand as the product of a process of development in which he reacted against some of his earlier views (as in the examples quoted above), without always quite giving them up.

His contemporaries, however, either failed to notice the new Montaigne, or found it necessary to excuse the change they saw. Montaigne was much admired and much read in his own day, and the *Essays* went through five editions between 1580 and 1588. But generally speaking, the Montaigne who was most appreciated and imitated was the early Montaigne, stoic and sententious, the Montaigne who most resembled his contemporaries. His friend Florimond de Raemond, writing in 1594, noted his 'courageous and almost stoic philosophy' (*sa philosophie courageuse et presque stoïque*). Another contemporary, Claude Expilly, called him a 'great-minded stoic'. Pasquier, another friend of Montaigne's, saw the *Essays* as a 'seedbed of beautiful and memorable maxims'. He did not much care for the third book. His verdict was that Montaigne was a bold man who allowed himself to be carried away by his wit and chose to mock the reader, and perhaps himself as well. In other words, a good deal of what we tend to find most interesting in Montaigne went unnoticed by his contemporaries or was dismissed as nothing but amiable eccentricity.

Even the term 'essay' had a warmer welcome on this side of the Channel, where it was taken up by Francis Bacon (1597) and Sir William Cornwallis (1600). However, in France in the late sixteenth century the 'discourse' form was popular and this popularity probably owes something to Montaigne's example. There were the *Serées* of Guillaume Bouchet (1584), which, like Montaigne, discuss impotence and torture; the *Matinées* of Nicholas Cholières (1585); and the *Bigarrures* of Etienne Tabourot (1584), who declared, in the manner of Montaigne, that he 'observed no order, but heaped up examples pell-mell as they came to mind', and went so far in imitation as to write discourses on the education of children and on pseudo-witches.

Pierre Charron (1541–1603), a priest who knew Montaigne well and was a house guest in his château, was even more of a disciple. His treatise on wisdom (1601), with its separate chapters on human vanity, misery, inconstancy, presumption, and so on, expresses the sceptical-fideist view of the world of Montaigne's apologia for Sebond in more systematic—and more dogmatic—form. The difference between them is expressed in the mottoes of the two men. Where Montaigne chose *Que sais-je?*, Charron preferred *Je ne sais*.

In the first two-thirds of the seventeenth century, Montaigne was still much appreciated in France. The *Essays* continued to be reprinted every two or three years; at least five times in 1608, six times in 1617, five times in 1627, nine times in 1636. The bishop of Belley, Jean-Pierre Camus (1584–1654), was, like Charron, a Counter-Reformation cleric who found fideism attractive. His *Diversités*—yet another synonym for 'essays'—drew heavily on Plutarch, Seneca and Montaigne, whose essays he called 'the gentleman's breviary'. The philosopher Pierre Gassendi (1592–1655), another priest, was an admirer of Montaigne and Charron and a declared disciple of Sextus Empiricus. Some of Gassendi's friends shared his enthusiasm, notably François La Mothe Le Vayer (1588–1672), who wrote dialogues on scepticism, and Cardinal Richelieu's librarian, Gabriel Naudé (1600–53). Gassendi, La Mothe and Naudé all had the reputation of *libertins*, a fashionable pejorative term of the seventeenth century with associations of atheism, cynicism, hedonism and sexual immorality. Cyrano de Bergerac (1619–55), another admirer of Montaigne, best known for his account of a voyage to the moon, was tarred with the same brush. How far this group went in their unorthodoxy it is difficult to say. Perhaps they were Catholics, despite their mockery of popular devotion. Perhaps they were deists, whose God was remote and impersonal, without interest in the world of men. Perhaps they were materialists who denied providence and believed the universe to be the result of chance, in the manner of Epicurus and Lucretius, authors they certainly admired.

What the group saw in Montaigne is somewhat easier to determine. His rejection of intellectual authorities appealed to them. Cyrano and La Mothe were attracted by his cultural relativism, while Naudé praised him for his style and his 'great abundance of maxims' and criticised credulous witch-hunters in a similar vein, while preferring the more methodical Charron. Naudé was too much the rationalist and too much the Aristotelian to accept Montaigne altogether. His motto was 'to square everything by the level of reason' (*esquarrer toutes choses au niveau de la raison*). The group incorporated important elements of Montaigne's thought into their own intellectual systems, inevitably giving these elements a somewhat different significance from their original one.

Montaigne was also well known outside France in the seventeenth century. In England, for example, Bacon's *Essays* owe something to the example of Montaigne, though his taut sentences and crisp generalisations are the antithesis of Montaigne in the sense that they seem designed to end a discussion rather than to provoke one. Florio's somewhat free translation of Montaigne goes back to 1603. It is likely that Shakespeare read him in this version, and that *The Tempest* owes something to the essay on cannibals. Sir Thomas Browne was another admirer of Montaigne and indeed a kindred spirit —essayist, fideist and explorer of himself. So was Joseph Glanvill, whose *Vanity of Dogmatising* (1661), dealt with a theme close to Montaigne's heart.

However, in the later seventeenth century there was a reaction against Montaigne. Descartes had something to do with it. In a sense Descartes was a sceptic in the tradition of Montaigne, for he began by doubting everything, but he ended very differently, with his picture of the universe as a vast machine. Montaigne regarded animals as intelligent in the same way that men are intelligent; Descartes thought of them as clockwork. Montaigne had helped undermine the traditional view of the hierarchical universe, but did not put anything systematic in its place. Those who accepted the new mechanical world picture inevitably saw Montaigne as old-fashioned.

The devout also turned against him. Montaigne had sometimes been attacked as an 'atheist' in his own day, but this seems to have been a minority view until the 1660s, when the leading churchman Bishop Bossuet preached against him. Blaise Pascal (1623–62) criticised Montaigne in his posthumously published *Pensées* for the 'foolish plan' of portraying himself, and also for his 'quite pagan attitudes to death'. He studied Montaigne carefully, taking over a number of his ideas and even phrases, but only to incorporate them into a very different moral and theological structure of his own. Nicolas Malebranche, Cartesian philosopher and Catholic theologian, was against Montaigne on both counts. The *Essays* were placed on the Roman Index in 1676 (the Spaniards, with their keener noses for heresy, had placed him on their Index in 1640). It has been argued with some plausibility that the reaction against Montaigne had much to do with the changing position of the Catholic Church. In the 1580s, the main threat to the Church came from the Protestants. Montaigne was clearly no Protestant; indeed, his scepticism could be used as a weapon against Protestants, to sap their confidence in private judgement. By the later seventeenth century, however, the sceptic or 'libertine' seemed the chief threat to the Church, and so Montaigne's own unorthodoxy seemed more questionable.

377

It should be added that the admiration which Naudé and his circle felt for Montaigne can have done him no good with the devout. It is a difficult question to decide whether the seventeenth-century censors, who put Montaigne on the Index, were more perceptive than their sixteenth-century colleagues, or whether they simply associated him with seventeenth-century misunderstandings of his work. His cultural relativism, which had so attracted Cyrano de Bergerac, was now forgotten. Bossuet's *Discourse on World History* (1681) is simply a history of western (classical-Jewish-Christian) civilisation, written as if China (and Montaigne) had never existed. Perhaps this collective amnesia was necessary for the intellectual stability of the age of Louis XIV. Only the Protestant sceptic Pierre Bayle (1647–1706) carried on the Montaigne tradition. His *Various Thoughts on the Comet* (1683) is a critique of human ethnocentrism in the same class as the apologia for Raymond Sebond.

There were also aesthetic reasons for the slump in Montaigne's reputation in the later seventeenth century. In the age of classicism, the loose construction of his essays was no longer pleasing. One leading French writer, Guez de Balzac (1597–1654), criticised Montaigne because his arguments were broken up by digressions (*son discours . . . est un corps en pièces*). Another writer, Charles Sorel (1602–74) complained that the essays 'lacked order and connection'. Pascal condemned what he called Montaigne's 'confusion'. These criticisms, religious and aesthetic, were effective; no French editions of Montaigne were published between 1669 and 1724, though a new English translation, more faithful than Florio's, was produced by Charles Cotton in 1685.

In the eighteenth century, Montaigne was rediscovered—and also reinterpreted. The 1724 edition, the first for more than fifty years, was published in London by a Frenchman who had translated Locke and thought of Montaigne primarily as Locke's precursor, particularly in his ideas on the education of children. The informal style came back into fashion at this time as part of the reaction against the values associated with Louis XIV. Denis Diderot (1713–84) appreciated Montaigne for the very disorder Pascal had condemned, seeing it as spontaneity. It is true that by the eighteenth century the language of Montaigne was beginning to seem quaint and even difficult, but it could always be modernised, and in some editions it was. The ideas were brought up to date as well as the prose. Readers of David Hume's *Essay on Miracles* (1748) almost inevitably interpreted Montaigne's remarks on miracles in a similar way. Was this to 'unfold' his meaning or to obscure it? Voltaire, who fought his own battles against western ethnocentrism and appreciated Montaigne as an ally, once compared him to Montesquieu, a much more systematic thinker. Diderot compared him to the eighteenth-century philosopher Helvétius. In short, Montaigne was seen as a *philosophe*. After 1789, we even find Montaigne the revolutionary. A certain Rabaut de Saint Etienne declared that when Montaigne doubted and Bacon experimented, 'they were preparing the French Revolution'.

Since the Enlightenment there have been several more Montaignes. For the German writer J. G. Herder (1744–1803), he stood for the appreciation of folksong and the return to nature. For the essayist William Hazlitt he was 'the first who had the courage to say as an author what he felt as a man'. Nietzsche admired him for his cultural relativism and his 'brave and cheerful scepticism', and tried to go beyond him in the same direction. Pierre Villey saw him as one who took 'a first step' in the direction of Bacon and a science based on empirical facts (in other words, the positivism of Auguste Comte). E. M. Forster, on the other hand, who once declared that 'My law-givers are Erasmus and Montaigne, not Moses and St Paul' saw him as representing the values of tolerance and loyalty to one's friends rather than to one's country.

We of the later twentieth century cannot afford to scoff at these past images, for we too have created a Montaigne of our own, or rather several. Claude Lévi-Strauss paid homage to Montaigne the ethnologist by calling one of his books *La Pensée sauvage*, a reference to the essay on cannibals. For R. A. Sayce, one of the most perceptive of the recent students of Montaigne, he is 'the first of the great modern bourgeois writers', who comes 'very close to Proust' in his analysis of feelings. Montaigne's disappointment on reaching Venice and finding it less marvellous than he expected is not at all unlike that of 'Marcel' at Balbec. Others have stressed Montaigne's anticipations of Freud, and his attitude to school has reminded one commentator of Ivan Illich. His stoic slogan 'follow Nature' is bound to acquire a new resonance in the next few years, and it can only be a matter of time before he is interpreted as a Taoist. Indeed, he does resemble the Taoists in his relativism, his trust in nature, his acceptance of death, just as the simple life lived by the Greek philosopher Diogenes, whom Montaigne often cites with approval, resembles that of the Taoist Hsü Yü, down to the detail of throwing away the unnecessary drinking vessel.

Such a variety of judgements would have amused Montaigne and ought to worry us. How can a book change its meaning for each successive generation? When we look at Montaigne's self-portrait, do we really see no more than our own reflection in the glass? This is of course a general problem. All the classics are reinterpreted afresh by every generation; if this does not happen, they cease to be classics.

However, it is the function of intellectual historians to warn their own generation of the distortions involved in this reinterpretation of the past, in treating Montaigne (like Shakespeare, or Dante) as our contemporary. We need to remember that he is not one of us, that his fideism, for example, or his use of classical antiquity as a point of reference, sets him apart from us. It is somewhat ethnocentric, not to say patronising, to treat Montaigne as an honorary member of the twentieth century. We would do better to ask ourselves how he would criticise society were he alive today.

And yet most of the interpretations of Montaigne which I have mentioned—perhaps all of them—do contain a kernel of truth. To see him as a *philosophe*, a psychologist or an ethnologist is to direct attention to ideas which he put forward and which some readers have neglected, even if it gives these ideas a disproportionate importance and locates them in a new context. There is a sense in which we are right to talk of the posthumous development of the *Essays*, of latent meanings gradually becoming manifest, of truth as the daughter of time. Some writers, thinkers, and artists seem to be particularly myriad-minded, multi-faceted, or 'polyvalent', and so they continue to appeal to a succession of very different posterities. Perhaps this is the secret of a 'past master'. In any case, there can be little doubt, after four hundred years, that Montaigne is, like Thomas More, like Shakespeare, like Socrates, like Michelangelo, a man for all seasons. Despite the hundreds of imitations which the *Essays* have inspired, it remains what its author once called it, 'the only book in the world of its kind'.

Further reading

The Pléiade edition of Montaigne (Paris, 1962) includes the letters and travel journal and has the advantage of making clear which portions of the *Essays* belong to the A-, B- and C-texts. A good modern translation is that by D. M. Frame (New York, 1957). John Florio's lively translation of 1603 has often been reprinted.

Among the best general studies of the man and the book are P. Villey, *Les Sources et l'évolution des essais de Montaigne* (2 vols, Paris, 1908); H. Friedrich, *Montaigne* (Bern, 1949, in German; French trans., Paris, 1968); D. M. Frame, *Montaigne: a biography* (London, 1965); R. A. Sayce, *The Essays of Montaigne* (London, 1972); J. Starobinski, *Montaigne in Motion* (Paris 1982; Chicago 1985).

1 *Montaigne in his time*

On Montaigne's social group, G. Huppert, *Les Bourgeois Gentilshommes* (Chicago and London, 1977—in English); on his generation, W. L. Gundersheimer, 'The Crisis of the late French Renaissance', in *Renaissance Studies in Honor of Hans Baron*, ed. A. Molho and J. Tedeschi (Florence, 1971). On the ideal of rural retirement—despite its focus on eighteenth-century England—M. Mack, *The Garden and the City* (London, 1969).

2 *Montaigne's humanism*

On humanism in general, P. O. Kristeller, *Renaissance Thought* (New York, 1961); C. Trinkaus, *In Our Image and Likeness* (2 vols, London, 1970), especially part 2, and *Humanism in France*, ed. A. H. T. Levi (Manchester, 1970). On Montaigne, Friedrich, chs 2–4; R. Trinquet, *La Jeunesse de Montaigne* (Paris, 1972), chs 12–14; D. M. Frame, *Montaigne's Discovery of Man* (New York, 1955). For samples of Montaigne's favourite classical authors, Plutarch, *Moral*

Letters from a Stoic (trans. R. Campbell, Harmondsworth, 1969).

3 *Montaigne's scepticism*

On the history of the movement, G. Leff, *Medieval Thought* (Harmondsworth, 1958), part 3; R. H. Popkin, *The History of Scepticism from Erasmus to Descartes* (second ed., Assen, 1964); C. Schmitt, *Cicero Scepticus: a Study of the Influence of the Academica in the Renaissance* (The Hague, 1972). For the key texts, Sextus Empiricus, *Outlines of Pyrrhonism* (trans. R. G. Bury, London, 1933), and Cicero, *Academica* (trans. H. Rackham, London, 1933). On Montaigne in particular, besides Popkin, ch. 3, C. B. Brush, *Montaigne and Bayle* (The Hague, 1966); Z. Gierczynski, 'Le Scepticisme de Montaigne', *Kwartalnik Neofilologiczny*, 1967; E. Limbrick, 'Was Montaigne really a Pyrrhonian?', *Bibliothèque d'Humanisme et Renaissance*, 39, 1977.

4 *Montaigne's religion*

H. J. J. Janssen, *Montaigne fidéiste* (Nijmegen and Utrecht, 1930); M. Dréano, *La Pensée religieuse de Montaigne* (Paris, 1936, new ed. 1969). On the Counter-Reformation, P. Spriet, 'Montaigne, Charron et la crise morale', *French Review*, 1965; on miracles, J. Céard, *La Nature et les Prodiges* (Geneva, 1977); on witches, A. Boase, 'Montaigne et les sorcières', in *Culture et politique en France à l'époque de l'humanisme*, ed. F. Simone (Turin, 1974).

5 *Montaigne's politics*

On the background, J. E. Neale, *The Age of Catherine de'Medici* (London, 1943): N. Z. Davis, *Society and Culture in Early Modern France* (London, 1975); Q. Skinner, *Foundations of Modern Political Thought* (Cambridge, 1979), especially vol. 2. R. N. Carew Hunt, 'Montaigne and the State', *Edinburgh Review*, 1927; E. Williamson, 'On the liberalizing of Montaigne', *French Review*, 1949; F. S. Brown, *Religious and Political Conservatism in the Essais of Montaigne*

(Geneva, 1963). Extracts from the thesis of J. P. Dhommeaux, 'Les idées politiques de Montaigne', are printed in the *Bulletin de la Société des Amis de Montaigne*, 1976.

6 *Montaigne as psychologist*

On the history of self-portrayal, G. Misch, *Geschichte der Autobiographie*, especially vol. 4 (Frankfurt, 1969), part 2.

On Montaigne, Friedrich, ch. 5; J. Chateau, *Montaigne psychologue* (Paris, 1966); L. R. Entin-Bates, 'Montaigne's remarks on impotence', *Modern Language Notes*, 1976; D. Coleman, 'Montaigne's "sur des vers de Virgile"' in *Classical Influences on European Culture, 1500–1700*, ed. R. R. Bolgar (Cambridge, 1976).

7 *Montaigne as ethnographer*

G. Chinard, *L'Exotisme américain dans la littérature française au 16e siècle* (Paris, 1911); M. T. Hodgen, *Early Anthropology in the Sixteenth and Seventeenth Centuries* (Philadelphia, 1964); D. F. Lach, *Asia in the Making of Europe*, 2 (Chicago, 1977), especially book 2, pp. 286–301; G. Gliozzi, *Adamo e il nuovo mondo* (Florence, 1977), pp. 199–219.

8 *Montaigne as historian*

On the background, D. R. Kelley, *Foundations of Modern Historical Scholarship* (New York, 1970); G. Huppert, *The Idea of Perfect History* (Urbana, 1970); R. J. Quinones, *The Renaissance Discovery of Time* (Cambridge, Mass., 1972).

On Montaigne, G. Poulet, *Etudes sur le temps humain* (Paris, 1950), ch. 1; F. Joukovsky, *Montaigne et le problème du temps (Paris, 1972)*; O. Naudeau, *La Pensée de Montaigne* (Geneva, 1972), ch. 3.

9 *Montaigne's aesthetics*

M. Croll, *Style, rhetoric and rhythm* (Princeton, 1966), collects his essays of the 1920s on the anti-ciceronian movement. Friedrich, ch. 8, a general study. On the prehistory of the essay, P. M. Schon, *Vorformen des Essays in Antike und Humanismus* (Wiesbaden, 1954). On Montaigne and the baroque, I. Buffum, *Studies in the Baroque* (New Haven, 1957), ch. 1. On Montaigne's rhetoric, M. McGowan, *Montaigne's Deceits* (London, 1974), and M. M. Phillips, 'From the *Ciceronianus* to Montaigne', *Classical Influences on European Culture, 1500–1700*, ed. R. R. Bolgar (Cambridge, 1976).

10 *The development of the* Essays

P. Villey, *Sources et évolution*; P. Villey, *Montaigne devant la postérité* (Paris, 1935); A. M. Boase, *The Fortunes of Montaigne* (London, 1935); D. M. Frame, *Montaigne in France, 1812–1852* (New York, 1940); C. Dédéyan, *Montaigne dans le romantisme anglo-saxon* (Paris, 1944); M. Dréano, *La Renommée de Montaigne, 1677–1802* (Angers, 1952).

Index

OXFORD

MORE OXFORD PAPERBACKS

This book is just one of nearly 1000 Oxford Paperbacks currently in print. If you would like details of other Oxford Paperbacks, including titles in the World's Classics, Oxford Reference, Oxford Books, OPUS, Past Masters, Oxford Authors, and Oxford Shakespeare series, please write to:

UK and Europe: Oxford Paperbacks Publicity Manager, Arts and Reference Publicity Department, Oxford University Press, Walton Street, Oxford OX2 6DP.

Customers in UK and Europe will find Oxford Paperbacks available in all good bookshops. But in case of difficulty please send orders to the Cash-with-Order Department, Oxford University Press Distribution Services, Saxon Way West, Corby, Northants NN18 9ES. Tel: 0536 741519; Fax: 0536 746337. Please send a cheque for the total cost of the books, plus £1.75 postage and packing for orders under £20; £2.75 for orders over £20. Customers outside the UK should add 10% of the cost of the books for postage and packing.

USA: Oxford Paperbacks Marketing Manager, Oxford University Press, Inc., 200 Madison Avenue, New York, N.Y. 10016.

Canada: Trade Department, Oxford University Press, 70 Wynford Drive, Don Mills, Ontario M3C 1J9.

Australia: Trade Marketing Manager, Oxford University Press, G.P.O. Box 2784Y, Melbourne 3001, Victoria.

South Africa: Oxford University Press, P.O. Box 1141, Cape Town 8000.

PHILOSOPHY IN OXFORD PAPERBACKS

Ranging from authoritative introductions in the Past Masters and OPUS series to in-depth studies of classical and modern thought, the Oxford Paperbacks' philosophy list is one of the most provocative and challenging available.

THE GREAT PHILOSOPHERS

Bryan Magee

Beginning with the death of Socrates in 399, and following the story through the centuries to recent figures such as Bertrand Russell and Wittgenstein, Bryan Magee and fifteen contemporary writers and philosophers provide an accessible and exciting introduction to Western philosophy and its greatest thinkers.

Bryan Magee in conversation with:

A. J. Ayer	John Passmore
Michael Ayers	Anthony Quinton
Miles Burnyeat	John Searle
Frederick Copleston	Peter Singer
Hubert Dreyfus	J. P. Stern
Anthony Kenny	Geoffrey Warnock
Sidney Morgenbesser	Bernard Williams
Martha Nussbaum	

'Magee is to be congratulated . . . anyone who sees the programmes or reads the book will be left in no danger of believing philosophical thinking is unpractical and uninteresting.' Ronald Hayman, *Times Educational Supplement*

'one of the liveliest, fast-paced introductions to philosophy, ancient and modern that one could wish for' *Universe*

Also by Bryan Magee in Oxford Paperbacks:

Men of Ideas
Aspects of Wagner 2/e

OPUS

General Editors: Walter Bodmer, Christopher Butler,
Robert Evans, John Skorupski

A HISTORY OF WESTERN PHILOSOPHY

This series of OPUS books offers a comprehensive and up-to-date survey of the history of philosophical ideas from earliest times. Its aim is not only to set those ideas in their immediate cultural context, but also to focus on their value and relevance to twentieth-century thinking.

CLASSICAL THOUGHT

Terence Irwin

Spanning over a thousand years from Homer to Saint Augustine, *Classical Thought* encompasses a vast range of material, in succinct style, while remaining clear and lucid even to those with no philosophical or Classical background.

The major philosophers and philosophical schools are examined—the Presocratics, Socrates, Plato, Aristotle, Stoicism, Epicureanism, Neoplatonism; but other important thinkers, such as Greek tragedians, historians, medical writers, and early Christian writers, are also discussed. The emphasis is naturally on questions of philosophical interest (although the literary and historical background to Classical philosophy is not ignored), and again the scope is broad—ethics, the theory of knowledge, philosophy of mind, philosophical theology. All this is presented in a fully integrated, highly readable text which covers many of the most important areas of ancient thought and in which stress is laid on the variety and continuity of philosophical thinking after Aristotle.

Also available in the History of Western Philosophy series:

The Rationalists   John Cottingham
Continental Philosophy since 1750   Robert C. Solomon
The Empiricists   R. S. Woolhouse

PAST MASTERS

General Editor: Keith Thomas

The *Past Masters* series offers students and general readers alike concise introductions to the lives and works of the world's greatest literary figures, composers, philosophers, religious leaders, scientists, and social and political thinkers.

'Put end to end, this series will constitute a noble encyclopaedia of the history of ideas.' Mary Warnock

HOBBES

Richard Tuck

Thomas Hobbes (1588–1679) was the first great English political philosopher, and his book *Leviathan* was one of the first truly modern works of philosophy. He has long had the reputation of being a pessimistic atheist, who saw human nature as inevitably evil, and who proposed a totalitarian state to subdue human failings. In this new study, Richard Tuck shows that while Hobbes may indeed have been an atheist, he was far from pessimistic about human nature, nor did he advocate totalitarianism. By locating him against the context of his age, Dr Tuck reveals Hobbs to have been passionately concerned with the refutation of scepticism in both science and ethics, and to have developed a theory of knowledge which rivalled that of Descartes in its importance for the formation of modern philosophy.

Also available in Past Masters:

PAST MASTERS

General Editor: Keith Thomas

Past Masters is a series of authoritative studies that introduce students and general readers alike to the thought of
leading intellectual figures of the past whose ideas still
influence many aspects of modern life.

'This Oxford University Press series continues on its encyclopae-
dic way ... One begins to wonder whether any intelligent person
can afford not to possess the whole series.' *Expository Times*

KIERKEGAARD

Patrick Gardiner

Søren Kierkegaard (1813–55), one of the most original thinkers
of the nineteenth century, wrote widely on religious, philosophical, and literary themes. But his idiosyncratic manner of presenting some of his leading ideas initially obscured their fundamental
import.

This book shows how Kierkegaard developed his views in
emphatic opposition to prevailing opinions, including certain
metaphysical claims about the relation of thought to existence.
It describes his reaction to the ethical and religious theories of
Kant and Hegel, and it also contrasts his position with doctrines
currently being advanced by men like Feuerbach and Marx.
Kierkegaard's seminal diagnosis of the human condition, which
emphasizes the significance of individual choice, has arguably
been his most striking philosophical legacy, particularly for the
growth of existentialism. Both that and his arresting but paradoxical conception of religious belief are critically discussed,
Patrick Gardiner concluding this lucid introduction by indicating
salient ways in which they have impinged on contemporary
thought.

Also available in Past Masters:

Disraeli   John Vincent
Freud   Anthony Storr
Hume   A. J. Ayer
Augustine   Henry Chadwick

PAST MASTERS

General Editor: Keith Thomas

Past Masters is a series of concise, lucid, and authoritative introductions to the thought of leading intellectual figures of the past whose ideas still affect the way we think today.

'One begins to wonder whether any intelligent person can afford not to possess the whole series.' *Expository Times*

FREUD

Anthony Storr

Sigmund Freud (1865–1939) revolutionized the way in which we think about ourselves. From its beginnings as a theory of neurosis, Freud developed psycho-analysis into a general psychology which became widely accepted as the predominant mode of discussing personality and interpersonal relationships.

From its inception, the psycho-analytic movement has always aroused controversy. Some have accepted Freud's views uncritically: others have dismissed psycho-analysis as unscientific without appreciating its positive contributions. Fifty years have passed since Freud's death, so it is now possible to assess his ideas objectively. Anthony Storr, psychotherapist and writer, takes a new, critical look at Freud's major theories and at Freud himself in a book which both specialists and newcomers to Freud's work will find refreshing.

Also available in Past Masters:

Homer   Jasper Griffin
Thomas More   Anthony Kenny
Galileo   Stillman Drake
Marx   Peter Singer

PAST MASTERS

General Editor: Keith Thomas

The people whose ideas have made history . . .

'One begins to wonder whether any intelligent person can afford not to possess the whole series.' *Expository Times*

JESUS

Humphrey Carpenter

Jesus wrote no books, but the influence of his life and teaching has been immeasurable. Humphrey Carpenter's account of Jesus is written from the standpoint of an historian coming fresh to the subject without religious preconceptions. And no previous knowledge of Jesus or the Bible on the reader's part is assumed.

How reliable are the Christian 'Gospels' as an account of what Jesus did or said? How different were his ideas from those of his contemporaries? What did Jesus think of himself? Humphrey Carpenter begins his answer to these questions with a survey and evaluation of the evidence on which our knowledge of Jesus is based. He then examines his teaching in some detail, and reveals the perhaps unexpected way in which his message can be said to be original. In conclusion he asks to what extent Jesus's teaching has been followed by the Christian Churches that have claimed to represent him since his death.

'Carpenter's *Jesus* is about as objective as possible, while giving every justifiable emphasis to the real and persistent forcefulness of the moral teaching of this charismatic personality.' Kathleen Nott, *The Times*

'an excellent, straightforward presentation of up-to-date scholarship' David L. Edwards, *Church Times*

Also available in Past Masters:

PAST MASTERS

General Editor: Keith Thomas

Past Masters is a series of concise and authoritative introductions to the life and works of men and women whose ideas still influence the way we think today.

'Put end to end, this series will constitute a noble encyclopaedia of the history of ideas.' Mary Warnock

SHAKESPEARE

Germaine Greer

'At the core of a coherent social structure as he viewed it lay marriage, which for Shakespeare is no mere comic convention but a crucial and complex ideal. He rejected the stereotype of the passive, sexless, unresponsive female and its inevitable concommitant, the misogynist conviction that all women were whores at heart. Instead he created a series of female characters who were both passionate and pure, who gave their hearts spontaneously into the keeping of the men they loved and remained true to the bargain in the face of tremendous odds.'

Germaine Greer's short book on Shakespeare brings a completely new eye to a subject about whom more has been written than on any other English figure. She is especially concerned with discovering why Shakespeare 'was and is a popular artist', who remains a central figure in English cultural life four centuries after his death.

'eminently trenchant and sensible . . . a genuine exploration in its own right' John Bayley, *Listener*

'the clearest and simplest explanation of Shakespeare's thought I have yet read' Auberon Waugh, *Daily Mail*

Also available in Past Masters:

Paine   Mark Philp
Dante   George Holmes
The Buddha   Michael Carrithers
Confucius   Raymond Dawson